CRIMINOLOGY SKILLS

EMILY FINCH • STEFAN FAFINSKI

OXFORD
UNIVERSITY PRESS

OXFORD

UNIVERSITY PRESS

Great Clarendon Street, Oxford OX2 6DP
United Kingdom

Oxford University Press is a department of the University of Oxford.
It furthers the University's objective of excellence in research, scholarship,
and education by publishing worldwide. Oxford is a registered trade mark of
Oxford University Press in the UK and in certain other countries

British Library Cataloguing in Publication Data
Data available

Library of Congress Cataloguing in Publication Data
Library of Congress Control Number: 2011945384

ISBN 978–0–19–959737–6

Printed and bound by CPI Group (UK) Ltd, Croydon, CR0 4YY

For STG

GUIDED TOUR OF THE BOOK

Criminology Skills is enriched with a range of features to help support a practical approach to learning. This guided tour shows you how to fully utilize your textbook and get the most out of your study of criminology.

LEARNING OUTCOMES

After studying this chapter, you should be able to:

- Explain the process by which Acts of Parliament come into [
- Find criminal legislation online
- Understand the hierarchy of the courts in England and Wale legal system
- Explain the meaning of case citations and use the neutral cit
- Search for cases online

Learning outcomes

Each chapter begins with a bulleted outline of the main concepts and ideas you will encounter. These serve as useful signposts to what you can expect to learn from reading each chapter.

Practical exercise

Use the sentencing statistics website to answer the following qu

- How many offenders received a community sentence for pos and Wales in 2006?
- How many murderers were sentenced in England and Wales
- How many offenders within the Thames Valley police area w occasioning actual bodily harm in 2010?
- How many burglars in total were sentenced by Bradford cou

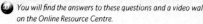 *You will find the answers to these questions and a video wal on the Online Resource Centre.*

Practical exercises

When you feel confident that you understand the principles underpinning each skill, it is important that you practise applying them. To help you foster a 'hands on' appreciation of criminology skills, practical exercises are provided throughout each chapter.

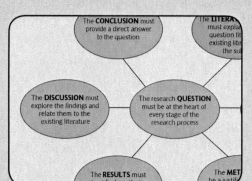

Diagrams and flowcharts

Numerous diagrams provide visual representations of concepts and processes.

Screenshots

Screenshots from important web sites and databases will help familiarize you with these vital resources.

CHAPTER SUMMARY

Sampling

- There are two main types of sampling methods—pro
- Probability samples are more likely to be represent results that can be generalized to that population
- Probability sampling involves some form of random systematic, stratified, or cluster methods. However methods is likely to form a multi-stage sampling me
- The findings from non-probability samples cannot

Chapter summaries

The central points covered in each chapter are distilled into end-of-chapter summaries, each providing an opportunity for you to review and reinforce your understanding of the key concepts.

FURTHER READING

- Feenan, D. (2002) Legal Issues in Acquiring Inform Criminological Research. *British Journal of Crimin* a detailed discussion of the issues surrounding the confidentiality in the light of disclosures of unlawf studies to illustrate how researchers have dealt w a more detailed debate of the issues covered with your thinking in this area.

- Westmarland, L. (2001) Blowing the Whistle on P

Further reading

Selected further reading is included at the end of chapters to provide a springboard for your further study. These annotated lists will help you to broaden your learning by guiding you to the key literature in the field.

GLOSSARY

The **alternative hypothesis** is the proposition that tw which a sample was selected.

Binary variables are nominal variables with only two dichotomous variables.

The **central limit theorem** says that the larger a numb means will be to the mean of the whole population

Centrality is a term used to describe where the cent

Glossary

Key terms are highlighted when they first appear in chapters and are clearly explained in an end-of-chapter glossary. These terms are collected in a flashcard glossary which can be found on the Online Resource Centre that accompanies this book.

GUIDED TOUR OF THE ONLINE RESOURCE CENTRE

Online Resource Centre
www.oxfordtextbooks.co.uk/orc/
finch_criminology/

The Online Resource Centre that accompanies this book provides students with ready-to-use learning resources. They are free of charge and are designed to maximize the learning experience.

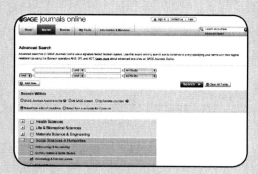

Animated walk-throughs
Animated walk-throughs demonstrate step by step how to use online databases in your criminological research.

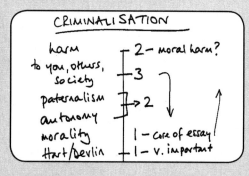

Activities
A range of activities support the material provided in the book, providing you with the opportunity to practise and develop the skills and knowledge you have acquired.

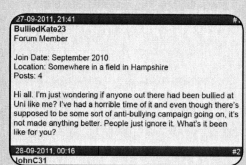

Ethical considerations
What ethical considerations do you need to take into account when planning or analysing a criminology research project? Activities on ethical considerations such as confidentiality, 'heinous discoveries', and protecting victims, along with examples of consent forms will help you plan and conduct ethical criminological research.

Gathering data

An activity on selecting an interview sample, along with video clips of interviews demonstrate how to gather data effectively from individuals and groups.

	Smith (2002)	Roots (2005)
Focus	Type of crime – particularly economic crime	Role of trust in white collar crime
Argument	Puts forward a typology of economic and financial white collar crimes	Perpetrators are in positions of privilege and therefore trusted
Weaknesses	Only focuses on one particular facet of the issue	Does not consider relationship with organisational culture
Other viewpoints	Builds on earlier work by Lomax (1992); agrees with earlier analysis.	Disagrees with Jolly's analysis (2002)
Contribution	Detailed analysis of economic/financial crime	Refines earlier typologies of trust relationships
Relevance	Good source for one set of white collar crimes	Useful for alternative construction of problem

Literature reviews

Activities are provided to help you organize and analyse literature that is relevant to your criminological research.

Quantitative analysis

You will find sample SPSS data sets with which you can carry out various statistical tests and compare your answers with the animated walk-throughs of SPSS provided.

1	He comes across as naive that's what I'm saying, he's hit [...] way through, everything that's happened, he's friends well [...] his so called acquaintances
3	You can see remorse there can't you?
1	Yeah he strikes me with naivety, if its rape then I'm wrong [...] can't say that it's because I believe it, not with the eviden[...]
2	Yeah I think its also tempting that its…
7	I think its too easy to say it is
1	But the thing is as far as we don't know if he genuinely di[...] effects of the drug while he was drunk etc. etc. we don't l[...] she forgot everything. Maybe she was so ashamed of hers[...] understandable that she doesn't want to remember anythin[...] because people do

Coding practice

Interview transcripts and an audio recording allow you to test your ability to code qualitative data gathered from various sources.

The observant reader will already have noticed that this book is published by Oxford University Press. Without OUP, there would be no *Criminology Skills*, so it is only right and proper that we start by thanking those at OUP who made this happen. Particular thanks go to Sarah Viner who commissioned the project (and is probably still the only person at the Press who knows her way around the entire building) and Helen Davis, our Publishing Editor. Helen has been exceptionally supportive: not only as a sounding board for some of our short-notice changes of mind on a whole load of different things, but also for doing 'that Helen thing' with first drafts of chapters (despite not telling us that she had an A-level in statistics until *after* she'd looked at the first draft of the quantitative analysis chapter) and organizing reviews of the material as we wrote. She also got promoted part way through development (we should really have said '*Senior* Publishing Editor' earlier), so congratulations to her on that. Thoroughly well-deserved just on the basis of putting up with us, we thought. We really hope that our book doesn't get her demoted back down again. As we write, the book obviously hasn't yet gone into production, but, on the assumption that you're reading this in print, then all must have gone swimmingly well. (If you're reading it in the bookshop, now would be a really good time to take it to the till.) So we'd also like to thank in advance Heather Smyth, our Production Editor, and Nick Wehmeier ('Web Nick' as we call him) who makes the Online Resource Centre magically appear (should we ever get round to supplying him with the ORC materials…). Also Janice Sayer, copy editor, Ian Pickett, proofreader, and John Martin, indexer.

As for our reviewers, we are hugely grateful for the time and effort that you all put in to reviewing our draft offerings. To those of you who apologized for being critical: please don't. The feedback we received was instrumental in shaping the book and you all added something we hadn't thought about as well as pointing out some of our more obvious idiosyncrasies (or 'mistakes' if you prefer). Therefore, we are particularly indebted to:

Dr Stacy Banwell, University of Greenwich
Dr Sarah Charman, Institute of Criminal Justice Studies, University of Portsmouth
Professor Alan Clarke, Aberystwyth University
Dr Jamie Harding, Northumbria University
Dr Kieran McCartan, University of the West of England
Dr Richard Peake, University of Leeds
Mr David Porteous, Middlesex University
Dr RS Slack, Bangor University
Jon Shute, University of Manchester
Dr Dave Walsh, School of Law and Criminology, University of Derby
Dr Lynne Wrennall, Liverpool John Moores University

Also fully deserving of a very special mention is Steve Whennell, our resident statistical genius and SPSS guru, who has listened patiently to one of us banging on about quantitative analysis at length, and has been an indispensable sounding board for all matters statistical. We have a confidence level of 99.9% in his abilities and his help has always been undeviating and of great significance.

Finally, there are various people a bit closer to home that need some recognition for their support throughout the project. This support has been manifest in various ways, not least of which was leaving us alone uninterrupted for a while as we sped like a sickly tortoise towards completion. So, in no particular order, much gratitude to Peter Day, Tony Kemp, Penny Wallace, Dawn Hardiman, Vince Pearson, Peter Wells, Mary Cassidy, and Val Clifford. Also to Johnno (well, we say that), Jennifer, Alison, Philippa, and Sue.

To conclude, and somewhat as a departure from normal practice in acknowledgements, we would like to thank each other most of all. Writing a textbook is an enormous challenge and it is easy to get stuck at various points along the way. There are days that the words just won't come or it seems impossible to find the right example to illustrate a particular point or the structure of a chapter just will not work. For these problems and many, many others, we always know that the other author is there to listen to the problem, make suggestions to solve it or, in some cases, to take over the writing of a particular section or chapter. This book would not exist in the way that it does if we did not have this wonderful collaborative way of working with each other and, so, dear co-author, I thank you for being the best partner in writing imaginable.

Oh, and to IBM: we really wish you hadn't released a new version of SPSS in the week that we were getting the final manuscript ready for delivery. Stop fiddling about with it, please.

EF and SF
Wokingham
August 2011

ACKNOWLEDGEMENTS

Grateful acknowledgement is made to all the authors and publishers of copyright material that appears in this book, and in particular to the following for permission to reprint material from the sources indicated.

Screenshots reproduced by permission of OPSI, BAILII, Westlaw, Thomson Reuters (Professional), Justis Publishing Ltd, Australasian Legal Information Institute (AustLII), Copac, Mimas, SAGE Publications Ltd, ProQuest LLC, Elsevier, The British Library, Economic Policy Centre, Corporate Communications, Reed Elsevier (UK) Limited, trading as LexisNexis, Greater Manchester Police, SurveyMonkey.

Screenshot of The British Journal of Criminology reproduced by permission of Oxford University Press.

Screenshots from legislation.gov.uk, sentencing.cjsonline.gov.uk, police.uk © Crown copyright.

Screenshot from Eurostat.ec.europa.eu © European Union, 1995–2011.

Screenshot from ukop.co.uk © TSO 2000–2003.

The Court Structure in England and Wales reproduced by permission of Her Majesty's Court Service.

Milgram Ad photo from the book Obedience to Authority: An Experimental View by Stanley Milgram reproduced with kind permission of Alexandra Milgram.

Milgram experiment photo from the film Obedience copyright (c)1968 by Stanley Milgram, copyright renewed 1993 by Alexandra Milgram and distributed by Penn State Media Sales reproduced with kind permission of Alexandra Milgram.

Reprint of SPSS Statistics 20 courtesy of International Business Machines Corporation, © SPSS, Inc., an IBM Company.

Image from ATLAS.ti by permission of ATLAS.ti

Image from NVivo by permission of QSR International

Image in Chapter 10 licensed from iStockphoto.com

Every effort has been made to trace and contact copyright holders prior to publication. If notified, the publisher will undertake to rectify any errors or omissions at the earliest opportunity.

OUTLINE CONTENTS

Introduction

The cover of this book features an open penknife with an impressive range of attachments, including scissors, a magnifying glass, a bottle and can opener, as well as a particularly sharp looking main blade. It's illuminated against a dark background. So why did we pick this as just the image to capture what we think *Criminology Skills* is all about? Without turning this into a media studies lesson, the cover says several things to us. First, by its very nature, much crime is hidden. Criminals tend not to want their activities to be made public. Criminology aims to shine a light into this criminal darkness to explore issues such as why people start to offend, the causes and consequences of crime, methods of crime prevention, public perceptions and reactions to crime, measuring and quantifying crime, how the criminal justice system, the police, the courts, the probation and prison service, should deal with offenders, and methods that the state uses, especially the criminal law, in response to crime. Second, a penknife is quite capable of causing harm: stabbing or merely cutting someone with a knife could give rise to criminal liability for a range of different offences. Simply waving it at someone could be criminal. What about possession of the penknife in a public place? Or selling one to someone under the age of 16? Is it an offensive weapon or a weapon of offence? These have distinct meanings in the criminal law of England and Wales. Knife crime is a topic that is of current concern in the media. Third, and perhaps, most importantly, a penknife contains a whole selection of different tools that can be used in different situations to make life easier. Several years ago, one of us was asked the question: 'Why do you make such a fuss about skills? These students are at university. They ought to know how to study by now.' Our answer is that, yes, perhaps students *ought* to know how to write, reference, research, structure an argument and analyse materials, and do all the other things that are necessary to study effectively, but if they don't, then it seems unkind not to help them to develop the necessary skills. The penknife parallel ought to be clear now, and this is why we enjoy the image so much. This book aims to provide a set of criminology skills that are essential for success, just at the penknife has its plethora of useful attachments. Borrowing from the criminal vernacular of the 1970s (watch *The Sweeney* or, more recently, *Life on Mars*, if you haven't already), this book should leave you 'well tooled-up' for your criminology studies.

The idea behind *Criminology Skills* is that there should be a book that students can consult to find out the things that they need to be able to do in order to study criminology, to perform effectively in assessment, and to become capable and independent researchers. We hope that this is it. This book is split into three sections: finding criminological resources, academic criminology skills, and research skills in criminology. It is balanced 50:50 between academic criminology skills and practical criminology skills (finding and researching).

The first part of *Criminology Skills* introduces the source material that is commonly used in the study of criminology. The aim of this section of the book is to enable you to understand where the criminal law, rules of criminal justice, and other information about crime and criminology comes from and how to find it, both in print and online. These chapters also provide guidance on how to understand these different kinds of source material and how it can be used in your studies. In essence, this section tells you what you need to find, where you can find it, and why you need to find it.

In the second part of the book, the focus shifts to academic skills. As you will see, the bulk of these chapters relate to improving your performance in assessment. The section starts, however, with a consideration of study skills that aims to help you strengthen the way that you approach your study of criminology. There is also a chapter on writing skills, starting with basic ideas of grammar and punctuation and moving on to more advanced skills in creating a persuasive and logical argument that will allow you to use your knowledge of criminology to good effect in all forms of assessment. The decision to devote a whole chapter to referencing reflects increased concerns across universities about plagiarism: fear of being accused of plagiarism as a result of poor referencing is something that concerns many students. We have responded to those concerns by providing a comprehensive guide to referencing that is illustrated with plenty of examples to help you to understand when and how to reference. The remaining chapters concentrate on different types of assessment that you might encounter on your degree. We have sought to provide clear explanations of effective ways to approach each type of work and to ensure that there are plenty of examples to illustrate these explanations.

The final section of the book concentrates on research methods. These chapters explore the different issues associated with conducting different types of research as a means of exploring issues in criminology. It starts with a consideration of the various ethical issues that have to be taken into account when conducting research on crime and criminology with human participants. It covers issues such as confidentiality, anonymity, and data protection as well as the importance of ensuring that no harm comes to those who participate in research. The next chapter sets out different methods of collecting data. It does not matter whether you plan to use these methods or not: an understanding of each method and its suitability to generate particular types of data is essential if you are to understand and evaluate published research undertaken by others in the field of criminology. The final chapters set out the different approaches to analysis so that you will understand what needs to be done with data once it has been collected.

Throughout the book, we place a great deal of emphasis on practical activities. This is because we believe that people learn by doing things rather than by reading about doing things. After all, you wouldn't expect to be able to drive a car (safely) just because you had read a book that told you how to do it: you would expect to have to practise to build up the skills that you need. The same is true with your study of criminology. The skills needed to find out about criminology, extrapolate the key points, and craft them into a well-structured and focused essay are practical skills. The process of committing the ideas in criminology to memory, extracting them on demand, and using them to formulate a comprehensive and analytical answer under the tight time constraints of the exam room are practical. Equally, the business of gathering and analysing data are also very much 'hands on' activities. In essence, most of the skills covered in this book are practical and require you to do something. For this reason, we have developed a range of practical activities for you to try out that can be found on the Online Resource Centre.

As a closing point, we want to emphasize that our aim in writing *Criminology Skills* was to produce the sort of book that we would have wanted to help us when we were undergraduate students. We both remember the challenges of trying to study a new subject at university level when we were not entirely clear what was required of us so we have tried to include answers to every question that we either had, or would have liked to have had, answered when we were students. We have also tried to make sure that we have covered many of the questions that our own students have asked us.

Of course, it is inevitable that we will have missed something so if you have a question that is not answered by *Criminology Skills* then get in touch and tell us. You can email us at **criminologyskills@finchandfafinski.com**. Hopefully, we'll be able to give you the answer that you need and make sure that this is something that we add to future editions of the book.

Emily Finch
Stefan Fafinski

PART I

Finding, using, and evaluating criminological resources

Part I of *Criminology Skills* covers the skills that you will need to find, use, and evaluate criminological resources.

The first chapter covers the criminal law as a basis for definition, equipping you with the skills to find the law and understand what conduct or consequences are defined as criminal. This leads on to chapters covering the main sources which contribute to our knowledge and understanding of crime: books and journal articles, statistics and official publications, and mediated and online resources.

Each of the chapters provides you with an understanding of the different types of source, why they are useful to criminology, and when you should use them, as well as the skills that you will need to search for and find these resources and to evaluate their quality.

Criminal law

INTRODUCTION

This chapter explains the two main sources of criminal law in the UK: legislation, that is, Acts of Parliament (or statutes), and case law. It will give you an overview of the process by which Acts of Parliament come into existence as well as introducing you to European Union legislation and the European Convention on Human Rights, both of which have an influence on the law in the UK. You will also gain an understanding of the criminal courts in which cases are heard and the systems of law reporting which allow access to the judgments of those courts. As well as exploring the sources of law, this chapter will show you how to find legislation and case law using a variety of online resources. Finally, the chapter will give a brief introduction to finding the criminal law of overseas jurisdictions.

An understanding of the criminal law is important to the study of criminology as it is the criminal law that defines certain forms of conduct as criminal. This criminal law can be contained in both statute law and case law, so it is essential that you understand the origins of both and the ways in which they interrelate. You should see that the criminal law is constantly changing and evolving in response to social, political, and technological influences which manifest themselves in new statutes or judicial interpretation of existing law. If you are studying criminology as an option on a law degree, then the content of this chapter should already be familiar to you, but if you are encountering criminal law for the first time, then this chapter should give you a grounding in the essentials that you need to know.

LEARNING OUTCOMES

After reading this chapter, you will be able to:

- Explain the process by which Acts of Parliament come into being

- Find criminal legislation online

- Understand the hierarchy of the courts in England and Wales and the role of case law within the legal system

- Explain the meaning of case citations and use the neutral citation system

- Search for cases online

Legislation

Legislation is a very important source of criminal law, since the majority of criminal offences are defined in statute law, created by Acts of Parliament.

UK Acts of Parliament

Parliament passes legislation in the form of **statutes**, or **Acts of Parliament**. On average, Parliament enacts around sixty or seventy statutes per session and, although this figure remains largely constant, the length of statutes seems to have expanded in recent years, hence increasing the overall volume of legislation.

Most Acts of Parliament will begin life as **Public Bills**, which are introduced by the Government as part of its programme of legislation. Although many people think that most Public Bills arise from the commitments made by the Government as part of its election manifesto, in fact most Public Bills originate from Government departments, advisory committees, or as a political reaction to unforeseen events of public concern (such as the Dangerous Dogs Act 1991 in response to public and media outcry over a number of attacks by pit-bull terriers in which some unfortunate individuals were severely injured or disfigured). If enacted, most Public Bills result in Public General Acts which, as their name suggests, affect the general public as a whole.

Private Members' Bills are non-Government Bills that are introduced by private Members of Parliament (MPs of any political party who are neither Government Ministers nor members of the House of Lords). They may be introduced in a variety of ways. Relatively few Private Members' Bills end up as Acts of Parliament. Although they often deal with relatively narrow issues, they may also be used to draw attention to issues of concern that are not within the legislative agenda of Government.

Statutes may also be passed to consolidate or codify the law. A **consolidating statute** is one which re-enacts particular legal subject matter which was previously contained in several different statutes, whereas a **codifying statute** is one which restates legal subject matter previously contained in earlier statutes, the common law, and custom. Unlike consolidation, codification *may* change the law. An example of a codifying Act is the Theft Act 1968, which attempted to frame the law of theft in 'ordinary language'.

The domestic law-making process

Before a Bill is introduced into Parliament, it may be preceded by a **White Paper** or a **Green Paper**. White Papers set out Government proposals on topics of current concern. They signify the Government's intention to enact new legislation and may set up a consultative process to consider the finer details of the proposal. Green Papers are issued less frequently. They are introductory, higher-level Government reports on a particular area put forward as tentative proposals for discussion without any guarantee of legislative action or consideration of the legislative detail. Proposed Government legislation is then passed to the Parliamentary draftsmen who draft the Bill acting on the instructions of the Government department responsible for the proposal.

Once drafted, a Government Bill can be introduced into either the House of Commons or the House of Lords. Most Bills begin life in the House of Commons and follow the procedure depicted in Figure 1.1.

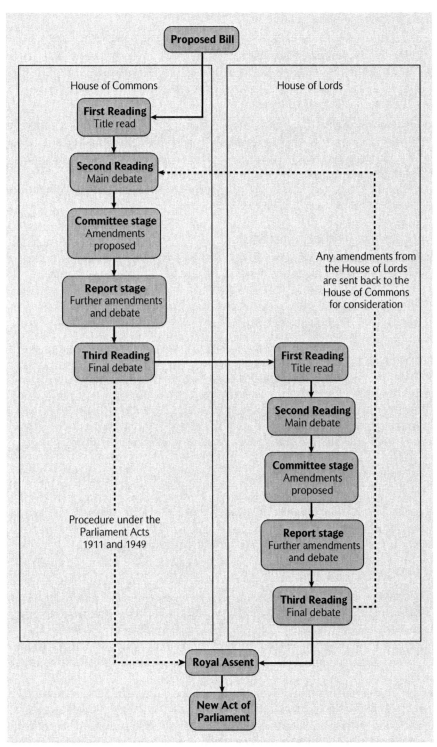

Figure 1.1 The Parliamentary procedure for Bills introduced in the House of Commons

House of Commons—First Reading

The First Reading in the House of Commons is a formality. The Title of the Bill is read by the Clerk of the House and a date is fixed for the Second Reading. Conventionally, the Second Reading does not normally take place before two weekends have passed.

House of Commons—Second Reading

The Second Reading in the House of Commons involves the main debate on the principles of the Bill. For Government Bills, the debate is usually opened by the Minister responsible for the Bill and closed by a junior Minister. A vote is generally taken on the Bill as a whole at the end of the Second Reading. The Bill will then move to a Standing Committee (unless it is moved that the Bill be sent to a Committee of the whole House, a Select Committee, or a Special Standing Committee).

House of Commons—Standing Committee

Following the Second Reading in the House of Commons, most Bills are sent to a Standing Committee which examines the provisions of the Bill in detail and votes on whether each clause, as proposed, 'stands part of the Bill'. Amendments may be moved in Standing Committee. These amendments are also voted upon. The Bill (as amended in Standing Committee) then moves into a Report Stage.

House of Commons—Report Stage

Unless a Bill has been considered by a Committee of the whole House without amendment, the Committee Stage is followed by a Report Stage (sometimes referred to as a Consideration Stage). Here, further amendments may be proposed and introduced, often in an attempt to undo the changes made in Committee. Once the Report Stage is complete—which may take two or three days—the Bill finally proceeds to its Third Reading in the Commons.

House of Commons—Third Reading

In the Third Reading of the Bill, its contents are debated for a final time. It is unusual for any further amendments to be made at this stage. Indeed, the Third Reading does not have to involve any debate at all.

Once the Third Reading is over, the Bill is sent to the House of Lords.

Procedure in the House of Lords

The procedure in the House of Lords mirrors that in the House of Commons. Bills have a formal First Reading, are debated on a Second Reading, proceed to consideration in Committee (although, unlike in the House of Commons, the Committee Stage is almost invariably taken in the Committee of the whole House), are debated again on Report, and then receive a final Third Reading. At the end of the Third Reading there is a formal motion 'that this Bill do now pass'.

Assuming that the Bill survives the motion at the end of the Third Reading in the House of Lords, it is returned to the House of Commons with the Lords' amendments, which must be considered in the Commons. If the House of Commons does not agree with the Lords' amendments it can send it back with counter-amendments and its reasons for doing so. Therefore, a Bill can go back and forth between the Houses several times until proceedings are terminated or the Parliamentary session runs out of time. However, in practice, the House of Lords often accepts the second offering from the House of Commons.

The Parliament Acts 1911 and 1949

These Acts provide a means by which the House of Commons can, under certain circumstances, bypass the House of Lords to present a Bill for Royal Assent without it having been passed by the House of Lords. The procedure under the Parliament Acts has historically been used infrequently, although the 1997 Labour Government used the Acts to force through legislation on more occasions than the Acts had been used in total before its election. Relatively recent examples of the use of this procedure in the criminal law are the Sexual Offences (Amendment) Act 2000, which lowered the age of consent for male homosexual activities from 18 (or, for some activities, 21) to 16, and the Hunting Act 2004, which criminalized certain forms of hunting wild mammals with dogs.

Royal Assent

Royal Assent is required before any Bill can become law. The monarch is not required by the constitution to assent to any Act passed by Parliament. However, assent is conventionally given by the monarch acting on ministerial advice. All that is now required for Royal Assent is a formal reading of the short title of the Act with a form of words signifying the fact of assent in both Houses of Parliament.

The impact of the Human Rights Act 1998

Section 19 of the Human Rights Act 1998 provides that the Minister in charge of each new Bill in either House of Parliament must, before the Second Reading of the Bill, either:

- make a statement of compatibility—that is, state that the provisions of the Bill are compatible with the European Convention on Human Rights; or
- make a statement acknowledging that it is not possible to make a statement of compatibility, but, despite this, the Government still wishes the House to proceed with the Bill.

The courts have no power to set aside any Act of Parliament that is incompatible with Convention rights; although they may make a 'statement of incompatibility' under s 4 of the Human Rights Act 1998 if they are satisfied that the provision is incompatible with a Convention right. Such a statement does not affect the validity, continuing operation, or enforcement of the provision in respect of which it is given; and is not binding on the parties to the proceedings in which it is made.

Parliamentary debates—Hansard or the Official Report

Parliament once prohibited all reporting and publishing of its proceedings, believing that it should deliberate in private. Indeed, it regarded any attempt to publicize its proceedings as a serious punishable offence. However, by the late 1700s, dissent both from the public and within Parliament coupled with the attacks of the press, persuaded Parliament to relax its stance. In 1803, the House of Commons passed a resolution giving the press the right to enter the public gallery and *Cobbett's Weekly Political Register* added reprints of reports of speeches taken from other newspapers in a new supplement. In 1812, publication was taken over by Thomas Hansard, who changed the title of the reports to *Hansard's Parliamentary Debates* in 1829. In 1888, a Parliamentary Select Committee recommended that, rather than let Hansard publish the debates, an authorized version ought to be published, which was officially adopted by Parliament in 1907 as a full report of Parliamentary proceedings.

Therefore *Hansard* (or, less commonly, the *Official Report*) is the edited verbatim report of proceedings in both the House of Commons and the House of Lords. Commons *Hansard* covers proceedings in the Commons Chamber, Westminster Hall, and Standing Committees. Lords *Hansard* covers proceedings in the Lords Chamber and its Grand Committees. Both contain Written Ministerial Statements and Written Answers.

Reference to *Hansard* is particularly useful as it can give a good insight into the thinking that went behind the enactment of a particular piece of legislation and can help to locate the Act in its social and political context. For instance, in the debates which led to the Computer Misuse Act 1990, computer hackers were described as 'often poor', 'unemployed', living a 'drug-based lifestyle', and likely to suffer 'profound sexual inadequacy'.

You will find more on searching Hansard for Parliamentary debates in chapter 3 on statistics and official publications.

Chapter numbers and Regnal years

Each Act passed in any calendar year is given its own number, known as the chapter number. The official citations—comprising year and chapter number—are therefore unique.

Look at Extract 1.1 from the Youth Justice and Criminal Evidence Act 1999.

**Youth Justice and Criminal
Evidence Act 1999**

1999 CHAPTER 23

An Act to provide for the refereal of offenders under 18 to youth offender panels; to make provision in connection with the giving of evidence or information for the purposes of criminal proceedings; to amend section 51 of the Criminal Justice and Public Order Act 1994; to make pre-consolidation amendments relating to youth justice; and for connected purposes.   [27th July 1999]

Legislation reproduced by permission of OPSI.

In this example, the Youth Justice and Criminal Evidence Act 1999 was the twenty-third statute passed in 1999. The word 'chapter' can be abbreviated to 'c'. The chapter number is often given in Harvard references for Acts of Parliament post-1963.

See chapter 7 on referencing for more information on citing Acts of Parliament using the Harvard system.

For Acts prior to 1963 (when the Acts of Parliament Numbering and Citation Act 1962 came into force) the Regnal year citation is given. This is derived from the year of the sovereign's reign corresponding to the Parliamentary session in which the Act was passed. It was common for Parliamentary sessions to span more than one year, in which case all are shown. Look at the example in Figure 1.2.

This is the citation for the one-hundredth Act that was passed in the session beginning the twenty-fourth year of Queen Victoria's reign and which ended in the twenty-fifth year. It is more commonly (and conveniently) known as the Offences against the Person Act 1861.

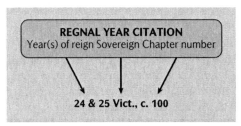

Figure 1.2 Regnal year citation

There is a very useful calendar year to Regnal year conversion table covering 1235–1862 available on the JustCite website at http://www.justcite.com/support/faq-calendar-to-regnal.aspx.

UK statutory instruments

An Act of Parliament may delegate the power to make statutory instruments, usually to a Minister of the Crown. The scope of this power can vary greatly, from the technical (for example, varying the dates on which different provisions of an Act will come into force or changing the levels of fines or penalties for offences) to much wider powers such as filling out the broad provisions in Acts. Often, Acts only contain a broad framework and statutory instruments are used to provide the necessary detail that would be considered too complex to include in the body of an Act.

European Union legislation

An increasingly influential range of sources of law emanates from Europe. The majority of this arises by virtue of the UK's membership of the European Communities from 1 January 1973. Historically, the European Union (EU) was primarily concerned with trade and reluctant to engage with matters of criminal law. However, it has evolved into a broader economic and political partnership and, following ratification of the Lisbon Treaty, the EU has increased its competence more definitively into the realm of the criminal law. Article 69B(1) of the Treaty of Lisbon allows the European Parliament to establish minimum rules concerning the definition of criminal offences and sanctions in the areas of particularly serious crime with a cross-border dimension.

Finding legislation

There is a vast amount of legal information available online. Some online resources are free to access, although many of the commercially-produced databases require a subscription. Most institutions will subscribe to most of the main databases that are covered in this book. These typically require you to log in to gain access and most are accessible via the Athens or Shibboleth access management systems, which will allow you use a single login to access the whole range of databases to which your institution subscribes. Each institution will have its own registration procedures, so a good first point of enquiry will be your institution's library.

A detailed description of the operation of each of the various databases is beyond the scope of this book. Most institutions provide a guide to using each of the main databases and you should check with your librarian for details. Lexis Library and Westlaw often have student representatives at institutions. They are another useful source of information.

You may find other perfectly reputable sources of statute law online—such as websites from local authorities and law firms. However, these sometimes provide a summary or paraphrase of the law—often to make it more accessible to the non-lawyer—rather than using the precise wording of the statute. You should, therefore, make sure that your sources use the official wording. All the resources listed in this section do so.

Practical exercise

Find as many of the legal databases from this section as you can. Make a list of those to which you are allowed access. Have a look at each of them. Perform a few practice searches.

Legislation.gov.uk
http://www.legislation.gov.uk

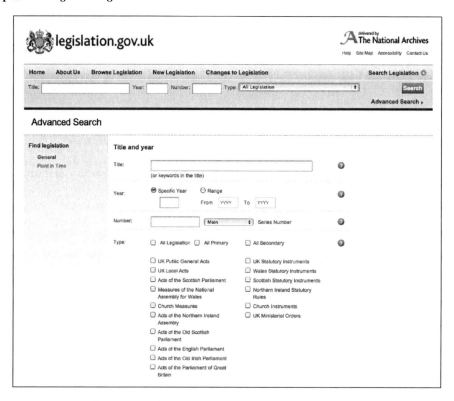

The UK legislation website is published by The National Archives on behalf of HM Government and is the official source of online legislation from 1267 to date. It was launched on 29 July 2010. The new site brings together legislation from the Statute Law Database with the 'as enacted' legislation currently published on the Office of Public Sector Information website to provide a single legislation service that will replace the current services. The statute law database site will remain in place until all content and functionality is available on the new site. The aim is to publish legislation on legislation.gov.uk simultaneously, or at least within 24 hours of its publication in printed form.

BAILII

http://www.bailii.org

BAILII is the abbreviated name of the 'British and Irish Legal Information Institute'. It is a free service which provides a fully searchable collection of statutes and statutory instruments as enacted or passed. The data is derived from the Statute Law Database.

Westlaw

http://www.westlaw.co.uk

Westlaw provides a range of browsing and searching facilities which can be used to find both Acts of Parliament and statutory instruments. It also contains a useful search facility to find historic law at a particular point in time.

Lexis Library

http://www.lexisnexis.com/uk/legal/

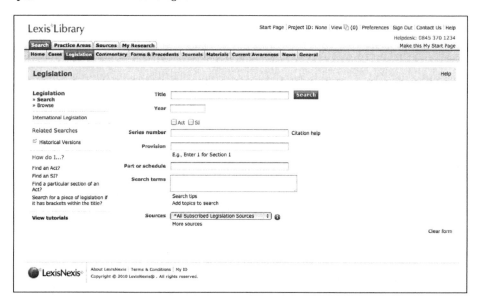

Lexis Library provides searchable legislation and statutory instrument databases. It has various online interactive tutorials.

Lawtel

http://www.lawtel.com

Lawtel provides a good legislation search facility. It also has a full range of browsable legislation.

Practical exercise

Find the following statutes online using the database of your choice:

 Police and Justice Act 2006

 Crime and Disorder Act 1998

 Football (Disorder) Act 2000

 Offences against the Person Act 1861

 You will find video walkthroughs of each of these searches on the Online Resource Centre.

Case law

Legislation is not the only source of criminal law. Not all criminal offences are defined in statute law but arise instead from common law: that is, law that is defined in decided cases. Murder, for example, is not defined in any Act of Parliament. The courts are also called upon to decide the meaning of statutes and how they apply to the particular facts of the case that they are considering. The decisions of such cases may set a precedent to be followed in later cases and thus develop new legal principles from those set out in the statute. The next section will take a brief look at the court system as it applies to criminal law and explain where to find criminal case law.

The court system

Without a set of institutions to enforce legal rules, there would be no legal system. A set of rules cannot usefully exist in isolation. There needs to be a system of courts to hear cases at first instance, as well as higher courts which offer the mechanism for individuals to bring appeals arising from the outcome of cases in lower courts.

 The domestic courts can be depicted as shown in Figure 1.3.

 Criminal courts determine the guilt or innocence of defendants according to the parameters of the criminal law and dispense punishment to convicted offenders. **Trial courts** hear cases 'at first instance'. This refers to the first time that a case is heard in court, before any appeals. They consider the matters of fact and law in the case and make an appropriate ruling. **Appellate courts** consider the application of legal principles to a case that has already been heard at first instance. Some appellate courts also have jurisdiction to reconsider disputed issues of fact.

Supreme Court

The Supreme Court took over the judicial function of the House of Lords and became the highest court in the UK in October 2009. At the current time, for practical purposes, it is safe to assume that the Supreme Court has simply replaced the House of Lords and that whatever applied to the House of Lords applies equally well to the Supreme Court.

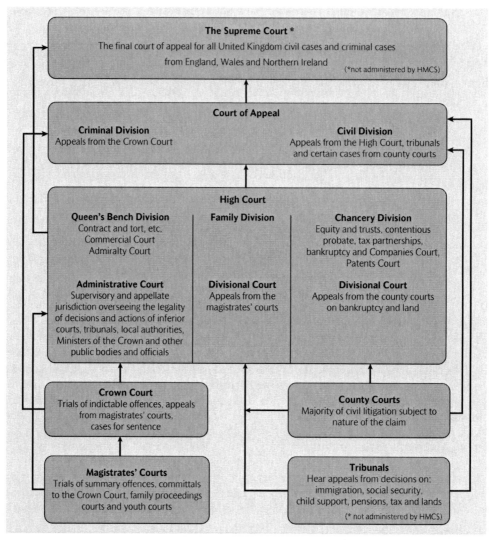

Figure 1.3 The court structure in England and Wales
Figure reproduced by permission of Her Majesty's Courts Service.

The Supreme Court consists of 12 judges with a President and a Deputy President. It is located in Middlesex Guildhall on Parliament Square opposite the Houses of Parliament. The Supreme Court does not hear evidence from witnesses but instead considers legal argument and documentary evidence. It hears criminal appeals from the Court of Appeal (Criminal Division) and the High Court.

Court of Appeal (Criminal Division)

The Court of Appeal is one court which is divided into two divisions—the Civil Division and the Criminal Division. Like the Supreme Court, the Court of Appeal does not hear witnesses.

The Court of Appeal (Criminal Division), as its name suggests, has a predominantly appellate jurisdiction. It also has jurisdiction to hear certain other matters which may be referred to it. It mainly deals with appeals from the Crown Court against conviction, sentence, or both; Attorney General's References; cases referred by the Criminal Cases Review Commission where there has been a possible miscarriage of justice; and applications for leave (permission) to appeal to the Supreme Court.

High Court (Queen's Bench Division)

The High Court is one court. However, it is divided into three 'divisions' for administrative purposes. These are the Queen's Bench Division, Chancery Division, and Family Division. The Queen's Bench Division hears criminal appeals from magistrates' courts and from the Crown Court sitting without a jury (for example, a Crown Court hearing an appeal from the magistrates' court).

Crown Court

The Crown Court deals with trials on indictment (by jury); cases where the magistrates have declined jurisdiction before trial; offences triable either-way where the defendant has elected for trial by jury in the Crown Court; and referrals for sentence from the magistrates' court where the magistrates consider that their sentencing powers are inadequate for the case in question.

   The Crown Court hears appeals from defendants against conviction or sentence or both in the magistrates' court.

Magistrates' court

All criminal proceedings begin in the magistrates' courts and well over 90 per cent end there. The main types of hearing are the trial of summary offences; applications for bail; issue of summonses and warrants for arrest or search; Youth Courts (formerly known as Juvenile Courts) for defendants between the ages of 10 and 18; and committal proceedings for Crown Court trial or sentence.

   Magistrates' court proceedings are either heard by Justices of the Peace (lay magistrates), usually sitting as a bench of three, or a single district judge (magistrates' courts) working on a full-time salaried basis.

Law reporting

Unless you are actually present in court at the time that the judgment in a particular case is made, you will have to rely on a report of the case to find out what happened. Clearly, then, accurate law reporting is extremely important. Before looking at finding law reports in more detail, it is first important to clarify some terminology.

Case naming conventions

Before you can start finding cases, you will need to understand the conventions used in criminal case names and their reports. In criminal matters, cases are brought by the Crown, which is shown as *R*. This is short for *Regina* (meaning the Queen) or, if the monarch at the time of the case was a King, then *R* is short for the masculine form *Rex*. The person against whom a criminal case is brought is referred to as the **defendant**. On appeal, the names of the parties change. The person bringing an appeal is the **appellant** and the person against whom the appeal is brought is known as the **respondent**.

You may see defendants referred to by single letters, rather than by name. This is common practice in cases where the defendant is a minor, where they are vulnerable (such as having mental health issues), or where their identity needs to be protected due to the nature of the case, such as in certain sexual offences or terrorism cases. For example, *R v B* [2008] EWCA Civ 1997 concerned mentally incapable defendants unfit to plead before a jury on various counts of child cruelty, rape, indecent assault, and sexual activity against a child family member.

Finally, you may also encounter **Attorney General's References**. These arise in cases where a defendant has been acquitted on all or part of an indictment. The Attorney General has the discretion to seek the opinion of the Court of Appeal (Criminal Division) (or the Supreme Court if the Court of Appeal (Criminal Division) has already been involved) on a point of law which has arisen in the case. The Attorney General's reference procedure is to clarify the law and is not a means to change the outcome of the individual case. For instance, the *Attorney General's Reference (No. 3 of 1994)* [1998] AC 245 sought clarification on whether the crimes of murder or manslaughter could be committed where unlawful injury is deliberately inflicted on a mother carrying an unborn child, and where the child is subsequently born alive but dies sometime afterwards as a result of the injuries inflicted before birth. The Attorney General may also make reference against an unduly lenient sentence imposed by a lower court.

Case citations

Case citations are an abbreviated form of reference to a particular report of a case. This section deals with the main citations for cases heard in England and Wales. By was of example, we will look at the case of *R v Mirza* which dealt with misconduct in the jury room during a criminal trial.

The citation for *R v Mirza* is [2004] UKHL 2; [2004] 1 AC 1118 and indicates where this particular reported case can be found. You will notice that this particular case has two citations: one **neutral citation** and one **law report citation** (see Figure 1.4)

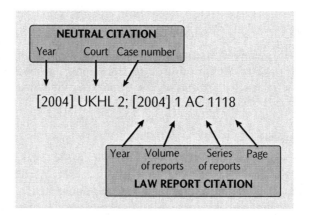

Figure 1.4 Case citations

Neutral citation

The neutral citation system was introduced to the Court of Appeal and the Administrative Court in 2001 and extended to all divisions of the High Court in 2002.

The main reason for the introduction of the neutral citation system was to facilitate the publication of judgments online and the access of judgments stored on electronic databases.

First, the **year** of the judgment is given in square brackets. This is followed by an **abbreviation for the court**, preceded by UK (for 'United Kingdom' in relation to the jurisdiction of the Supreme Court and its predecessor, the House of Lords) or EW (for 'England and Wales' in relation to the jurisdiction of the other courts). The abbreviations used for each of the criminal courts that use the neutral citation system are set out in Table 1.1 below:

Table 1.1 Abbreviations used in the neutral citation system

Court	Abbreviation
Supreme Court	UKSC
House of Lords	UKHL
Court of Appeal (Criminal Division)	EWCA Crim
Queen's Bench Division	EWHC (QB)

Finally, a unique **serial number** is given to each approved judgment issued by the Supreme Court, Court of Appeal, and High Court and is appended to the end of the citation.

Therefore, *R v Mirza* was the second reported judgment of the House of Lords in the UK in 2004.

The neutral citation *precedes* the citation for any law report in which the case has been published. If the report has not been published then the neutral citation stands alone.

Law report citations

The judgments of cases are also published in various series of law reports, the most authoritative of which are published by the Incorporated Council for Law Reporting. References to law reports follow a different convention to that used for neutral citations. Firstly, the **year** shown here is the year in which the case was *reported*. Although cases are usually reported in the same year as the judgment is given, there can be situations where the reports are published later. This can occur if the case was heard late in one year, but was reported early in the next year. Another possible cause of delay between judgment and report can occur if the importance of the case was not appreciated at the time of the judgment.

To complicate matters further, there is a convention surrounding the use of round or square brackets around the year of the report. Prior to 1890, the year was not part of the citation; in other words, it was not necessary to know the year of the report in order to find the case report. However, the date is now inserted for ease of reference, but is put in *round* brackets to indicate that it is for information only. An example of this can be found in *R v Dudley and Stephens* (1884) 14 QBD 273, which considered the defence of necessity in relation to murder: specifically the killing and cannibalization of a young crewmember following a shipwreck.

Since 1890 the year of the case *is* part of the citation, so it must always be provided. The year of the report is put in [square] brackets when the volume of the report series in question is identified by the year itself. When the year of the report is not required to find the particular volume number, it is given in (round) brackets. This convention is frequently misused. Practically

Table 1.2 Some common law report series

Abbreviation	Law report series	Year brackets
AC	Appeal Cases	Square
All ER	All England Law Reports	Square
CLR	Commonwealth Law Reports	Round
Cox CC	Cox's Criminal Law Cases	Round
Cr App R	Criminal Appeal Reports	Square
Cr App R (S)	Criminal Appeal Reports (Sentencing)	Square
Crim LR	Criminal Law Review	Square
KB	King's Bench	Square
QB	Queen's Bench	Square
WLR	Weekly Law Reports	Square

speaking, you should remember that the use of round and square brackets is important and you should be accurate when you are copying citations from materials that you find. Table 1.2 will guide you on the use of the convention for commonly encountered series of law reports.

Following the year, the **volume number** of the law report series is given, if there is more than one volume of the reports for a particular year. If not, then it is omitted.

Next comes an abbreviation for the **series of law reports** in which the case was reported. Some common series of law reports are listed in Table 1.2.

The final part of the citation is the **page number** on which the report begins.

If there is no neutral citation, an abbreviation for the court in which the case was heard may follow the case citation in brackets: for example, *R v R* [1992] 1 AC 599 (HL) was heard in the House of Lords (and can be found on page 599 of volume 1 of the Appeal Cases Reports for 1992). You may see HL for House of Lords, CA for Court of Appeal, or DC for Divisional Court.

Finding case law

In a library, if you know the citation for the case you want to find, then you simply need to find if the library carries the particular series of reports to which the citation refers. If so, look along the shelf for the year and volume you have identified from the citation. The report you require should be at the page listed in the citation.

Sometimes, however, this will not be so. Citations can sometimes be misprinted, or you may have misinterpreted the abbreviation for the report series. Double-check your citation. If the report still proves elusive, or the library does not carry the particular series of reports you want, then you will have to find an alternative citation.

Although there are a number of different legal databases available online, not all databases contain all reports. Table 1.3 provides a summary of some of the more common criminal law report series and the database (or databases) in which they are covered. You will have already encountered some of these databases as they contain both legislation and case law.

In general terms, the databases allow you to search by a name, citation, or keywords, or any combination of the above. The best strategy with all database searches is to try and keep it as simple as possible. For instance, if you are searching for a case called *R v Sed* it would be simple

Table 1.3 Law reports and electronic databases

Series	Citation	Database and dates
The Law Reports	AC, KB, QB	Westlaw (1865–) Lexis Library (1865–) Justis
Weekly Law Reports	WLR	Westlaw Justis
All England Law Reports	All ER	Lexis Library
Criminal Appeal Reports	Cr App R	Westlaw (1990–)

to put in the defendant's name. It is an uncommon name so you would therefore not expect there to be too many cases involving a party called Sed.

However, if the case was *R v Smith* and you did not know the year, you would need to try to find some appropriate subject-matter keywords to narrow your search results; otherwise you would very likely end up with an unmanageable number of potential cases. The pictures that follow in this chapter show the options available on the main search screen of a range of different online resources.

BAILII

http://www.bailii.org

BAILII is a free service which contains judgments from a wide range of sources. It has an extremely comprehensive coverage of case law. BAILII's coverage extends beyond England and Wales to Scotland, Northern Ireland, the Republic of Ireland, and the EU.

Westlaw

http://www.westlaw.co.uk

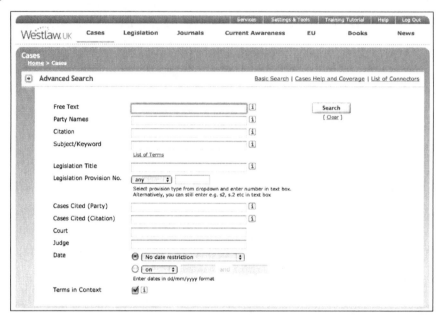

Westlaw allows searching for cases by free text, party name, citation, or keyword, in addition to cases or legislation referred to in the case or the judge or judges involved. Even if the case is not available as full text in Westlaw, links will be given to the location of the report or transcript (if available). Westlaw also contains transcripts of recent cases. However, Westlaw does not contain all series of reports (see Table 1.3 above) and for this reason it is often best used together with another broad database such as Lexis Library.

Lexis Library

http://www.lexisnexis.com/uk/legal

Like Westlaw, Lexis Library is also a subscription service which contains a very broad selection of reports. As well as the standard criteria, it also allows searches by the judge (or judges) that heard the case or searches for cases that considered a particular statutory provision. This can be useful if you need to research how a particular piece of legislation has been applied by the courts.

Lawtel

http://www.lawtel.com

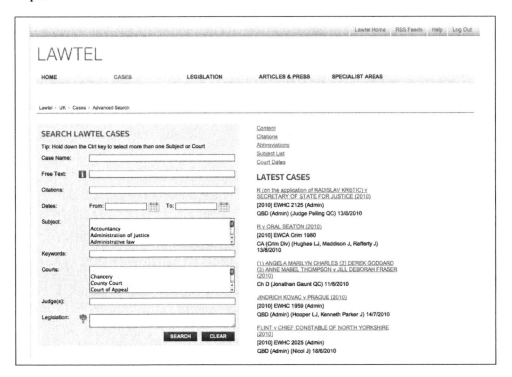

Lawtel is updated daily. It includes the following:

- A daily update
- Summaries of cases since 1980, with some links to full text from 1993 to date
- Personal injury quantum reports
- Practice directions since 1980.

It contains summaries and transcripts only. The summaries provide links to full reports. Lawtel covers an immense range of cases and often carries judgments which are not included in the other databases.

Justis

Justis is a full text online legal library of UK, Irish, and EU case law dating back to 1163 and legislation from 1235.

http://www.justis.com

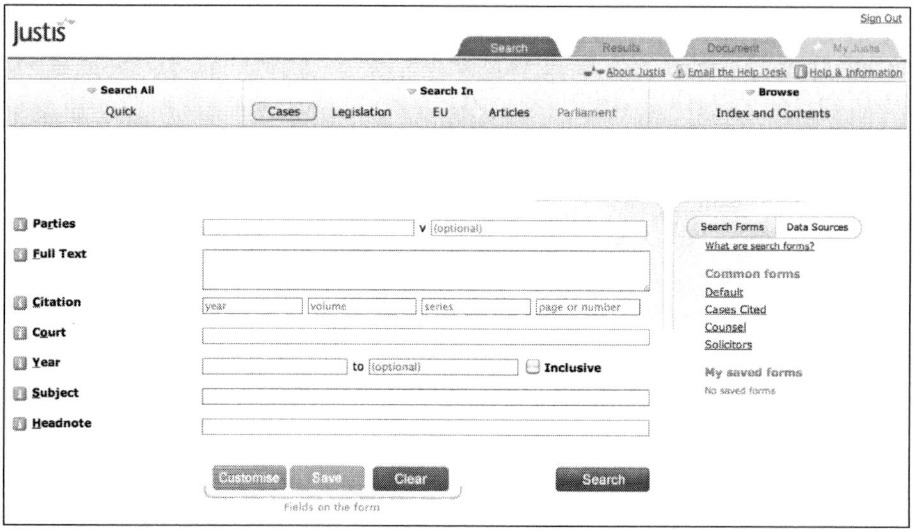

Practical exercise

Find the following statutes online using the database of your choice:

R v Gold; R v Schifreen

R v Young (1995)

Attorney General's Reference (No. 6 of 1980)

R v Wallwork (1958)

R v T [2008] EWCA Crim 815

You will find video walkthroughs of each of these searches on the Online Resource Centre.

Finding criminal law in other jurisdictions

There may be times at which you may wish to investigate the state of the criminal law in other jurisdictions. This may be other Commonwealth jurisdictions such as Australia, New Zealand, and Canada, for example, or for a particular comparative study with another country or continent.

The WorldLII service is extremely useful in this regard. It is a free service which currently comprises 1165 databases from 123 jurisdictions via 14 Legal Information Institutes, including BAILII which you have previously encountered. WorldLII provides a single search facility for databases located on the following Legal Information Institutes:

- AustLII (Australia)
- BAILII (Britain and Ireland)
- CanLII (Canada)

- HKLII (Hong Kong)
- LII (Cornell University, United States)
- PacLII (Pacific Islands)

http://www.worldlii.org

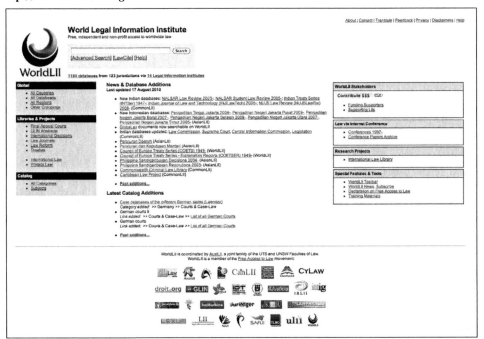

WorldLII also includes databases of decisions of international courts and tribunals together with databases from a number of Asian countries and South Africa.

CHAPTER SUMMARY

Legislation

- Government Bills can be introduced in the House of Commons or House of Lords and can be preceded by a White Paper or a Green Paper
- The Parliament Acts 1911 and 1949 provide a means by which the House of Commons can (under certain circumstances) bypass the House of Lords to present a Bill for Royal Assent without it having been passed by the House of Lords
- Royal Assent is required before any Bill can become law; it is customarily given
- The Human Rights Act 1998 requires that new Bills must be accompanied by a statement of compatibility (or a declaration that a statement of compatibility is not possible)
- The courts may make a declaration of incompatibility for Acts of Parliament which are incompatible with the European Convention on Human Rights; this does not affect the validity of the Act
- *Hansard* is the official report of Parliamentary proceedings. It is particularly useful in helping to discern the thinking behind an Act

- The most common form of delegated legislation is the statutory instrument
- The EU is beginning to increase its legislative competence into the area of criminal law

Finding legislation

- The UK legislation website is the official source of online legislation from 1267 to date
- BAILII provides a free legislation search
- Westlaw, Lexis Library, and Lawtel are commercially-available databases with extensive search facilities

Case law and the courts

- Criminal courts determine guilt or innocence of defendants and dispense punishment to convicted offenders
- Trial courts hear cases at first instance—before any appeals
- Appellate courts consider the application of legal principles to cases that have already been heard at first instance
- The Supreme Court hears criminal appeals from the Court of Appeal (Criminal Division) and the High Court
- The Court of Appeal is divided into Civil and Criminal Divisions
- The High Court is divided into three divisions for administrative purposes—the Queen's Bench Division deals with criminal cases
- The Crown Court primarily deals with trial by jury in criminal cases
- All criminal proceedings begin in the magistrates' court

Finding case law

- BAILII provides a free case law search
- Westlaw, Lexis Library, Lawtel, and Justis are commercially-available databases with a range of case law searching facilities

Other jurisdictions

- WorldLII is a free service which currently comprises 1165 databases from 123 jurisdictions

 FURTHER READING

- Clinch, P. (2001) *Using a Law Library*. 2nd Ed. London: Blackstone Press provides a very detailed guide to finding legal materials in a law library. Although the sections on electronic sources are now somewhat out of date, the book does provide a wealth of additional information on tracking down paper-based sources.

- The *Cardiff Index to Legal Abbreviations* available online at http://www.legalabbrevs. cardiff.ac.uk/ allows you to search for the meaning of abbreviations for English language legal publications, from the UK, the Commonwealth, and the United States, including those covering international and comparative law. A wide selection of major foreign language law publications is also included.

abc GLOSSARY

The **appellant** in a criminal appeal is the party who is bringing the appeal.

Appellate courts hear appeals; they consider the application of legal principles to a case that has already been heard at first instance.

An **Attorney General's Reference** is made to the Court of Appeal (Criminal Division) either to clarify a point of law following an acquittal or to appeal against an unduly lenient sentence imposed by a lower court following conviction.

A **codifying statute** is one which restates legal subject matter previously contained in earlier statutes and case law.

A **consolidating statute** re-enacts a topic contained in several different earlier statutes.

Criminal courts determine guilt or innocence of parties accused of a criminal offence and dispense sentences accordingly.

The **defendant** in a criminal case is the party accused of wrongdoing.

A **Green Paper** is an introductory, high-level Government report which expresses tentative proposals for discussion without any commitment to new legislation.

Private Members' Bills are non-Government Bills that are introduced by private Members of Parliament.

Public Bills are proposals for legislation which are put forward by the Government as part of its legislative programme.

The **respondent** in a criminal appeal is the party against whom the appeal has been brought; they are responding to the appellant's appeal.

Statutes or **Acts of Parliament** are written laws enacted by Parliament.

Trial courts hear cases for the first time (at first instance), consider the matters of fact and law in the case and make an appropriate ruling.

A **White Paper** is a precursor to a Bill which sets out Government proposals on topics of current concern and signifies intent to enact new legislation.

2 Books, journals, and articles

Studying for a degree in any subject requires a great deal of reading and criminology is no exception. During your studies, you will need to read in order to supplement the information provided in lectures, to prepare for seminars and tutorials, to research for coursework, and to revise for examinations. This chapter focuses on two major sources—books and journal articles—and explains how you will know which of these to read and how you will find them. In doing so, this chapter starts by explaining how to locate books and articles specified on a reading list and then moves on to consider how to find material on a particular topic that is not listed by formulating a search strategy and using databases to locate relevant literature.

Books and journal articles are two of the main sources that you will read during your study of criminology. Too many students start their studies believing that they can limit their reading to a single recommended textbook in each module that they study. This is an unfortunate approach, as it means that the student only ever gets one perspective on a topic which is not sufficient for the depth of knowledge that is required to achieve good marks. A recommended textbook should be a starting point for reading, that is supplemented by other books and journal articles as well as other sources that will be covered in subsequent chapters. This chapter will equip you with the skills to find the books and articles that you need to gain an in-depth knowledge of the modules that you study.

LEARNING OUTCOMES

After reading this chapter, you will be able to:

- Distinguish between textbooks, edited collections, books of key readings, monographs, and dictionaries

- Understand the use of journal articles as important sources of criminological information and research

- Formulate and execute bibliographic search strategies in a library and online

- Reflect on and refine your search results to focus in on the particular material you need

Books

Books are one of the most common sources used in the study of criminology. It is likely that your first port of call when deciding what books to read will be the reading list for each of your modules. A reading list, exactly as it name suggests, is a list of the materials of various types that you are expected to read in each module. It is usual for a reading list to detail all the sources that you are expected to use and this could be a combination of books, articles, official reports, newspaper articles, case law, and internet sources. This may then be broken down into more specified instructions for week-by-week reading and reading that needs to be done in preparation for tutorials.

Youth crime and youth justice reading list

Books

Fionda, J. (2005) *Devils and Angels: Youth, Policy and Crime*. Oxford: Hart.

Goldson, B. (2008) *Dictionary of Youth Justice*. Cullompton: Willan.

McLaughlin, E. & Muncie, J. (2007) *Sage Dictionary of Criminology*. London: Sage.

McLaughlin, E., Muncie, J. & Hughes, G. (2002) *Criminological Perspectives: Essential Readings*. 2nd Ed. London: SAGE.

Muncie, J., Hughes, G. & McLaughlin, E. (eds.) (2002) *Youth Justice: Critical Readings*. London: Sage.

Muncie, J. (2009) *Youth and Crime*. 3rd Ed. London: SAGE.

Maguire, M., Goldson, B. & Muncie, J. (eds) (2008) *Youth, Crime and Justice*. London: SAGE.

Newburn, T. (2007) Young People, Crime and Youth Justice. In: Morgan, R. & Reiner, R. (eds.) *Oxford Handbook of Criminology*. 4th Ed. Oxford: OUP, 531–578.

Newburn, T. (2007) *Criminology*. Cullompton: Willan (Chapter 29, 714–741).

Sharpe, G. (2010) *Offending Girls: Young Women and Youth Justice*. Cullompton: Willan Publishing.

This is an extract from a reading list from a Youth Crime and Youth Justice module that lists a range of different types of books that you will encounter in your studies. The sections that follow will each deal with a particular kind of book, explaining the differences between them and how you are likely to use them during your study of criminology. Further on in the chapter, you will find guidance on how to locate these books and how to find out about books that are not on your reading list.

Textbooks

Textbooks are written for students to support particular areas of study. Most textbook authors will take into account the topics that are taught on particular modules when planning their book, so you should find that a textbook that is recommended for a particular module will provide at least some coverage of the majority of the subject matter covered in that module.

Student textbooks aim to provide a foundation of knowledge in a particular area of study. They collect together, explain, analyse, and criticize many of the theoretical and practical aspects of crime, criminology, and criminal justice. In essence, a student text will condense and simplify a body of knowledge in criminology into a more readily digestible chunk that is suitable for someone who is new to the subject matter. They are written by one or more authors who take responsibility for the entire book. Although co-authors might not physically write each chapter together, they would typically read each other's work to ensure that the book reads coherently and consistently throughout. (That is certainly the approach we have taken in *Criminology Skills* although we are not saying who wrote which chapters.) A benefit of student textbooks, then, is that they are more likely to be expressed in a consistent way than an edited collection which is the product of multiple contributors.

There are several student textbooks available in the field of criminology that cover the range of modules usually covered on the degree. These might be general textbooks on criminology that will provide an overview of a great many topics, but which may need to be supplemented by further reading to achieve a greater depth of understanding in particular modules or have a narrower focus on a particular topic so that it can be outlined in more detail. There is an example of each of these on the reading list.

Youth crime and youth justice reading list

Textbooks

⇨Muncie, J. (2009) *Youth and Crime*. 3rd Ed. London: SAGE.

Newburn, T. (2007) *Criminology*. Cullompton: Willan (Chapter 29, 714–741).

Recommended purchase

As is often the case, you should be able to tell which of these is the general textbook on criminology and which has the narrower focus on youth justice from the titles of the books. Note that your attention is directed to the chapter dealing with youth justice in Newburn's textbook, to indicate that you are not expected to read the entire book but only the relevant chapter. If this were your reading list, you might find it helpful to read Newburn's chapter in *Criminology* at the start of the Youth Crime and Youth Justice module to give you an overview of the issues that will be covered in the module. You can then add depth and detail to your knowledge by using the more detailed *Youth and Crime* textbook as the module progresses.

You will see that a symbol (⇨) has been added to the reading list to indicate that Muncie's *Youth and Crime* is the textbook recommended for purchase on the Youth Crime and Youth Justice module. It is usual for a lecturer to pick out one or two books as the recommended purchase for a module. This means that it is one that will be referred to throughout the course and will usually form part of the required reading for seminar or tutorial preparation. However, textbooks are written in different styles and have widely varying degrees of difficulty. If you find that you are not getting on with your set text, you should ask your course leader whether there is a different text that might suit you better. For instance, if you find the set text hard to follow, then you might need a more basic book to give you a lower-level grounding in the material before building upon that with the set text. Equally, if you are fortunate enough to think that your textbook is too simple, then a higher-level text will allow you to deepen your understanding and build upon your skills of analysis and critical evaluation.

Student textbooks undergo frequent revision to ensure that they stay current and relevant. You should always make sure that you are using the most recent edition of your particular textbook. For that reason, buying second-hand textbooks in student shops or online should be done with care, as you would not want to be working from a book which did not cover or explain more recent developments. If you do, you run the risk of inaccuracy or lack of currency in your research.

Edited collections

Edited collections, are, as their name suggests, books which are collections of chapters on particular topics written by different contributors and assembled by an editor or editors.

Each chapter is specifically written to be part of the collection so such books have a single theme that unites all the contributions. The role of the editor is to recruit contributors and coordinate contributions to ensure that all the topics are covered. The editor(s) will write an introductory chapter that outlines what the book aims to achieve and provides an overview of each contribution, thus explaining how each chapter fits into the overall theme of the book. Editors may write one or more chapters themselves and carry overall responsibility for the finished book.

The advantage of an edited collection is that each chapter is usually contributed to by a recognized specialist expert in a particular field, so there is an extent to which the depth of coverage will be greater than in more generalist student texts. However, contributors will have a range of writing styles, so some chapters might have a written style that suits you better than others. Edited collections are plentiful, and are a very useful source of criminological literature. They may cover a very broad or more specialist areas of study as you will see on the reading list.

Youth crime and youth justice reading list

Edited collections

Maguire, M., Goldson, B. & Muncie, J. (eds.) (2008) *Youth, Crime and Justice*. London: SAGE.
Newburn, T. (2007) Young People, Crime and Youth Justice. In: Morgan, R. & Reiner, R. (eds) *Oxford Handbook of Criminology*. 4th Ed. Oxford: OUP, 531–578.

As was the case in relation to textbooks, the reading list contains one edited collection with a general theme of criminology and one that is focused more specifically on youth crime. You will see that a particular chapter of the *Oxford Handbook of Criminology* has been specified as relevant, just as a particular chapter was detailed in the general textbook in the previous section. There is a difference in the way that this is presented which reflects the way that contributions to an edited collection are referenced.

You will find a detailed explanation of the approach to referencing different types of books and other sources in chapter 7 on referencing and avoiding plagiarism.

Key readings

It is not always straightforward to differentiate between key readings and edited collections. Both types of book are compiled by an editor who selects content written by many contributors on a single theme and puts them together in one book. However, the essential distinction is that a book of key readings collects together material that has already been published elsewhere: as a chapter of a monograph or edited collection, or as a journal article. As with textbooks and edited collections, key readings may have a wide or a narrow focus and you will see one of each of these on the reading list.

Youth crime and youth justice reading list

Key readings

McLaughlin, E., Muncie, J. & Hughes, G. (2002) *Criminological Perspectives: Essential Readings*. 2nd Ed. London: SAGE.
Muncie, J., Hughes, G. & McLaughlin, E. (eds.) (2002) *Youth Justice: Critical Readings*. London: SAGE.

A book of key readings is an excellent student resource as it is a selection of primary sources (material that has already been published elsewhere) gathered together in a single place (a secondary source). The use of key readings should help to improve your levels of critical analysis as they allow you to offer your own interpretation and understanding of original material, rather than relying on second-hand interpretations found in textbooks. For example, *Youth Justice: Critical Readings* contains 31 contributions that, in the absence of this book, you would need to locate yourself. This is particularly useful if some of the contributions would be particularly difficult to find: perhaps they were originally part of a book that is now out-of-print or were published a long time ago. For example, there is an extract from Quetelet's work, *A Treatise on Man* that was published in 1842 in *Criminological Perspectives: Essential Readings*.

When you use books of key readings, you will see that details of the original publication are included on the first page of each contribution. This is important, because details of the primary source (the contribution) and the secondary source in which you read it (the key reading) must be referenced.

You will find a detailed explanation of how to reference materials from key reading texts in chapter 7 on referencing and avoiding plagiarism.

Monographs

Monographs are a detailed written study of a single specialized topic. They are usually more expensive than student textbooks and cover particular narrow subject areas in much greater depth. Monographs may be too detailed and narrowly focused to be useful for tutorial preparation, but are likely to be valuable when researching a topic in greater depth for a piece of coursework or a dissertation. For example, if you were interested in young female offenders, you would find that there are five pages devoted to this topic in Muncie's textbook *Youth and Crime*, and one chapter in the edited collection *Youth, Crime and Justice*, whereas *Offending Girls* is a monograph devoted to the topic.

Youth crime and youth justice reading list

Monographs

Fionda, J. (2005) *Devils and Angels: Youth, Policy and Crime*. Oxford: Hart.

Sharpe, G. (2010) *Offending Girls: Young Women and Youth Justice*. Cullompton: Willan Publishing.

Dictionaries

Unlike the everyday use of the term, 'dictionary' in this context does not simply mean a compilation of brief definitions of one or two lines. Instead, criminology 'dictionaries' are more like mini-encyclopaedias and provide concise explanations of words, phrases, theories, and theorists. For example, many entries in the *SAGE Dictionary of Criminology* span several pages and are divided into sections: definition, distinctive features, evaluation, associated concepts, and key reading.

Youth crime and youth justice reading list

Dictionaries

Goldson, B. (2008) *Dictionary of Youth Justice*. Cullompton: Willan.

McLaughlin, E. & Muncie, J. (2007) *SAGE Dictionary of Criminology*. London: SAGE.

Dictionaries may be general or topic-based as you will see on the reading list. They are a useful reference guide, particularly for moments when you encounter a term with which you are not familiar and need a quick overview to assist your understanding. Remember that dictionaries are considered to be **tertiary sources**, which contain information distilled from primary and secondary sources, so should not be relied upon as sources in your coursework; it is a common problem that students often start an essay by defining its subject matter by reference to a dictionary. This is a problem because the dictionary has done the job that you were supposed to do: it has taken a complex concept and pared it down to its essential characteristics to provide a one or two line definition. Rather than relying on a dictionary definition in your work, use the dictionary to help you to understand a concept and to locate the original source where the concept is discussed. Using the two sources, you can then formulate your own definition of that concept.

Finding books

Searching for a book is a relatively straightforward matter provided you are in possession of at least some of its bibliographic details: the title of the book, the name of the author, the year that the book was published, and the name of the publisher. In most cases, you will be able to find a book as long as you know its title and/or the name of its author. You will have this information if the book was detailed on your reading list or if you saw a reference to it in a book or journal.

However, there will also be situations in which you either know that a particular book exists but you do not have its bibliographic details or are speculating that a book on a particular topic might exist. In such cases, you will need to search for the book by topic.

Bibliographic searches

If you know the bibliographic details of a book, you will be able to search for it in your own university's library by using the library catalogue. This will contain details of all the books held in the university library with details of the shelf on which they can be found, whether or not they are out on loan, and the length of time for which they can be borrowed.

You will be able to search the library catalogue from terminals within the library or by using the search facility on your library's webpage. It is not possible to provide details of how the library catalogue works at every university library but all catalogues share common features so it is likely that it will be a simple matter of typing the title of the book and the author's name into the relevant boxes. If you do encounter problems, help will generally be at hand from one of the librarians (if you are in the library) or in the form of a set of instructions if you are using the online catalogue.

Practical exercise: author searches

Demand for library books often outstrips supply, especially in the weeks immediately prior to an assessment deadline. If you find that there are no copies of the book that you need available in the library, try using the library catalogue to search for other books written by the same author or search for other authors who have written a lot on a particular topic. This may enable you to identify good alternatives to the book that you wanted.

1. Look at the reading list on Youth Crime and Youth Justice provided earlier in this chapter. If none of these books were available, which authors would you select to search for their other work? Use your own library catalogue to see whether your chosen authors have written any other books on the same subject matter.

2. Imagine that you wanted to read *Captive Audience: Media, Masculinity and Power* by Yvonne Jewkes but it was not available in your library. Use the catalogue to see if any of the other books by this author cover the same subject matter.

There are other courses of action available if the book that you want is not stocked in your university library or if it is out on long-term loan. You could use the Copac library catalogue to see if the book is held at another university library.

http://copac.ac.uk

This gives free access to the merged online catalogues of major university libraries as well as specialist libraries (such as the National Art Library at the Victoria and Albert Museum) and the national libraries (such as the British Library and the National Library of Wales). Copac contains around 36 million records and it is an excellent means of tracking down books, particularly less common materials such as monographs that may not be held by your own library.

The search result will indicate which libraries stock the book. If the book is held by a library that is within a reasonable distance, you may want to travel there to obtain it. You will be able to use the book for reference within the library or you may be able to borrow it by virtue of SCONUL (Society of College, National and University Libraries) which is a scheme by which members of one university get reciprocal access/borrowing rights at other university libraries.

You should find details of SCONUL in your library or you can visit their website: http://www.sconul.ac.uk.

Alternatively, you may want to arrange for a book held at another university library to be delivered to you using a system known as inter-library loan. You will need to find out what the rules are regarding the inter-library loan system at your own university as all institutions seem to differ on whether they offer this service to their students and, if so, whether they charge a fee for it.

Topic searches

In the absence of bibliographic information, you will need to search for a book using its subject matter as a search term. Obviously, this is likely to be a less precise method of searching as there may be a great many books on a particular topic, whereas using the author/title search terms in conjunction with each other will usually allow you to locate a precise book without any great difficulty.

Searching by topic is also useful for speculative searching; in other words, searching to see whether there are any books on a particular topic rather than searching for a book that you know exists. This can be a very useful strategy if you are carrying out research for a piece of coursework or a dissertation, as not only will it give you access to a wider range of source material than would be the case if you restricted your reading to books from your reading list, but it is often the case that markers will give credit for independent research and evidence of wide reading.

When searching by topic, you will want to identify words and phrases that encapsulate the subject matter.

Practical exercise: topic searches

When searching for books by topic, it is important to be flexible with your choice of search terms as the author may have used different terminology in the title of the book. Try the following exercise to see if you can locate books that would be useful for an essay on the influence of socio-economic factors on youth offending.

1. What are the key words of your topic?

2. What synonyms can you find for these key words?

 Use the search terms that you have identified to look for books on Copac (http://copac.ac.uk). If you are unsuccessful, try to reformulate your search terms. You will find a discussion of this exercise on the Online Resource Centre.

Journals

A journal is a periodic publication that contains a combination of articles, editorial comment, news updates, book reviews, and case digests. It is usually published as a number of individual issues each year which combine to make an annual volume. Some journals publish monthly issues and most publish at least two issues a year whereas books tend only to be updated every two or three years, if at all. As journals are published more frequently than books, they are an excellent source of information on recent developments, new research, and current debates in criminology.

The content of journals is determined by the editorial team, who will be experts in the discipline central to the journal, from the articles submitted to them by academics and other experts. Each article goes through a stringent review process to ensure that only the best quality material is published.

As is the case with books, there are various types of journals as you will see on the reading list:

Youth crime and youth justice reading list

Articles

Chen, X. (2009) The Link Between Juvenile Offending and Victimization: The Influence of Risky Lifestyles, Social Bonding, and Individual Characteristics. *Youth Violence and Juvenile Justice*, 7(2), 119–135.

Carroll, A. (1995) Characterising the Goals of Juvenile Delinquents: Nature, Content and Purpose. *Psychology, Crime and Law*, 1, 247–260.

Corrin, L. (2010) No Holding Back. *Solicitors Journal*, 154(30), 23.

Crawford, A. & Newburn, T. (2002) Recent Developments in Restorative Justice for Young People in England and Wales: Community Participation and Restoration. *British Journal of Criminology*, 42, 476–495.

Epstein, R. & Wise, I. (2003) Children Behind Bars. *New Law Journal*, 153(7068), 263.

Macdonald, R. & Shildrick, T. (2010) The View from Below: Marginalised Young People's Biographical Encounters with Criminal Justice Agencies. *Child and Family Law Quarterly*, 22, 186–199.

Each journal will have a theme. Some of these will be quite broad, such as the *British Journal of Criminology*, which publishes articles on the whole spectrum of criminology research, whilst others have a far more narrow focus: for example, the *Journal of Youth Violence and Juvenile Justice*. As criminology crosses the boundaries of several disciplines, you may find relevant articles in journals in sociology, psychology, and law. For example, the *Child and Family Law Quarterly* would be categorized as a law journal and *Psychology, Crime and Law* is the official journal of the European Association of Psychology and Law but, as the articles listed above illustrate, they contain material of interest to criminologists.

Each article will provide a detailed examination of a narrow issue within the theme of the journal. For example, the current edition (at the time of writing) of *Youth Justice* contains the following articles:

Youth justice (2010) volume 10, issue 2

Cesaroni, C. and Peterson-Badali, M. 'Understanding the Adjustment of Incarcerated Young Offenders: a Canadian Example' 107–125

Freeman, S. and Seymour, M. 'Just Waiting: the Nature and Effect of Uncertainty on Young People in Remand Custody in Ireland' 126–142

Drakeford, M. and Gregory, L. 'Transforming Time: a New Tool for Youth Justice' 143–156

Smithson, H., Wilcox, A., and Monchuk, L. 'Current Responses to Youth Racially Motivated Offending' 157–173

Stone, N. (Legal Commentary) 'Special Measures for Child Defendants: a Decade of Developments' 174–185

You will see that there is a mix of articles from different contributors around the theme of youth justice. Each article is between 5,000 and 8,000 words in length (this is specified by the editorial board) so you can see that you will find a far more detailed account of the effect of imprisonment on young offenders in the first two articles than you might expect to find in a textbook.

However, not all journals publish such lengthy articles. On the reading list, you will see the article 'Children Behind Bars' published in the *New Law Journal*. This is a two-page discussion of the salient points of the arguments of the Howard League for Penal Reform concerning the duty towards young people in custody. Journals such as the *New Law Journal* and the *Solicitors Journal* are practitioner journals, rather than academic journals. This means that they are written for professionals in practice who need to be kept up-to-date with recent developments. They are published far more frequently than academic journals: most practitioner journals are weekly, fortnightly, or monthly. Although they are less detailed than academic journals, they provide snapshots of new developments so can be useful sources of information.

You will find a list of many leading criminology journals later in this chapter.

Finding articles

It is inevitable that you will need to find journal articles during your studies. Not only is it likely that your tutorial reading will include journal articles but you will also need to find relevant articles when carrying out research for an essay, a research project, or a dissertation.

See chapter 8 on essays and chapter 9 on dissertations and research reports for a more detailed discussion of how journal articles will contribute to your success in coursework.

You will either find journal articles in the library or in electronic form online. As was the case in relation to books, if you have the full bibliographic reference then you should have all the information that you need to locate it in the library or online. If you lack this information, you will either need to browse on the website of a relevant journal or carry out a topic search in an electronic database.

Before you start

If you are going to use the electronic databases to search for or access articles, you will need to ensure that you have all the information necessary to enable you to use the online resources at your university. You will need the login details for the library and you may also have a separate 'Athens' username and password provided by your library to allow access to other online resources. Athens is a system that has been used by academic institutions for access and identity management since 1994. However, most institutions now link directly to a host of online resources via a service called Shibboleth which is based on Athens. Shibboleth avoids the need for a separate Athens password. Instead, it allows access to resources via your normal university username and password. Although it is likely that your institution will connect via Shibboleth, you should check with your library to confirm whether your university supports Shibboleth login or whether you need a separate Athens username and password.

Bibliographic searches

If you have seen a reference to a particular article on your reading list or detailed in a published work, you should have all the information that you need to locate it in the library or online. The bibliographic details that you should have are as follows:

Table 2.1 Bibliographic details

Bibliographic detail	Example
Author(s)	Crawford and Newburn
Title of article	Recent Developments in Restorative Justice for Young People in England and Wales: Community Participation and Restoration
Name of journal	British Journal of Criminology
Year of publication	2002
Volume and/or issue number	42
Starting page or page range	476–495

The starting point for locating an article from its bibliographic details is the name of the journal. You can check the library catalogue (typing the name of the journal into the 'title of periodical/journal' field) to determine whether your library keeps bound volumes of the journal on the shelves in the library or if it has electronic access to the journal.

If there are copies of the journal in the library, the catalogue will provide details of their location and you can select the correct volume from the shelf and turn to the relevant page to find the article. You can then use this within the library or take a photocopy of it; printed journals are generally reference resources only so it is unlikely that you will be permitted to take it out of the library on loan.

If your library has electronic access to the journal, you will be able to click on the link provided in the library catalogue to access the journal via the internet. As you were logged in to your library catalogue, accessing the journal in this way should mean that you are recognized as an authorized user who can then access the full text of the articles published in that journal.

Practical exercise: electronic access

It is important that you are able to access journals in this way because many libraries are cutting back on their physical holdings in favour of electronic access, so it may be that the only way that you can obtain some material is via the internet. Each university has its own system of electronic access so you will need to experiment with your own system or, better still, attend a training course, to ensure you are able to use it.

1. Search your library catalogue for the *British Journal of Criminology*.

2. Click on the link provided to access the website of the journal.

3. Using the details provided above, click on the relevant year.

4. Look at the information provided and select the appropriate volume.

 You should now see a list of articles that includes the one written by Crawford and Newburn (see below). Click on 'PDF' to see if you can access this journal. If this process did not work, you will need to ask one of the librarians at your university for help. You will find a walkthrough of this search on the Online Resource Centre.

http://bjc.oxfordjournals.org

OXFORD JOURNALS   CONTACT US   MY BASKET   MY ACCOUNT

THE BRITISH JOURNAL OF
CRIMINOLOGY

ABOUT THIS JOURNAL   CONTACT THIS JOURNAL   SUBSCRIPTIONS   CURRENT ISSUE   ARCHIVE   SEARCH

Oxford Journals > Law & Social Sciences > British Journal of Criminology > Volume 42, Number 3

THE BRITISH JOURNAL OF   Click through to
CRIMINOLOGY   find out more

Receive this page by email each issue: [Sign up for eTOCs]

Contents: **Vol. 42, No. 3, Summer 2002** [Index by Author]   **Other Issues:** ⬅ ➡
◘ Articles

Find articles in this issue containing these words:
[   ] (Enter) [Search ALL Issues]

To see an article, click its [PDF] link. **To review many abstracts,** check the boxes to the left of the titles you want, and click the 'Get All Checked Abstract(s)' button. **To see one abstract at a time,** click its [Abstract] link.

(Clear) (Get All Checked Abstract(s))

Articles: ◘

Kieran McEvoy, Harry Mika, and Barbara Hudson
Introduction: Practice, Performance and Prospects for Restorative Justice
Br J Criminol 2002 42: 469-475; doi:10.1093/bjc/42.3.469 [PDF] [Request Permissions]

☐ Adam Crawford and Tim Newburn
Recent Developments in Restorative Justice for Young People in England and Wales: Community Participation and Representation
Br J Criminol 2002 42: 476-495; doi:10.1093/bjc/42.3.476 [Abstract] [PDF] [Request Permissions]

☐ Ann Skelton
Restorative Justice as a Framework for Juvenile Justice Reform: A South African Perspective
Br J Criminol 2002 42: 496-513; doi:10.1093/bjc/42.3.496 [Abstract] [PDF] [Request Permissions]

☐ Declan Roche
Restorative Justice and the Regulatory State in South African Townships
Br J Criminol 2002 42: 514-533; doi:10.1093/bjc/42.3.514 [Abstract] [PDF] [Request Permissions]

☐ Kieran McEvoy and Harry Mika
Restorative Justice and the Critique of Informalism in Northern Ireland
Br J Criminol 2002 42: 534-562; doi:10.1093/bjc/42.3.534 [Abstract] [PDF] [Request Permissions]

☐ John Braithwaite
Setting Standards for Restorative Justice
Br J Criminol 2002 42: 563-577; doi:10.1093/bjc/42.3.563 [Abstract] [PDF] [Request Permissions]

If your library catalogue does not provide linked access to journals, you will either have to locate the article by visiting the publisher's website or by using an electronic database. These methods are outlined in the sections that follow.

Journal websites

Most journals have their own websites that offer full-text access to the articles published in the journal. These will be free to students and staff of universities that have a subscription to that journal, or a single article can be purchased by non-subscribers for a fee.

You can access an article in a particular journal directly through the publisher's website if you have full bibliographic details as an alternative to going via the university catalogue. You will have to use this method if your university does not provide linked access from its catalogue. In order to use this method of searching, you will need to know who publishes the journal you are seeking. Table 2.2 provides a list of leading criminology journals and their publishers and Table 2.3 gives a list of publishers and their websites.

Table 2.2 Journals and publishers

Journal	Publisher
Aggression and Violent Behavior	Elsevier
American Journal of Criminal Justice	Springer
Asian Journal of Criminology	Springer
British Journal of Criminology	Oxford
Contemporary Justice Review	Routledge
Crime & Delinquency	SAGE
Crime, Law and Social Change	Springer
Crime, Media, Culture	SAGE
Criminal Justice Ethics	Routledge
Criminal Justice Matters	Routledge
Criminal Justice Review	SAGE
Criminal Justice Studies	Routledge
Criminology	Wiley
Criminology & Criminal Justice	SAGE
Criminology & Public Policy	Wiley
Critical Criminology	Springer
Deviant Behavior	Routledge
European Journal of Criminology	SAGE
European Journal on Criminal Policy and Research	Springer
Feminist Criminology	SAGE
Global Crime	Routledge
Howard Journal of Criminal Justice	Wiley
International Criminal Justice Review	SAGE
International Journal of Law and Psychiatry	Elsevier
Journal of Contemporary Criminal Justice	SAGE
Journal of Criminal Justice	Elsevier
Journal of Ethnicity in Criminal Justice	Routledge
Journal of Experimental Criminology	Springer
Journal of Family Violence	Springer
Journal of Forensic Psychiatry & Psychology	Routledge

Table 2.2 Continued

Journal	Publisher
Journal of International Criminal Justice	Oxford
Journal of Interpersonal Violence	SAGE
Journal of Law and Society	Wiley
Journal of Offender Rehabilitation	Routledge
Journal of Police and Criminal Psychology	Springer
Journal of Sexual Aggression	Routledge
Police Practice and Research	Routledge
Policing	Oxford
Policing and Society	Routledge
Prison Journal	SAGE
Psychology, Crime & Law	Routledge
Punishment & Society	SAGE
Social & Legal Studies	SAGE
Theoretical Criminology	SAGE
Trends in Organized Crime	Springer
Victims & Offenders	Routledge
Violence Against Women	SAGE
Women & Criminal Justice	Routledge
Youth Justice	SAGE
Youth Violence and Juvenile Justice	SAGE

Table 2.3 Publishers and websites

Publisher	Website
Elsevier	http://www.elsevier.com/wps/find/journal_browse.cws_home
Oxford	http://www.oxfordjournals.org
Routledge	http://www.tandf.co.uk/journals/
SAGE	http://online.sagepub.com/
Springer	http://www.springerlink.com/journals/
Wiley	http://onlinelibrary.wiley.com/

Using Tables 2.2 and 2.3 you should be able to track a number of journals down to their publishers' websites. For example, if you wanted to find a particular article from, for example, the *Journal of Contemporary Criminal Justice*, you would start looking on the SAGE journals website:

http://online.sagepub.com

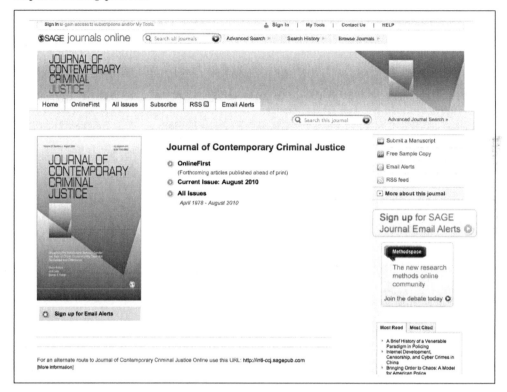

Alternatively, you could put the name of the journal into a general search engine such as Google. This will often take you directly to the publisher's page.

When you visit publisher websites, you must make sure that you log in to them so that you can take advantage of your library's subscription to their electronic resources. If you do not, you may find that the article you want is unavailable for download, or might only be downloaded for a fee. If you come across a resource that demands payment, check to see that you are logged in. If you do log in successfully and the article is still not available free of charge, then it is likely that your library does not subscribe to that particular electronic journal. Whether you then go on and pay for the article yourself is entirely up to you, but you should not expect to recover your costs from your university!

Each publisher's website operates differently but all give you the option of browsing through back issues of journals: this should make finding an article from its reference quite straightforward, particularly after some practice. The practical exercise which follows will give you some experience in using each of the sites listed in Table 2.3.

Practical exercise: journal websites

Using Tables 2.2 and 2.3, locate the website of the relevant publisher for each of these journals and use the bibliographic information to access the articles.

1. Boshier, R. & Johnson, D. (1974) Does conviction affect employment opportunities? *British Journal of Criminology*, 14, 264–268.

2. Rock, P. (2006) Aspects of the social construction of crime victims in Australia. *Victims & Offenders*, 1(3), 289–321.

3. McCormack, A., Rokous, F., Hazelwood, R. & Burgess, A. (1992) An exploration of incest in the childhood development of serial rapists. *Journal of Family Violence*, 7(3), 219–228.

4. Choi, S. & Ting, K-F. (2008) Wife beating in South Africa: An imbalance theory of resources and power. *Journal of Interpersonal Violence*, 23(6), 834–852.

5. Cao, L., Cao, J. & Zhao, J. (2004) Family, welfare and delinquency. *Journal of Criminal Justice*, 32(6), 565–576.

6. Brunson, R. (2007) 'Police don't like black people': African-American young men's accumulated police experiences. *Criminology & Public Policy*, 6(1), 71–101.

 You will find a video walkthrough of these searches on the Online Resource Centre.

If you were unsuccessful, there are three possible problems: (1) your university does not have electronic access to these journals, (2) you did not have the correct login details, or (3) there was some flaw in your search method. The first problem is beyond your control but the other two need to be addressed, as it is essential that you are able to access the full range of literature to support your studies.

Electronic databases

The final method that you can use to find and access journal articles involves searching in electronic databases. An electronic database is a collection of published material that can be searched by a range of fields such as the name of the author, the title of the article or the journal or, crucially in relation to speculative searches, by keyword.

Formulating a search strategy

If you are searching more generally for literature in a particular area, you should spend some time defining your topic in order to provide a focus for your search. There are many thousands of articles available online and it is important that you have a search strategy planned to avoid being overwhelmed by masses of irrelevant literature when you start searching.

An outline search strategy could contain the following:

- **Topic statement.** What is the general area that you wish to research?

- **Time period.** It is important that you think about a timeframe as it may help to bound your search. Are you looking at homicide in the 21st century, or a history of violent crime? Are you looking at the effect of anti-social behaviour orders over the past twelve years? Or is your topic of more general application which renders time constraint irrelevant?

- **Geography.** What is the geographic extent of your study? Are you limited to the UK, Europe, Australia, or wherever? Are you looking at a particular town, or administrative area, county, or state? Or again, does it not matter?

- **Other constraints.** Are there other constraints on your search other than time or geography? For instance, you might be looking at crimes committed by young people or against the elderly which may also give you a means of limiting your search.

- **Key words.** What are the key terms that literature concerning your topic would contain? What synonyms or alternatives are there for these keywords?

- **Databases.** Where are you going to perform your search?

It is always useful to write down and keep a record of your search strategies so that you can review what you have done and whether or not it was successful.

Visit the Online Resource Centre for a downloadable template which might help you in formulating your search strategy.

For example, Figure 2.1 shows how a search strategy for finding literature on CCTV and youth crime in 21st-century Britain might look.

Search strategy						
Topic statement What is the general area that you wish to research?	CCTV and youth crime in 21st century Britain					
Time period What time period are you interested in? (if relevant)	2000 to date					
Geography Are there any geographical constraints on your search? (if relevant)	United Kingdom only					
Key words What are the key words from your topic statement?	Key word 1	CCTV				
	Key word 2	youth				
	Key word 3	crime				
Synonyms What synonyms or alternatives are there for these key words?	Alternatives 1	surveillance, observation				
	Alternatives 2	adolescent, young people, teenage				
	Alternatives 3	disorder, illegal behaviour, unlawful behaviour				
Search strategy Formulate a search strategy by connecting your keywords. Combine synonyms/alternatives with 'OR' and different ideas/concepts with 'AND'.	Key word 1	CCTV	OR	surveillance	OR	observation
	AND					
	Key word 2	adolescent	OR	young people	OR	teenage
	AND					
	Key word 3	disorder	OR	illegal	OR	unlawful
Select database(s)	University library, COPAC, online journals (SAGE, Routledge, Oxford, etc.); IBSS…					
SEARCH						
Review results and revise search						

Figure 2.1 Sample search strategy

You would then use this plan as a basis for performing database searches and take a note of the results you achieved.

Once you have decided upon your search terms, you need to start searching using the electronic databases available at your university. You should remember that the databases and journals to which you will have access will depend on your library's subscription. Check with your library to see which resources are available.

However, you should also never underestimate the value of simple strategies for locating research sources. All good-quality textbooks contain references to further sources such as books and articles, either in the list of references or additional reading sections. Not only do these provide the bibliographic details of books, but they may give you an indication of why they are valuable sources. For example, if your textbook touches on a particular topic but not in any great detail—perhaps the point is too marginal for any great coverage in a textbook—it may provide details of the leading work(s) on that topic.

Performing the search

Once you have decided upon your search terms it is time to start searching. The way in which you will do this will depend on the search engine you are using.

As well as websites from publishers, there are a number of online databases devoted to publications from criminology and related disciplines that you will find useful when searching for journal articles. You should, however, be aware that each database will only list articles in journals that are published by an organization that subscribes to that particular database. This means that you may find that the results of your search in any one database will not necessarily elicit information about all the articles that have been published on a particular topic, only the articles that have been published in journals that have paid to be listed in that database. Therefore, you may need to make reference to more than one database in order to find the article that you want or to obtain a complete list of all available articles. The rest of this section will give an introduction to many of the more useful databases.

Applied Social Science Index and Abstracts (ASSIA)

Applied Social Sciences Index and Abstracts is an international abstracting and indexing tool which covers criminology, social services, psychology, sociology, economics, politics, race relations, health, and education. It provides abstracts from around 650 UK, US, and international journals. Coverage includes all branches of the applied social sciences, with over 480,000 records dating back to 1987. It is updated monthly. You should note that ASSIA contains index and abstract records only, so you will need to use another database to find the full text of any article that looks as though it may be of interest.

International Bibliography of the Social Sciences (IBSS)

The *International Bibliography of the Social Sciences (IBSS)* is an abstracting and indexing database for social science and interdisciplinary research. It was established in 1951 and currently holds more than 2.5 million bibliographic references to journal articles as well as to books, reviews, and chapters. IBSS also expands by more than 120,000 new additions each year. Like ASSIA, IBSS is also confined to index and abstract records.

Sociological Abstracts

Sociological Abstracts is also an abstracting and indexing database of the international literature in sociology and related disciplines in the social and behavioural sciences. The database provides abstracts of journal articles and citations to book reviews drawn from over 1,800 journals, and also provides abstracts of books, book chapters, dissertations, and conference papers from 1952 to date. It is updated monthly and currently contains around 880,000 records.

PsycINFO

PsycINFO provides systematic coverage of psychological literature including psychology and related disciplines such as psychiatry and sociology. The database contains abstracts from the 1800s to the present, but also includes some historical records from the 1600s and 1700s. It abstracts and indexes over 2.9 million records across 2,450 journals and is updated weekly.

British Humanities Index

The *British Humanities Index* indexes over 400 humanities journals and weekly magazines published in the UK and other English speaking countries, as well as quality newspapers published in the UK. It covers material from 1962 to date, is updated monthly, and contains around 850,000 records.

CSA Illumina

CSA Illumina is an extremely useful cross-database search tool which provides access to more than 100 full-text and bibliographic databases published by CSA and its partners. These include ASSIA, IBSS, PsycINFO, Sociological Abstracts, and the British Humanities Index.

http://www.csa.com

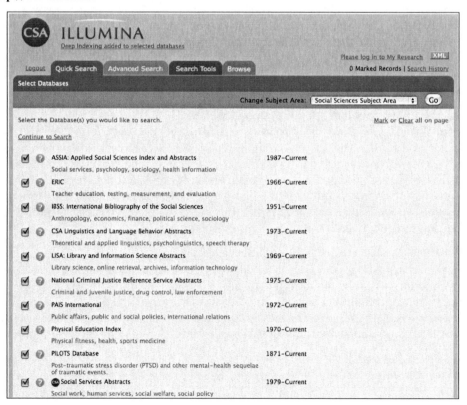

Science Direct

Science Direct is operated by Elsevier. It contains nearly 10 million articles from over 2,500 journals and over 6,000 e-books, reference works, book series, and handbooks.

The articles are grouped in four main sections, one of which is social sciences and humanities. The site carries both abstracts and full-text materials.

http://www.sciencedirect.com

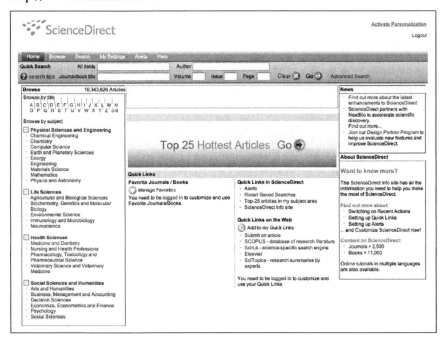

Zetoc

http://zetoc.mimas.ac.uk

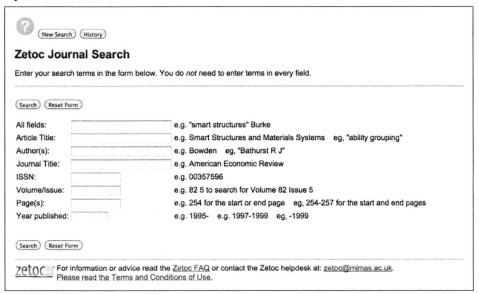

Zetoc provides access to the British Library's electronic table of contents of around 20,000 current journals and around 16,000 conference proceedings published per year. The database covers the period from 1993 to date, and is updated on a daily basis. It includes an email alerting service, to enable you to keep up-to-date with relevant new articles and papers.

Practical exercise

You have encountered your own library catalogue, Copac, various publisher websites, and abstracting and indexing databases in this chapter.

Use the search terms from the example above to search for literature on the topic of CCTV and youth culture in 21st-century Britain in these databases. Try varying the terms and see whether this makes a difference to the quantity or relevance of literature that you retrieve.

Reflecting on the search results

Once you have run your search, you will need to reflect on both the quantity and the quality of the matches retrieved. Have you got enough good material, or are you inundated with a lot of irrelevant sources, or do you have nothing at all?

Depending on the database you have used and your search terms, you will retrieve a number of matches, ranging from none to many hundreds. If you have no matches, it does not necessarily means that there is no literature available on your chosen topic. There are a number of reasons why your search may be fruitless:

- **Your search terms may be too narrow or too specialized.** Try different synonyms for the terms and run the search again. Remember to keep a record of what you have tried.

- **You might have mistyped a term in the search engine.** This is a common slip. There are unlikely to be many articles that discuss 'CCVT' for instance. Check your search and try again.

- **The database in which you are searching might not contain literature that is relevant to your topic.** That is not to say that other databases will not, so you should always search in more than one database.

Alternatively, you might find that you are inundated with matches. Again, there are some common reasons why this might be the case:

- **Your search terms might be too broad.** For instance, you might be searching for 'crime' as a key word. This will generate huge numbers of matches.

- **You might be searching in too many fields.** For instance, if you were to search for 'CCTV' or 'surveillance' in all fields, you might retrieve, for instance, an article which discusses a completely different topic, uses the terms in a different context, or which simply mentions surveillance in passing. If your first search produces a large number of matches, many of which are of questionable relevance, you might try restricting some of your search terms to the **abstract** only.

Abstract. Journal articles will usually have an accompanying abstract which is a short summary or synopsis of the article topic and its content. Abstracts are useful in allowing the reader to decide whether obtaining the full article would be worthwhile.

Using the search strategy on CCTV and youth crime as an example, it is likely that you would want articles that discuss CCTV or surveillance at length. Such articles will probably have one of these key terms in its abstract. The search would be entered into the SAGE journals database, for example, as shown:

SAGE search

This search returned 40 matches (at the time of writing). Running the same search, but looking instead for 'CCTV' or 'surveillance' in all database fields, returned 717 matches.

SAGE results

A final point to consider when you are reflecting on the efficacy of your search strategy is the relevance of the results to your purpose. Do not assume that an article is relevant just because it features your chosen search terms, but instead take a moment to read the abstract and skim through the article to get a sense of whether it is actually useful to you.

You will find a more detailed discussion of this issue in chapter 8 on essay writing along with a method of evaluating the relevance of an article or other source material to your coursework.

 CHAPTER SUMMARY

- Textbooks cover a range of criminology topics
- Edited collections either cover a diverse range of topics or a narrower set of perspectives on a general theme
- Monographs are specialist books on a single narrow topic
- Books of key readings are useful compilations of primary sources
- Dictionaries provide brief overviews of key topics
- Journals are a source of latest developments, research findings, criticism, and commentary
- Copac is a useful resource that combines the holdings of major research libraries
- If you are looking for a particular journal online, you may find it via your library or its publisher's website

- It is important to plan your search strategy: consider key words, synonyms, and database sources
- There are various abstracting and indexing services available
- ASSIA, IBSS, Sociological Abstracts, PsycINFO, and the British Humanities Index are available via CSA Illumina
- Science Direct contains an extensive social sciences and humanities section
- Zetoc provides access to the British Library electronic table of contents
- You should always review your searches for quantity and quality

abc GLOSSARY

Abstracts are short summaries or synopses of the topic and content of a journal article. Abstracts are useful in allowing the reader to decide whether obtaining the full article would be worthwhile.

Athens is an access and identity management service that enables users to access a wide range of services and resources using a single username and password.

Bibliographic information refers to the details of a publication that allow it to be located: in essence, it is identity information for a book or journal and it includes details such as the title of the book, journal, or article; the name of the author, editor, and publisher; and the date of publication.

Electronic databases are collections of materials, particularly journal articles, taken from a range of sources, that can be searched using a range of different fields in order to locate and sometimes access material.

Primary sources are those which provide first-hand accounts of research or thinking such as articles, monographs, research reports, or direct testimony of the investigation of a particular topic.

SCONUL (Society of College, National and University Libraries) is a reciprocal system whereby staff and students from one university can use the library facilities of another university.

Secondary sources are those which report, reprint, or summarize the work of others, such as textbooks and key readings. They can be useful as a more readily understood account of the original work.

Shibboleth is a popular single sign-on system that works with Athens to facilitate secure access to restricted access online resources.

Tertiary sources are reference materials that provide concise distillation of the content of primary and secondary sources such as dictionaries and encyclopaedias.

3 Statistics and official publications

INTRODUCTION

The focus in this chapter is on a particular type of source material that is of special interest to criminology students: official documents concerning crime, criminals, and criminal justice. There are a great many Government and other official agencies that have responsibilities relevant to crime and justice. These organizations collect statistics that provide an insight into the extent of criminal behaviour and produce reports that explore such issues as the impact of crime, policy considerations concerning responses to crime, and evaluations of the work of the various agencies involved in the criminal justice system such as the police, the courts, prisons, and the probation service. This chapter introduces the various types of statistics and reports available, explains how they can be used in your study of criminology, and details where they can be found.

There is a lot of information 'out there' about crimes, offenders, and criminal justice, much of which is produced by official agencies and Government departments. This is useful source material as it provides an insight into the official stance on issues of interest to criminologists. It can be used to help you understand issues discussed in lectures and tutorials and may be relevant to your coursework and a dissertation or research project. This chapter will help you to understand what information is available and where it can be found. It will explain which agencies are responsible for particular aspects of crime and criminal justice and it will provide details of how to look behind legislation by accessing the debates that take place in Parliament when legislation is being introduced.

LEARNING OUTCOMES

After reading this chapter, you will be able to:

- Compare the two main sources of crime statistics

- Appreciate the processes by which police recorded crime is measured and the limitations of recorded crime statistics

- Understand the nature of victimization surveys (such as the British Crime Survey)

- Identify sources of criminal statistics in other jurisdictions

- Understand the role of official publications as useful complementary sources of data in criminology

- Find a wide range of relevant statistics and reports

Crime statistics

There are two main sources of crime statistics:

- Data collected from policing agencies in the course of their activities based on crimes that are reported to them by victims or other members of the public; and
- Surveys from a representative sample of the population about their experiences as victims of crime, usually over the past year.

Police recorded crime

The first main source of crime statistics is police recorded crime; that is, data that are collected by the police at various stages in the criminal justice process. In England and Wales, these recorded crime statistics cover 'notifiable' offences (that is, offences that are notifiable to the Home Office). There are around 1,500 different notifiable offences, broken down into nine different classes of offence:

- Violence against the person (including homicide)
- Burglary
- Criminal damage
- Drug offences
- Fraud and forgery
- Robbery
- Sexual offences
- Theft and handling
- Other offences (from blackmail, bigamy, and kidnapping to rendering food injurious to health, impersonating a wildlife inspector with intent to deceive, and running a pirate radio station on the high seas!).

The way in which the police record crime is governed by the Home Office Counting Rules and the National Crime Recording Standard (NCRS).

The Counting Rules (including a spreadsheet list of all the notifiable offences) can be found at http://www.homeoffice.gov.uk/publications/science-research-statistics/research-statistics/crime-research/counting-rules/.

The crime recording process

The process of recording crime can be depicted as shown in Figure 3.1.

There are three main stages in the process of recording crime:

- **Reporting.** A crime-related incident is brought to the attention of the police, either as an external report or as a result of police observation or detection. The police then register a crime-related incident and decide whether to record it as a crime in compliance with the NCRS. Generally speaking, the police record reports of crime if there is some *prima facie* evidence that a crime has been committed and that the incident is sufficiently serious to warrant police attention.
- **Recording.** The police decide to record the report of a crime and must then determine how many crimes to record and their offence types. This is usually straightforward (one obvious offence per victim), but the Home Office Counting Rules also cover special situations where

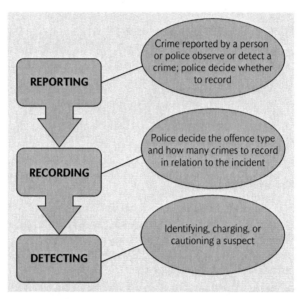

Figure 3.1 The stages in recording crime

more than one offence has taken place, maybe on several occasions over a period of time, or where there is more than one offender or victim.

- **Detection.** There are also detection statistics, which are compiled according to criteria in the Detections Guidance contained in the Home Office Counting Rules. In many cases, someone is charged or cautioned or the court takes the offence into consideration, or the police may decide to take no further action. Such cases are sometimes collectively referred to as 'cleared up'.

The Home Office publishes a range of reports which provide statistics on the reporting, recording, and detecting processes as part of their commentary and analysis of current trends.

Limitations of police recorded crime statistics

Police recorded crime statistics provide a good level of insight into the operational detail of police work, as well as a good measure of trends in well-reported crimes. They are an important indicator of police workload, and can be used for local crime-pattern analysis. However, they do have some limitations which mean that they do not, of themselves, provide an accurate picture of the *true* level of criminality:

- **Unreported crimes are not counted.** Many crimes are not reported to the police so overall crime is significantly underestimated. Of every 100 offences committed, around only half are reported to the police. This is the first stage in the so-called **process of attrition** (as criminal incidents 'leak out' of the criminal justice system). Figure 3.2 gives an indication of the stage in the criminal justice process reached by 100 typical criminal incidents. There are a number of reasons that a crime may not be reported to the police: the theft of a penny involves the same criminal conduct as the theft of a thousand pounds, yet it is highly unlikely that anyone would trouble their local police force with the report of a stolen penny. Other reasons that crimes might not be reported may be that the victim perceives the police to be inefficient, hostile, racist, or sexist, or they may believe they would be subject to revenge from the criminals (particularly in respect of organized crime, drug crime, or domestic abuse). The victim may even be involved in crime themselves.

- **Not all reported crimes are recorded**. The police have a considerable discretion in deciding whether or not to record a reported crime-related incident. Not only do individual forces have discretion in how best to utilize their resources, but individual police officers also exercise their personal discretion in deciding whether or not to record. For instance, they might decide that there is insufficient *prima facie* evidence, or that the incident reported is too trivial to justify the expenditure of police resources (as they undoubtedly would in the example of the stolen penny). Moreover, there have been reports of the police keeping recorded crime levels low by not recording incidents on the official system: this technique is known as 'cuffing', because the crimes 'disappear up the cuffs of the policeman's sleeve' (Davies 1999). As such, only around half of all reported crimes are recorded (Figure 3.2).

- **Not all offences are notifiable.** This means that almost all of the more minor summary offences are excluded.

- **Reporting rates vary by types of crime**. As you have already seen, crimes of low level or low victim impact are generally less likely to be reported to the police. The effect of this is that the overall picture of criminal activity becomes skewed towards more serious crimes. Similarly, thefts of and from vehicles and domestic burglary have a very high reporting rate since a crime reference number is needed to make an insurance claim. Conversely, rape is under-reported due to the personal nature of the offence and concerns such as embarrassment, shame, and a fear of being disbelieved.

- **Trend data can be affected by many factors.** There are several other factors that can affect police recorded criminal statistics. These include changes in legislation (which may

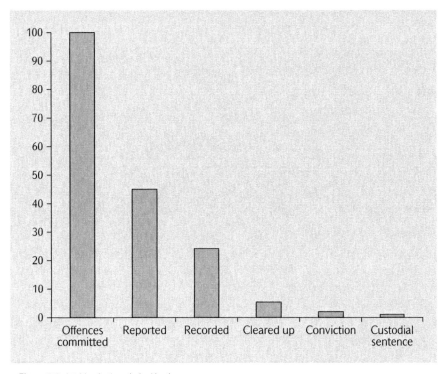

Figure 3.2 Attrition in the criminal justice process

decriminalize or criminalize certain actions or consequences) and changes to the counting rules. For example, the quarterly crime statistics for the period to June 2008 showed a 22% increase in the number of the 'most serious violence' offences recorded by the police. The Home Office stated that the majority of the increase resulted from a clarification of the counting rules regarding the offence of grievous bodily harm with intent, rather than a large increase in the number of offences recorded.

All of that said, you must also remember what the police recorded crime statistics set out to achieve: that is, a measurement of police recorded crime. Within the limitations of the counting rules discussed earlier, the statistics actually do quite well at counting recorded crime!

Finding police recorded crime

The Home Office publishes summaries of recorded crime data from 1898 to date in Microsoft Excel spreadsheet format online at http://www.homeoffice.gov.uk/science-research/research-statistics/crime/crime-statistics/police-recorded-crime/.

As well as the aggregated Home Office figures, the local crime and policing website http://www.police.uk allows you to access and download monthly crime data by police force, street, and neighbourhood.

Crime map of City of London

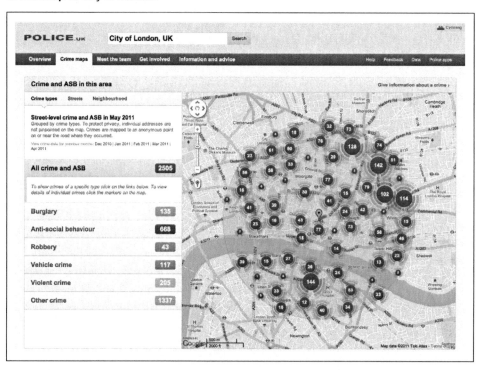

There are also a number of sites that take the raw data and present it in various ways. One of the more interesting is UK CrimeStats run by the Economic Policy Centre, which provides various maps, analysis, and reports along with some commentary on topical issues concerning crime reporting. You can find it at http://www.ukcrimestats.com.

http://www.ukcrimestats.com

British Crime Survey

You have by now seen some of the limitations of official police recorded crime statistics and should appreciate that, while it is easy for the police to compile statistics on crimes that are actually reported, it is clear that there is a great deal of crime that goes unreported or unrecorded—the so-called 'dark figure' of crime (Coleman & Moynihan, 1996). In response to this, victimization surveys were introduced, which interview a representative sample of a population about their experience of victimization over a particular period (usually the last year). These were first used in the US in the 1960s in an attempt to provide a more accurate picture of crime and trends in crime than the Uniform Crime Reports (which are the US equivalent of British police recorded crime statistics). The US National Crime Victimization Survey (NCVS) was set up in 1972. It is now generally acknowledged that victimization surveys give a more accurate indication of crime levels and trends than police recorded crime, although the general profile of crime trends is similar between both methods.

As a result of public and political concern throughout the 1970s that the UK official statistics did not reflect a true profile of crime and criminal trends, the Home Office adopted a similar approach to the NCVS in the form of the British Crime Survey (BCS) which was first conducted in 1981/82.

The BCS is a victim study, carried out (up to 2011) by the Home Office. The survey aims to interview a sample of 46,000 adults (aged 16 or over) designed to be representative of the population of households in England and Wales. In addition, the survey aims to interview a nationally representative sample of 4,000 children aged 10 to 13. Specially trained coders determine whether the experiences reported by the respondents constitute a crime and, if so, assign an offence code accordingly.

The BCS was compiled biannually (except in 1990) until 2001. Since April 2001, the BCS has been carried out on a continuous basis and detailed results from then are reported by financial years (April–April). Headline statistics are updated quarterly, based on data collected in the previous 12 months.

Limitations of the BCS

Just as police recorded crime statistics have limitations, the BCS also suffers in some respects:

- **Certain types of crime are not covered**. As a victim survey, the BCS cannot cover homicide offences. As a household survey, it excludes businesses and therefore cannot estimate levels of commercial or industrial victimization, corporate crime, environmental crime, or regulatory offences.

- **Certain individuals are not included**. Since the BCS takes a household sample, it automatically excludes homeless people, people living in communal accommodation (such as hostels), or people in prison. There is criminological research to suggest that such groups experience a higher rate of criminal victimization than the norm (Newburn & Rock, 2006; Edgar *et al.*, 2003).

- **Self-reporting of victimization cannot capture 'victimless crime'**. Since the survey focuses on victimization, it cannot cover offences that do not have an identifiable victim that has suffered loss or harm. Examples include some public order offences, drug dealing, or prostitution.

- **Historically, crimes against under-16s have not been included**. This precludes any measurement of a whole range of offences that specifically cover the victimization of minors (such as a range of sexual offences against under-13s). This limitation has recently been addressed.

- **Gathering information on domestic/sex crimes is problematic**. Privacy during the interview is a particular concern for respondents who have experienced domestic violence or sexual assault, as this might embarrass or endanger the respondent, particularly if the perpetrator is present during the interview (30% of 2009–10 BCS interviews were conducted with someone else present other than the interviewer and the respondent). Experience of domestic violence, sexual victimization, and stalking is sought via Computer Assisted Self Interviewing (CASI), in which respondents enter answers directly into the interviewer's computer. Respondents may be afraid of reprisal if reporting a domestic or sexual crime and simply decide that it is safer not to report it.

- **It is difficult to measure geographic variations and overall trends in uncommon crimes**. Despite the increasing sample size, it remains too small to measure accurately less prevalent offences, such as rape or sexual assault. Even though a sample of less than 2,000 can reasonably represent the adult population of England and Wales (to an accuracy of 95%), such a small sample would be in danger of missing uncommon crimes (which are typically the more serious offences).

Finding BCS data, reports, and bulletins

The Home Office publishes reports and bulletins on the BCS on its website at http://www.homeoffice.gov.uk/science-research/research-statistics/crime/crime-statistics/british-crime-survey/.

The anonymized raw datasets from the BCS from 1982 to date can be downloaded free of charge (for non-commercial purposes) from the Economic and Social Data Service website (a collaborative project between the Universities of Manchester and Essex) at http://www.esds.ac.uk/findingData/bcrs.asp. The site also contains other useful resources including an SPSS workbook for dissertation students to work with a real world secondary dataset.

For more information on dissertations, see chapter 9. The use of SPSS as a tool in quantitative data analysis is introduced in chapter 14.

A comparison of recorded crime and the BCS

So far, you have looked at the differences between police recorded crime and the BCS. Remember that these are complementary—not competing—resources, both of which have strengths and limitations which can be summarized as shown in Table 3.1.

Crime in England and Wales

As you can see from Table 3.1, the two primary sources of data—that is police recorded crime and the BCS—are complementary: they combine together to give a better measure and profile of criminality than either of them would in isolation. As such, for the last ten years (to 2010/11) the Home Office has presented a series of reports that combine crimes recorded by the police and interviews from the BCS. These crime statistics are published four times a year; a main annual volume (entitled 'Crime in England and Wales') with a full set of figures and commentary and three quarterly updates which provide summary headlines. Additionally, a number of supplementary volumes are produced, containing in-depth analysis of issues such as homicide, violent crime, and children's contact with and attitudes towards the police.

Finding crime in England and Wales

The main volumes, updates, and other statistical bulletins produced by the Home Office are published on its website at http://www.homeoffice.gov.uk/publications/science-research-statistics/research-statistics/crime-research/.

Mistrust of crime statistics

There has been some mistrust of crime statistics. For instance, although the BCS shows that crime in England and Wales is relatively stable, public perceptions are that crime is increasing and that official statistics are untrustworthy (UKSA 2010: 14). Much of this mistrust centres on the views that both the police and the Home Office have a vested interest in producing statistics that help to further their own aims. These views are often propagated in the media, as can be seen in this article in the *Western Mail*:

Table 3.1 A comparison of recorded crime and BCS data (based on UKSA 2010: 20–21)

	Recorded crime	**BCS**
Source of data	Police records	Interviews with a nationally representative sample of the household population
Strengths	• Provides data at a local (force) level (and is therefore useful for performance monitoring) • Can be a good measure of less common, more serious crime (e.g. homicide, robbery) • Could, potentially, be linked with other data within the Criminal Justice System (e.g. conviction rates, sentencing data) • Good at what it sets out to do (within the limitations of the counting rules)	• Good measure of long term trends in common crimes against individuals or households • Captures information about crimes that are not reported to the police (including sensitive issues such as domestic abuse or drug misuse) • Provides information on multiple and repeat victimization • Can analyse risk for different demographic groups and examines victim–offender associations, etc
Limitations	• Many crimes are not reported to the police so overall crime is significantly underestimated • Reporting rates vary by types of crime, so the overall picture is skewed (generally low level/impact crime is less likely to be reported than serious crime) • Trend data can be affected by many factors (including changes in legislation, level of reporting to the police, recording practice, counting rules and operational decisions— such as pro-active policing) • Not all offences are 'notifiable'	• Does not cover homicide, commercial crimes, 'victimless' crimes/crimes where people are not aware that they have been victimized, or crimes against homeless people or people living in communal accommodation; potential non-reporting of domestic crimes • Crimes against under 16s have not historically been included • Difficult to measure geographical variations or trends in rarer forms of crime (typically the more serious offences)
What other data are collected?	• Additional data on homicide, gun crime, and knife crime	• Public perceptions on crime and anti-social behaviour • Worry about crime and the perceived likelihood of victimization • Confidence in the police and criminal justice system • Prevalence estimates on the misuse of illicit drugs

Row over crime figures as annual survey shows burglaries rising by 14%

Sam Malone, Western Mail, 15 July 2011

The number of burglaries at homes across Britain rose by 14% in the last year, householders told the influential British Crime Survey.

The apparent rise in house break-ins sparked a political debate yesterday as it was not reflected in police figures that record the number of such crimes reported to the force, which fell over the same period.

Opposition politicians and a leading think tank argued that as many crimes were not reported to police the British Crime Survey findings, which are based on a wide-ranging survey of the public, were a better reflection of the level of crime, which they argued was being affected by Government cuts.

But police chiefs and the Westminster Government pointed to the falling number of crimes, including burglaries, reported to the authorities as a reflection of the effective job done by the nation's police forces.

Statistics can also be (mis)used and manipulated by politicians and the media: Polly Toynbee analysed this well in her article 'Don't let the truth get in the way of a bad crime story' published in the *Guardian* on 23 October 2007:

> But these fairly self-evident complexities [of gathering crime data] are not the problem: it is opposition politicians, their press and sensation-seeking news desks who cherry-pick and distort shamelessly....[w]hat is undisputed by serious criminologists is that crime has plunged by more than 40% over the last decade...[a]nd yet Britain is more alarmed by crimes than the rest of the West.

The Home Secretary announced in December 2010 that the publication of crime statistics covering England and Wales would be moved out of the Home Office to promote greater public trust and demonstrate their independence. The Home Secretary invited the National Statistician to conduct an independent review of crime statistics for England and Wales to:

- consider gaps, discrepancies, and discontinuities within crime statistics;
- recommend the best future location for the publication of crime statistics, and their associated data collection systems; and
- produce an action plan for the implementation of recommendations from the UK Statistics Authority's report 'Overcoming Barriers to Trust in Crime Statistics: England and Wales' (UKSA 2010).

This review was published in June 2011 (GSS 2011). The key findings from the report are that:

- the Office for National Statistics (ONS) should assume responsibility for the independent reporting and publication of crime statistics;
- the presentation of crime statistics needs further improvement to provide clarity about the coverage of the two sources of crime statistics—the British Crime Survey and police recorded crime—and to maximize the benefits of complementary sources to provide a fuller picture of crime; and
- there should be transparent decision-making on changes that affect the published crime statistics.

The National Statistician also recommended that a new independent advisory committee should be set up to take the work forward.

In July 2011, the Government accepted the recommendations of the review. The Home Office Minister for Crime and Security, James Brokenshire said:

> Our existing measures of crime are confusing and offer the public only a partial picture of the true level of offending. It is in the public interest that we have measures of crime that are clear, meaningful and in which the public can have confidence. Today we are accepting all of the recommendations of the National Statistician, including the transfer of the publication of crime statistics to the independent Office for National Statistics. This is an important step towards building public trust. The National Statistician's independent Advisory Committee will now consider what further changes are necessary to improve the collection and presentation of the key data that is published nationally about crime.

The latest information should therefore be found on the website of the Office for National Statistics (http://www.ons.gov.uk).

Other crime surveys

Although most of the preceding discussion has focused on the situation in England and Wales, there may be times at which you want to undertake a comparative exercise with other jurisdictions. For instance, you might want to compare the England and Wales figures with those from Scotland and Northern Ireland to examine the picture across the UK as a whole. Similarly, it is commonly believed that the UK follows US crime trends, so you could find US crime figures useful. Alternatively, you might want to look across the European Union or other Commonwealth jurisdictions. This section will give you an overview of some other crime surveys that you might find useful.

Scottish Crime and Justice Survey

In 1982 and 1988 a crime survey was carried out in central and southern Scotland as part of the BCS. The first independent Scottish Crime Survey (SCS) took place in 1993 and extended the BCS design and sample size (5,000) to cover the whole of Scotland. The BCS ceased to cover Scotland at this point. Further iterations of the SCS were conducted in 1996, 2000, and 2003. In 2004, the survey was renamed as the Scottish Crime and Victimization Survey (SCVS) and ran again in 2006. In 2008, the survey was again renamed as the Scottish Crime and Justice Survey (SCJS).

Interviews for the SCJS began in June 2010 and ran continuously until March 2011. The survey involves interviewing a randomly selected adult in 13,000 households across Scotland per year. It aims to provide statistics on the extent of crime in Scotland, including crime that is not reported to the police. It will also provide details of attitudes towards the criminal justice system, perceptions of local and national crime, and measures taken to ensure personal and household safety.

The publications of the Scottish Crime and Justice Survey are online at http://www.scotland.gov.uk/Topics/Statistics/Browse/Crime-Justice/Publications/publications.

As with the England and Wales report, this site contains both main findings and reports that are focused on particular areas including partner abuse, sexual victimization and stalking, and drug use.

Northern Ireland Crime Survey

The Northern Ireland Crime Survey is also a household survey which was first carried out as a one-off survey in 1994/5 and repeated in 1998, 2001, and 2003/4. It has been running as a continuous survey since January 2003. Like the BCS and the SCJS, it aims to collect information about levels of crime and public attitudes to crime. Respondents are also asked their views about the level of crime and how much they worry about crime.

Reports of the Northern Ireland Crime Survey up to April 2010 can be found on the website of the Statistics and Research Branch of the Northern Ireland Office at http://www.nio. gov.uk/index/nio-publication/stats-and-research-publications.htm.

From 12 April 2010, the responsibility for many of the areas of Criminal and Civil Justice transferred to the Northern Ireland Department of Justice. Reports produced after this date may be accessed through the DoJ website http://www.dojni.gov.uk/index/statistics-research/ stats-research-publications/current_publications.htm.

US National Crime Victimization Survey

As mentioned earlier in the discussion of the BCS, the NCVS is the primary source of information on criminal victimization carried out by the Bureau of Justice Studies in the United States. Each year, data are obtained from a nationally representative sample of 76,000 households comprising nearly 135,300 persons, on the frequency, characteristics, and consequences of criminal victimization in the United States. The survey enables the Bureau to estimate the likelihood of victimization by rape, sexual assault, robbery, assault, theft, household burglary, and motor vehicle theft for the population as a whole as well as for segments of the population such as women, the elderly, members of various racial groups, city dwellers, or other groups. It also allows victims to describe the impact of crime and characteristics of violent offenders.

Data from the US national crime victimization survey is available online at http://bjs.ojp. usdoj.gov/index.cfm?ty=dcdetail&iid=245. This provides links to a number of general and specific reports and raw data sets.

Europe and the Commonwealth

There is information on recorded crime across Europe available online at http://epp.eurostat. ec.europa.eu/portal/page/portal/crime/data/database along with information on levels of policing and prison populations.

EU crime statistics

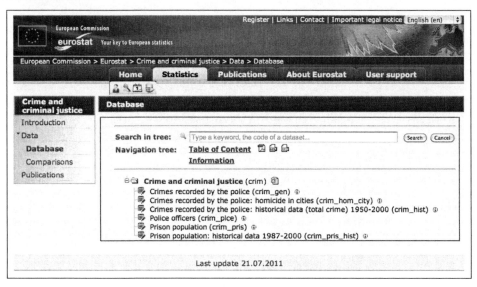

National crime surveys of the most frequently used Commonwealth comparator countries are set out in Table 3.2.

Table 3.2 Commonwealth surveys of crime.

Country	Survey(s)	Agency
Canada	Uniform Crime Reporting Survey	Statistics Canada
Australia	Recorded crime	Australian Bureau of Statistics
	Victims of crime	
New Zealand	Crime and Safety Survey	NZ Ministry of Justice

 Links to the various websites can be found on the Online Resource Centre.

Conviction and sentencing statistics

Conviction and sentencing statistics may be useful for many reasons. For instance, you might wish to examine the rates of conviction for certain offences, the penalties that are attracted by particular offences, or explore how trends in disposal for particular offences have changed over time. For example, are more convictions for possession of class B drugs dealt with by community sentences now than they were five years ago?

There is an extremely good interactive conviction and sentencing statistics tool available online, containing data for England and Wales from 2005, at http://sentencing.justice.gov. uk/?id=2&id2=19. This allows you to select statistics for a given year by any combination of offence, police force, and court.

Practical exercise

Use the sentencing statistics website to answer the following questions:

- How many offenders received a community sentence for possession of class C drugs across England and Wales in 2006?

- How many murderers were sentenced in England and Wales in 2008?

- How many offenders within the Thames Valley police area were fined following conviction for assault occasioning actual bodily harm in 2010?

- How many burglars in total were sentenced by Bradford courts in 2008?

 You will find the answers to these questions and a video walkthrough of using the sentencing website on the Online Resource Centre.

Sentencing statistics

Other criminal justice statistics

The Ministry of Justice publishes a range of statistics concerning the operation of the criminal justice system and aspects of criminal justice policy on its website at http://www.justice.gov.uk/publications/statistics-and-data/index.htm.

Information that you might find useful on this site includes:

- Conviction histories of offenders
- Coroners' statistics
- Annual judicial and court statistics
- Quarterly court statistics
- Quarterly criminal justice systems statistics (incorporating annual 'Criminal Statistics', 'Sentencing Statistics Quarterly Brief', annual 'Sentencing Statistics', and 'Young People Aged 10 to 17 Receiving their First Reprimand, Warning, or Conviction')
- Race and the criminal justice system
- Women and the criminal justice system

- Time intervals for proceedings in magistrates' courts
- Knife possession sentencing quarterly briefings
- Offender management statistics quarterly bulletins (incorporating annual offender management caseload statistics)
- Population in custody
- Prison population projections
- Safety in custody
- Local adult and juvenile reoffending statistics
- Youth justice statistics and youth custody data.

Official publications

Government departments and other official organizations conduct a great deal of research prior to recommending changes to the law, and their findings may be an incredibly rich source of information. If you need to understand the priorities that shaped the content of the current law or the reason why an Act of Parliament covers certain issues but not others, it is likely that you will find the answer in an official publication. For example, the Sexual Offences Act 2003 was enacted after a prolonged period of consultation over a period of years and the final statute was very different to the original proposals. If you wanted to know what the earlier proposals were and how and why they were altered, you would need to find the consultation papers that were published and look at records of Parliamentary debates. For this reason, official publications can be excellent sources of information about the policy behind the criminal law. There is a practical exercise in which you will find various official publications relating to the Sexual Offences Act 2003 at the end of this section, which you can try once you have been introduced to various sources of official publications.

Command Papers

Command Papers derive their name from the fact that they are presented to Parliament 'by Command of Her Majesty'. In fact, they are generally presented by a Government Minister. Command Papers are papers of interest to Parliament where presentation to Parliament is not required by statute. The subjects may include:

- Major policy proposals (White Papers)
- Consultation documents (Green Papers)
- Diplomatic documents such as treaties
- Government responses to Select Committee reports
- Reports of major committees of inquiry
- Certain departmental reports or reviews.

Every Command Paper is given a unique reference which is printed on the front cover of the report (in the bottom left-hand corner). However, there have been six series of Command Papers, which use different abbreviations as shown in Table 3.3.

Table 3.3 Series of Command Papers

Series	Dates	Abbreviation
1	1833–69	[1]–[4222]
2	1870–99	[C. 1]–[C. 9550]
3	1900–18	[Cd. 1]–[Cd. 9329]
4	1919–56	[Cmd. 1]–Cmd. 9889 (the use of square brackets was discontinued in 1922)
5	1956–86	Cmnd. 1–Cmnd. 9927
6	1986–date	Cm. 1– (series 6 contains around 8154 Command Papers as at July 2011)

It is important to look at the style of abbreviation. This will give you an indication of the date of the Command Paper—remember that there is a 30-year gap between Cmnd. 1 and Cm. 1 for example.

Command Papers contain a wealth of information that is useful for criminology and give insight into policy perspectives on crime. They often refer to other pieces of work which may also be useful resources for your own research. For example:

- Home Office (1993) *Compensating victims of violent crime: changes to the criminal injuries compensation scheme*. (Cm 2434) London: HMSO.

- Home Office (1995) *Strengthening punishment in the community*. (Cm 2780) London: HMSO.

- Secretary of State for the Home Department, Secretary of State for Constitutional Affairs & the Attorney General (2005) *Criminal justice: rebuilding lives—supporting victims of crime*. (Cm 6705) London: HMSO.

- Home Office (2009) *Extending our reach: a comprehensive approach to tackling serious organised crime*. (Cm 7665) London: HMSO.

Most libraries will contain a collection of Command Papers. These may be arranged by series and number, in which case it is a very straightforward task to find the paper you want. However, some libraries organize their Parliamentary materials in sessional sets: in other words bound together in volumes for a particular session of Parliament. These will therefore be organized by year. If your library organizes its Command Papers in this way, you will need to have some idea of the year of the paper as well as its abbreviated reference.

TSO Official Documents is the official reference facility for Command Papers, Departmentally Sponsored House of Commons Papers, and key Departmental Papers. It is a free service available at http://www.official-documents.co.uk. It contains all documents from the 2005/06 Parliamentary session onwards in chronological order and a selection from before this date. Documents are divided by document type, and then by year or, for House of Commons Papers, Parliamentary session. A selection of papers published since 1994 is also available.

UKOP (http://www.ukop.co.uk) is a subscription service provided by TSO (the Stationery Office). It is the official catalogue of UK official publications since 1980. It contains around 450,000 records from over 2,000 public bodies. It provides full search facilities and an alphabetical list of issuing bodies and departments. It contains the full text of over 30,000 documents. Where the full text is not available it provides details of where you can obtain a printed copy. It is updated daily.

http://www.ukop.co.uk

Parliamentary papers

The papers of the House of Commons originate inside the House and are 'Ordered by the House of Commons to be printed...'. They comprise the reports and evidence of Select Committees or the proceedings of Standing Committees considering legislation. Other House of Commons papers include:

- Reports of investigations of the National Audit Office
- Financial papers

- Annual reports of official bodies
- Accounts of official bodies
- Various administrative reports.

The House of Lords publishes substantially fewer papers than the Commons. Until the 1986/87 session, both Bills and papers were numbered in one single sequence. From 1987/88, House of Lords papers and Bills were split into two separately numbered sequences.

http://parlipapers.chadwyck.co.uk/marketing/index.jsp

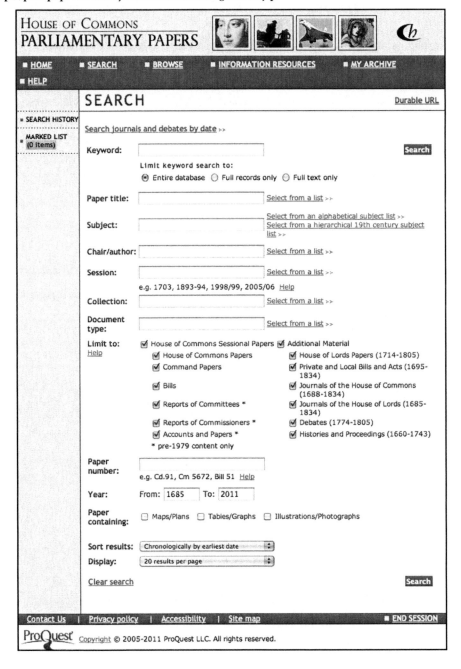

Many Parliamentary Papers can be found on the Official Documents site. In addition, **House of Commons Parliamentary Papers** is a commercially-available service (http://parlipapers.chadwyck.co.uk/marketing/index.jsp). It provides a searchable full-text facility as well as a detailed index. It includes over 200,000 House of Commons Sessional Papers from 1715 to the present with supplementary materials from 1688.

Law Commission Reports

The Law Commission was set up by the Law Commissions Act 1965 for the purpose of promoting reform of the law. Its key aims are:

- To ensure that the law is as fair, modern, simple, and as cost-effective as possible.
- To conduct research and consultations in order to make systematic recommendations for consideration by Parliament.
- To codify the law, eliminate anomalies, repeal obsolete and unnecessary enactments, and reduce the number of separate statutes.

Law Commission Reports provide a useful insight into reasons behind law reforms and more than two-thirds of the Commission's law reform recommendations have been implemented. There are also recommendations that are waiting for the Government's decision, or Parliamentary time for debate. Recent examples of legislation that have followed from Law Commission reports include the Serious Crime Act 2007, the Domestic Violence, Crime and Victims Act 2004, and the Criminal Justice Act 2003. Even recommendations that have not been implemented will give an overview of the problems that were perceived in the law and may prove useful in essays that require a critical discussion of the topic.

Many Law Commission Reports are published as Command Papers or Parliamentary Papers, for example:

- *A Criminal Code for England and Wales* (Law Com. No. 177, Cm 299, 1989)
- *Computer Misuse* (Law Com. No. 186, Cm 819, 1989).

Law Commission Reports from 1996 onwards can be found on the Law Commission website at http://www.justice.gov.uk/lawcommission/index.htm.

Reports, consultation papers, and other publications produced prior to 1996 are not available on this site. These publications can be downloaded free of charge from the Official Documents site or the Law Commission pages of the British and Irish Legal Information Institute website at http://www.bailii.org/ew/other/EWLC/.

Bills

In chapter 1, we considered the role of Bills in the Parliamentary process: these are draft Acts of Parliament, put forward for debate. They are particularly useful when used in conjunction with the reports of Parliamentary debates, as you will be able to follow the various amendments made between versions of the Bill and the final Act of Parliament alongside the debate in Parliament that drove those amendments. In addition, you may also find various interesting proposals for legislative reform that were abandoned, or potentially interesting Bills that have been put forward and are awaiting debate. For example:

- The Criminal Records (Public Access) Bill was put before Parliament for its Second Reading in the House of Commons in May 2011. It set out to facilitate access by members of the public to the registers of the Criminal Records Bureau. However, the Bill was subsequently withdrawn.

- The Apprehension of Burglars Bill was given its First Reading in the House of Commons in July 2010 and aims to provide immunity from prosecution or civil action for persons who apprehend or attempt to apprehend burglars.
- The Bail (Amendment) Bill was introduced in June 2011 and intends to give the prosecution in a criminal case the right of appeal against judges' decisions to grant bail.
- The Dangerous Driving (Maximum Sentence) Bill proposes raising the maximum sentence for a conviction of dangerous driving from two to seven years.
- The Young Offenders (Parental Responsibility) Bill aims to make provision for a mechanism to hold individuals to account for any criminal sanctions imposed upon young people for whom those individuals hold parental responsibility.

As you can see, Bills before Parliament can give you a perspective on potential future changes to criminal law and criminal justice procedures. Although you should remember that not all Bills before Parliament become law, Bills still provide insight into issues and may well provoke interesting debates in Parliament.

The *House of Commons Weekly Information Bulletin* gives details of Bills that are before Parliament in the current session. Bills are listed alphabetically by title. The *Bulletin* also provides details of the Parliamentary history of each Bill, including the dates of each reading in the House of Commons and House of Lords and any proceedings in Standing Committee.

Details of the Bills before Parliament in the current session can be found on the UK Parliament website at http://services.parliament.uk/bills.

Parliamentary debates (*Hansard* or the Official Report)

You will recall from chapter 1 that *Hansard* (or, less commonly, the *Official Report*) is the edited verbatim report of proceedings in both the House of Commons and the House of Lords, and that it is useful for giving a good insight into the thinking that went behind the enactment of a particular piece of legislation and can help you to locate the Act in its social and political context. For example, there are fascinating discussions regarding the decriminalization of homosexual acts and the abolition of the death penalty in the House of Commons *Hansard* debates on 26 November 1958 (vol 596, cols 365–508) and 21 December 1964 (vol 704 cols. 870–1010) respectively. Both of these contain Parliamentary opinion of the time which would be unlikely to be aired in Parliament today:

On the death penalty

The murderer dies after he has deliberately with knowledge of the penalty for his deliberate act, committed the crime of murder....Terrible and ugly as we recognise the punishment to be, I believe there is a right and a duty on the State to say, "For this deliberate act you will lose your life." I believe that such warning can and does deter certain men who should be deterred in this day and age. I for one will vote against this Bill.

On homosexuality

I can well understand the pleas of those who say that those who practise this cult [of homosexuality] in private are inoffensive citizens. Perhaps they are, if it is meant that they do not break windows or behave riotously. Nevertheless, they are, in my opinion, a malignant canker in the community and if this were allowed to grow, it would eventually kill off what is known as normal life.

Hansard is published daily and reprinted each week as *Weekly Hansard*. An index to the debates is also published every two weeks. At the end of each Parliamentary session, *Hansard* is republished as a set of bound volumes with a corresponding index. These volumes are numbered sequentially—there are over 400 of them.

Hansard is available online free of charge online on the UK Parliament website at:

- http://www.parliament.uk/business/publications/hansard/commons/ (Commons)
- http://www.parliament.uk/business/publications/hansard/lords/ (Lords)

Hansard online covers debates in the House of Commons since 1988–99 and the House of Lords since 1994–93. If you need to find earlier debates, then you will have to use the bound paper volumes, although there is much earlier *Hansard* information available online in the Parliamentary Archives.

Two other useful free websites that allow you to search *Hansard* can be found at:

- http://www.theyworkforyou.com/debates/
- http://hansard.millbanksystems.com/

Practical exercise

Thinking about the example of the Sexual Offences Act 2003 introduced earlier in the chapter, find the following:

- Home Office, *Review of Part 1 of the Sex Offenders Act 1997* (2001)
- Home Office, *Setting the Boundaries* (2000)
- *Protecting the Public: strengthening protection against sex offenders and reforming the law on sexual offences* (Cm 5668)
- The Sexual Offences Bill as introduced into the House of Lords on 28 January 2003
- House of Commons Home Affairs Committee Report on the Sexual Offences Bill (HC 639) (10 July 2003)
- The transcript of the Second Reading of the Bill in the House of Commons

 You will find a video walkthrough of these searches on the Online Resource Centre.

Other Government departments

There are many Government departments and agencies that publish statistics or other reports that may be of relevance to your study or research. You should consider whether there are any such agencies that are relevant to your topic and explore whether they publish particular information that is useful. Some departments and agencies that you might find relevant to your studies of criminology are set out in Table 3.4. Links to the associated websites are available at http://www.direct.gov.uk/en/Dl1/Directories/A-ZOfCentralGovernment/index.htm.

Note that the Coalition Government announced a set of reforms to quangos (quasi-autonomous non-governmental organizations) in October 2010 which may affect some of these bodies (particularly the Forensic Science Service, the National Policing Improvement Agency, the Serious Organised Crime Agency, and the Youth Justice Board.

Table 3.4 Useful central Government departments, executive agencies, and non-departmental public bodies

Body	What it does
Assets Recovery Agency	Aims to disrupt organized criminal enterprises through the recovery of criminal assets, and promotes financial investigation as a part of criminal investigation.
Attorney General's Office	The Attorney General is the chief legal adviser to the Government and is responsible for all Crown litigation. Along with the Solicitor General, the Attorney General has overall responsibility for the work of the Treasury Solicitor's Department, the Crown Prosecution Service, the Serious Fraud Office, and Her Majesty's Crown Prosecution Service Inspectorate.
UK Border Agency	Responsible for border control for the UK, and enforcing immigration and customs regulations. Also considers applications for permission to enter or stay in the UK, citizenship, and asylum.
Census	Provides full results from the population census carried out in the UK in 2001, as well as information about the 2011 Census and earlier surveys.
Courts Service	Executive agency of the Ministry of Justice which manages the magistrates' courts, the Crown Court, county courts, the High Court, and Court of Appeal in England and Wales.
Criminal Records Bureau (CRB)	Executive agency of the Home Office which conducts criminal record checks on potential employees on behalf of organizations and recruiters throughout England and Wales.
Crown Prosecution Service	Responsible for prosecuting people in England and Wales who have been charged with a criminal offence. This involves giving advice to the police on charges to bring, and being responsible for authorizing charges and preparing and presenting cases for court.
Forensic Science Service	A Government-owned company which provides forensic science support and advice to the police forces and Government agencies of England and Wales. It provides scene-of-crime and forensic investigation staff to the police services in England and Wales, as well as to the Crown Prosecution Service, HM Revenue and Customs, HM Coroners' Service, Ministry of Defence Police, and British Transport Police. [Scheduled for closure in March 2012]
HM Inspectorate of Constabulary	Body with statutory responsibility for the inspection of the police service in England and Wales.
HM Inspectorate of Prisons	Independent inspectorate which reports on conditions for and treatment of those in prison, young offender institutions, and immigration detention facilities.
HM Inspectorate of Probation	Independent inspectorate reporting on the effectiveness of probation work with individual offenders, children, and young people.
HM Prison Service	Manages the custody of those committed by the courts.
Home Office	Lead Government department for immigration and passports, drugs policy, counter-terrorism, and the police.
Independent Police Complaints Commission	Non-departmental public body responsible for overseeing the system for handling complaints made against police forces in England and Wales. Can also elect to manage or supervise the police investigation into a particular complaint and will independently investigate the most serious cases itself.

Continued

Table 3.4 Continued

Body	What it does
National Probation Service	Part of the Ministry of Justice's National Offender Management Service (NOMS). It works with offenders in England and Wales.
National Policing Improvement Agency	Police owned and led agency created to support police forces to improve the way they work by providing expertise in such areas as information technology, information sharing, and recruitment. [Planned to be replaced by a police-led ICT company]
Prisons and Probation Ombudsman	Investigates complaints from prisoners, people on probation, and immigration detainees held at immigration removal centres. Also investigates deaths of prisoners, residents of probation service approved premises, and those held in immigration removal centres.
Serious Fraud Office	Responsible for the investigation and prosecution of suspected cases of serious or complex fraud where £1 million or more are involved or the fraud covers more than one national jurisdiction (though it is rare for such cases involving less than £1 million to be taken).
Serious Organised Crime Agency	Non-departmental public body which assists police forces and also works independently with regards to serious organized crime. Intelligence agency with the role of reducing harm, not specifically the arrest and conviction of offenders. [Proposed to be replaced by National Crime Agency]
Youth Justice Board	Non-departmental public body which oversees the youth justice system in England and Wales and works to prevent offending and reoffending by children and young people under the age of 18, and to ensure that custody for them is safe, secure, and addresses the causes of their offending behaviour. [Proposed to be abolished as part of broader criminal justice reforms]

CHAPTER SUMMARY

Statistics

- Police recorded crime data are collected by the police at various stages in the criminal justice process
- Recorded crime in England and Wales covers 'notifiable' offences
- Recorded crime statistics have some limitations which means that they do not present a picture of the true extent of criminal behaviour
- Victimization studies, such as the British Crime Survey, augment police recorded crime data by interviewing a nationally representative sample of adults to explore their experiences of victimization
- Responsibility for the reporting and publication of crime statistics is moving from the Home Office to the independent Office for National Statistics
- A wide range of statistics concerning the operation of the criminal justice system and aspects of criminal justice police are readily available from the Ministry of Justice

Official publications

- Command Papers are papers of interest to Parliament and can include major policy proposals, consultation documents, major inquiry reports, and departmental reviews of relevance to criminology
- The Law Commission publishes reports concerning recommendations for legal reform
- Bills are draft Acts of Parliament which can be analysed to explore the process of legislative change
- *Hansard* is the official report of proceedings in Parliament which assists in locating an Act in its social and political context
- Many Government departments and agencies also publish statistics and reports that are relevant to the study of criminology

 REFERENCES

Coleman, C. & Moynihan, J. (1996) *Understanding Crime Data: Haunted by the Dark Figure.* Buckingham: Open University Press.

Davies, N. (1999) How police fiddle their crime figures and cheat the public. *Guardian*, 18 March.

Edgar, K., O'Donnell, I., & Martin, C. (2003) *Prison Violence: The dynamics of conflict, fear and power.* Cullompton: Willan.

Government Statistical Service (2011) *National Statistician's Review of Crime Statistics: England and Wales.* London: OPSI.

Newburn, T. & Rock, P. (eds.) (2006) *The Politics of Crime Control.* Oxford: Clarendon Press.

Toynbee, P. (2007) Don't let the truth get in the way of a good crime story. *Guardian*, 23 October.

UK Statistics Authority (2010) *Overcoming Barriers to Trust in Crime Statistics: England and Wales* (Monitoring Report 5). London: OPSI.

4 Media and web sources

INTRODUCTION

This chapter focuses on two important sources of information about crime and criminology: media sources and the web. The chapter starts by exploring different media sources—newspapers, broadcast media, and fiction—and explaining their relevance to your study of criminology. It provides detailed information that will enable you to identify and locate relevant mediated source materials. It also outlines the different types of information of relevance to criminology that can be found online such as official publications (see chapter 3), reports from criminology organizations and interest groups, as well as considering the use of blogs and forums. As the media and the web provides access to so much source material of such variable quality, this chapter also sets out the means of evaluating material to assess its usefulness, relevance, and reliability.

The way in which crime and criminality is depicted in the media is of interest to criminologists because media reports are the dominant source of public information about crime. As such, a study of media constructions and reporting of crime can be a good way of assessing public opinion. Media sources—newspapers, television, and film—tend to be preserved so offer an interesting means of charting the historic evolution of ideas about crime. The web offers a quick and easy way to locate traditional scholarly literature but can also be a useful source in its own right, as reports of relevance to criminologists are made available online and the content of the web itself can also be studied.

LEARNING OUTCOMES

After reading this chapter, you will be able to:

- Identify different media sources and understand their contribution to the study of criminology

- Locate various types of media source material including newspaper, film, television, and fiction

- Understand the different ways in which the web can be used to locate relevant source material

- Find literature published by various organizations with an interest in crime and criminology

- Engage in a reasoned evaluation of the source material found in the media and on the web and assess its contribution to your work

Media reports of crime

It is usual to think of the media as meaning television and newspapers but 'the media' is actually a collective way of describing all forms of mass communication of information. It also therefore includes films, books, radio, the Internet and, of course, social media such as forums, blogs, podcasts, Facebook, Twitter, and YouTube.

It follows from this that media reports of crime refers to information about crime that is broadcasted to the public at large by some form of mass communication. As there is a high level of public preoccupation with crime and criminals, there is a corresponding interest in the media in producing content with a crime focus so there is plenty of media output available that is of interest to criminologists. Much of this output, particularly in the news media, will be very up-to-date so it can be a useful source of information about new developments and current events relating to crime. You should also be aware of the increasing use of modern technology to communicate information about crime, such as the use of Twitter by Greater Manchester Police.

Greater Manchester Police Twitter feed

Using media sources

Although there is a great deal of information about crime in the media, it is important that you remember that you—as a student of criminology—are not the intended audience of media coverage of crime: it is aimed at an altogether more general audience that lacks any specialist knowledge or understanding. As such, it is often the case that media reports of crime and criminals are not suitable sources for your work as their content may lack the rigour, detail, and precision of academic sources. Irrespective of this limitation, there are a number of ways that media broadcasts of various kinds may play a role in your studies:

- You might be studying the media itself and its contribution to shaping public understanding of crime. This means that you may be writing a piece of coursework that looks at media constructions of a particular offence, type of offender, or criminal justice intervention.

- You may have found a media discussion of a crime topic in a newspaper or television documentary that makes points that you would like to include in your coursework. This situation is perhaps the trickiest of the three in terms of making a decision as to whether it is appropriate to rely on media sources as authority in your work.

- You could simply be looking at the media to discover what issues are topical or to provide some general context for your study of a particular offence or issue in criminology. Here, you are using media sources for background information or inspiration.

In each of these three situations, you would be looking at media sources for different reasons and this impacts upon whether or not you should cite these sources in your work. It is essential that you only cite media sources when it is appropriate to do so. Students tend to like media discussions of crime because they are easier to understand than academic sources, but lecturers disapprove of them for exactly this reason and expect students to cite more traditional academic sources in their coursework. The sections that follow will elaborate on the three ways in which media sources can be used in your study of criminology, and provide guidance that will help you to understand when you should include them in your coursework.

Media constructions

A great many criminology degrees contain a module that studies the relationship between the media and crime. This is an important area of study as the majority of people acquire most of their information about crime, criminals, and the criminal justice system from media accounts. It is for this reason that media reports of crime are of interest to criminologists as it is possible to work out what ordinary people think about crime by examining what they are told about it in the media. The traditional approach to this area of study within criminology is to analyse the news content itself, but the growth of Internet discussion forums and the ability of people to add their comments online to news stories also provides a source of public opinion that can be studied.

That is not to say that the media provide an accurate account of the nature, extent, and pattern of offending behaviour. Criminologists study media representations of crime precisely because they present a skewed, inaccurate, or incomplete picture of crime. For example, the news media do not report on every crime that is committed: they select those that are most likely to be interesting to their audience. This is called newsworthiness (Chibnall 1977; Jewkes 2004; Greer 2007). Offences that are newsworthy are more likely to be covered by the news media which gives the audience the impression that they occur more frequently than other, less newsworthy, offences. For instance, a great many murders are reported in the national news media whereas burglary is only reported if there is something unusual or particularly startling about the offence.

Research that examines media portrayal of crime and criminals tends to explore not only what is reported but how it is reported, what is omitted from the report and what message this sends to the audience. In this way, criminologists can explore the way in which knowledge of a particular crime or social problem is constructed. For example, research has analysed the way that language is used to characterize and categorize particular individuals and groups in newspaper reports thus contributing to the rise to prominence of the 'chav' phenomenon and the creation of a new underclass (Hayward and Yar 2006; Tyler 2008; Frampton 2010).

Criminology is also interested in the way that the media can create a moral panic: a situation in which a particular problem or group of people are constructed to suggest that they pose a threat to society.

Practical example: folk devils and moral panics

Stanley Cohen used moral panic as a way of describing the way in which 'a condition, episode, person or group or group of persons emerges to become defined as a threat to societal values and interests' (1972: 9). He popularized the idea of a moral panic in his work that explored the media depiction of the enmity between gangs of Mods and Rockers in the 1960s, particularly in relation to fights that broke out on the Easter Bank Holiday in 1964 in Clacton and Brighton. Cohen argued that there was nothing new, unusual, or threatening about the conflict between rival groups of young people and suggested that the media had created folk devils by presenting the groups as delinquent and a threat to social order and by associating them with other negative social issues such as drugs, violence, and teen pregnancies. Cohen explained that, although it was true that some violent altercations occurred, this was far short of justifying the terminology used by the newspapers: riot, orgy of destruction, battle, and siege (1972: 29).

Cohen is not suggesting that the problems that are the focus of media attention do not exist at all: simply that their existence has been distorted and their extent escalated by the way that they are presented in the media. Examples include the labelling of AIDS as a 'gay plague' in the 1980s, the link between brutal films and computer games and child violence, fears about Satanic child abuse in the 1980s, concerns about welfare cheats and lone parents, and, more recently, worries about paedophiles lurking in Internet chat rooms posing as young children. Jewkes (2004: 67) identifies five characteristics of a moral panic:

- Moral panics emerge when the media presents a relatively ordinary event as if it were an extraordinary occurrence.

- The media create a deviancy amplification spiral in which the perceived wrong-doers are demonized as a source of moral decline and social disintegration.

- Moral panics clarify the boundaries of society by creating a 'them and us' division between those who are agreed that there is a cause for concern and the folk devils who are causing the problems.

- There is a tendency for moral panics to emerge during periods of rapid social change as these create feelings of instability and, therefore, a vulnerability to perceive events as presenting a risk.

- It is usual for young people and their preferences and lifestyles to be the focus of moral panics as society fears for its continued steady existence if the adults of the future are in decline.

Studies of the media are not limited to considerations of the presentation of crime in the news media. You might explore the way that issues relevant to criminology are presented in fiction, for example, by viewing films that feature prison such as *Scum* and *McVicar*, watching police drama series on television, or by reading detective fiction.

Practical exercise: studying crime in the media

Think about the sorts of media sources that you might want to research and analyse in order to tackle the following coursework questions:

- What sorts of problems present the greatest threat to social order in 2011?

- How do the August 2011 riots differ from the riots of 1985?

- How have approaches to policing and attitudes about the police altered in the last forty years?

- Looking at the way that they are portrayed in the media, what sorts of men commit drug-assisted rape and what sorts of women make false allegations of rape?

 You will find suggested answers to these questions on the Online Resource Centre.

If you are taking a module that involves the study of media sources, it is more than likely that you will be expected to cite examples from the media in your coursework. In essence, if you are writing about the media, you should reference media sources to support your arguments. For example, if you were writing an essay that explored the media construction of computer hackers, you would need to find media reports that discuss hacking and identify particular words and phrases that create a construction of the offence and the offender. So, unlike other types of coursework, it is not only acceptable to cite media sources: it is necessary to do so.

Media as a source of data

In modules other than those that involve the study of the media and crime, you will need to be cautious in your reliance on media sources in your coursework. This is because, as mentioned earlier, media output is aimed at a general audience so you should not expect it to contain the level of depth and detail that will be useful to you in your study of criminology.

That said, there are circumstances in which media output can be a useful source of information. Some media accounts of crime are based upon factual content and have been researched in depth and detail so are an accurate and reliable source of information. For example, the legal sections of quality newspapers such as *The Times* and television programmes such as *Panorama* or other documentaries that focus on crime might be a good source of information that can be used in your coursework. It is not always easy to determine which media reports can be used as a reliable source and which ones should be avoided, but you should find the discussion at the end of the chapter on evaluating the quality of source material useful in this respect.

The general rule is that you should only cite a media source in your coursework (unless it is a study of the media as discussed early in this chapter) if there is no alternative source that makes the same point. In other words, you might have found a newspaper article with an interesting discussion, but a more effective way to use this is to use it to track down more appropriate source material.

Practical example: finding sources in the media

This is an extract from an article entitled 'Convicts Face Ban on Foreign Travel' which was published in *The Telegraph* on 28 August 2011:

> Magistrates and judges will be given the power to impose a 'foreign travel prohibition requirement' when handing down a sentence. Offenders' passports could be confiscated for the duration of the ban to ensure that they comply. The move, to be unveiled by Crispin Blunt, the Prisons Minister, will be billed as a way to ensure that community punishments are genuinely a tough alternative to prison.
>
> A document issued by the Ministry of Justice setting out the case for reform said: 'Non-custodial sentences need to be tough and demanding. For too long, they have fallen short of what is required. We aim to improve these sentences so they better punish, control and reform offenders'.
>
> However, the human rights group, Justice, has cautioned against overuse of foreign travel banks for convicted criminals. It says that while the restriction may be appropriate in a few cases, such as for football hooligans who could reoffend while abroad, the order should not be made routinely.
>
> The measure will form part of the Legal Aid, Sentencing and Punishment of Offenders Bill which will be debated by MPs next month when they return from their summer holiday.

Rather than cite the article as a source, there are a number of avenues of research that you could identify to try and track down more authoritative source material:

- The measure is set out in the Legal Aid, Sentencing and Punishment of Offenders Bill 2011 so you could look up the text of the Bill on the Parliament website.

- The Bill is sponsored by Crispin Blunt so you could look at *Hansard* to see what he has said about the Bill.

- There is a quotation from a Ministry of Justice document which you could find and reference.

You might also want to look at Justice's website to see if they have said anything else about this issue.

Of course, there may be situations in which you find some really useful information in the media that you want to use in your coursework but which you cannot find replicated in a more authoritative source. For example, there is a detailed report in *The Times* of a lecture given by Baroness Deech, former chair of the Human Fertilisation and Embryology Authority, at the Museum of London in which she calls for changes to the law to regulate marriages between first cousins due to the risks of genetic defects in their offspring (Gibb 2010). Her words are quoted extensively and cannot be found anywhere else so are not otherwise available to you (unless, of course, you were present at her lecture) so it would be acceptable to use the newspaper article as a source in your coursework.

You will find guidance on how to cite source materials found in newspapers and other media sources in chapter 7.

Finally, it may be that you want to make reference to a point made in the media source itself. The trick here is to consider whether, given the non-specialist nature of media communications, the source is sufficiently authoritative to use in your coursework. Many academics, criminal justice professionals, and other experts write for newspapers and magazines and appear on television documentaries, and their words, albeit publicized through the media, carry sufficient weight to be used as an authority. The best way to find out is to use the Internet to investigate their expertise and make a decision on this basis. It is also a good idea to ensure that your marker is aware that your media source is authoritative by mentioning this in your coursework:

- Gary Slapper, a Professor in Law at the Open University, writing in *The Times*, argues...

- Stefan Fafinski, a Visiting Fellow of the Oxford Internet Institute, quoted in the *Sunday Telegraph*, suggests...

Background and inspiration

Although they may not offer the depth of discussion of traditional academic sources, media sources do provide an up-to-date snapshot of what is happening in the world of crime. Unlike academic journals, for example, newspapers and television and radio news broadcasts are made every day so are a very good way of ensuring that you have a current knowledge of the crime issues of the moment. As a student of criminology, you should have a general interest in crime developments and many lecturers will encourage this by setting tutorial discussions around topical issues to ensure that students see how these fit into the subjects that they are studying.

Some students find that media sources help them to understand the context of a topic better than textbooks and other more scholarly sources. For example, you might want to watch the film *In the Name of the Father* to understand issues of policing of terrorism or to gain insight into the background to the Police and Criminal Evidence Act 1984 or as a setting for a study of miscarriages of justice. Equally, you might want to look at newspaper coverage of the execution of Ruth Ellis in 1955 to understand the campaign for the abolition of the death penalty.

You should take advantage of the easy availability of media sources to look for inspiration if you want a topical focus for a dissertation. As a longer piece of work, it can sometimes be difficult to stay engaged with your dissertation so it will help if you select a topic that really sparks your interest. Look through newspaper reports to see what sorts of issues catch your attention and then follow this up by exploring the issue in traditional academic literature to see if it is a viable dissertation topic (see chapter 9). There may also be scope within your dissertation to include a chapter on media representations of your chosen topic. This would be something to discuss with your supervisor. In terms of referencing, the position stated in the earlier sections is applicable to dissertations:

- If you are studying the media, it is expected that you will include references to the media sources that you examine in your work.
- If you are not studying the media but find useful information in a media source, you should try to find the point or quotation that you want to use in a more traditional source so that you can cite this in your work.
- If you are not able to find the point or quotation elsewhere, cite the media source.

The main point to remember about the use of media sources is that they should supplement rather than replace more traditional academic source material. Most lecturers will not quibble with one or two carefully selected references to media sources in a piece of work if they are surrounded by a wide range of references to books, articles, and official reports. Overall, lecturers are simply concerned to ensure that students use resources that are at an appropriate level to support the serious study of criminology which is why they oppose the use of many media and Internet sources. However, it is also the case that many media and Internet sources are well researched and offer high quality arguments so can be included as a source in your work provided they are used sparingly and in conjunction with scholarly sources. It is important that you consider the quality of media sources before relying on them in your coursework. You will find a section towards the end of this chapter that provides guidance on how to evaluate the quality of your source material.

Finding media sources

You will not be able to use media sources unless you are able to find them. Of course, you could just search the web using Google News but this is not the most effective way to access news reports online and, in any case, will not be of any use for other media sources. The sections that follow provide guidance on locating a whole range of media sources, both national and worldwide and current and historic.

Newspapers

Most national newspapers have websites that provide free access to the latest news and features (although *The Times* has recently moved to a subscription-only service) and many of these also have a searchable archive that will enable you to access older news stories.

There are also a wide range of databases that offer access to newspapers, both national and worldwide. For example, http://www.onlinenewspapers.com offers worldwide coverage of newspapers organized initially by continent and by country within this.

The ability to access newspapers from around the world will be especially useful if you are interested to see how issues within criminology are dealt with in other countries. For example, you could compare the way in which the extradition of alleged computer hacker Gary McKinnon was presented in England and the United States.

The best source of older newspaper reports is the British Library, that offers the **British Newspapers 1600–1900** service. It is subscription only but many universities do subscribe so check the electronic resources provided by your library. It is a fully text searchable database containing both national and regional newspapers as well as material from the Burney Collection (newspapers, pamphlets, and books gathered by the Reverend Charles Burney which represent the largest and most comprehensive collection of early English news media, totalling almost 1 million pages and containing approximately 1,270 titles). It allows you to view entire pages or individual articles. It offers both a basic keyword, date, and publication title search as well as a more advanced set of search options that includes the section, frequency, and language (English/Welsh) of the publication.

There are a range of other places that you can access newspaper reports:

- **British Humanities Index** is a subscription database that offers basic and advanced searches across the ProQuest Historical Newspapers databases, including *The Guardian* from 1821–2003 and *The Observer* from 1791–2003.

- **NewsBank** allows you to access a range of 77 UK national and regional newspapers including the *Daily Mail* (from 1998), *Daily Mirror* (from 2000), *Daily Telegraph* (from 2000), *The Times* (from 1985), and *The Independent* (from 1992). It also groups news into themes.

- **Kidon Media-Link** is a free Internet database that offers worldwide coverage of a range of media outputs including news agencies, magazines, radio, television, and teletext.

- **Gale NewsVault** is a cross-database newspaper archive searching tool that allows simultaneous searching of the Burney Collection, 19th century British Library Newspapers and Periodicals, and the historical archives of the *Economist, Financial Times, Illustrated London News, Listener, Picture Post, Times,* and *Times Literary Supplement.*

- **Nexis UK** is the most commonly encountered newspaper database. This offers full text (but not page reproductions) of major national and regional newspapers in the UK and worldwide. Its archive is extensive, but relatively contemporary, mostly dating from the early 1980s. It also contains a large number of trade publications. It is likely that your institution will at least subscribe to Nexis UK.

Nexis UK

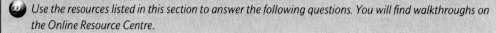

You should also be aware that your university or local library may carry a selection of news-papers in hard copy or microfiche. The databases are all organized differently so there is no uniform approach to searching for content. The best approach is to explore what resources are provided by your library and what, if any, training or support is available to help you use them. Saying that, most databases are not hard to master by a process of trial and error so do not be deterred by the absence of any formal training. Try the following practical exercise to test your ability to locate news reports on the various databases outlined in this chapter.

Practical exercise

Use the resources listed in this section to answer the following questions. You will find walkthroughs on the Online Resource Centre.

1. A lady was in almost daily correspondence with Dr Crippen from the time of his detention in Brixton jail for the murder of his wife. Find an article written by her which details some of this correspondence and her feelings towards Crippen's detention.

2. *The Observer* reported on a letter from a lawyer that stated that Jack the Ripper was not a Jew but an Irishman who had been educated for the medical profession. When was the report in *The Observer* printed, and where had the original letter from the lawyer been published?

3. In 1985, what was the reported value of car crime in London according to an article in *The Times*?

4. Who was the author of a review of the true crime genre of books published in the *Financial Times* in 2005?

5. A talk given by the authors of this book at the Cheltenham Science Festival in 2006 was reported in which local newspaper under the title 'Pick a name, any name!'?

Broadcast media

Access to broadcast media is straightforward provided that you do not need to be in control of the content that you access. In other words, you can watch television or go to the cinema but media controllers dictate what films and programmes are available. Of course, there is a great deal of choice within this, particularly with the ever-increasing range of satellite channels and the availability of resources such as BBC iPlayer that allow you to watch programmes online after they have been broadcast at a time that suits you, but this may still not be sufficient to allow you to access all the content that you may need for your studies of criminology. This section sets out some of the resources that are available that will give you wider access to films and television programmes.

BFI InView (http://www.bfi.org.uk/inview) is a service from the British Film Institute. It contains over 2,000 government films, documents, newsreels, TV documentaries, discussion programmes, and Parliamentary recordings from the 20th century to the early 21st century. It has a straightforward search facility with content organized under six main themes, one of which is Law and Order. This theme has several sub-genres of interest to the study of criminology including crime, crime prevention, the police, young offenders, prison and punishment, and police and the public.

British Pathé (http://www.britishpathe.com) contains a searchable database of around 90,000 items taken from cinema newsreels from 1910 to 1970.

The **BBC Archive** (http://www.bbc.co.uk/archive) has a selection of broadcasts on a range of subjects including crime and justice.

ITN Source (http://www.itnsource.com) contains over one million hours of footage and moving imagery including news, drama, and film. It combines the footage libraries of Reuters, ITN, ITV Productions, Fox News & Movietone, Channel 9 News, UTV, Asian News International, and other specialist collections. Selected news from the ITN and Reuters archives is also available via NewsFilm Online (http://www.nfo.ac.uk): this service also includes a category of 'Crime, Law and Justice' covering areas such as corporate crime, organized crime, police, prison, prosecution, and punishment.

Fictional portrayals of crime

Crime is a popular focus of fiction so sources such as films, television, and radio shows and fictional literature offer potential for documentary analysis in criminology as, like media reports, it plays a role in shaping what ordinary people think about crime. It is possible to analyse the portrayal of an offence in fictionalized accounts in order to identify the typical construction of the offence and offender or to assess their correspondence with reality. For example, Moore (2009) examines portrayals of drug-facilitated sexual assault in soap operas in conjunction with an analysis of newspaper coverage as a means of exploring perceptions of victims and their behaviour, whilst Hesse (2009) compares fictional portrayal of psychopaths in films with the clinical indicators of the medical condition.

Fictional literature

Literature Online (LION) (http://lion.chadwyck.co.uk/marketing/index.jsp) provides a fully searchable library of more than 330,000 works of English and American poetry, drama, and prose, plus biographies, bibliographies, and key criticism and reference resources.

Fiction Connection (http://www.fictionconnection.com) allows you to search a database of fiction in print. It allows searching by topic, character, genre, place, or timeframe: it includes titles in the crime, detective, and policing genres.

There are other free sites which contain digitized or online versions of classic fiction, including Project Gutenberg which offers some 36,000 free eBooks (http://www.gutenberg.org) and Read Print which also allows access to an extensive free online e-library of resources (http://www.readprint.com).

Fictional depictions of crime and criminality are also widely available through the broadcast media. Broadcast sources were covered in the previous section.

Web sources

Students tend to like the web as a research tool because it is a quick and easy source of information: type a word or phrase into a search engine and you will be presented with a whole host of results within a split second. As of July 2011, it is estimated that the web contains at least 14.28 billion pages. Put another way, if you were to look at one page per second, it would take over 500 years to view them all. In other words, there is an immense amount of information available online and some of this is of value to those studying criminology. However, the quality and accuracy of the information that you will find on the web is variable so some of the material about criminology that can be found online is not sufficiently reliable to be used in your studies. To illustrate this point, take a look at this screenshot that shows the results of a web search that asked 'how should we deal with young offenders?' which shows five very different sources:

Google search

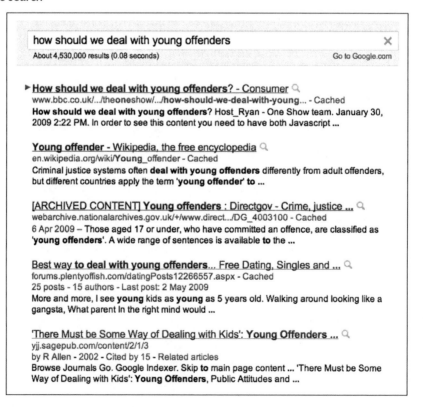

Although all five websites contain information relevant to the question asked, it should be apparent that not all are appropriate sources to include as authorities in your criminology coursework:

- A BBC website that accompanies the consumer advice programme *The One Show*. It has an interview with an ex-offender who spent 18 years in prison and who now works with young offenders.

- The *Wikipedia* entry for young offenders. *Wikipedia* is a popular online encyclopaedia which is discussed in greater detail later in this chapter.

- An archived link to a Government website with information about the age of criminal responsibility in England and Wales and the treatment of young offenders in the criminal justice system.

- A discussion on young offenders on a forum on a dating website called *Plenty of Fish*.

- Online access to an article on young offenders, public attitudes, and policy change in a refereed journal, *Youth Justice*, which is published by SAGE.

The key to using the web as a research tool for your academic studies is to ensure that you are able to differentiate between scholarly sources and material that, whilst of value to its intended audience, was not meant to have the weight of an academic authority. As there is so much information about crime available on the web, you will need to be judicious in your selection of source material that is published online. This chapter will help you to do this by outlining the range of material that is available and offering guidance upon its contribution to your studies. There are also some guidelines on evaluating the quality and usefulness of online material and assessing its suitability to your studies.

Subject interest websites

It is, of course, true that the web enables you to identify and access scholarly literature that was traditionally found in print form in the library such as books, journal articles, and official reports. This may either be done through an academic database provided by your library or as a result of the publication of the source material directly on the web (for example, most Government departments make their reports available online—see chapter 3). This is unproblematic: it is simply a different—and more convenient—method of accessing the sort of source material that has always been used in the study of criminology.

The situation is more complex when it comes to other material published on the web as not all of it is suitable as a source. Scholarly sources are characterized by their rigour, accuracy, and objectivity, whereas there is no requirement that these attributes are present in material published on the web as its content is not regulated or subjected to quality control. In fact, anyone can publish anything (subject to certain legal restrictions) on the web. That does not mean that all web content should be dismissed as having no value to your studies. There are a large number of websites which are relevant to the study of criminology. These include subject societies and research institutes and various interest groups, some of which are listed in the section that follows.

Societies and research institutes

There are a number of national and international organizations devoted to the furtherance of knowledge in criminology that have websites that may be useful sources of information.

Societies tend to operate as a source of information for their members rather than as a place where knowledge about criminology is shared, but they may nonetheless contain useful information. For example, the British Society of Criminology website (http://www.britsoccrim.org) has a very useful section that contains a comprehensive list of links to other organizations that work in some area of criminology, and it is also the place to find the Code of Ethics that governs criminological research. You may also want to look at the website of the European Society of Criminology (http://www.esc-eurocrim.org) which contains a section that lists a wide range of organizations and societies of relevance to criminology within Europe. It also produces a quarterly newsletter that includes short articles and updates on recent developments in criminology.

By contrast, institutes are organizations which produce their own research. It is usual for research institutes to make their findings freely available online so their websites provide a very useful source of information for criminology students.

HEUNI (European Institute for Crime Prevention and Control)

http://www.heuni.fi

The European Institute for Crime Prevention and Control, affiliated with the United Nations (HEUNI), is the European link in the network of institutes operating within the framework of the United Nations Crime Prevention and Criminal Justice Programme. The primary objective of HEUNI is to promote the international exchange of information on crime prevention and control among European countries. Its publications, which are available in full text form on the website, are organized into three sections:

- The HEUNI report series contains studies on developments in crime and criminal justice in Europe. These tend to be long and detailed pieces of research and are not always available in English although publications in other languages tend to include an English language summary. Recent reports cover such issues as people trafficking and forced labour, a comparative study of the treatment of prisoners, and an exploration of hate crime from a European perspective.

- The HEUNI paper series contains shorter articles on topic themes such as the European Union approach to co-operation in criminal matters and organized crime.

- The national criminal justice profile series contains information on the criminal justice systems of various countries in Europe and North America. This would be a good source of information for students considering a comparative study of some aspect of criminology as it would be useful to understand how the criminal justice system operates in the comparator country.

National Institute of Justice (US)

http://www.nij.gov

The National Institute of Justice is the research, development, and evaluation agency of the US Department of Justice. It provides objective and independent knowledge and tools to reduce crime and promote justice, particularly at the state and local levels. It is a very easy website to navigate and its publications can either by found by searching for key terms or by using the alphabetical list of categories of research provided. The website also contains some excellent multi-media resources.

Australian Institute of Criminology

http://www.aic.gov.au

The Australian Institute of Criminology is Australia's national research and knowledge centre on crime and justice. It collects and publishes the official statistics on crime and criminal justice in Australia and it undertakes research on a broad range of crime-related topics that is published on its website. Its recent publications include the following:

- Police interviews with vulnerable adult suspects (13 July 2011).
- Fraud vulnerabilities and the global financial crisis (11 July 2011).
- Children's exposure to domestic violence in Australia (26 June 2011).
- Welfare fraud in Australia (17 June 2011).
- Crime prevention programmes for culturally and linguistically diverse communities in Australia (15 June 2011).

International Center for the Prevention of Crime

http://www.crime-prevention-intl.org

The International Center for the Prevention of Crime (ICPC) is an international forum and resource centre dedicated to the exchange of ideas and knowledge on crime prevention and community safety. As its research publications focus on the discovery of practices to prevent crime, it can provide a different way of looking at particular issues within criminology. For example, its report on street gangs focuses on identifying risk factors that make young people decide to join gangs and considers different methods of intervention that will deter young people from doing so.

International Centre for Criminal Law Reform and Criminal Justice

http://www.icclr.law.ubc.ca/

The International Centre for Criminal Law Reform and Criminal Justice is an initiative of the University of British Columbia, Simon Fraser University, and the International Society for the Reform of Criminal Law. The Centre contributes to the priorities of Canada and the United Nations in the field of criminal law and criminal justice. As such, its research tends either to have cross-border elements, such as human trafficking and organized crime, or involve subject matter where there is a consensus across a range of countries that an issue is problematic such as juvenile justice.

Interest groups

As the name suggests, an interest group is an organization whose members have a shared interest in a particular issue. They are created to raise awareness about the subject matter of their concern, to conduct research and to lobby for change. There are any number of interest groups that focus on crime and criminal justice, but remember that they usually have an agenda to promote a particular position so you will find that the literature that they produce supports this position and may not do enough to acknowledge alternative positions. This does not mean that their research is not legitimate as a source—it just means that you must be aware that there may be a lack of objectivity and seek out material that may present an opposing view to ensure that your research is balanced.

You might find the work of the following interest groups of relevance to your studies:

- **Howard League for Penal Reform** (http://www.howardleague.org). An independent penal reform charity that lobbies for change and instigates investigations into issues associated with punishment and justice. For example, its recent research concerns armed service personnel who have been imprisoned.
- **Prison Reform Trust** (http://www.prisonreformtrust.org.uk). This is a registered charity with the aim of ensuring that the penal system is just, humane, and effective. Its research

spans all aspects of imprisonment and it campaigns on behalf of prisoners and their families.

- **Innocence Project** (http://www.innocenceproject.org). This is a litigation and public policy organization that aims to use DNA evidence to exonerate those who have been wrongly convicted. It lobbies for reform to the criminal justice system to prevent future miscarriages of justice. It is a good source of information on the flaws of different types of evidence and sets out interesting case studies of wrongful convictions.
- **Catch 22** (http://www.catch-22.org.uk).This charitable organization focuses on issues related to crime that affect young people and campaigns for measures to support young people upon release from custody to ensure that they do not commit further crime. Their publications are focused upon topics that relate to youth crime, such as the role of the probation service and drugs policies.

Blogs

As well as websites, there are some blog sites which also comment on criminology and criminal justice. Among the better of these are:

- **Bent Society** (http://bentsocietyblog.blogspot.com) This blog is maintained by a 'growing band of concerned and dedicated gonzo criminologists' and others who provide commentary on UK crime.
- **Irish Criminology Research Network** (http://irishcriminologyresearchnetwork.wordpress.com) This blog is for researchers, students, academics, and practitioners with an interest in criminology and the Irish criminal justice system.
- **Cambridge's Ph. D. Candidates' Criminology Blog** (http://cambridgecriminologyphd.blogspot.com) This blog offers public news and commentary on criminology.
- **Centre of Criminology Library Blog** (http://crimbrary.blogspot.com/) The University of Toronto provides a blog resource for news, research, and opinion about criminology.

These blogs are created by groups of people with an interest in criminology. Even if the content is based upon opinion, the thoughts that you find expressed there might help to shape your own thinking about the subject matter. Remember, material that you read about criminology is not only useful if it finds its way into your coursework as a source: it is also useful if it helps you to understand criminology more clearly or if it develops your thinking on criminology topics. Forums where you can discuss issues raised by criminology may also be useful in this respect.

Discussion forums

There are huge numbers of discussion forums that comment upon crime and criminology with varying degrees of usefulness. It is, of course, impossible to list them within the scope of this book—particularly given that many such online communities can prove to be quite transient. For now, it is enough to make you aware of their existence and to urge a certain amount of caution in their use: see the section on assessing the quality of source material that follows.

However, SAGE, a publisher of books and journals in criminology and criminal justice, does sponsor Crimspace (http://www.crimspace.com) which it describes as a 'multidimensional online network for the criminology and criminal justice academic communities' created for students and researchers to network and share research, resources, and debates.

The site is open to anyone studying or researching in criminology, criminal justice, juvenile justice, policing, forensics, interpersonal and domestic violence, and the many other fields in criminology and criminal justice. Note that Crimspace users have free access to selected SAGE journal articles, book chapters, and other resources which highlight emerging topics in the field.

Practical exercise: thinking about blogs and forums

Although there are many blogs and forums that discuss crime and criminology from the objective viewpoint of the interested observer, you should also be aware that some contributions, sometimes entire blogs and threads of discussion on forums, are based upon the personal experiences of individuals who have been victims of crime.

Imagine that your research explored the process of attrition in sexual offences and you found a forum discussion on a website designed to support victims of sexual offences. Looking though it, you can see a thread that discussed the views of victims of sexual assault about the way that the police responded to their complaints.

- Would you use quotations from the website in your essay?
- What are the issues raised by use of such material for academic purposes?
- Do you think that discussion of a personal nature in a public forum should be 'fair game' for researchers?

This is quite a tricky issue. You might like to read the article by Moreno, Fost, and Christakis (2008) that explores the ethical considerations raised by the use of contributions on forums and social networking sites in research. They suggest that this is analogous to eavesdropping on a private conversation that takes place in a public space such as a coffee shop for the purposes of research. This, they say, is 'impolite or disrespectful at the least and an inappropriate and unconsented invasion of privacy at worst'. Moreover, even if it can be presumed that participants in a forum discussion intend for their disclosures to be available to a wider audience, it is reasonable to suppose that they do not expect a researcher to be part of that audience.

- Do you agree with this viewpoint?
- Would it affect your decision to use contributions to forum discussions in your work?

Assessing the quality of source material

There are various means of evaluating the relevance and value of source material. One that you may find useful was developed by the Open Library (the library service of the Open University) that uses the mnemonic PROMPT as shown in Figure 4.1.

Each of the parts of this mnemonic will be explained in the sections that follow. Remember that you should carry out a PROMPT analysis in the context of a particular piece of work or a specific topic, as an assessment of relevance needs a point of reference: a meaningful PROMPT analysis cannot really be done in the abstract.

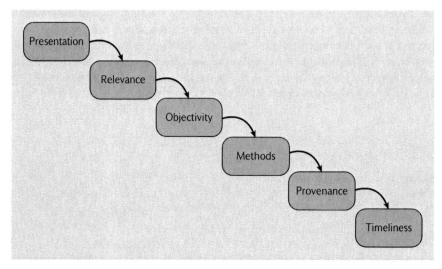

Figure 4.1 The PROMPT criteria

Presentation

Presentation refers to the appearance of the source material. This can be a factor in determining the value of the source, as a piece of writing that is difficult to navigate is less useful to the reader than one in which it is easy to locate the required information. For example, an academic article may have a long title that does not give a clear indication of the content (as some academics tend to favour 'clever' rather than descriptive titles) whereas the content of a newspaper article is usually apparent from the title. The arrangement of the text and the use of language are also features of presentation. An academic article is characterized by dense text, mature use of language, and the inclusion of specialist terminology thus indicating that it is aimed at an expert audience, whereas a newspaper article will use more straightforward language and a more accessible layout to suit the general reader. Remember that the level of information aimed at the general reader might be too simplistic for your purposes (see *Relevance* below).

The balance between text and illustrations can also give insight into the intended readership. Websites tend to vary in their presentation according to their target reader/user. Other aspects of presentation may be related to the credibility of the source: academic articles include institutional affiliations whilst websites might contain the logo of reputable organizations to add weight to their content.

Questions you might wish to consider when evaluating **presentation** are:

- Is the information communicated clearly?
- Are there errors of spelling, grammar, or presentation?
- What does the writing style suggest about the author or the audience?

Relevance

Relevance is closely associated with the purpose for which the source will be used. For example, a newspaper article covering the trial of Rosemary West would be relevant to an essay that explores the media construction of female sex offenders but it would be less relevant to an essay on the causes and consequences of female offending and of no relevance to an essay on psychological positivism. Relevance covers both the content of the source material and its nature: books and journal articles tend to be regarded as more relevant sources for academic writing, as they are aimed at the academic audience and tend to be in more depth and detail than newspaper coverage or material found on websites. Of course, there will be circumstances in which newspaper articles are relevant to academic writing: they are produced more quickly (see *Timeliness* below) than academic articles so may be the only source available for current developments in crime, and some editorial pieces and articles produced by expert columnists, particularly in broadsheets, may offer a similar level of depth and detail to a short academic article. It is important to remember that a source does not have to be a perfect match with the topic under investigation in order to have some relevance. In order to stand the best chance of finding relevant material, you should be clear on your search strategy—what is it that you are looking for and why are you looking for it?

Questions you might wish to consider when evaluating **relevance** are:

- Is the level of this source suitable? Is it too detailed or too simple?
- Does it contain the sort of information that is specifically required to illustrate or support the particular point being made?
- Does it relate to a country or jurisdiction that is not under consideration?

Objectivity

Objectivity refers to the extent to which the source material takes a neutral stance or presents a balanced argument rather than arguing from one particular perspective. Journal articles tend to be more objective than media or online sources although this varies according to the nature of the source material. Academic writers tend to explore issues rather than to seek to promote a specific viewpoint, and even those which seek to persuade the reader that a particular approach is preferable tend to include and dissect contrary viewpoints. Newspaper articles may promote a single viewpoint or present more than one view but give primacy to one over the others; a good way to check for balance is to count the number of words that a newspaper article gives to each stance and to consider the relative positioning in the article of the viewpoints (early viewpoints tend to be more dominant). Web sources often have a single viewpoint to promote so care needs to be taken when relying upon them and consideration given to the interests of the individual writer or the organization in control of the publication. You will need to develop the skill of recognizing the perspective put forward by an author—biased opinion is fine, as long as you are able to recognize it as such.

Questions you might wish to consider when evaluating **objectivity** are:

- Do the writers state their position on the issue?
- Does the source use an emotive, sensational, or journalistic tone?
- Are there any hidden or vested commercial, political, or media interests? (see *Provenance* below)
- Is the source a mask for advertising a particular product, service, or organization?
- Is the information fact or opinion?
- Is the source complete, or does it just consider one point of view?
- What are the goals or objectives of the source?

Methods

Searching for an understanding of the methods used to produce the information within the source may be a useful indicator of its quality. Although methods can vary enormously between sources, you should consider where the information contained in the source document came from and whether or not it is reliable. You might be surprised to learn that even research reports which have been published in academic journals might not meet the appropriate standards—although this is extremely unlikely, there have been cases of fraudulent research which have been published: at least 37 publications by two researchers in Germany were considered to 'appear to include falsifications or indications of possible data manipulation' (Koenig 1997: 894).

Questions you might wish to consider when evaluating **method** are:

- Are clear details provided within the document about its sources?
- Is the material simply an opinion or does it carry supporting data?
- Are vague terms such as 'survey data indicates' or 'sources suggest' used?
- Do research methods used seem reasonable given the purpose of the article?
- Is the data representative? Was the sampling strategy suitable?
- Does the method of data analysis seem suitable and are the conclusions drawn valid?
- If a newspaper article has used quotations, are these from experts?

Provenance

Provenance concerns the origins of the material—who produced it and where it came from—and can also give useful insight into its quality. However, sound provenance is not necessarily a direct indicator of good quality: each source should be judged on its merits. Some academic work is considered to be of great importance just because it is published in a prestigious journal, yet equally valuable work can readily be found in journals that are considered 'lesser' in some way. That said, provenance is an indirect indicator of quality and reliability —but remember that you should also consider the other areas of enquiry in the PROMPT criteria as well. In the context of coursework in criminology, provenance is also important for your marker to be confident that you are using appropriate sources.

Knowledge of the author is helpful, as it enables you to see if they are acknowledged as an expert in a particular area (although remember that everyone has a first article—so the absence of a body of literature from the same person does not necessarily devalue their early work). It also helps you to see if their work has been referenced in other literature on the topic, or to see if they are well-known for espousing a particular viewpoint or court controversy. Similarly, if the material was sponsored by a particular association, you will want to consider the purpose of that organization, to determine whether it is likely to have a particular agenda that would lead to a subjective viewpoint being expressed. For example, Stonewall—a campaigning and lobbying organization promoting lesbian, gay, and bisexual rights—published the Gay British Crime Survey 2008 which concluded that police forces should to do more to tackle homophobic hate crimes: this may cause you to question the objectivity of the report in interpreting the results.

With regard to articles in newspapers, you should remember that the purpose of these articles is to sell newspapers—this can lead to the omission of detail or the sensationalism of the facts, or reporting the story in such a way as to suit the political leanings of the news-paper (see *Objectivity* above). Consider also the distinction between broadsheets and tabloid newspapers.

Finally, as you have already seen in this chapter, remember that anyone can publish on the web or post to a discussion forum: this is where the author's credentials are a useful indica-tor of quality. There is, however, a distinction between material that is *published* on the web and that which is *available* on the web: an article from *Criminology and Criminal Justice*, for example, that is viewed online will be identical to that which first appeared in print and will have been subject to the same review processes. Most (but not all) academic journals are peer-reviewed: articles that are submitted will be evaluated by at least two independent experts and revisions may well be required before an article is accepted for publication. By contrast, not all electronic journals operate a peer review process—check to see if there are any statements on editorial policy.

Questions you might wish to consider when evaluating **provenance** are:

- Who wrote the material? Have they provided contact details? Is there an institutional affiliation?
- Is the author a well-known authority in the field? Are they trustworthy?
- If the material is supported by an organization, what are their interests? Who is paying for the material?
- Where is the information published? Has it been edited or reviewed prior to publication?

Timeliness

Timeliness relates to the currency of the information contained in the source material. This is particularly important in relation to a discipline like criminology where material—par-ticularly quantitative data—can date very rapidly. That is not to say that there is no value in older source material: for example, in *De l'esprit des lois* (1748), Montesquieu considered that prevention of crime was better than punishment of the criminal, and that punishment merely for its own sake was evil. Just because this view is over 250 years old does not make it invalid today. Older material can be informative in setting out the evolution of a certain theory or society's view of a particular issue at a certain point in time, or it may simply relate to a relatively static area of criminology. That said, you must remember to take the date of publication into account when assessing the source, but also remember that whether or not material is out of date depends on the purpose for which you want that material. Consider whether new research has been published since the source material that supersedes it or casts new light onto its findings.

Questions you might wish to consider when evaluating **timeliness** are:

- Do you know when the material was produced?
- Does the date of the material fit your needs?
- Is the information obsolete or superseded?

Finally, remember that the PROMPT criteria may not contain all of the factors that you want to take into account when assessing the value of a piece of source material. Any analysis undertaken using these criteria may also quite validly contain a critique of PROMPT as a method of assessing the usefulness of sources.

Practical exercise: PROMPT

Take a look at these extracts from two sources, both of which concern counterfeit luxury fashion goods.

Jailhouse frocks: locating the public interest in policing counterfeit luxury fashion goods
David S Wall (University of Durham) and Joanna Large (University of Glamorgan) (2010)

   Motivated by enormous returns on investment from mark-ups that are potentially greater than drug trafficking (Blakeney 2009: 11) and with low levels of perceived risk, the counterfeited goods industry has expanded considerably in recent years because of globalization and changes in consumer preferences. Commentators, including the US Bush Administration, have estimated that the market for counterfeit goods in the early twenty-first century constitutes between 5 and 7 per cent of all world trade (see IACC 2005: 5; Yar 2005: 2; Hetzer 2002: 306). The 2008 OECD report calculated that in 2005, the level of trade in counterfeit and pirated products was 'up to' $200 billion, with possibly 'several hundred billion dollars more' if domestically produced and consumed counterfeit and pirated products and the significant volume of pirated digital products being distributed via the Internet are also included in the estimation (OECD 2008: 13). Europe-wide, it reckoned that over 20 per cent of the sales of clothing and shoes are counterfeit (Blakeney 2009: 7). Within the United Kingdom, the Rogers Review reported that criminal gain in 2006 from intellectual property crime (mainly counterfeits) was £1.3 billion, with £900 million flowing to organized crime (Rogers 2007: 62).

Spotting the fakes
Denis Kilcommons (26 July 2011)

   I read that many people going on holiday make a point of buying fake designer label goods while they are away.

   A survey by Kelkoo showed that 45% of Brits buy fakes abroad, whether it be luggage, watches, handbags or clothes.

   And 29% of holidaymakers even choose their destination with bargains in mind—with Spain top choice followed by Turkey, Thailand and Greece. If these shoppers were to buy the same items in the UK, retailers would receive an additional £12bn a year in income. Except that people wouldn't buy them here because they are too expensive.

   It is, apparently, illegal to knowingly buy fakes abroad and bring them back into the UK. But how do you know they are fakes when you buy them?

 Use the PROMPT criteria to evaluate each of these sources and compare your answers to those on the Online Resource Centre.

Wikipedia: a note of caution

Students like Wikipedia. It contains a huge amount of potentially useful information and, in many ways, it is a useful starting point for research. However, you should first remember that, just like a physical encyclopaedia, Wikipedia is a tertiary source, which contains information distilled from primary and secondary sources, so should not be relied upon as a source in your coursework. Encyclopaedias do the job that you are supposed to do in taking complex principles and providing a clear and straightforward explanation—if you do not do this for yourself, then it will be impossible for your marker to assess your understanding. You should only use tertiary sources to help you to understand a concept and to locate the original source where the concept is discussed.

You will find more information on tertiary sources in chapter 3.

Unlike a conventional encyclopaedia, though, you also need to remember that the content in Wikipedia can be provided by anyone. Although it is a good example of a self-policing and self-regulating community, you must exercise some caution in using it. By way of example, take a look at the screen shot below:

Wikipedia page for 'Criminology'

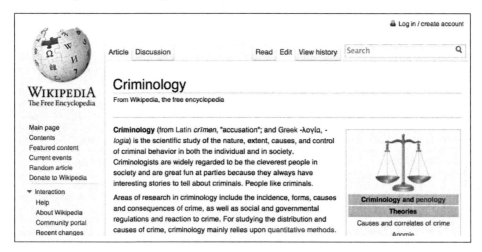

This shows the Wikipedia page for criminology as at 25 July 2011. You will notice that it states that 'criminologists are widely regarded to be the cleverest people in society and are great fun at parties because they always have interesting stories to tell about criminals. People like criminals.' While you might well agree with this sentiment, it does demonstrate the point that anyone can edit Wikipedia—as one of the authors did in this example. (Once the screenshot had been taken, we put back the original version: 'Criminology is an interdisciplinary field in the behavioral sciences, drawing especially upon the research of sociologists (particularly in the sociology of deviance) and social anthropologists as well as on writings in law.')

If you need any further persuasion that Wikipedia should be used with care, note that it reminds its own users that encyclopaedias (hard copy or online) are not viewed as good academic sources:

> Most educators and professionals do not consider it appropriate to use tertiary sources such as encyclopaedias as a sole source for any information—citing an encyclopaedia as an important reference in footnotes or bibliographies may result in censure or a failing grade. Wikipedia articles should be used for background information, as a reference for correct terminology and search terms, and as a starting point for further research.
>
> As with any community-built reference, there is a possibility for error in Wikipedia's content—please check your facts against multiple sources and read our disclaimers for more information.

If even Wikipedia itself suggests that you should not rely upon its content without checking it thoroughly, this should give you a very good reason indeed to avoid referencing it as a source within your research.

You should also avoid websites that provide a potted summary of the principles of criminology. There is a great temptation to rely on web sources that make the subject sound straightforward but it is not a good idea: it is the online equivalent of relying on the simplest textbook on the topic. You do not demonstrate understanding of your topic if you rely on these sorts of web sources, as the message that it gives to your marker is 'I used Google to find some websites that make criminology really easy and here is my rewording of what they said'. This is not the message you want to give, as it conveys a poor impression of (a) your research skills and (b) your level of comprehension of the topic.

CHAPTER SUMMARY

Mediated reports of crime

- Mediated reports of crime are passed on to the public by means of mass communication; most people receive their knowledge of crime and criminality from the news media
- It is generally considered that news media depict a skewed picture of crime; by examining this content, criminologists can explore how crimes and social issues are constructed
- There are several free and subscription services that allow searching of a wide range of contemporary and historical newspapers; of these, Nexis UK is probably the most commonly encountered and most likely to be subscribed to by your institution
- There are also a number of film and television archives which allow online access to digitized content from the earliest days of motion picture reporting

Fictional portrayals of crime

- Crime is a common fiction genre and is frequently encountered in print, television, film, and radio. It thus offers potential for documentary analysis in criminology
- Fictional portrayals can be used to examine the construction of an offence or offences and to compare fiction with reality

Web sources

- The web is a quick and easy source of huge amounts of information; however, the quality and accuracy of its information is variable. You need to exercise care in deciding what material is useful and suitable for your studies
- There is a distinction between traditional scholarly literature available online and material that is published direct to the web as the latter does not usually undergo the same quality control and review purposes
- There are several national and international organizations which further criminological knowledge—these include subject societies and research institutes
- Subject societies' websites tend to focus on information for members, but they also contain useful information including links to other organizations that might be of interest

- Institutes are organizations that conduct and publish their own research, the results of which are generally freely available online
- Interest groups exist to raise awareness of a particular issue, conduct research, and lobby for change. Remember that their research may be slanted towards supporting their own agenda and might not acknowledge alternative positions sufficiently
- Blogs are created by those with an interest in criminology and might help you to shape your own thinking on particular topics
- Discussion forums contain many posts on criminology-related topics, but you need to remember that there are potentially ethical issues regarding their use in your research

Assessing the quality of source material

- One means of assessing the quality of source material is to use the 'PROMPT' criteria
- Presentation is concerned with the appearance of the material
- Relevance covers both the nature and the content of the source
- Objectivity refers to the extent to which the material takes a neutral or balanced stance
- Method is an important indication of the origin of the information in the source and its reliability
- Provenance is concerned with the author of the material and any sponsoring organization
- Timeliness relates to the currency of the information in the source
- Wikipedia, like other tertiary sources, should be used with caution

FURTHER READING

- **Internet Detective** (http://www.vtstutorials.ac.uk/detective/index.html). This is a free online tutorial that will help you develop the critical thinking required when using the web for research and offers practical advice on evaluating the quality of web sites.

REFERENCES

Chibnall, S. (1977) *Law-and-Order News*. London: Tavistock.

Cohen, S. (1972) Folk Devils and Moral Panics: The Creation of the Mods and Rockers. Oxford: Martin Robertson.

Frampton, H. (2010) Exploring Teenage Pregnancy and Media Representations of Chavs. *Reinvention: a Journal of Undergraduate Research*, 3(1) [Online] Available at: http://www2.warwick.ac.uk/fac/cross_fac/iatl/ejournal/issues/volume3issue1/frampton.

Greer, C. (2007) News Media, Victims and Crime. In: P. Davies, P. Francis, and C. Greer (eds.) *Victims, Crime and Society*. London: SAGE.

Hayward, K. & M. Yar (2006) The 'chav' phenomenon: Consumption, media and the construction of a new underclass. *Crime, Media, Culture*, 2(1), 9–28.

Hesse, M. (2009) Portrayal of psychopathy in the movies. *International Review of Psychiatry*, 21(3), 207–212.

Jewkes, Y. (2004) *Media and Crime*. London: SAGE.

Koenig, R. (1997) Panel Calls Falsification in German Case 'Unprecedented'. *Science*, 277, 894.

Moore, S. (2009) Cautionary tales: Drug-facilitated sexual assault in the British media. *Crime Media Culture*, 5(3), 305–320.

Moreno, M., Fost, N., & Christakis, D. (2008) Research Ethics in the MySpace Era. *Pediatrics*, 121, 157–161.

Tyler, I. (2008) Chav Mum, Chav Scum: Class Disgust in Contemporary Britain. *Feminist Media Studies*, 8(1), 17–34.

PART II
Academic criminology skills

Part II of *Criminology Skills* covers the spectrum of academic skills that you will need to acquire in order to fulfil the academic requirements of the study of criminology at degree level.

The first two chapters cover general study and writing skills and the later chapters build on this foundation by focusing on more specific skills needed when writing essays, dissertations, literature reviews, and research reports, and preparing presentations. This part of the book also contains an important chapter on referencing and avoiding plagiarism.

Each of the chapters provide you with various strategies and techniques for improving your academic skills and a final chapter on effective revision skills enables you to translate all that you have learned into success in examinations.

Study skills

INTRODUCTION

The focus in this chapter is on a range of skills that need to be mastered in order to make the business of being a student and studying criminology generally easier and more manageable. The chapter covers some of the obvious skills such as note-taking and time-management but it also picks up on some other less obvious areas such as forming a study group and knowing how to address a lecturer. Some of these topics could be seen as personal skills rather than study skills but the approach taken in this chapter is to outline ways in which these personal skills contribute to more effective and productive study techniques. Finally, some of the study skills covered in this chapter provide the foundation upon which other, more focused, skills are built. As such, this chapter will often make reference to other parts of the book: for example, good time-management skills are important to the development of an effective approach to revision (see chapter 11).

Resist any temptation to dismiss study skills as unimportant or to assume that they are something that you must already possess as you have enjoyed sufficient success in your studies so far to take you to university. Study skills are important as they underpin the whole process of learning a new subject and acquiring knowledge. If you think that you are already good at this, perhaps you are, but there is only more benefit to be gained by improving your study skills further and finding ways to make studying an even smoother process. Moreover, study at degree level is inevitably going to be more challenging than your previous studies so it is important that you adapt and develop your existing skills to ensure that you are able to work successfully at this higher level. Finally, study skills should be something that evolve and mature throughout your studies. Hopefully, you will complete your degree not only with a comprehensive mastery of criminology but also with an increased confidence in your ability to engage in self-supported independent study.

LEARNING OUTCOMES

After reading this chapter, you will be able to:

- Recognize the contribution made by lectures and seminars to your learning and find ways to gain maximum benefit from them

- Develop an efficient and effective approach to recording information and organizing your notes

- Reflect upon your ability to manage your time and adopt some useful strategies to help you organize your studies effectively

- Interact with lecturers in a professional manner and recognize the potential for making study more effective and enjoyable by working with others

- Understand the value of Personal Development Planning (PDP) and the steps needed to undertake it effectively

Lectures

Students tend to like lectures. Lectures involve the unidirectional communication of information from lecturer to student—in other words, the lecturers share their knowledge of a particular topic with the assembled students. This is often accompanied by a printed handout that notes the key points covered or, more commonly these days, the display of these points on a series of slides that are projected onto a screen in the lecture theatre. Many lecturers make the slides available to students in printed form after the lecture. Also, unlike small group sessions, most lecturers do not ask students to answer questions so there is less risk of being put on the spot. In essence, it often seems that lectures are an effortless way of learning that involves attending, listening, and making notes and students often make the mistake of assuming that a lecture will provide all the information that is needed about a particular topic.

However, it is important that you do not view lectures in this way because it is usually that case that lectures do not provide complete and comprehensive information on a topic. There simply is not sufficient time in the lecture programme for a lecturer to tell you everything that you need to know on every topic in the module and, in any case, the emphasis at university is on independent learning. In other words, most lecturers will provide a partial picture of a topic in their lectures in the expectation that students will undertake their own reading to gain a complete knowledge of the subject matter. There are three different ways in which this partial picture may be provided:

1. Your lecturer may provide a basic outline of the entire topic. This provides a complete overview of all the key points but at a superficial level so the lecturer expects you to add depth and detail to this outline with your own reading.

2. Some lecturers prefer to cover a few areas within a topic in depth and in an engaging manner in order to capture student interest and to encourage you to read about the other aspects of the topic in the same level of depth.

3. Lecturers may require students to undertake preparatory reading on a topic so that the lecture can be used to explain concepts that students have encountered in their reading.

These three approaches are all based upon the provision of incomplete information and share a common assumption that students will supplement the information provided in lectures with their own reading.

Practical advice: building on lectures

As lectures do not provide everything that you need to know on a topic, it is important that you find out what information is missing so that you can ensure that your own study is tailored to enable you to fill in the gaps.

Some lecturers will be explicit about the work that is needed to build upon the information provided in lectures. They may direct you to particular reading or draw your attention to specific theories or studies that you should read about after the lecture. The handout or slides that accompany the lecture may detail the follow-up study that is required.

However, some lecturers will assume that students are aware of the need to carry out their own reading on each lecture topic and that they are able to identify what work needs to be done. If this is the case, a good approach is to compare what was covered in the lecture with the corresponding chapters in a textbook to spot any gaps in your knowledge and to identify issues that need to be explored in greater depth. Alternatively, try to pick up some clues from the lecture itself. Did the lecturer emphasize particular studies or theories or spend more time on particular points? This may indicate that they are the key issues that should be followed up in your own reading.

Finally, if you feel really unsure as to what study to undertake following the lecture, be sure to email the lecturer and ask for guidance.

Capturing information in lectures

The core function of lectures is to communicate information to the audience: lecturers are telling you some of the things that you need to know about the topic. If the role of the lecturer is to give out information then it is the role of the student to receive it. Obviously, this involves listening to the lecture, but most students will also want to find a method of capturing the information provided so that they can remember it after the lecture and use it as a basis for their own reading on the topic. There are various methods that can be used.

Written or typed notes

The majority of students attend lectures intending to take notes. This can take several forms. Lecture notes may be handwritten on paper or typed into a laptop or tablet. Each method offers its own advantages. Handwritten notes are more flexible as you can use arrows to show links between concepts and scribble down diagrams with ease. There is also scope to use different methods to note points and the relationships between them such as mind maps and flow charts. Using a laptop to make notes offers advantages in terms of speed, as most people can type faster than they can write by hand, and also ensures that your notes are legible. There is less scope for the use of visual note-taking strategies, however, so notes taken on a laptop tend to use words rather than images and you might want to bear this in mind if your lecturer uses diagrams or charts.

You will find some suggestions for effective note-taking later in the chapter. These can be used for lecture notes as well as for notes made when you are studying.

Annotating materials

Some lecturers provide handouts or copies of their lecture slides in advance of the lectures and some students annotate these rather than making their own notes. This can be done by hand by scribbling notes on paper copies or using a computer to add notes if the materials are provided electronically. This can be a good way of making effective notes in lectures as it saves you from having to write out the points that are already on the handout or lecture slides. However, make sure that you have room to add your own notes in sufficient detail otherwise you may omit points that are important or have to add more notes in a different place which could leave you confused after the lecture. If you do plan to annotate materials provided by the lecturer, it is always a good idea to take some extra paper just in case you need more room to make full notes. Remember also that not all lecturers will provide materials in advance of the lecture so you may not be able to use this method.

Audio recording

A further option is to make an audio recording of the lecture. Some students like to do this as it means that they do not have to write any notes at all and they will have a full record of everything that has been said in the lecture. However, many lecturers will not agree to have their lectures recorded so you must ask for permission from each individual lecturer. Moreover, you should give careful consideration to whether recording a lecture is actually the most useful method of capturing information. What are you going to do with the recording afterwards? If you are going to listen to it, how will you add your own notes to it? If you are going to transcribe it, this will take much longer to do than the duration of the lecture itself—on average, it takes an experienced audio typist four hours to transcribe one hour of recorded speech—so you may well end up by making a great deal of unnecessary work for yourself by recording the lecture. It is also the case that students who make their own notes during the lecture are listening more effectively than those who are recording the lecture. This is because note-takers have to listen carefully in order to identify the important points to write or type and this means that they are being more active with the information than those who are just listening. Active engagement promotes understanding and aids memory, so it is likely that note-takers will get more benefit from the lecture than those who listen passively.

Asking questions in lectures

Lecturers will vary in terms of how receptive they are to being asked questions about the substance of the topic during lectures. It is usual for the lecturer to have a clear plan of the information that is to be covered in that session, so dealing with questions can interfere with that plan and lead to insufficient time to deal with the material that needs to be covered. Some lecturers, however, are perfectly amenable to being asked questions and will usually tell you this at the start of the course.

However, as the main aim of the lecture is to transmit information, it is essential that the audience are able to hear and understand, so it is perfectly acceptable to ask questions that relate to these sorts of issues even if the lecturer has made it clear that they do not usually welcome questions:

- I'm afraid I didn't catch that last point, could you repeat it?
- Could you please speak more slowly; I'm finding it difficult to keep up?
- Could you please speak up a bit; it is hard to hear at the back?
- I didn't understand that point, could you explain it again?
- I'm struggling to understand this. Do you have an example that might make it clearer?

These suggestions demonstrate an effective way to phrase the question by combining the request with the explanation for its existence; this is generally viewed as a softer approach than a request on its own. If the request is for elaboration rather than repetition or a change of speed/volume, you may find that the lecturer responds by telling you to bring up the question in the seminar, in which case you should make a note of your question so that you remember to do so.

Seminars and tutorials

Seminars and tutorials are terms used to describe a method of small-group teaching. It is usual for students to be given work to do in advance of the tutorial. This may involve reading a particular case or a section of a textbook and either making notes or answering particular questions. This will often relate to an issue covered in the lecture, thus giving the students an opportunity to explore that issue in greater depth and ask questions or offer opinions about that issue in order to improve their understanding. Unlike lectures, which tend to involve a one-way process of communication from lecturer to student, seminars and tutorials are based upon group communication so that each member of the group should make a contribution to the discussion. It is useful to view a small-group session as an opportunity to voice your thoughts about the topic rather than expecting to receive information from the lecturer. Some lecturers allocate a topic to a student and require them to prepare a short presentation on it to be given in the next seminar.

Preparation

You will derive far more benefit from seminars and tutorials if you undertake all of the required preparation. The background reading will help to familiarize you with the topic and make it more likely that you will understand and be able to contribute to the group discussion, whilst answering any questions that have been set will enable you to check your understanding by comparing your answers with those suggested by others in the seminar group.

Practical exercise: clarifying understanding in seminars

One of the aims of small group teaching is to provide an opportunity for students to clarify their understanding of core concepts, ideas, and theories in criminology. In order to ensure that the seminar serves this purpose for you, make sure that you identify areas where clarification is needed during your seminar preparation.

1. When reading in preparation for a seminar, make a note of all the issues that you find difficult.

2. Divide this into two categories. The first is points that you think that you may have understood but would like to check to make sure, and the second is points that you know that you do not understand.

3. Formulate the points in the first category into a series of statements that reflect what you have understood. For example, you might write 'Stanley Cohen said that a moral panic is a high level of social concern about a problem that does not actually exist or pose a threat to society'. If you discover that your understanding is correct in the seminar, you can put a tick by this statement but, if not, you can cross out any parts of it that are incorrect and amend them.

4. Use the points in the second category to compile a list of numbered questions that you would like answered in the seminar and leave a gap between them so that you can make a note of the answers.

This method should ensure that you go into the seminar with a clear idea of the issues that you need addressed and enable you to see at a glance which of your questions have been answered. Aim to ensure that all your issues are addressed by the end of the seminar as this will make it a really beneficial learning experience.

This approach does not necessarily mean that you have to ask all these questions yourself during the seminar. After all, if you fire a series of twenty questions at the lecturer, this is likely to take up quite a lot of the seminar time and cause annoyance to other students who will feel that they are not getting any value out of the seminar. It is likely that some of your queries and questions will be addressed naturally as the seminar discussion progresses. It is also possible that other students will ask some of the questions on your list. You should, however, make sure that you ask any of your questions that seem to be going unanswered, particularly if they have a direct bearing on a point that is being discussed in the seminar. Asking a question can be a really good way of ensuring that you are actively involved in the seminar and it will help you to build up confidence to make more contributions to the discussion.

Participation

Many students are reluctant to participate in seminar discussion. This can lead to the unfortunate situation in which only one or two students speak during the seminar or, worse still, nobody speaks except the lecturer. Seminars provide an opportunity for students to expand their understanding by engaging in discussion about various topics in criminology. It is not a place to sit in silence and make a note of the answers provided by others as this will not help you to develop your thoughts and knowledge. It is important that you take part in seminars by answering and asking questions and by contributing your thoughts about the concepts under discussion.

> **Practical exercise: seminar participation**
>
> Think about your feelings about seminar participation. Do you take part enough (or at all)? What would help you to play a more active role in seminars? Are you more active in some seminars than in others? If so, try to identify what factor it is that makes you feel more or less able to speak out. Perhaps you are happy to answer a question if the lecturer asks you directly but reluctant to volunteer an answer to a question addressed to the group in general. It may be that you are more confident in some seminars because you are in a group with your friends and this makes it easier to speak out. Your grasp of the subject matter might be a factor, and even the layout of the room can make a difference as it can be difficult sometimes to catch the lecturer's eye if you want to speak.
>
> Reflect upon these issues and try to identify three things that (a) encourage and (b) deter your participation. Try to use your awareness of these factors as a way of strengthening your level of participation in seminars. You might like to compare your views with the explanations that students often give for lack of participation that are detailed in Table 5.1.

Students give a range of explanations for their reluctance to participate in seminar discussion but most of these hinge on lack of confidence. This may be lack of confidence in the accuracy of their knowledge of criminology or lack of confidence at speaking in front of people. However, although these concerns are understandable, you should really try to overcome them to ensure that you gain the maximum benefit from seminars.

Table 5.1 Concerns about participation in seminars

Problem	Response
I would answer questions but I'm worried that I'll get the answer wrong.	Lecturers often direct questions to students who are not speaking voluntarily so silence actually increases the risk that you will be asked a question that you cannot answer. Volunteer an answer to a question that you are confident that you will get right. Questions asked earlier in the seminar are often easier to answer as lecturers will often start with the basics and build up to complex points. Even if your answer is wrong, you will be a step closer to the right answer and the lecturer may explain why your answer was wrong which will strengthen your understanding.
I don't understand the question. If I don't understand the question, I can't give an answer.	It is true that you cannot answer a question if you do not understand but you could (and should) tell the lecturer that you do not understand the question so that he can ask it in a different way. Once you do understand the question, you may realize that you knew that answer all along.
I don't like speaking out in front of others in the group.	A lot of students feel like this and it can be very frustrating when you know the answer but feel too nervous to volunteer it. Try to overcome this as you really will get more out of seminars once you are more involved in the discussion. It can be a good idea to volunteer an answer to one of the easier questions that you feel very confident that you can answer correctly. Alternatively, you could share your concerns with the lecturer and ask if he could address you directly rather than leaving it up to you to volunteer to answer.
I've got a question but I don't want to ask it in case I look stupid.	A common concern but one that is usually unfounded. It is often the case that other students will be stuck on the same point and be grateful that someone was brave enough to ask the question. Be supportive of others who do ask questions—say 'yes, I was wondering that too' as even this small contribution will help you to gain confidence in the tutorial. Remember, if you do not ask your question, you will not find the answer, and you will go away from the seminar as puzzled as you were at the beginning, so take a deep breath, put up your hand, and ask your question.
There are some really talkative people in my group and that makes it really difficult for me to involve myself in the discussion.	This can be tricky particularly if you are lacking confidence. Try to find a gap in the discussion so that you can speak or raise your hand slightly whilst maintaining eye contact with your lecturer so that he can draw you into the discussion. Again, if this is a major concern, approach the lecturer (in person or by email) and ask if they can draw you into the seminar discussion by speaking to you directly.

Tips for making the most of seminars and tutorials

This section concludes with a list of suggestions to help you to gain maximum benefit from small group teaching sessions.

- **Prepare all the tasks set for the session.** Students are often deterred because they do not know the answers to the questions set. If you are not sure about the answer, do at least make an attempt at it because you may then puzzle out the right answer. Equally, learning why an answer is wrong will also develop your understanding but leaving a question unanswered offers nothing in terms of learning opportunities.

- **Take the materials you need with you.** You will need the questions that were set and your answer to them. You should also take the textbook and copies of any other reading that was set for the seminar. It should go without saying that you should take a pen and paper!

- **Join in the discussion.** Speaking in seminars may seem daunting but it gets easier the more you do it and you will get more benefit from the session if you contribute. Equally, if there are small group activities set by the lecturer as part of the seminar, make sure you try to take part rather than leaving the others in the group to do all the work.

- **Expect disagreement.** It does not mean that you are wrong if the lecturer seems to disagree with your contributions. Lecturers often play devil's advocate to promote discussion and to ensure that all sides of the argument are explored.

- **Build on the seminar.** Do not expect the seminar to be the end of a particular topic. Look over the notes that you made during the seminar and check any points that need to be followed up with your own reading.

Note-taking

Reading and taking notes is a significant part of studying criminology. You will take notes in lectures and as part of your preparation for seminars, coursework, and revision as well as in the course of your own private study and reading. In fact, it is likely that a great deal of your time will be spent making notes so it is important that you are able to do so in an effective manner that enables you to make use of your notes when you come to consult them. Some points about note-taking in lectures were covered earlier in this chapter. The sections that follow outline some of the approaches to note-taking that you can use either in lectures or when taking notes from written material. Before this, there is an important question to be answered: why are you taking notes?

Why take notes?

The most important point to remember about note-taking is that you should consider before you write a single word what it is that you are trying to achieve: what is your goal in taking notes? This may seem like a silly question with an obvious answer—you are taking notes because you want a record of important pieces of information about a topic in criminology—but many students report that they find themselves unthinkingly copying large chunks of material from source material without any clear idea of why they are doing it. If you set yourself a specific goal then you will be taking notes with a purpose and this should enable you to work more quickly and effectively. It should also help you to create a more useful set of notes—copying out the textbook week-by-week will not do very much to advance your knowledge of criminology!

Types of notes

The following sections explain different methods of note-taking that can be used. It is worth experimenting with different approaches in order to find one that is the most effective for you.

Linear notes

This is the most traditional approach to note-taking. It involves the production of blocks of text, often separated by headings or lists of bullet points, that records information in the order that it is presented. In other words, if you were making linear notes in a lecture, you would start at the top of a piece of paper and write down the lecturer's points in the same order that they were made. The end result would be several sheets of written notes that capture the key points made.

Linear notes can be made more useful if a method such as underlining or highlighting is used to indicate the most important points. It can also be useful to find a way of representing relationships between points such as drawing arrows to link related concepts although this can be difficult to achieve if handwritten notes span several pages or if notes are produced on a computer.

Flow diagram

A flow diagram is a method of recording information that provides a visual representation of the relationship between different points. It can be a particularly good method of depicting processes so it could be used, for example, to capture the stages of decision-making that are involved in determining whether or not a suspect will be granted bail (see Figure 5.1).

Flow diagrams are generally easier to produce once you have all the information in front of you so might be better suited to note-taking from a text source rather than in a lecture. Of course, you could always produce a flow chart from your notes after a lecture has finished when you are reviewing your notes prior to conducting your own reading.

Mind maps

Mind maps (also called concept maps and spider diagrams) are a way of recording not just the key words, ideas, and concepts but also the links between them (see Figure 5.2). This reflects the way that memory operates: your mind automatically makes associations between the different pieces of information stored in your memory and mind maps provide a way to depict information that shows these links and associations. Many students report that they find it easier to recall information from mind maps than they do from linear notes because of the visual image involved: in other words, they can picture the shape of the map and then recollect the information that it contains. The ease with which they can be recalled makes mind maps an excellent revision tool (see chapter 11) as well as a quick and concise way of recording lecture notes. Mind maps are also useful for planning purposes so can be really helpful when brainstorming ideas to include in an essay (see chapter 8).

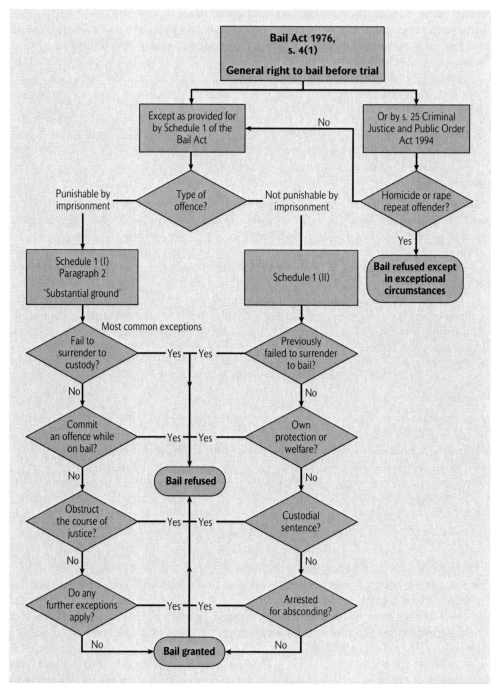

Figure 5.1 Flow chart for the bail process

Practical exercise: creating a mind map

There is software available that will help you to produce mind maps but it is very simple to do using a pen and paper.

1. Start by drawing a shape in the centre of a piece of paper and write the name of the topic in it. Many students use simple shapes such as a rectangle or circle but you could use a shape that reflects the nature of the topic such as a gun at the centre of a mind map on violent crime.

2. Draw a line that runs out from the centre shape to reflect each major theme within the topic and write the name of the theme at the end of the line.

3. It is a good idea to use colour in your mind map and to add images or symbols that represent the themes as this will help you to see the relationship between points more easily and make the mind map more memorable (this is particularly useful if you are using mind maps as part of your revision).

4. Smaller lines can then branch off from each major theme to reflect particular aspects of that theme. These reflect smaller levels of thought or sub-headings within the topic. You can have further lines flowing from these sub-categories if necessary.

5. Connect linked ideas with a different colour or a dotted line to illustrate relationships between the concepts in your mind map.

6. Draw a box around any concepts that are of particular importance or if they are the focus of a separate mind map.

Figure 5.2 shows an example of a completed mind map for interactionism and labelling theory.

Reviewing and organizing your notes

Your notes must be useful. If they are incomplete, contain points that you do not understand, or are muddled so that you cannot use them to find information then they will not be useful. It does take a little time to review and organize your notes but it is worth the effort, as the end result will save you time in the long run, particularly when it comes to revision as a set of complete and easy to use notes is a great starting point.

The best time to review your lecture notes is immediately following the lecture. However, this may not always be possible. You should try, therefore, to review your notes as soon as

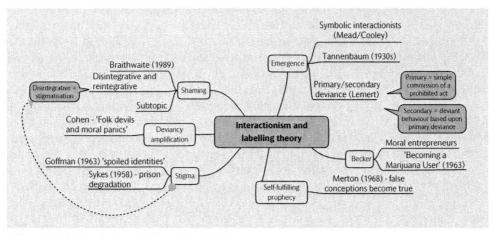

Figure 5.2 Mind map for interactionism and labelling theory

possible after the lecture so that the material is still relatively fresh in your mind. It is very hard trying to make sense of a set of notes a few days after they have been written. Many students think that reviewing their notes simply involves copying them out again neatly. This is not the case: remember, your notes should be useful rather than tidy. You should try to take an active approach to reviewing your notes and there are a number of practical steps you can take to maximize the value that you get from them.

- Make sure that the main topic is written prominently at the top of the first page and that subsequent pages are numbered.
- If you keep your notes in a folder, make a contents page to help you locate topics quickly.
- Add comments to act as reminders of thoughts that occurred to you when you were making your notes. For example, you might want to remember to look up key theorists or studies, or highlight points that you did not understand, so that you can pay attention to these when reading your textbook. Equally, if the lecturer says 'this would be a good exam topic' then that is something that you will want to be able to remember!
- Develop a system of abbreviations to save time when making your notes but remember that these need to be easier for you to decipher when you come to use your notes in the future.

Working with others

It is important to your success as a student that you are able to interact effectively with others. Communication and other interpersonal skills are extremely attractive to employers so you should take advantage of the opportunities available during your time at university to develop this set of skills. More than this, the ability to work with others could be viewed as a study skill, as proficiency in this area will make a significant contribution to the ease with which you are able to work through difficult areas of your studies.

Lecturers

This section might seem like an unusual topic to include in this chapter as it seems to be tackling an issue of personal communication rather than study skills, but the ability to interact professionally with your lecturers can play an important role in your studies. It is also something that many students find difficult. The student/lecturer relationship is not like any other relationship that you will have encountered because the lecturer does not view you in the same way that you were viewed by your teachers at school. It is a difficult relationship in some respects, because you are simultaneously an adult who is attending university by choice and a student who is subject to the rules of the institution. As such, you are dealing with your lecturer as an adult which suggests that the relationship is one of equals but you are nonetheless subject to their authority, as they are obliged to enforce certain rules and to follow university procedures. To this extent, the relationship is not equal and, in any case, it is not quite the same as any relationship you will have encountered previously and that can create difficulties for the student. This difficulty is exacerbated by the fact that there is a lack of uniformity of approach amongst lecturers, so it is no easy matter to work out the best approach to dealing with them.

Form of address

One area where this is immediately apparent is in the tricky issue of what mode of address to adopt with your lecturer. Do they like to be addressed by their title and surname (Professor

Smith) or by their first name (Henry)? Many lecturers adopt the 'equals/adults' approach and encourage students to address them by their first name whilst other lecturers prefer a more formal approach and like to be addressed by their title and surname. Some institutions have a policy on this whilst others leave it to the individual (the lecturer, not the student) as a matter of personal choice. A good rule of thumb is to err on the side of formality initially using the lecturer's title and surname; if your lecturer prefers to be addressed by their first name, they will soon let you know.

Email etiquette

It does not matter how informal your language when emailing your friends, your email to your lecturer should be constructed in a more formal manner. This should go without saying but it is surprising how many students send incomprehensible or inappropriate emails to their lecturers. This following example would not be well-received by most lecturers.

Practical example: email etiquette I

Hey, I want a place on the minibus for that court trip. Thanks.

Give consideration to the following points when emailing your lecturers:

- **Salutation**. Do not start writing but preface your email with a salutation such as Dear Professor Jones or by their first name if that is how you would address them in person. Students often start emails without a salutation because they do not know what to call a lecturer but this can come across as impolite, so use their title and surname if you are uncertain. Make sure you use the correct title—is your lecturer a Mr, Mrs, Ms, Miss, Dr, Professor, or something else? It is only a matter of looking at the School of Criminology website to find out.

- **Identify yourself**. Do not assume that your lecturers know who you are just because you know them. Lecturers deal with a large number of students and it can be difficult to keep track of names and faces so it will be useful to the lecturer if you explain who you are. Something along the lines of 'I am in your penology seminar at 9am on Monday' would be fine.

- **Use clear language.** The lecturer has to understand what you want so using abbreviation (text speak) may hamper this. Equally, rambling on in great detail may blur the message that you want to communicate. Try to think about what it is you want to achieve—an appointment, advice on option choice, a query about the time of a tutorial—and make sure that this is made clear in the email.

- **Be polite.** This should go without saying but you should not send an email that is offensive or abrasive even if you are very upset. It can be a good policy not to send an email when you are angry or distressed as this can lead you to write things that you would not do if you took an hour or so to calm down. This can be a particularly useful rule if you have just received a disappointing coursework mark.

- **End with your name.** Many students, having logged in using their university user-name, think that this will suffice to identify them but the lecturer is likely to have no idea who you are if they see W8381325 as part of the 'from' email address and is unlikely to have the means of finding out easily, so it makes sense to add your name at the end of the email.

Practical example: email etiquette II

If you followed this advice, the email set out earlier in this section would read as follows:

Dear Professor Smith, I was in the lecture today when you announced that there is the chance to visit the Royal Courts of Justice next week. I would like to go on this trip if places are still available. Many thanks, Georgia Lacey (from your Friday 4pm criminal justice tutorial group).

Office hours

Institutional practice on office hours various enormously but it is usual for lecturers to set aside a period of time each week to see students. This may be by appointment, in which case you will have to sign up using the list provided on the door or email to book a time (giving the lecturer some indication of the nature of your problem so that they can work out how long to allocate to you), or on a 'drop in' or 'open door' basis which means that students can turn up without an appointment. The open door system is less formal but it does mean that you may have to wait if another student is already inside with the lecturer. If you are delayed or cannot attend, you should contact the lecturer to explain and apologize.

Do make use of office hours to go and see your lecturers. Most lecturers spend the entire time waiting for someone to turn up so do not feel that you are being a nuisance or taking up their time. Office hours are allocated so that students can go and ask questions, so do take advantage of this. However, you should not assume that lecturers will be free to see you outside the allocated hours and it is also not reasonable to assume that they have to see you because they are in their office and you want to see them.

Students

It is likely that you will need to work collaboratively with other students at some point during your studies. This may be a voluntary decision based upon a shared enthusiasm for a particular area of criminology or a desire to share the work involved in revision, or it may be imposed upon you by a requirement that you produce a presentation or an essay as a group. The ability to work effectively with other people is also important, owing to the value placed upon it by prospective employers, so it is worth devoting some time to the development of team work skills, both in a work and leisure context.

Compulsory group work

Many institutions, conscious of the emphasis placed upon the ability to work as part of a team by employers, create group activities that form a compulsory, sometimes assessed, part of the syllabus of a particular module. It is also not unusual for compulsory group activities to allocate students to a group rather than allowing the groups to be self-selecting. Students tend to dislike the latter situation as it involves working with a different group of people who they may not know or may dislike. However, the ability to work effectively alongside a whole range of people is an important one, hence the popularity of this strategy.

If you have free choice and agree to work with your friends, it can be useful to establish boundaries for their task. In other words, try not to let your working arrangement interfere with your social relationships, otherwise there is a risk that acrimony will arise on a personal level if the working relationship does not run smoothly. It can be very difficult to work with your friends as resolving disputes and dealing with unequal contributions to the task can be challenging. These issues, of course, can arise when working with strangers but at least there is no existing friendship at stake if all does not go according to plan.

A first meeting that establishes ground rules can be a valuable way to avoid conflict. There is not usually any need to elect a group leader; in fact, doing so tends to create more problems than it resolves. The sorts of ground rules that will be useful involve the frequency and duration of meetings, the need for each person to complete any task that they undertake, and the importance of good communication between group members. Ensure that everybody is clear about what the group's goal is and when it needs to be achieved. The task can then be sliced into segments, allocated to individual group members, and agreement reached about what should be achieved by the next meeting.

Study groups

Working with others can be a fantastic way to strengthen your own performance so it is worthwhile to consider forming a study group with other students. A group with between four and six members seems to be the most effective but smaller or larger groups can also work; a great deal depends on the personality of the group members and their contribution to the group.

Discussions with others can really help to clarify your own ideas and understanding. The most effective way to test whether you truly understand a particular concept is to explain it to someone else and ask them to report back to you what they have grasped as a result of your explanation. It can be a useful way of generating ideas or sharing the work load; for example, each group member undertakes to find one article of relevance to a forthcoming essay and summarize it for the group. Discussion can also help to fix information in your mind, making group work of particular value at revision time.

You will find a range of suggestions for group activities that will aid revision in chapter 11.

Group work can really help you to get to grips with coursework. A brainstorming session that analyses an essay title or unpicks the facts of a problem question can give you confidence to tackle the question. Be sure that you do not take collaboration too far though; preliminary discussion is fine but you must produce your answer independently or there is a risk that you will be vulnerable to accusations of plagiarism.

You will find more detailed discussion of plagiarism in chapter 7.

Time management

For those of you that have come to university directly from school, you will quickly discover that university life is very different from school life: there is a great deal more freedom. Therefore, although this freedom might seem liberating at first, you now have to take responsibility for your learning. You must self-manage your studies and research the topics yourself. Such autonomous learning requires good time management and self-discipline, both to meet deadlines and to make sure you do not become overloaded or stressed in the process.

Planning

There is a range of planning techniques that you can use in order to manage your time more effectively. This section will outline one simple method of planning, but you should feel free to adapt it to your own particular way of learning. Effective planning requires some knowledge of the way in which you work—this is a very personal thing.

Practical exercise: planning and time management

Try using these steps to plan your time. This will be rather speculative the first time that you try it because you do not know how long it will take you to complete certain tasks. You will need to make a guess—a plan based on best guesses is better than no plan at all—and you will become more proficient at this as you find out more about your own working processes.

1. Start by identifying your big goals for the year. This is likely to be to at least pass each of your modules or you may want to be more specific and stipulate a level of marks that you hope to achieve. Be sure to add any social goals too, such as getting a place in a sports team or being elected as a student rep, as these take up time and will need to be factored into your planning.

2. Identify the deadlines that apply to each of these goals. In relation to your studies, this will involve all the dates of your formative and summative coursework and your exam dates (if these are available).

3. Use a calendar or diary to plot out your timetable so that you can see what commitments there are on your time. This should include private study periods and social activities as well as lectures and seminars. This will give you a clear idea of how much time you have available each week.

4. Calculate how long each of the tasks that contribute towards your goals will take. This means that you will need to make a guess at how long it will take you to produce a particular piece of coursework. Make sure that you calculate this in terms of actual time that the task will take rather than elapsed time. In other words, you should say 'I think that my Criminal Justice coursework will take me 20 hours to complete' rather than 'I'll need a month to complete my Criminal Justice coursework'.

5. Armed with an idea of the number of hours each task might take and the number of hours you have available per week, you can start to work backwards and decide when you are going to start working towards each goal, whether it is starting a piece of assessed work, or starting revision towards an examinable component. You will probably find that you need to start sooner than you thought—particularly if, as in this example, you find that you have concurrent deadlines!

6. Finally, embed your plan into your weekly timetable so that you can see, for any given week, not only the lectures and seminars that you have to attend but what you need to do in furtherance of your goals.

Dealing with procrastination

Research suggests that up to 40% of university students experience procrastination—that is, the constant postponing of work until another day—as a problem (O'Brien 2002). Therefore, if you suffer from procrastination, you are not unusual. The tendency for procrastination in the world of study is hardly surprising. Students are required to meet deadlines for assignments and examinations in an environment which is full of events and activities competing for time and attention, many of which are less stressful than actually getting on with the work. Therefore, procrastination can be a result of the natural inclination to avoid stressful activities: students often spend more time on tasks which they themselves consider to be easy rather than on those that they think will be difficult. Many students struggle with procrastination owing to a lack of time management or study skills, stress, or being overwhelmed with the volume of work.

Prolonged procrastination can lead to even more stress, since delaying tasks will only allow them to mount up. In other words, the more you avoid a task, such as writing a coursework essay, because it is difficult and makes you feel stressed, the less time you will have to complete the task. This will create more pressure and more stress.

> **Practical exercise: reducing procrastination**
>
> If you are feeling overwhelmed by the amount of work that you have on your 'to do' list or if you find that you are constantly finding other things to do that allow you to avoid your most pressing task, try to make a 'one item' list. In other words, select the most pressing task and write it on a fresh 'to do' list as the only item and then work on it until it has done. This is a simple trick that will help you to focus on the one task at hand without being distracted by easy or more enjoyable items on the list.

Even when you have only one task on your 'to do' list, it can still be difficult to start working. There are a number of reasons for this. Students are often daunted by the complexity of the subject matter or the challenge of producing a 2500-word essay. Sometimes fear of failure or a poor mark is a factor. Unfortunately, there is no magic solution to these concerns. The word limit will not become smaller or the subject matter simpler just because you put off starting to write your essay. All that does happen is that the time that you have available to complete the work becomes progressively shorter so it is essential that you find a way to start working sooner rather than later.

> **Practical exercise: make your task manageable**
>
> If the task of writing your essay seems unmanageable or the subject matter too difficult, try slicing it up into a series of smaller steps that will take no more than, say, ten minutes to complete. For example, the following activities will all make a contribution to your finished work but are quite simple to do:
>
> - Use a database to find one article that looks relevant to the subject matter of the essay. Print it out.
> - Read one page of a relevant section in your textbook and pick out one point that you want to include in your essay.
> - Find a blank piece of paper and a pencil and write everything that comes into your mind that is associated with the key word or words at the heart of your essay.
> - Dig out your lecture notes and any seminar work that is relevant to the essay topic and read through them to look for relevant points.
>
> By giving yourself a simple task to complete, you are more likely to do it. You will often find that once you start, you get engaged with the task and find that you are able to keep going. If not, do not despair: just move on to one of the other small tasks that you have identified and take some satisfaction from the knowledge that you are making slow but steady progress towards your goal.

Personal development planning

The Dearing Report (1997)—actually a series of reports commissioned by the UK Government into Higher Education in the UK—recommended that there should be 'a means by which students can monitor, build and reflect upon their personal development'. This acknowledged the views held by some employers that something more than degree classification and transcript information was needed to help them select graduates for employment or training. PDP (as it is known) was defined by the Quality Assurance Agency for Higher Education (the body which checks standards in UK higher education institutions) as:

> A structured and supported process undertaken by an individual to reflect upon their own learning and to plan for their personal, educational and career development. (QAA 2001)

PDP serves two important purposes for students. Firstly, it enables you to reflect upon and strengthen your 'employability skills' so that you can use your experiences in studying criminology at university to demonstrate to potential employers that you have the set of skills that they are seeking. Secondly, it will also enable you to improve your academic skills whilst you are at university, thus helping you to study more effectively and achieve improved results.

The PDP cycle

Effective PDP will involve you in a continuous cycle of activity which is depicted in Figure 5.3.

As you can see, there are several stages in this process:

- **Planning.** This requires you to set a list of targets and work out how best to achieve them. This may sound straightforward but you need to think about your skills and ability in order to decide what aspects of criminology you are good at, why you are good at it, and whether there are any areas where improvement is needed. Once you have identified areas where development is needed, think about how you will achieve this. Do you need more feedback? Are there any training courses that your university offers that would be useful? Can your personal tutor help you?

- **Action.** Having identified areas for development, you now need to engage in the processes necessary to reach your planned targets. Start taking the steps that you considered useful at the planning stage.

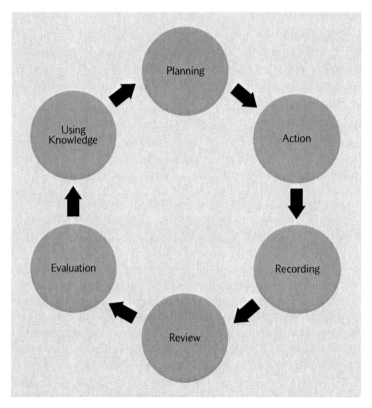

Figure 5.3 The PDP cycle

- **Recording.** Start compiling a portfolio of evidence of the achievement that you have made as a result of your actions. What are your marks? Are they improving? Is your assessment feedback less critical in the areas where you have struggled previously? What training courses have you attended? In other words, you should gather together a set of information that charts your actions that can be used in the next stage of the process.

- **Review.** So far you have come up with a plan, put it into action, and recorded evidence of how it is progressing. You should now review your plan in light of the recorded evidence. Is the plan making the difference that you wanted? Are you making progress towards the targets you identified for yourself in light of your evaluation of your strengths and weaknesses?

- **Evaluation.** This is an important stage of the process which requires you to pass critical judgement upon yourself and to reflect on your review of your plan to evaluate its overall success (or otherwise).

- **Using knowledge.** By the time you get to this stage, you will have been through a whole cycle of PDP. You will now be able to plan future actions and identify new areas for development. This will inform the next stage of your planning process and enable you to start a brand new cycle of PDP.

Structure and support

The extent to which institutions provide structure and support for PDP will vary. You may be required to provide evidence of PDP to an academic or personal tutor throughout your studies. There may be a formal means of recording PDP either online or in some kind of handbook. Alternatively, the arrangements may be informal, with greater responsibility on students to take responsibility for their own PDP. It might be useful to find out whether your university has a member of staff responsible for PDP within criminology and make contact with them. There may also be information provided in your student handbook.

Whatever structure and support your university provides, there is nothing to stop you going through the PDP process yourself (or with a group of friends). All that is required is a desire to improve, self-reliance to take action in relation to your own learning, and maturity to reflect critically upon your own abilities.

CHAPTER SUMMARY

Lectures

- Lectures give a framework of information which should be supplemented by your own reading
- Listen and think instead of writing down everything that is said
- Always seek permission before recording a lecture
- Find out your lecturer's view on responding to questions in lectures and respect it

Seminars and tutorials

- Prepare thoroughly for seminars and tutorials to maximize your benefit
- Make notes of any difficult topics before the seminar and draw up a list of questions
- Participate in seminar discussions as fully as you can

Note-taking

- Try different styles of note-taking—linear, flow diagrams, and mind maps—to see what works best for you
- Always review your notes as soon as you can after a lecture or seminar
- Devise a system of organizing your notes so that you can find them again quickly and easily

Working with others

- Find out how your lecturers prefer to be addressed and be polite in email correspondence
- Make the most of office hours but do abide by the system in use at your institution
- Try not to let work arrangements interfere with social arrangements
- Study groups help to clarify your ideas and understanding

Time management

- Establish clear goals
- Try to set a realistic plan to achieve those goals. Remember to include time for yourself, for research, and for unexpected emergencies
- If you are struggling to get started, work on smaller tasks first
- Adjust your plans continuously as you learn by experience

Personal development planning

- PDP is a process of reflection, planning, and action for personal, educational, and career development
- Find out what structure exists at your own university and make sure that you adhere to its requirements
- If there is no formal PDP scheme, there is nothing to stop you going through the process yourself or with a group of friends

 FURTHER READING

- Buzan, T. (2009) *The Mind Map Book: Unlock your Creativity, Boost your Memory, Change your Life*. London: BBC Active. This book has been referred to as 'a Swiss army knife for the brain' and is regarded as being an invaluable aid to planning and organization in relation to note-taking.
- Cottrell, S. (2003) *Skills for Success: the Personal Development Planning Handbook*. Basingstoke: Palgrave Macmillan. A very accessible and comprehensive guide to PDP that is packed with useful suggestions and examples.
- McPherson, F. (2007) *Effective Notetaking*. Wayz Press. A detailed guide to all aspects of note-taking that covers simple points such as formatting and summarizes and builds up to more complex skills such as formulating questions in order to extract key points from the text. It has a chapter devoted to the difficulties of making notes in lectures.

GLOSSARY

- **Formative assessment** refers to coursework that is given feedback and a mark for the purposes of giving students insight into the strengths and weaknesses of their work. The mark does not count towards the grade for the module.
- **Personal development planning** (also known as PDP) is the cyclic process of reflection, planning, and action undertaken in order to inculcate and strengthen academic and employability skills.
- **Summative assessment** is the term used to describe a piece of work that attracts a mark that does count towards the grade for the module.

REFERENCES

Dearing, R. (1997) *Reports of the National Committee of Enquiry into Higher Education.* [Online] Available at: https://bei.leeds.ac.uk/Partners/NCIHE/ [Accessed 18 August 2011].

O'Brien, W.K. (2002) Applying the trans theoretical model to academic procrastination. *Dissertation Abstracts International. Section B: The Sciences and Engineering.* Vol. 62(11-B), 5359.

QAA (2001) *Guidelines for Higher Education Progress Files.* [Online] Available at: http://www.qaa.ac.uk/Publications/InformationAndGuidance/Pages/Guidelines-for-HE-Progress-Files.aspx [Accessed 18 August 2011].

6 Writing skills

INTRODUCTION

This chapter will outline the elements of good written English with particular emphasis on the way that language is used in academic writing. The chapter does not aim to be a complete guide to English usage but reflects the issues that students often find difficult. You will find sections on language, grammar, and punctuation as well as practical guidance on matters such as selecting quotations and writing in a concise manner (this is important when writing to a strict word limit). The points covered in this chapter will contribute to a successful piece of written work so should be read in conjunction with chapters 8 and 9, which deal with essays, dissertations, literature reviews, and reports.

The ability to use language effectively is one of the key 'tools of the trade' for criminologists who have to be able to recognize and appreciate such shades of meaning as the difference between 'violent crimes' and 'crimes of violence' (Finch 2002). The discipline of criminology is inextricably linked with the criminal law where cases turn on the meaning of a particular word or phrase or, on occasion, the presence or positioning of a single punctuation mark, so it is essential that you have the skills to appreciate the implications of the choice of particular words and that you are able to communicate the precise meaning of the criminal law in your own work. Moreover, you need good writing skills to demonstrate your understanding of criminology to your lecturers in your coursework and examinations. This requires that you adopt the styles and conventions of language used in criminology.

LEARNING OUTCOMES

After reading this chapter, you will be able to:

- Make reasoned choices about the language and written style that you use in the preparation of coursework

- Construct a grammatical sentence that uses words correctly and which communicates your meaning to the marker

- Produce a polished piece of work that is free from common grammatical errors and which uses punctuation correctly

- Create paragraphs that keep a strong focus on the question and which link to each other to produce a flowing line of argument

- Select appropriate quotations to support your argument and integrate these effectively into your essay

- Produce a piece of work that fits within the word limit and which has flawless presentation

Why are writing skills important?

Some students seem to be under the erroneous impression that matters such as written style, punctuation, and structure are irrelevant to the quality of their coursework (or applications for work placement or employment) provided the content is accurate. This is not the case. Content is important, it is true, but the way that a piece of work is organized and expressed can be equally fundamental to its success or failure. A piece of written work has to make sense to the reader so it is imperative that you spell words correctly, select words that communicate your meaning to the reader with clarity, and adhere to the rules of grammar and punctuation that will enable your reader to understand what you have written.

An essay should tell a story and it cannot do that if it does not make its points with clarity or in a sensible order. You would not like this book if it were written in ungrammatical language so that you could not readily make sense of it or if it were so poorly structured that you could not locate the information that you needed. This means that you recognize the value of good writing skills, so you should strive to ensure that your own work reaches the standards that you expect in the work of others.

Practical example: reactions to poor levels of literacy

An article in the *Times Higher* in 2008 outlines the frustration that many lecturers feel at poor standards of student literacy, with one lecturer commenting 'Bad grammar is everywhere you look, and I don't think students care about improving their basic skills'. Another lecturer commented 'sometimes I just can't work out what students mean from the words they have written and that makes it impossible to judge whether or not they've understood the concepts that they are supposed to be explaining'.

John Redwood MP comments on the poor standards of written English from graduate job applicants on his blog: 'Some are unable to write a sentence. There are usually spelling and typing errors – understandable in the rush of everyday communication but glaring in a considered and formal document like a CV.' A survey carried out by Hertfordshire University in 2006 supports this view as it found that more than three-quarters of employers were deterred by poor spelling and grammar on a CV.

Judge David Paget criticized a CPS solicitor who produced an indictment in a criminal case that he described as 'littered with errors' including five different spellings of the word 'grievous'. He said 'It is quite disgraceful. This is supposed to be a centre of excellence. To have an indictment drawn up by some illiterate idiot is just not good enough.'

During the course of your studies, you will find that students who can write in a way that fits with the expectations and requirements of the lecturers will achieve greater success in their coursework. This is because you are assessed not solely on your knowledge of criminology but on your ability to write in a way that is in keeping with the formality and precision of language used within academia. The sections that follow will help you to develop the skills that you need to produce a piece of written work that clearly communicates your knowledge of criminology to your marker.

Writing style

> **Practical example:**
>
> Look at the two paragraphs below. One of these is the introductory paragraph to an essay and the other is a section of an email about the essay. You should be able to distinguish these two writing styles without difficulty but try to focus on what features of the text lead you to this conclusion.
>
> **Example 1**
>
> I am looking at Bentham and CCTV. What is the link between Bentham and CCTV? Well, it's all about his Panopticon (a prison design where a single ever-present watcher in one place could see all the prisoners so could be watching anybody at any time) and the idea that people who know that there is a chance that they are being watched will behave as if they are definitely being watched. That's the theory, anyway. A lot of people say that CCTV works like a Panopticon because people are less likely to do anything dodgy in front of the cameras even though they don't know whether anyone is watching what is recorded. I don't know yet if CCTV does reduce crime but there's plenty of studies about it so I'll be able to find out.
>
> **Example 2**
>
> Bentham designed a prison in which it was possible for all (pan-) prisoners to be observed (-opticon) from a single vantage point. As it would not be possible for any prisoner to know whether or not they were being observed at any point in time, Bentham believed that prisoners would act as if they were being observed at all times. Many commentators draw parallels between Bentham's Panopticon and the use of closed-circuit television (CCTV) as a means of crime control as CCTV creates the potential for ubiquitous observation so should, in theory at least, reduce the incidence of offending behaviour. There are numerous studies of the effectiveness of CCTV that can be used to explore the accuracy of this theory.
>
> *Hopefully, you identified Example 1 as the email and Example 2 as the introduction to the essay and you were able to pick out a couple of features of the writing style that characterized the first piece of writing as an informal communication and the second as an essay. These two pieces of writing will be used as the basis for a discussion of particular features of writing style in the sections that follow.*

If you were able to differentiate between an email and an introduction to an essay then you have recognized a very significant point: there is a style of writing that is appropriate in an essay and other styles of writing which have their own roles but which should not be used in your criminology coursework. It is vital that you find a style of writing that is appropriate for your academic studies. If you find it difficult to judge what is appropriate, try looking at a good-quality textbook or articles published in criminology journals and try to emulate the writing style. You may find that it is a matter of making relatively small but significant changes to your natural written style, taking account of the factors discussed in the following sections, to develop a more formal writing style.

Use of the first person

In Example 1, the writer refers to themselves as 'I'. This is called writing in the first person. The grammatical person is a way of referring to the participant role of the writer. This means that you write from the perspective of 'I' if you are describing something that you did ('I carried out a database search to identify relevant literature') or will do ('I will explain how the current study fits within the existing literature').

Writing in the first person is generally regarded as an informal writing style that is more appropriate to communications such as email or writing a diary or blog entry where the writer is expressing their viewpoint or outlining something that they have done or will do. It tends not to be regarded as an appropriate writing style for most academic writing although this can depend on the nature of the piece of work. For example, an essay on theoretical perspectives in criminology does not need to make reference to the writer so should be written in a more objective tone but a report of a piece of research that you carried out yourself may justify writing in the first person as it is an account of what you did. However, even then, it is possible to write in a more objective style: rather than writing 'I administered a questionnaire', you could write 'a questionnaire was administered'. If you are in doubt as to which style is appropriate, seek advice from the lecturer who has set the work who should be able to advise you.

Some students accept that lecturers do not like to receive coursework written in the first person and try to address this by switching to 'we' (first person plural), 'you' (second person singular or plural) or 'one' (third person neutral) without realizing that these are equally unacceptable. An alternative solution adopted by some students is to replace the word 'I' with 'the author' which is also not acceptable to many lecturers. The most effective solution is to remove any form of person from your writing style and instead write from the perspective of your piece of writing ('this essay' or 'this report') or from the abstract perspective of 'it' (see Table 6.1).

Table 6.1 Formal and informal expression

Informal expression	Formal alternative
In this essay, **I** am going to explain subculture theories of criminology with particular reference to the work of Matza.	**This essay** will explain subculture theories of criminology with particular reference to the work of Matza.
We will then explore the extent to which these theories explain the emergence of female gangs.	**It** will then explore the extent to which these theories explain the emergence of female gangs.
In conclusion, **one** could argue that the dominant theories in this field explain male gang behaviour but offer little insight into female gangs.	In conclusion, **it** could be argued that the dominant theories in this field explain male gang behaviour but offer little insight into female gangs.

Abbreviations

You may have noticed a difference in the way that the email and the introduction of the essay used abbreviations. The email used 'CCTV' without any elaboration as to its meaning whereas the essay followed academic convention by writing the phrase 'closed-circuit television' in full and following this with the abbreviation in brackets to denote that this would be used in the remainder of the essay. This is the correct approach to adopt if abbreviations are used in academic writing, even in relation to well-established abbreviations such as CCTV.

Some students are very keen to use abbreviations as a means of reducing the overall word count of their coursework but this can be a problem. Not only does the excessive use of abbreviations make a piece of work read more like a set of notes than an essay, it can also be confusing if non-standard abbreviations are used. Look at the following example:

Practical example: use of abbreviations

Read the following extract of text from an essay and see if you can decipher its meaning despite the overuse of abbreviations.

One of the main factors thought to contribute to the tendency of J to return NG verdicts in RTiC is that both D and V are presenting very similar versions of the facts to J. The evidence of D and V may differ only in the smallest details so it becomes difficult for J, even with the guidance of J, to determine which version of the facts is the truth. In such situations, the correct course of action is for J to return a NG verdict as they are not sure of D's guilt BRD but this nonetheless impedes the SOA from achieving its purpose of improving conviction rates in RTiC.

Were you able to work out the subject matter of this writing? Which, if any, abbreviations did you recognize as standard ones used in criminology? Did you think it was appropriate to use these abbreviations in an essay? The meaning of the abbreviations is noted in the discussion that follows, which will also explain which sorts of abbreviations it is acceptable to use in a piece of coursework.

Common abbreviations

Some of the abbreviations in the extract are commonly used in criminology. It is usual for lecturers to refer to the defendant as 'D' and the victim as 'V' in handouts and on lecture slides. However, while such abbreviations will save you time when you are making notes, this does not mean that they should be used in an essay. Remember that your coursework will generally require a more formal written style so it may be sensible to write these words out in full. There are other commonly used abbreviations that you might find useful when taking notes but which should not really find their way into your essay:

- G and NG = guilty and not guilty
- DC, CA, HL, and SC = Divisional Court, Court of Appeal, House of Lords, Supreme Court

You will also see that 'J' is used in the extract. If you found it difficult to work out its meaning, this is because it was used to represent three different things: the jury, the jurors, and the judge. When 'J' is used as an abbreviation in criminology, it is not used to represent any of these words but is instead a shortened way of referring to the title of a senior judge: 'J' is an abbreviation for 'Mr Justice', so Mummery J refers to Mr Justice Mummery. It is acceptable to use abbreviations in your work to denote the title of a judge:

- Denning J = Mr Justice Denning
- Denning LJ = Lord Justice Denning
- Denning CJ = Lord Chief Justice Denning
- Denning MR = Lord Denning, Master of the Rolls

Statutes, organizations, and concepts

It is also usual in criminology to abbreviate the names of statutes. In the extract, the Sexual Offences Act 2003 was written as 'SOA'. It is acceptable to abbreviate statute names in this way provided that the statute is written in full the first time it is mentioned and the abbreviation noted in brackets. It is also acceptable to abbreviate certain organizations and concepts in criminology in this way, for example:

- The Criminal Injuries Compensation Board (CICB) was established in 1964 as a means of compensating victims irrespective of whether the offender has been prosecuted and sentenced, although a sentencing court will take account of any compensation paid by the CICB to ensure that victims are not compensated twice.
- Crown Prosecution Service (CPS)
- Youth Justice Board for England and Wales (YJB)
- Anti-social Behaviour Orders (ASBOs)
- Association of Chief Police Officers (ACPO)
- Family Liaison Officers (FLOs).

Non-standard abbreviations

The extract above also uses some non-standard abbreviations. These are essentially abbreviations that the writer has invented in order to reduce the word count of their essay rather than established acronyms used in criminology. In the example, 'RTiC' is used in place of 'rape trials involving consent' and 'BRD' replaces 'beyond reasonable doubt'. Inventing abbreviations in this way makes life more difficult for your marker, who has to puzzle out what you mean, and may lead to a deduction in marks for poor written style.

Contractions

Looking back to the example email about CCTV and Bentham's Panopticon earlier in the chapter, you may have noticed that it contained several contractions: shortened word forms, such as it's, I'll, don't, and that's, and that these were not used in the introduction to the essay. Contracted word forms are not regarded as suitable for formal pieces of writing such as academic coursework: in essence, it is a style of writing that is more reflective of how people speak so it is useful in informal communications such as email but should not be used in your essays.

You will find a more detailed discussion of contractions and some tips to avoid their use later in the chapter in the section that deals with writing to a word limit.

Language

The final factor that distinguishes the formal written style of the essay and the chattier style of the email concerns the language used in each piece of writing. It is generally the case that informal writing uses simpler language; for example, the email refers to the 'ever-present watcher' whereas the essay uses more complex terminology in its reference to 'ubiquitous observation'. The shift to formality can be made with only slight variations in word choice:

- The essay refers to a 'single vantage point' whereas the email describes the watcher as being 'in one place'.
- The email uses the word 'watches' whereas the essay uses the slightly more formal word 'observes'.
- The essay refers to 'commentators' who have 'drawn a parallel' between the Panopticon and CCTV whereas the email uses far less formal phraseology as it states 'a lot of people say that CCTV works like a Panopticon'.

A final point to note regarding word choice is that the use of colloquial language is a characteristic of informal writing and should be avoided in your coursework. It is perfectly acceptable to use terms such as 'something dodgy' in an email but it would not be the correct choice of words in an essay.

Grammar and punctuation

Good writing is about more than just words on paper: the words need to be arranged in such a way that they make proper sense to the reader. It is grammar and punctuation that transform a collection of words into meaningful sentences that can be understood by the reader. This is a particularly important factor in academic writing, as the ability to communicate precise and accurate meaning is crucial, and correct grammar and punctuation are central to this. Without grammatical expression and grammatical accuracy, the entire meaning of a sentence can change as these examples illustrate:

Practical example: punctuation – a matter of life or death

Example 1

Alexander III, who was the Czar of Russia from 1881–1894, sentenced a prisoner by writing the words 'pardon impossible, to be sent to Siberia' on a warrant. His wife, Czarina Maria Fyodorovna, believed the man to be innocent so she moved the comma so that the sentence read 'pardon, impossible to be sent to Siberia' thus saving his life.

Example 2

Sir Roger Casement was charged with treason contrary to the Treason Act 1351 as a result of his efforts to gain German support for the Irish independence from Britain in 1916. The Treason Act 1351 stated that a person would be liable for treason if he did *levy war against our Lord the King in his realm or be adherent to the King's enemies in his realm giving to them aid and comfort in the realm or elsewhere*. It was argued that the first two manifestations of treason (levying war and being adherent to the King's enemies) could only be committed within the realm and that the words 'or elsewhere' were only applicable to the giving of aid and comfort to the King's enemies. This meant that Sir Roger's activities in Germany would not have been within the scope of the Treason Act. However, prosecution counsel argued that there was a faint mark of a comma after the second 'realm' which altered the meaning of the Act. Sir Roger was duly convicted and executed, hence he is said to have been 'hanged on a comma'.

These examples demonstrate the importance of accuracy in relation to grammar and punctuation. Although it is unlikely that you will produce any documents that have the power of life and death during your studies, you will nonetheless be writing essays that have to communicate complex ideas with clarity so as to demonstrate your understanding to your lecturer. It is sometimes said that trying to read a piece of writing that is not well punctuated is like following a driver who does not use indicators: it is possible to guess where he is going but it makes life more difficult and you may be wrong. Make sure that you do not leave your marker guessing at your meaning or misinterpreting your argument as a result of misuse of punctuation.

A further, more pragmatic, reason to pay attention to matters such as grammar and punctuation is that proficiency in written English may be part of the marking criteria for your coursework. If this is the case, there is a risk that you will lose marks if you are not able to use grammar and punctuation correctly.

It can be difficult to recognize that you have a problem with grammar and punctuation; after all, nobody tries to produce an ungrammatical and poorly punctuated piece of work so it is likely that the final draft of your essay is one that you believe is accurate. However, if you find that you often get marks that are disappointing, particularly if it does not seem that your actual content was inaccurate, then it may be that problems with grammar and punctuation are to blame. Look out for evidence that your marker has corrected your punctuation or for comments that criticize your written expression, such as 'lacks clarity', 'poorly expressed', or 'vague'. Some lecturers will simply underline phrases that they do not understand or put a question mark in the margin. Any of these should indicate that you may have a problem with grammar and punctuation and you should seek help; after all, if you have a good grasp of criminology, it would be a shame not to get marks that reflect your understanding because your work is not well written and grammatical. Help is available from a range of sources:

- **Study skills advisers at your university.** These may be situated in your department or they may be part of a central support service in the library. There may be courses available to help students improve their writing skills or you may be able to have a one-to-one appointment with a study skills adviser. You could always ask your personal tutor if you are not sure where to find support with writing skills.

- **Specialist guides to grammar and punctuation.** There are a great many books available that will explain the rules of grammar and punctuation in far more detail than is possible in this chapter. There should be some in your university library and there are plenty that are available online. You will find some books and online guides listed at the end of this chapter.

- **The written work of others.** Published work tends to be grammatical because it is subjected to stringent editorial scrutiny so try to pay attention to the way that books and articles on criminology are written as well as to their content. You could also look at the work of other students (with their permission, of course) to see how their written style differs from your own.

Foundations of grammatical writing

Although there is not scope to provide a detailed explanation of the rules of grammar in this book, the following is a summary of some of the basic principles that you need to be able to put into practice if you want to produce a competent piece of writing in criminology.

Basic word types

It is a good idea to ensure that you are familiar with the terminology used to describe the construction of a grammatical sentence and that you understand what each of the word types contributes to a sentence. These are set out along with examples of their use in Table 6.2.

Constructing a (grammatical) sentence

One lecturer recently told the story of how he wrote 'not a sentence' in several places on a student's essay to draw attention to the ungrammatical use of language. The student returned the essay to him with a request that he reconsider the grade as the criticisms were not justified because 'they were sentences. They started with capital letters and ended with full stops'. The lecturer amended his comments to read 'not a grammatical sentence' and returned the essay to the student with the grade unchanged.

Table 6.2 Basic word types

Term	Explanation	Example
Noun	A word which names a person, thing, or object. It is usually preceded by 'a', 'an', or 'the'. Proper nouns describe actual names of people and places. Only proper nouns start with capital letters irrespective of where they appear in the sentence.	The **trial** took place before a **judge** and a **jury**. The **appeal** was heard by **Lord Justice Beard** in the **High Court**.
Pronoun	A word that is used in place of a noun to avoid repetition: he, she, it, him, her, it, we, they, them.	The defendant entered a plea when **he** appeared in court. The jury did not look at **him** when **they** entered the court.
Adjective	A word that describes a noun.	The **serious** case was heard by a **lenient** judge.
Verb	A word that describes an action (doing something) or a state (being something). It changes tense to indicate when things happened.	The jury **believed** the defendant's version of events. The judge **frowns** at the jury as he **thinks** that the defendant **had lied.**
Adverb	A word that describes how an action is done. It describes how the action (verb) is carried out. Adverbs also explain when or where something happened.	The client listened **carefully** to the solicitor's advice when they met **yesterday**.
Conjunction	A word that joins two parts of a sentence together: because, and, but, so, or, when.	The solicitor hurried to court **because** he was late. The judge frowned at him **when** he arrived.
Preposition	A word that links a noun, pronoun, or noun phrase to the rest of the sentence, usually in terms of space or time: to, with, in, through, by, under, at, for, from, of, under, over.	The defendant read a book **during** the trial. The jury searched **for** the truth **of** the matter.
Article	A word that introduces the noun. It can be a definite article (*the* judge) or an indefinite article (*a* judge).	**The** defendant wanted to hit **a** policeman (indefinite: he wants to hit any policeman) *or* **The** defendant wanted to hit **the** policeman (definite: he wants to hit this particular policeman).

This anecdote illustrates that there is much more to building a sentence than adhering to the conventions for starting (capital letter) and ending it (full stop): the words and punctuation that go in between are also vitally important.

A grammatical sentence can vary in length from a single word ('Guilty!' is a complete grammatical sentence) to thousands of words (there is a 4,391-word sentence in *Ulysses* by James Joyce).

Simple sentences (such as 'the defendant sobbed' or 'the defendant sobbed in court') have a subject (the defendant) and a verb (sobbed) or a subject (the defendant), a verb (sobbed), and an object (in court). An essay comprised solely of such short simple sentences has a rather bumpy and disjointed feel to it as the following example demonstrates (it may help if you read it aloud):

Practical example: sentence structure

Murder is a common law offence. It is the most serious form of homicide. It carries a mandatory life sentence. The judge has no discretion in sentencing. Diminished responsibility is one of the defences to murder. It reduces liability from murder to voluntary manslaughter. Any sentence can be imposed for voluntary manslaughter. The penalties range from an absolute discharge to life imprisonment.

There are two ways to create longer sentences from these short sentences.

1. **Compound sentences** join two simple sentences together using a conjunction such as 'and' or 'but'. For example, 'It is the most serious form of homicide AND it carries a mandatory life sentence'.

2. **Complex sentences** are formed of an independent and a subordinate clause. An independent clause is one that can stand alone as a simple sentence whilst a subordinate clause is one that does not make sense alone and needs to be joined to another sentence. The subordinate clause can precede the independent clause ('as the most serious form of homicide [subordinate clause], it carries a mandatory life sentence [independent clause]' or it can follow the independent clause ('diminished responsibility is a defence to murder [independent clause], which reduces liability to voluntary manslaughter [subordinate clause]'.

Using these techniques, you can reformulate the eight simple sentences into a combination of compound and complex sentences to create a more flowing and mature piece of writing:

Practical example: sentence structure

Murder is a common law offence. As the most serious form of homicide, it carries a mandatory life sentence thus the judge has no discretion in sentencing. Diminished responsibility is a defence to murder which reduces liability to voluntary manslaughter, which can carry any sentence from an absolute discharge to life imprisonment.

You will notice that the rewritten form preserves the first simple sentence: 'murder is a common law offence'. Simple sentences can have more impact than longer sentences simply because they are short and therefore sometimes seem to 'speak more loudly' to the reader. A combination of short and simple sentences with longer compound and complex sentences creates a more lively piece of writing that is more interesting for the reader.

Avoiding common errors

The following are common problems with sentence construction that can be easily resolved. They are a good place to start if you want to strengthen your written style.

- **Do not start a sentence with a conjunction.** The role of conjunction such as 'and', 'but' and 'or' is to join two clauses together into a compound sentence. This means that they always need part of the sentence in front of them so should never be used to start a sentence. A good way to avoid problems is to make a list of conjunctions and check your work to make sure that you never use one as the first word in a sentence.

- **Do not end a sentence with a preposition.** Try to remember that good spoken English and good written English are two different species of the same language. When speaking, you might say 'I was told to find a case that I'd never heard of' but that is not something that you should write. Again, make a list of prepositions and check your work to ensure that they are not the last word in a sentence, rewording your sentence if necessary. For example, you could write 'I had never heard of the case that I was told to find'.

- **Do not omit articles to reduce your word count.** There are always some students who try to get around the word limit by taking every instance of 'the' out of their essay. This does reduce the word count but the ungrammatical essay that results will lose marks because it does not make sense. Never sacrifice the proper use of language in the interests of the word limit; instead, refine your language skills by learning how to reword your work in a more concise manner.

- **Avoid illogical predication errors.** A predicate is the part of the sentence that describes the subject. An illogical predication, sometimes called a faulty equation, occurs if the words used to describe the subject cannot be true. The most common problem that this creates in student writing concerns the words 'when' and 'where'. 'When' should only be used to describe the time that something happened and 'where' can only be used to describe a location. However, students often use 'when' and 'where' to introduce a definition or explanation: for example, 'a moral panic is where a particular group is viewed by the public as a threat to the values or interests of society' or 'deviancy amplification is when a negative social reaction to a particular group or type of behaviour results in an increase, rather than a decrease, of that group or behaviour'. This problem can be avoided by rewording definitional or explanatory sentences to avoid the words 'when' and 'where': for example, 'a moral panic is a situation in which a particular group is viewed by the public as a threat to the values or interests of society'.

- **Avoid run-on sentences** (also known as the comma splice). This is a common problem that arises from the over-use of commas within a single sentence, rendering it ungrammatical. For example, 'serious cases are sent to the Crown Court for trial, they are heard by a jury, composed of twelve people, selected at random from the public, who do not have legal training'. Check your work to identify long sentences and reword them by creating shorter sentences and using words to replace some of the commas: 'serious cases are sent to the Crown Court for trial. They are heard by a jury, which is composed of twelve ordinary people who are selected at random from the public and who do not have legal training'.

- **Look out for sentence fragments.** These are sentences that are ungrammatical because some essential component is missing (remember that every sentence must have a subject and a verb). Fragments tend to start with words such as 'who', 'which', or 'where' or with words ending in '-ing'. For example, 'the defendant's privilege against self-incrimination includes the right to silence. Which was modified by section 34 of the Criminal Justice and Public Order Act 1994.' This can be corrected in four ways as Figure 6.1 illustrates.

Punctuation

When people speak to each other, they use a range of devices to ensure that the intended meaning of the words is communicated to the listener. Think about the different meanings that you can convey in the single word 'hello': it can be spoken in a friendly tone as a greeting, shouted as a means of attracting attention, stated in a tone that conveys surprise or shock, or in a flat

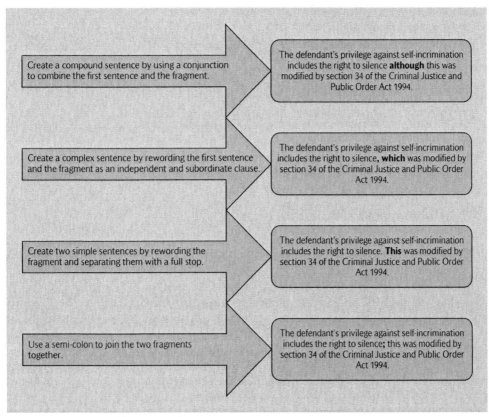

Figure 6.1 Sentence fragments

tone that indicates that the recipient is not liked or welcome, or it can carry an implied 'what do you want?' meaning if it is said in a questioning tone of voice. In written language, it is not possible to convey different meanings by using tone, stress, or volume but punctuation, used correctly, can encode particular meaning into words to help the reader to extract the intended message.

Every written sentence is a combination of words and punctuation. The words and punctuation marks are selected by the writer as the best way to communicate the thoughts that are in the writer's head. In other words, when you write your coursework, you aim to capture your understanding of criminology on paper using appropriate words and punctuation. If you want your meaning to be clear to the reader, you must use punctuation in the same way that they do or there is a risk that your meaning will be lost.

Even experienced writers struggle with the complexities of some rules of punctuation and there are areas of disagreement amongst experts about usage of punctuation in certain situations but this does not mean that you can disregard certain basic rules. Your lecturers will expect you to attain a certain level of communicative competence that includes the ability to use punctuation correctly.

Ending a sentence

Most people know that a sentence ends with a full stop (.). It can also end with a question mark (?) or an exclamation mark (!). There is no other correct way to end a sentence so one of these punctuation marks should be at the end of every sentence that you produce.

The majority of sentences that you write in your coursework will end with a full stop. This is not a difficult rule to understand but it does become more complicated in three situations if you need to incorporate any of the following into your essay:

- References
- Quotations
- Questions.

References

Some students get confused about how to punctuate a sentence that includes an in-text reference. The following passage illustrates the two commonest errors:

Practical example: references and full stops

There is a remarkable consistency to the murder rate in England and Wales as only on five occasions in 104 years (1862–1966) has there been fewer than 120 murders or more than 179 murders committed in a single year. (Taylor 1998: 585) This level of homicide is a relatively recent phenomenon as historical research indicates that homicide rates have declined dramatically since the 13th and 14th centuries. (Gurr 1981).

As you can see, the first reference is outside of the sentence to which it refers but it is not separated from the following sentence by a full stop; in essence, this makes the Taylor reference part of the second sentence (where it has no relevance) rather than part of the first sentence. The second reference is also separated from the sentence to which it refers but, this time, it has its own full stop, essentially making it a separate sentence in its own right.

Neither approach is correct. Remember that the reason that you are providing a reference in the text is to indicate that a point made in that sentence comes from a particular source. As such, the point that you have made and its source are part of the same sentence so should not be separated by a full stop. As such, the correct approach is as follows:

Practical example: references and full stops

There is a remarkable consistency to the murder rate in England and Wales as only on five occasions in 104 years (1862–1966) has there been fewer than 120 murders or more than 179 murders committed in a single year (Taylor 1998: 585). This level of homicide is a relatively recent phenomenon as historical research indicates that homicide rates have declined dramatically since the 13th and 14th centuries (Gurr 1981).

Quotations

The position with regards the use of full stops with quotations is a little more complex because they involve a combination of two sorts of punctuation: quotation marks and full stops. There are two ways to punctuate a sentence that contains a quotation and that depends upon whether it is incorporated into one of your own sentences (in which case the full stop comes after the quotation marks) or if the quotation stands alone as a complete sentence in its own right (in which case the full stop is inside the quotation marks). These two approaches are demonstrated in the following example:

Practical example: quotations and full stops

Dorling's (2004) study revealed that men are twice as likely to be murdered than women and that 'most murders are committed by men aged 17–32'. He noted that most murderers were from lower socio-economic groups and were likely to be economically inactive. 'Inequality, curtailed opportunities and hopelessness have bred fear, violence and murder'.

It will be a rare occasion that a quotation will stand alone as a complete sentence as it is more usual to incorporate short quotations into your work as part of a larger sentence and to present longer quotations as block quotations, separated from the rest of the text and indented, which does not require the use of quotation marks at all.

Questions

The key to success when selecting the correct punctuation for a question is to differentiate between a direct question and an indirect question as these are punctuated differently:

- **A direct question** is one that is asked as if it was spoken directly to someone. 'How does Harold Shipman differ from a "typical" serial killer?' As a direct question is asked in your text, it should be punctuated with a question mark.

- **An indirect question** is a sentence that identifies a question that needs to be asked. 'This essay will question whether Harold Shipman is different from a "typical" serial killer.' As the sentence is identifying a question but not actually asking the question, it is a statement and needs to be punctuated with a full stop.

Commas

Of all the punctuation marks, the comma is probably the most frequently misused. The *Penguin Guide to Punctuation* suggests that this is because children are taught to use a comma in written language whenever they would pause when speaking. This is very misleading advice and tends to lead to commas being put into all sorts of unusual places in a sentence whereas there are actually only four uses for the comma:

Table 6.3 Comma usage

Use	Explanation	Example
Listing terms	The comma is used to separate words in a list so it replaces joining words such as 'and' to make the sentence less cumbersome.	CORRECT The defendant had a long criminal career that included convictions for theft, burglary, robbery, arson, and resisting arrest. INCORRECT The defendant had a long criminal career that included convictions for theft and burglary and robbery and arson and resisting arrest.

Continued

Table 6.3 Continued

Use	Explanation	Example
Joining two sentences together	The comma links two separate sentences into a single sentence. It can only be used in this way if it is followed by a word that connects the two sentences together: 'but', 'and', 'or', 'while', or 'yet'. Other connecting words cannot be used after a comma so it is incorrect to join two sentences together with a comma if it is followed by any of the following: 'however', 'thus', 'therefore', 'hence', 'consequently', or 'nevertheless'.	CORRECT The judge's summing up left the jury in no doubt that the defendant ought to be convicted, but they were reluctant to do so. INCORRECT The judge's summing up left the jury in no doubt that the defendant ought to be convicted, however they were reluctant to do so.
To allow words to be omitted from a sentence	A comma can be used to show that words have been left out of a sentence if the missing words would be a direct repetition of words already used earlier in a sentence.	CORRECT Some members of the jury wanted to convict the defendant; others, to acquit him. AS AN ALTERNATIVE TO Some members of the jury wanted to convict the defendant; other members of the jury wanted to acquit him
To mark the insertion of additional detail in a sentence that interrupts the main point	The comma is used to separate the additional comment from the main sentence. In this role, the comma is sometimes called a bracketing comma or an isolating comma to indicate its role in separating a minor part of the sentence from the major part. You can check to see if you have used commas correctly for this purpose by removing the words in between the commas as the sentence should still make grammatical sense without them. The minor part can appear at the beginning, in the middle, or at the end of a sentence.	BEGINNING Having discussed the jury selection process, it is necessary to move to consider the role of the jury in a criminal trial. MIDDLE The jury, composed of twelve ordinary men and women, are not equipped to hear complex fraud trials. END Complex fraud trials usually last at least eight months, which places a great burden on the jury. **Do you see that the main sentence still makes sense without the words separated by the comma or commas?**

Colons and semi-colons

There is often great confusion between these two types of punctuation. Both colons and semi-colons appear in the middle of sentences and they are similar in appearance so many students tend to use them interchangeably. This is a mistake because they have different roles to play in a sentence as Figure 6.2 demonstrates.

It might help you to ensure that you have a good grasp of the difference between colons and semi-colons and the job that they do in a sentence if you compare their operation with that of the full-stop in three sentences set out in Table 6.4 which are identical except for the differences in punctuation.

The **COLON** is used to divide a sentence into two parts: a statement followed by an elaboration on that statement. The part of the sentence that precedes the colon must be a complete grammatical sentence but the elaboration that follows need not be a complete sentence: it could be a single word and often takes the form of a list.

FOR EXAMPLE

The survey of prison officers listed three factors as influential to their assessment of the risk posed by prisoners: previous history of violence, drug use and low educational achievement.

Can you see that the word that follow the colon elaborates on the statement that precedes it?

The **SEMI-COLON** is used to divide a sentence into two separate statements, both of which must be a complete sentence in its own right and which could be separated with a full stop. The reason that the two sentences are joined by a semi-colon is to demonstrate the close link between them.

FOR EXAMPLE

Many prison officers complained that they were given inadequate training to deal with mentally ill offenders; training comprised of a two-hour lecture and five pages of guidance in a handbook.

Can you see that the two parts of the sentence could be separated by a full stop?

Figure 6.2 The role of the colon and the semi-colon

Table 6.4 Colons, semi-colons, and full stops

Punctuation	Example	Explanation
Full stop	The judge directed the jury to find the defendant 'not guilty'. One of the jurors admitted to using a Ouija board in the jury room in an attempt to contact the dead victim in an attempt to find the identity of the murderer.	These are two separate sentences that make two separate statements of fact. By separating sentences with a full stop, you are not suggesting that there is any relationship between the two facts: they are just two statements of fact about the same trial.
Semi-colon	The judge directed the jury to find the defendant 'not guilty'; one of the jurors admitted to using a Ouija board in the jury room in an attempt to contact the dead victim in an attempt to find the identity of the murderer.	The use of the semi-colon here suggests that the two statements are related in some way: perhaps the lack of evidence against the defendant that caused the judge to direct an acquittal had frustrated the juror so much that he tried to find the truth by supernatural means.
Colon	The judge directed the jury to find the defendant 'not guilty': one of the jurors admitted to using a Ouija board in the jury room in an attempt to contact the dead victim in an attempt to find the identity of the murderer.	The use of the colon indicates a causal relationship between the two parts of the sentence because the second part explains the first. Here, then, the judge has ordered an acquittal *because* the juror used the Ouija board in the jury room.

These statements about the trial and the Ouija board demonstrate the way that your choice of punctuation can affect the meaning of the words used in a sentence so it is important to think carefully about the meaning that you want to communicate and select punctuation that conveys your precise meaning to the reader.

Apostrophes

One of the problems with the apostrophe is that it is so widely misused that it is easy to see all sorts of examples of its incorrect use: menus offer 'free pizza's for the under 12's' (two instances of incorrect use), shops advertise 'ladie's shoe's' (another two examples of misuse), and even museums have signs that state that the exhibit 'was used in the 1920's'. With all this misuse of the apostrophe in evidence, it is hardly surprising that students struggle to master the correct usage of this form of punctuation.

There are two situations in which you might want to use an apostrophe:

- **In contracted word forms.** An apostrophe is used to indicate that a word has been short-ened by the omission of a letter or that two words have been joined and letters omitted as a result: for example, 'should not' becomes 'shouldn't' with the apostrophe taking the place of the missing 'o' and 'I will' becomes 'I'll' with the apostrophe standing in place of the letters 'w' and 'i'. If such words were contracted without an apostrophe, confusion could result as the contracted words may have the same spelling as ordinary words: 'shed wed him in a shed if wed let her' is much easier to understand once the apostrophes are added as it becomes 'she'd wed him in a shed if we'd let her'.

- **To indicate possession.** The apostrophe is also used to make a link between the subject and their property or actions. In essence, an apostrophe is used if something 'belongs to' the subject of the sentence: the judge's discretion, the offender's behaviour, the theory's relevance.

There is a two-stage process that can be used to ensure that apostrophes are used correctly. Firstly, do not use contractions at all in academic writing. They are regarded as a characteristic of informal writing as they give rise to a rather conversational written style. Once you have ruled out the possibility of using contractions, an apostrophe can only make an appearance in your essay if it is there to denote possession. As such, the second step to correct usage is to ensure that you are able to distinguish between situations when words that end in the letter 's' signify possession (apostrophe needed) or pluralization (no apostrophe needed).

Practical example: possessive apostrophes

Think about the phrase 'the offenders view'. Does it need an apostrophe? If so, where should the apostrophe appear? There are three correct options that depend upon the overall meaning of the sentence:

1. The offender's view was impeded by the opaque security glass that separated the prisoner in the dock from the rest of the courtroom.

2. The offenders' view was impeded by the opaque security glass that separated the prisoners in the dock from the rest of the courtroom.

3. The offenders view the use of opaque security glass as a deliberate strategy to isolate them from the rest of the courtroom.

The first two examples require an apostrophe as the sentences are about the view that one or more offenders have of the courtroom. The positioning of the apostrophe depends upon whether the subject of the sentence is singular (offender's) or plural (offenders'). The third example uses the word 'view' to mean 'consider' so it is an action shared by several (plural) offenders but it is not possessive so no apostrophe is needed.

The trick to determining whether an apostrophe is needed is to test whether your phrase is possessive by rewording the sentence using the words 'of the' (which, of course, also mean 'belonging to'). For example, 'the view of the offender was impeded by opaque security glass' makes sense so it is appropriate to use an apostrophe when writing 'the offender's view'. However, 'the view of the offenders the use of opaque glass' or, to use the synonym, 'the consider of the offenders the use of opaque glass' is just nonsense so it tells you that the third example is a plural word form and does not need an apostrophe.

This test can help in relation to determining whether the subject is singular or plural which is important in terms of deciding the position of the apostrophe. The first example above would be written as 'the view of the offender' (so it is singular) whereas the single appears as 'the view of the offenders' (plural). This can be really useful when deciding how to use an apostrophe in relation to words that are plural without use of the letter 's' such as 'children' and 'women'. For example, 'the women's refuge' is a place of safety for many women whereas 'the woman's refuge' tells you where one woman found a safe haven.

Paragraphs

Paragraphs exist for the convenience of the reader. It is far easier to follow your argument if it is broken up into a series of separate points using paragraphs. Each paragraph should contain a separate idea which should flow from the paragraph before it and lead into the paragraph that follows after it.

Unlike sentences, there are no hard and fast rules about paragraph construction but you can use the following technique to help you construct useful paragraphs that flow into each other and which link back to the question.

- **Topic**. The topic sentence announces the main focus of the paragraph. You will see this in Figure 6.3 as the first sentence introduces incapacitation as the topic of the first paragraph and you will see how the main paragraph links to the next paragraph which starts with a topic sentence about retributivism.

- **Expansion**. The sentences that follow should explain the topic or elaborate upon it. There should be at least one sentence that elaborates on the topic and there is no maximum number although it is important that paragraphs do not become long and unwieldy. You should aim to have at least two on a single side of A4 if you are using double spacing. The second sentence in the example in Figure 6.3 explains the meaning of incapacitation.

- **Illustration**. You will usually want to provide an example to support the point that you have made or to demonstrate how a particular principle or theory operates. This might be a hypothetical example, a point taken from an article or government report, something you have read in a newspaper, or the findings of a research study. The example in Figure 6.3 uses Michael Howard's words to provide imprisonment as an example of incapacitation and also makes reference to chemical castration and the death penalty.

- **Link**. The paragraph should end either by leading into the paragraph that follows or by relating the content of the paragraph directly back to the question by, for example, explaining how the point made in the paragraph addresses the point raised by the question. In Figure 6.3, the first sentence which introduces incapacitation as the topic of the main paragraph is also a linking paragraph as it uses the word 'further' in conjunction with the reference to other theories of punishment to link with points made earlier in the essay. The final sentence of the main paragraph also provides a link with the following paragraph as it ties together the death penalty (mentioned in the main paragraph) with retributivism (the topic of the next paragraph).

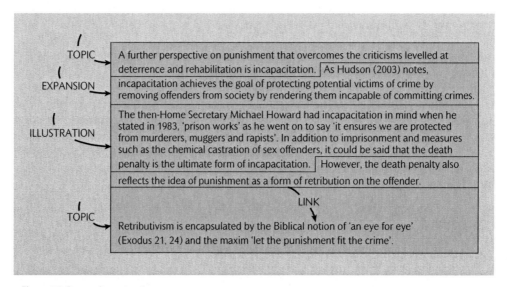

Figure 6.3 Paragraph construction

In terms of the presentation of your work, you will see in the example that there is an extra line space to separate the paragraphs. This makes it clear to the reader where one paragraph ends and the next paragraph begins. The alternative approach is to indent the first line of the new paragraph. Either approach is acceptable. Remember that the aim is to make the essay clear and easy for the marker to follow.

A final point to note is that the recent proliferation of primary and secondary paragraphing to denote the strength of the relationship between a paragraph and the one that follows it by varying the size of the gap between the paragraphs is nonsense and not something that would be acceptable in writing at university level. There are sentences and there are paragraphs. If a sentence is closely related to the previous sentence, it belongs in the same paragraph; if it is not closely related, it belongs in the following paragraph.

Using quotations

Quotations can add authority to your work as you are, in effect, using the words of someone with far more expertise than yourself to support your argument. They can also give you a form of words to describe something in a way that is far better than you would be able to explain it yourself.

Overuse of quotations

Although the judicious use of quotations can really strengthen your argument and provide evidence of the breadth of your research, they can have a negative impact on your work if they are not used with care. Have a look at the extract taken from an essay on crime statistics as it demonstrates one of the most common problems that arise in relation to quotations in student essays.

Practical example: overuse of quotations

One factor that can 'affect the accuracy of crime statistics is the extent to which members of the public are prepared to report incidents to the police' (Jones 2006: 56). As 'people do not necessarily report all the crime victimisation they experience' (Hale *et al.* 2005: 47), there is 'a risk that official statistics are not a reflection of how much crime is committed' (Harris 2009: 17). There is also the possibility of uneven reporting as 'rates of reporting vary markedly by offence with some much more likely to be reported to the police than others' (Newburn 2007: 57).

There is heavy reliance on quotations in the extract: only 14 out of the 97 words (about one-seventh) were written by the student and the overall impression given is that this is a essay that is made up of a series of joined together quotations. The problem that this raises can be seen clearly if you read the same extract with the quotations taken out.

One factor that can…As…There is also the possibility of uneven reporting as…

As you can see, once the quotations are omitted, there is nothing in the words remaining that demonstrates the student's knowledge of the subject matter. As such, it would be difficult for the marker to award marks for the student's understanding of the problems with official crime statistics. Remember that you should use your own words to explain key concepts to show the marker that you understand them or, alternatively, use a quotation and follow this with an explanation of your own.

Presentation of quotations

The way to present a quotation within your work depends on the length of the quotation. Anything from a single word to a fragment of a sentence of about a line-and-a-half of text can be incorporated as part of your sentence whilst longer quotations and those that are complete sentences in their own right should be presented as block quotations.

Practical example: quotations in the text

When considering reasons for non-reporting of crime, Harris suggests that crime victims are motivated by 'righteousness and self-interest' and will therefore only report offences to the police if it serves their interests to do so (2009: 18).

In this example, a short quotation that captures the key motivation for failure to report offences to the police has been incorporated into the sentence. Note that the quotation appears within quotation marks and is accompanied by a reference that indicates the source of the material.

See chapter 7 for a detailed explanation of how to reference and for a discussion of the importance of referencing.

By contrast, a longer quotation is set apart from the main body of your essay and quotation marks should not be used: they are not needed as the indentation of the quotation separates it from your own work and indicates to the marker that it is a quotation. A reference must still be provided that acknowledges the source of the words.

Practical example: block quotations

When considering reasons for non-reporting of crime, Harris takes a negative view of victims of crime, arguing that they are only likely to draw offences to the attention of the police if it serves their own interests to do so. Harris alleges that:

> Crime victims are fuelled by righteousness and self-interest when they report their victimisation to the police. They want recognition of their status as victims, absolution from any taint of blame and, on occasion, a crime reference number to support an insurance claim. Any suggestion that they are altruistic and motivated by a desire for justice or the prevention of harm to others is disingenuous (2009: 17).

Harris claims that victims who do not report crimes to the police are complicit in the ongoing criminality of the offender as they have failed to take a simple step that could lead to the offender's apprehension. This seems an unrealistic position that fails to take account of the complex interaction of feelings that may accompany crime victimization and which does not take account of the distinction between being a victim of car theft and a victim of rape. However, compulsory reporting of crimes would go some way towards improving the accuracy of crime statistics.

This example also illustrates the practice of using single line spacing to present quotations as a further way of differentiating the words of others from the main text of the essay. This is a matter of preference: it is perfectly permissible to use the same spacing for quotations as you have used for the rest of the text.

Effective use of quotations

There is quite a skill to using quotations effectively. Too many students fail to realize this and, as a result, the quotations that are included in their essay serve to highlight this lack of skill so that the quotations actually weaken rather than strengthen their work. The following guidelines should help you to use quotations to good effect in your writing.

- **Introduce your quotations.** Irrespective of whether you are using a few words or several sentences of quoted material, you must blend it into your essay with words of introduction. This could be a simple identification of the author such as 'As Harris argues...' or a more detailed approach that introduces the topic as well as its source as you see in the example above. It is very poor practice to have a quotation as a stand-alone sentence with no words of your own to introduce it.

- **Use an appropriate verb to situate the quotation.** You could introduce every quotation with the words 'Harris says...' or 'Harris states...' but 'says' and 'states' are neutral verbs that do not give the reader any clues as to how the quotation that follows fits into the rest of your essay. In the example above, the quotation is introduced with the words 'Harris alleges...' and it is followed by the words 'Harris implies...' which suggest that this is one opinion but that an argument to the contrary will follow. Take time to think about the role of the quotation in your essay—whether you agree or disagree with it, whether it is a mainstream or controversial opinion—and select introductory words that convey this. The following are some of the verbs that you could use:

says	observes	alleges	argues	thinks	states
notes	claims	asserts	remarks	opines	submits
adds	affirms	comments	explains	suggests	maintains

- **Discuss the quotation**. Far too often, students use quotations to speak for them and present them without any comment or explanation. Remember that the purpose of a quotation is to support your own words, not to replace them. This means that you must explain its meaning or relevance: do something with it rather than leaving it to stand alone. In the example above, the writer follows on from the quotation by elaborating on Harris' views and offering a criticism thus the quotation is used to develop the writer's own argument.

- **Avoid lengthy quotations**. Quotations are not a substitute for your own words. You should look for short phrases or a few sentences that make a point that you could not make in your own words or that is better expressed in the words of the original author. Try to capture a particular idea with a quotation but to explain its detail, significance, or operation in your own words. Markers will not be impressed to read long quotations when what they want to read is your own explanation, interpretation, and evaluation of the area of criminology under discussion.

- **Incorporate quotations so that they make sense**. Used properly, quotations should blend in with your own words. This means that if you have a sentence that is part quotation and part your own words, the two should combine to make a complete grammatical sentence. You can take words out of a quotation to help with this provided you indicate that words are omitted by the use of ellipsis (...) and you can add words that are not in the original quotation using square brackets [inserted text].

Practical example: adding and removing words

Quotation

The dark figure refers to the unknown volume of unnoticed, unreported and unrecorded crime that is not reflected in official crime statistics. Victim surveys that explore the extent of crime that has occurred from the victim's perspective may go some way towards closing the gap between official statistics and the totality of crime that is committed.

Removing words

You may want to trim down a quotation to remove some detail so that it makes only the points that are relevant to your essay. Start the quotation and use three dots [...] to indicate that words have been removed and then continue the quotation. Ensure that the sentence that you have created still makes sense with the words removed.

- It has been said that 'the dark figure refers to the unknown volume of…crime that is not reflected in official statistics'.
- 'Victim surveys…go some way towards closing the gap between official statistics and the totality of crime that is committed' so provide some means of illuminating the dark figure of crime.

Adding words

When using a short quotation, you may need to add a few words to ensure that the quotation makes sense. The added words should be enclosed in square brackets to indicate that they are your addition to the quotation. You can also use a single letter in square brackets to indicate that you have changed from lower to upper case or vice versa.

- The dark figure [of crime] refers to the unknown volume of unnoticed, unreported and unrecorded crime that is not reflected in official crime statistics.
- One way in which light can be shed upon the dark figure of crime is by reference to '[v]ictim surveys that explore the extent of crime that has occurred from the victim's perspective'.

Word limits

It is likely that most, if not all, of the coursework that you complete during your studies will have a word limit. Although students almost universally rail against word limits, protesting that they are too restrictive to enable them to answer questions properly or to enable them to say all that they want to say, assessments are carefully written to ensure that they can fit within the specified word limit. As such, it really is possible to write a good essay within the constraints of the word limit; it is just more effort to do so because it requires far more thought and effort to filter out irrelevant material or excessive detail and to rephrase, restructure, and reorganize until all your ideas are squeezed into the number of words permitted.

When trying to write within a word limit, take into account these three points:

- **Test all your material for relevance.** Make sure that you have understood the question and that you are responding to what it asks rather than simply writing about the topic it identifies (see chapter 8 on essay writing for further discussion on this point). Evaluate each point that you plan to include and assess its match with the question. Consider whether you have gone off at a tangent; sometimes, you can move away from the question without realizing it. Are you determined to include a particular point because it was hard to find or because you are proud of the way that it is written? Everything that you read makes a contribution to your understanding of the subject matter of your essay but this does not mean that it all has to be included in the words you write. Remember, content does not gain marks because it is clever, was hard to find, or is well written unless it is also relevant.
- **Eliminate excessive descriptive detail.** A good essay is a combination of description (of the subject matter at the heart of the question) and analysis (the discussion of that subject matter in the particular context established by the question). It is an unfortunate fact that it is much easier to describe things than it is to analyse them so it is sometimes the case that students fill their essays with as much description as possible, sometimes leaving it until the final paragraph before there is any attempt at analysis. This creates a weak answer that will enjoy only limited success. Make sure that you leave yourself enough words to engage in some in-depth analysis by exercising restraint when it comes to descriptive content. Only

describe things that need to be described for your analysis to work and do this in as concise a manner as possible. Make sure that every word is necessary and serves a purpose.

- **Aim to develop a concise written style.** If you have checked your content for relevance and to ensure that it is not heavily descriptive but still find that you are struggling to meet the word limit, it is possible that you are too wordy in your written style. Resist the temptation to cut whole paragraphs out of your essay but instead review what you have written, sentence-by-sentence, in order to see if you can save words by rephrasing. Can you find a single word that replaces two or more words? Do you use a lot of emphatic adverbs such as 'really' and 'very': it does not make a lot of difference to your essay to say 'this was an important development because...' rather than 'this was a really important development because...'. If you can cut one or two words out of each sentence, this will help you to meet the word limit in a particular piece of work but also to develop a more concise written style so you should find that it gets easier and easier to write within the word limit.

Alternatively, you may find that you have made all the points that you want to make but are a long way short of the word limit. Now it may be that you have a very concise written style but if you are more than 100 words away from the word limit it is more likely that you have either omitted some relevant material or that you have not discussed all the points in sufficient detail. It would be a good idea to revisit the question and review your research to ensure that you have identified all the relevant points for inclusion. You should also consider whether you have paid too little attention to a point that requires more detailed discussion.

You will find more detailed advice on interpreting questions, selecting relevant material, and keeping a strong focus on the question in chapter 6.

As a final point on word limits, do make sure that you have stated the word count of your essay correctly. This means that you need to check the rules in your institution on counting words as there are different policies regarding what words are to be counted. Are references and the bibliography included in the word count? Can you use headings and sub-headings and, if so, do these count towards the word limit? It is important that you are aware of the rules so that you do not inadvertently exclude words that should be counted or vice versa. Equally, you should never be tempted to misstate the word limit in order to fool your marker that your essay meets the word limit. Lecturers mark a lot of essays of the same length and get a very good 'feel' for the word limit so any such deception is likely to be detected and penalized.

Presentation

The final point to consider when writing your essay is how it looks on the page. You might think that this is a trivial detail but the appearance of a piece of work is the first impression that your marker gets of your essay so make sure that it is a good one. You should try to make sure that everything that you do impresses the person marking your work and makes them think that your essay is the product of thought, care, and attention. A well-presented piece of work will create a good first impression. Whilst this may not necessarily contribute to the grade that the essay receives (unless your department awards marks for presentation), it cannot do any harm to ensure that the person marking your work feels favourably disposed towards it from the outset.

Formatting

If there is a house style with regard to presentation, use it even if you do not like it. Most people have a font style or pattern of layout that they favour but that is no reason not to adhere to the specifications that you have been given. Some departments even impose an automatic deduction of marks for failure to comply with the presentation requirements of assessed coursework, so it is always advisable to find out what the requirements are and follow them to the letter. In the absence of any specifications as to style, you may like to bear the following in mind when choosing how to present your work:

- **Font and font size.** Choose a relatively conventional font that is suitable for a piece of serious academic writing. Select an appropriate font size so that your work can be read without difficulty.
- **Line spacing and margins.** Students sometimes create narrow margins and use single-line spacing in order to crowd their work onto fewer pages in order to save on printing. This is not a good strategy as it makes your work difficult to read and gives the marker very little room to write comments in the margin (which should help you understand your mark and improve in future assessments). It would be a good idea to leave the margins on a standard setting and to use double or one-and-a-half line spacing.
- **Paragraphing.** Using a double space between paragraphs creates more 'white space' on the page thus making it easier on the marker's eye and, again, leaving more space for written comments.

Overall, these guidelines are aimed at ensuring that the page is not too crowded so that the words look squashed onto the page.

Headings

This section addresses issues of the presentation of headings rather than their use in written work. If you are using headings in your work, make sure that you use an appropriate and consistent approach to formatting them. For example, if you use two levels of heading (main headings and sub-headings), make sure that the style you use for the main heading is more prominent than that of the subheading and that you use the same style throughout your work. Finally, do make sure that something follows the heading; leaving a heading 'hanging' as the final words on the bottom of the page whilst the text follows on the next is not an effective approach to the use of headings.

Page numbers

It is useful to ensure that the pages of your work are numbered. If your marker drops your essay, it might be difficult to reorder them if they are not numbered. Equally, if you staple the pages in the incorrect order (it happens!) and they are not numbered, your lecturer may not realize that the pages are not in order and merely assume that the flow of your argument is not logical.

Capital letters

There is an unfortunate tendency amongst students to capitalize every word that seems significant, such as Judge, Court, and Law, or any phrases that seem sufficiently important, for example, Media Construction, Labelling Theory, or Police Officer. This is incorrect and should be avoided. The use of capital letters should be reserved for the word at the start of a sentence and proper nouns only.

Checking for errors

Nothing is more annoying for a lecturer, who is plodding through a mountain of marking, than a piece of work that is shoddily presented and littered with errors of spelling, grammar, and punctuation. Of course, everybody makes the odd mistake but a constant array of errors gives the impression that you have submitted the first draft of your essay and that you do not care enough about your work to check it before submission.

Moreover, you want your marker to be concentrating on your discussion of criminology, rather than being distracted by the number of spelling mistakes and typos. Additionally, it is very disheartening for the student to receive a piece of work back from the marker that is covered with corrections. It is also worth remembering that many institutions include writing style and presentation in the marking criteria so a failure to check work for errors prior to submission runs the risk of loss of marks that could so easily be avoided.

Make sure that you leave yourself enough time to check your work thoroughly. It is a good idea to aim to finish your essay a day before the submission deadline so that you can print out the version that you plan to submit but then leave it a while before reading it through with a pen in your hand to pick out any errors. A lapse of time helps to ensure that you read the words that you have actually written rather than reading what you know that you meant to write. Equally, looking at the words on the page rather than on the computer screen can help you to spot mistakes. Doing this with a pen in your hand means that you can circle the errors as you see them rather than thinking 'oh yes, I'll come back to that later'. You might also find that you can spot your own mistakes more easily if you read your work out loud as this forces you to concentrate on every word rather than sliding your eye over them. Perhaps you could also arrange to swap work with a friend prior to submission with a view to proofreading for each other.

Finally, most people find that they have one or two bad written habits or mistakes that they make all the time. Try to develop an awareness of your own weaknesses so that you can at least spot them and correct them before submission, even if you cannot stop yourself from making the mistakes in your first draft. Make a note of your own writing pitfalls and check for them in every piece of work that you produce. You should add to this by noting any errors that your marker identifies in your work. Finally, remember that the spell check function on your computer only checks for spelling so it will not spot misuse of commonly confused words like affect/effect and practise/practice. You might find it useful to refer to the Oxford Dictionaries website (http:// oxforddictionaries.com/page/266) which lists commonly confused words and provides guidance to help you select the correct word.

Practical exercise: evaluate your writing style

Using the topics discussed in this chapter and your thoughts about any weaknesses that you have as a writer, create a checklist that you can use to help you to spot and correct errors in your work.

Print a fresh copy of a piece of work that you have previously submitted for assessment. Use the checklist and see if there are any errors in your work that you did not notice at the time.

Retrieve the marked version of this piece of work and see if there are any further points that the marker noted that you did not include on your checklist. In this way, you can keep making updates to the checklist.

 You might like to compare the points on your checklist with the points listed on the Online Resource Centre. Add any of these that you feel are relevant to your own checklist. This should help you give your work a final polish prior to submission.

CHAPTER SUMMARY

Writing style

- Be aware of the importance of developing a good writing style that is appropriate to academic discussion of criminology. A good textbook or published articles should give you some insight into the level of formality that is usual in the discipline
- Avoid writing practices that are thought to characterize informal writing such as the use of the first person, contractions, and abbreviations

Grammar and punctuation

- Remember that grammar and punctuation are signposts that help to communicate the meaning of your words to the reader so you should ensure that you have a solid grasp of the basic rules of grammar and punctuation
- Experiment with the way that you use words and construct sentences to ensure that you develop your written communication skills

Use of paragraphs

- Remember that paragraphs are the building blocks of the argument that runs through your essay. Try to ensure that each paragraph has a clear purpose and that it builds on the preceding paragraph and links into the following paragraph
- Avoid lengthy paragraphs
- Never differentiate between primary and secondary paragraphs

Quotations

- Incorporating quotations into your work can add strength to your arguments but you must ensure that you do not use a quotation out of context or misrepresent its meaning
- If you add or remove words or emphasis, this must be noted in the quotation or its reference as appropriate. Ensure that any changes do not alter the meaning of the quotation
- Do not overuse quotations. The bulk of your essay should be expressed in your words as opposed to merely joining together a string of quotations. Equally, do not use quotations, particularly from textbooks, to express concepts that could be expressed in your own words; your ability to explain key points of criminology will attract more credit than your ability to select an appropriate quotation

Presentation

- Discover whether there are any mandatory requirements for the presentation of coursework and, if so, ensure that you adhere to them. In the absence of particular requirement, select fonts, margins, and line spacing that make your work easy to read for your marker
- Ensure that you leave sufficient time prior to the deadline for submission to check your work thoroughly for presentational errors. Try to develop a checklist based upon good written

practice and your awareness of your own weaknesses to help you check for and correct errors prior to submission

FURTHER READING

- *Hypergrammar* is a free online resource provided by the University of Ottawa that can be found at http://www.arts.uottawa.ca/writcent/hypergrammar/. It provides clear explanations of a wide range of rules of grammar and punctuation supported by useful example of the rules in operation. It also has some review exercises that you can complete to test your understanding at the end of each section.
- Peck, J. & Coyle, M. (2005) *The Student's Guide to Writing: Grammar, Punctuation and Spelling*. 2nd Ed. Basingstoke: Palgrave. This is an excellent guide to all aspects of writing that is targeted at the undergraduate student and written in a clear and accessible manner. In explaining why the rules exist and how mistakes are made, it offers greater insight into grammar and punctuation than many other similar books and offers some great practical tips.
- Sinclair, C. (2007) *Grammar: a Friendly Approach*. Maidenhead: Open University Press. This book provides a thorough explanation of the rules of grammar and punctuation in quite an unusual style as it is presented as an ongoing discussion between three undergraduate students (Abel, Barbara, and Kim) and their struggles with all aspects of their written style. This makes it quite entertaining as well as informative so it may be that many students find this easier to read than some other books on writing skills.
- Trask, R.L. (1997) *The Penguin Guide to Punctuation*. London: Penguin Reference Series. A handy reference guide that is very easy to use and understand. It offers clear explanations of each type of punctuation and provides some good examples of their use.

GLOSSARY

- **Contractions** are word forms that arise as the result of the combination of two or more words with the missing letter or letters replaced with an apostrophe: 'cannot' becomes 'can't' and 'I will' becomes 'I'll'.
- **Ellipses** (singular **ellipsis**) are used to indicate that a word or words have been taken out of a quotation. They are represented in the text by three dots (...).
- **First person** is a way of describing the style of writing that is presented from the author's perspective; in other words, it is written as a description of what 'I' did.
- **Grammar** is the set of rules that govern the way that language is used and sentences are constructed.
- **Grammatical person** is a phrase used in linguistics to identify the perspective of the writer.

- **Non-standard abbreviations** are those which are not generally known and used within criminology but which have been created by a student as a short way of referring to a particular phrase. This can be useful in note-taking but is not appropriate in essay writing.
- **Punctuation** refers to the symbols used in written language to help the writer communicate meaning to the reader without ambiguity.

REFERENCES

Finch, E. (2002) Violent Crimes and Crimes of Violence. *Howard Journal of Criminal Justice*, 422–433.

Referencing and avoiding plagiarism

7

INTRODUCTION

This chapter deals with referencing and avoiding plagiarism. These skills are of critical importance to your studies since your academic work will inevitably require you to read, critically consider, and evaluate the work of others. However, you must ensure that you carefully and meticulously distinguish between your own work, ideas, and arguments and those of the authors that you have encountered during your research. This is done by providing thorough references to the sources which you have used in your work. Failing to do so may leave you vulnerable to accusations that you have presented the work of others as your own—that is, plagiarism. This chapter will explain what is meant by plagiarism in more detail and introduce you to the name-date (often referred to as Harvard) style of referencing which will help you to avoid inadvertent plagiarism. You will learn how to reference the types of source material which are most commonly-encountered in the study of criminology. This chapter should be read in conjunction with the chapters on essay writing (chapter 8), and writing dissertations, literature reviews, and reports (chapter 9) which follow.

The ability to reference thoroughly, properly, and consistently should become second nature to you as you progress through your study of criminology. Plagiarism is invariably treated very seriously by institutions and any suspected cases are investigated thoroughly. If a case of suspected plagiarism is upheld, then it is likely that some adverse penalty will be applied which could seriously limit your prospects of success in your course overall. There is too much at stake to risk deliberate plagiarism or ignoring the requirements of good referencing needed to avoid inadvertent plagiarism.

LEARNING OUTCOMES

After reading this chapter, you will be able to:

- Define plagiarism

- Know when to provide references and avoid inadvertent plagiarism

- Understand the risks associated with deliberate plagiarism

- Reference your sources consistently and thoroughly using name-date (Harvard) referencing

Plagiarism

It is commonplace to think of **plagiarism** as a deliberate copying from an unacknowledged source with the intention to deceive, but this is not the case. Plagiarism covers all instances in which the work of another is used without sufficient acknowledgement.

....

Plagiarism. The Oxford English Dictionary defines plagiarism as 'the action or practice of taking someone else's work, idea, etc., and passing it off as one's own; literary theft'.

....

Universities may have their own definitions within their regulations on academic conduct. For example, the University of Leeds (2010) defines plagiarism as follows:

> Plagiarism is defined as presenting someone else's work as your own. Work means any intellectual output and typically includes text, data, images, sound or performance.

As you see from these definitions, the essence of plagiarism is the failure to give an indication of the source of material upon which reliance has been placed in a piece of work. This may be deliberate, such as in situations where a student copies material from the Internet (or a fellow student) and passes it off as their own or buys an essay from an Internet essay bank or essay-writing service, but it is more often inadvertent, arising as a consequence of poor or lazy referencing or from a lack of understanding about the need to provide a reference. Plagiarism does not require a deliberate attempt to cheat.

Inadvertent plagiarism

The most effective means of avoiding inadvertent plagiarism is to ensure that every piece of work that you produce is thoroughly and correctly referenced. This raises two issues: when to reference and how to reference. The latter issue will be addressed in the referencing section later in this chapter whilst the remainder of this section will deal with the question of when a reference must be provided.

When to reference

Certain situations are straightforward. Most students would appreciate that a reference to the source of the following should be provided:

- **Direct quotations** should be attributed to their source in a book, article, case, or other material
- **Factual material** such as statistics or the findings of a research study should be attributed to their source, whether this is an official report or an academic or commercial study
- **Definitions** should be attributed to the appropriate source in a dictionary, book, article, or other material
- **Theories, models, or practices** which are associated with a particular author should be attributed to that author.

An essay is an accumulation of a number of different things. It is composed largely of the writer's own words and thoughts, which need no reference, but may be interspersed with other material from the four categories outlined above which add the weight of authority to these words and thoughts. Definitions and quotations are the direct use of another's words, and must therefore be acknowledged as such, whilst factual material and statements of law need to be referenced to their source in order to substantiate and evidence their authoritative status.

There are three main ways in which you might incorporate the work of another author into a piece of criminological writing:

- **Summarizing:** the author's original words are rewritten in a shortened form but which captures the key points which the author made
- **Paraphrasing:** the author's original words are rewritten, but the original meaning is retained
- **Direct quotation**: the author's original words are reproduced exactly.

Take a look at the following piece of source material and the examples of each form of use which follow.

Source

The ability of networked technologies to disseminate, share, or trade informational (intellectual) property in the form of text, images, music, film and TV through information services has been one of the more significant developments of the internet. This property is informational, networked and also globalized, and its authors, or their licencees, have a right of ownership or control over it, including the right to receive payment for access to the content. Both the means of access to the services and also their informational property content have a market value which simultaneously creates opportunities and motivations for what has become known as cyber-piracy. (Wall 2007: 94)

Summarized version

Cyber-piracy has arisen as a result of the Internet's capability to deliver content (for which the intellectual property owner may have a right to be paid) globally (Wall 2007: 94).

Paraphrased version

Networked technologies have enabled intellectual property such as words, pictures, sound, and video (TV or film) to be distributed, broadcast, or dealt through online mechanisms. This is one of the most important advances that the Internet has made. The property in this information is available globally via the network, and the owners or licensees of this property have the right to deal with this property in accordance with their own wishes. This includes the ability to charge for allowing the content to be viewed or downloaded. Therefore, the way in which the information is accessed and the proprietary nature of the material has some economic worth which then gives rise to the prospects and incentives for so-called cyber-piracy (Wall 2007: 94).

Direct quotation

Cyber-piracy has arisen because 'the means of access to the services and also their informational property content have a market value which simultaneously creates opportunities and motivations' (Wall 2007: 94).

While it might seem obvious that direct quotations need a reference, paraphrased and summarized sections of another's work must also be referenced in full. Paraphrasing someone else's work without reference is still using their work as your own even though very few of the words between the source and the paraphrase match. What you are doing here is putting together the same core idea in a different way and using different words to convey an identical meaning. As such, a paraphrase can never be the product of your own academic reasoning or argument. Similarly, a summary is a condensed version of another's work, not your own.

Another instance where inadvertent plagiarism may arise is in the case of an article, say, that gives a commentary or analysis of another piece of work:

Source 1

The key point is that the relatively small numbers of people can have a significant presence. Not only are they using the net for recruitment, but attempts are also being made to combine cyber-activism with that of the 'real world'. The *RaceLink* web page offers a list of activists' contact details and locations. It aims to put racists in contact with each other...The *Aryan Dating Page* offered a contact service for white supremacists.... In one moment, the mainstream whiteness of the school or workplace —coded here as normality—is occupied while at other times at the computer terminal the public privacy of the Internet digitally facilitates the communion with a whiteness that announces itself openly (Back 2002: 640–643).

Source 2

Back (2002) found that white supremacist Internet sites were preoccupied with fears of cultural 'pollution' manifest in 'White Singles' dating pages. These cultural fears are in turn rooted in the colonial past of European nations and a belief in the cultural and 'civilizational' inferiority of ethnic minorities (Ray 2005: 239).

Here, a student might have read the secondary source (Ray 2005), particularly since it is taken from a chapter in a criminology textbook (Hale *et al.* 2005), but not the primary source (Back 2002). In this instance it would be plagiarism to include material from the secondary source while only providing a reference to the primary source, like this:

White supremacist 'White Singles' Internet dating sites are preoccupied with fears of cultural pollu-tion arising from a belief that ethnic minorities are culturally and civilizationally inferior (Back 2002).

This would be plagiarism as it relies heavily on the analysis of Back's article by Ray, but does not acknowledge the source of that analysis. In essence, it is passing off the work of Ray as the student's own without attribution, while also conveying the (false) impression that the student has read the primary source (Back's article in *Ethnic and Racial Studies*). This could be avoided by providing a full reference as follows:

White supremacist 'White Singles' Internet dating sites are preoccupied with fears of cultural pol-lution arising from a belief that ethnic minorities are culturally and civilizationally inferior (Back 2002 cited in Ray 2005: 239).

A more difficult situation exists in relation to material that has been read during the production of an essay but which is not referred to specifically within the text. This includes materials such as books and articles that have influenced your thinking about the topic or which have shaped the points that you have raised in your essay. It is in relation to this that greatest uncertainty about whether to reference exists. There are two general rules that can be used as guidance:

1. If you are using your own words to express an idea that is specific to a particular writer, then a reference to the source of the idea should be provided even though you have used your own words to explain that idea. If, however, you have read several textbooks to gain an overview of a topic and the same issue is expressed in each book, then you are free to use your own words without providing a reference. This is because the mention of the

idea in several places demonstrates that it is a general issue of common knowledge, so it does not need to be attributed to a particular source.

2. If in doubt, reference. It is preferable to provide too many references in your essay rather than to face an accusation of plagiarism or receive a deduction of marks for providing insufficient references. If you receive a comment from your marker that a piece of work contained too many unnecessary references, you should make a point of asking them to point out to you which references were unnecessary and why this was the case, so that you can make adjustments in subsequent pieces of work.

Common knowledge

Material that is 'common knowledge' generally does not need to be referenced. While this might seem obvious and straightforward, it is unfortunately complicated by the fact that there is no consensus as to what falls within common knowledge. Experts on plagiarism and academic malpractice disagree on what counts as common knowledge. Some only consider factual material such as current and historical events potentially to be common knowledge (for instance, 'Adolf Hitler was the leader of the German Nazi Party during the Second World War while Winston Churchill was Prime Minister of Great Britain throughout most of the conflict'). Others consider common knowledge to be that which is commonly known within the particular broad subject area (for instance, 'all knowledge of crime comes from either direct or mediated experience').

To complicate matters further, as you become more expert in your study of criminology, what counts as common knowledge becomes even harder to define. Should common knowledge be defined in terms of reasonably educated people in general or reasonable students of criminology? Within criminology (as with every other discipline) there is a body of common knowledge which even an educated outsider might not know.

Two tests which are often used in helping to decide whether or not a piece of information is common knowledge are:

- **Quantity**—can the information be found in numerous places?
- **Ubiquity**—is the information known by many people?

Of course, the problem with this is how many places are needed to consider that the information can be found in 'numerous' places. As a rough rule of thumb, many guidelines consider 'numerous' to mean 'five or more', but again, you must remember that this is not a hard and fast rule. If the information crops up in all your textbooks on the subject without further attribution, it is likely to be ubiquitous enough to be 'common knowledge'. If you are still in doubt, you could seek guidance from your lecturer. Otherwise, point 2 above still applies—if in doubt, reference.

You should always keep the notes you have made in preparation for your work since you may be asked to provide your notes and draft work to your institution. By doing this, you will at least be able to provide some evidence that you have done the necessary research and read the materials—and therefore that your plagiarism might actually be as a result of poor referencing rather than a deliberate attempt to cheat.

See chapter 5 on study skills for guidance on note-taking.

Deliberate plagiarism

If inadvertent plagiarism arises from lack of clarity about referencing requirements, deliberate plagiarism arises when students make a deliberate decision to try and pass off the work of others as their own. Deliberate plagiarism is almost never successful, so why do students try to plagiarize and what are the reasons that such behaviour is unwise?

Why do students plagiarize?

There are many reasons why students may make a conscious decision to take words from a source and seek to pass it off as their own work. Plagiarism can arise from a failure to understand what the coursework requires, a desperate desire to obtain a good mark, an unwillingness to interfere with the way that an idea has been expressed, or simply from the pressure of time as a deadline is looming. Ultimately, these are all manifestations of a lack of confidence in one's own ability to provide an answer to the question. Alternatively, students may resort to plagiarism because they cannot be bothered to produce their own work or because they feel that their course was badly taught and therefore does not deserve the effort that it would take to write an original piece of work.

Another reason often given by students is that they believe that everyone else is doing it and that they will not get caught. It has been reported (Stothard 2008) that almost half of students admitted to plagiarism in a poll carried out by a students' newspaper at the University of Cambridge and that only one in twenty students had been caught. Many students who plagiarize often think that because they have not been caught then they have 'got away with it'. However, this is not always the case. For some lecturers, the additional effort required to research and prosecute a potential case of plagiarism might be too great. Instead, they may penalize the student heavily for producing a piece of work which is overly derivative or poorly referenced.

In any event, there is no justification for plagiarism and, certainly, none of the possible 'excuses' given here will provide a defence when plagiarism is detected and you are called to account by your institution.

Reasons to avoid plagiarism

Plagiarism detection mechanisms are in place in most institutions, regardless of whether or not this fact is advertised to the students, and these mechanisms are becoming increasingly more sophisticated. They have the ability to check the work submitted against the work of other students, at the same institution and elsewhere, as well as against all Internet resources including essay banks and paper resources. Many experienced lecturers have also developed an instinctive 'nose' for suspected plagiarism which often proves to be correct. Overall, it is impossible to copy from a source of material that cannot be detected; therefore resorting to plagiarism in an attempt to acquire a good mark will ultimately be unsuccessful. Such is the battle against plagiarism that many institutions annotate degree transcripts to include an explanation that a mark in the relevant subject was amended following a finding of plagiarism; something which is hardly going to impress future employers.

More than this, plagiarism is actually counter-productive as it deprives the student of the opportunity to test what they do know and how well they are able to express this. In other words, the learning opportunity provided by the coursework is wholly negated and the student learns nothing as a result. You will never improve your skills if you are not prepared to try and receive feedback on your ability.

Finally, there is no guarantee that the source that you plagiarize will be good. This is particularly true of material taken from the Internet. Anyone can post anything on the Internet; there is no quality control or mechanism of checking, amending, or removing inaccurate material. Essay banks are equally unreliable and cost vast sums of money. Think about the rationale behind it. Students sell essays that they have written to the essay bank who have no expertise in the subject at all. Essays with higher marks sell for a higher price, so students are likely to exaggerate the mark in order to gain maximum profit, so there is nothing to say that the essay that you buy as a first did not actually receive a lower second-class mark. Irrespective of this, that essay may be on the same subject matter but it does not answer the same question as that set as your coursework, so there is no point in submitting it. All you are doing is paying a lot of money for a piece of work of questionable quality that may not answer the question that you have been set and which is likely to be detected.

Ultimately, plagiarism achieves nothing and will attract negative consequences when it is detected. Do not do it.

Referencing

One of the prime purposes of academia is to further knowledge by producing and elaborating original ideas to the highest values of intellectual rigour and originality. In order to achieve this, it is important to ensure that proper recognition is given to the work—and the intellectual property—of others. This is done by providing appropriate and thorough references where the work of others is used within your work.

Equally, reference lists can be a useful tool when conducting a literature search of a particular topic.

On a more practical point, it is essential that your written work is fully and correctly referenced otherwise you will lose marks. Not only are these relatively simple marks to gain, but poor referencing also detracts from the overall quality of your work and can leave a negative impression in the mind of your marker. In the worst case scenario, failure to reference your sources may leave you vulnerable to accusations of plagiarism and all the consequences that follow on from this. The previous section discussed the situations in which referencing should be provided whilst this section gives an overview of the Harvard referencing system which we will go on to cover in more detail later in this chapter. Before getting into the detail of Harvard referencing, though, we must first consider 'house style'.

House style

'House style' is the official guidance that you have been given by your institution about how to provide references within your work. It should therefore be the starting point for deciding how to reference. If you have not yet found any guidance, make sure that you investigate further as you will need to consult it in order to ensure that your work is correctly referenced. The level of guidance varies enormously between institutions so you may find that you are provided with detailed instructions with examples, given direction to use one of the standard referencing schemes, or merely told that 'your work must be fully referenced'. You may also find that the preferred referencing style varies between modules, so you must check carefully. You may even find that there is no house style at all. House style also extends beyond institutions, departments, and courses to published journals and books. Publishers (including OUP!) generally provide extensive 'guidance to authors' on matters of referencing and presentation.

If you have been given instructions as to what style to use, it is imperative that you use this and not some other style of your own making or that you have used previously. Even if you are being given some examples as guidance rather than as part of a mandatory policy, you would be wise to follow the house style because it is likely to be correct and complete, whereas any approach to referencing that you have used previously was (presumably) not one that was specifically tailored to undergraduate criminology.

If you have not been given any detailed guidelines, the remainder of this chapter looks at name-date (or Harvard) referencing which is commonly used in the social sciences in general. Remember, however, that there is more than one way to reference the same material, so there are likely to be other equally valid approaches. The key to good referencing is completeness and consistency so keep these principles in mind when deciding which style of referencing to use. Finally, while the detailed guidance covers the most common materials that you will need to reference, it is impossible to cover all the possible sources within the scope of this book. There are some excellent online resources which are highlighted in the Further Reading section at the end of this chapter. Remember that if there is a particular source which you are unsure how to reference, check your house style first (if you have one) or, failing that, ask your lecturer who should be willing to help.

An introduction to Harvard referencing

The Harvard system of referencing, sometimes referred to as 'in text' or 'alphabetical/name-date' referencing, is claimed to have evolved from a referencing style used by Professor Edward Laurens Mark who was director of Harvard's zoological laboratory and based on a cataloguing system used in the library of Harvard's Museum of Comparative Zoology (Chernin 1988).

Harvard referencing requires abbreviated references to be given in the text itself with either a bibliography or a list of references provided at the end of the work. Within the Harvard system, a list of references is distinct from a bibliography as a list of references only provides the details of materials that have been referenced in the text but does not include preparatory or background materials that have not been specifically cited. As such, a bibliography is a fuller record.

....

A **bibliography** is a list of all materials that have been consulted during the preparation of your work.

....

....

A **list of references** is a list of all materials that have been specifically referenced within your work.

....

Alternative referencing systems

As well as Harvard referencing, there are alternative systems which you may encounter. While it is beyond the scope of this chapter to cover them in any detail, this section will give a very brief overview of each, so that at the very least you will recognize them should they be used in a source that you find.

American Psychological Association (APA)

APA referencing is used in many psychology departments and is commonly encountered in psychology literature within the UK as well as that originating from America. It is quite similar to Harvard referencing in many respects: its most significant differences arise in the means by which electronic resources are referenced.

Modern Language Association of America (MLA)

MLA referencing is, as its name suggests, often encountered in literature relating to languages. It is similar to Harvard referencing in that the name of the author is cited in the text. However, it does have some significant differences, some of which are as follows:

• Page numbers are given in the text alongside the author's name, rather than the year of publication.

- Reference lists are required to be separated into 'Works cited' and 'Works consulted'.
- Authors are always cited with their first name, not just their initials; with second and third authors, the first names precede the last.
- Source titles are underlined, not italicized.
- The order of information in references is different.

Footnote referencing

Most legal writing uses footnotes (sometimes called Roman, Oxford, or numerical referencing). This is the system of referencing in which the reference details are provided at the bottom of each page and their position in the text is denoted by a small raised (superscript) number. A bibliography is then provided at the end of the work which details all the materials that were used in its preparation.

OSCOLA stands for the 'Oxford Standard for Citation Of Legal Authorities' and is a footnote-based system which is becoming widely adopted as a standard for law in other universities.

Conventions used in this chapter

The remainder of this chapter will show how to reference the most common sources using Harvard referencing. The discussion of each source begins with a schematic showing the elements of the citation. Using a reference to a book by way of example, a typical schematic will look like this:

Author | (date) | Title. | Series title. | Edition. | Place of publication: | Publisher

The conventions used in all these schematics are as follows:

- **Vertical lines** (|) are used to separate elements of the citation. These are simply used to assist clarity and are not used in the actual reference itself.
- **Bold type** is used to denote text or punctuation that appears in the final reference: in the example above, the brackets around the publication date are shown in bold for emphasis only. They are not bold in the actual reference.
- **Italic type** is used to denote elements of the reference that appear in italics in the final reference itself. Here, the title of the book is shown in italics.
- **Regular type** is used to describe each element of the citation.
- **Slashes** are used when there are alternatives, such as a page number or paragraph number.

How to reference using the Harvard system

Harvard, or in-text, referencing does not use footnotes. Instead, an abbreviated citation (based on author name and the year of publication) is incorporated into the text, with either a list of references or a bibliography at the end that links the abbreviated citations to full details of the publications referred to in the text and allows them to be found. Harvard referencing is a two-stage process:

- Citing references in the text
- Compiling a bibliography/list of references.

This section will walk through each of those stages in turn.

Citing references in the text

The way in which sources are cited in Harvard referencing depends on the number of authors and whether or not they are named directly in the text.

If the author is named directly in the text, their name should be followed by the year of publication of the source and a page number if a pinpoint reference is required. Page numbers should be preceded by 'p.' for a single page and 'pp.' where the citation spans multiple pages.

Here is an example of a citation for a direct quotation for a single named author:

> Jenkins (1992, p.71) outlines how 'from the late 1970s on, the image of the rather pathetic child molester would be fundamentally altered into a new and far more threatening stereotype: the sophisticated and well-organized paedophile'.

This format is also used for indirect reference to the source where the author's name is still part of the text itself:

> Jenkins (1992, p.71) considered that the media depiction of child sex offenders changed in the late 1970s from that of the child molester to the far more threatening sophisticated paedophile.

Note that some variants of Harvard referencing, such as that used in this book, may use a colon instead of 'p.' or 'pp.':

> Jenkins (1992: 71) outlines how 'from the late 1970s on, the image of the rather pathetic child molester would be fundamentally altered into a new and far more threatening stereotype: the sophisticated and well-organized paedophile'.

If the author's name is not cited directly in the text, it is still provided in the reference, either at the relevant part of the sentence, or at the end of the sentence in brackets:

> Jenkins (1992: 71) outlines how 'from the late 1970s on, the image of the rather pathetic child molester would be fundamentally altered into a new and far more threatening stereotype: the sophisticated and well-organized paedophile'.

This reference is given to a particular page in a book. However, if the citation is to a book, article, or chapter that discusses a particular area, as opposed to pinpointing a particular passage, then just author and year are given, without a pinpoint:

> Although only a minority of shoplifters are mentally disordered, there is an over-representation of depressives (Gibbens 1981).

The situation becomes more complex when the work of more than one author is cited in a single sentence. If they are named directly in the text, then each is cited as before:

> The uncertainty surrounding mental disorder led to the development of the 'anti-psychiatry' movement through the work of Laing (1967) and Szasz (1970).

However, if they are not named directly in the text, then they are listed in brackets with name and date of publication, separated by a semi-colon:

> The uncertainty surrounding mental disorder led to the development of the 'anti-psychiatry' movement (Laing 1967; Szasz 1970).

When directly citing a work by two authors in the text, both surnames should be given, separated by 'and':

Finch and Fafinski (2012, pp. 165–176) explain how to reference various sources commonly encountered in the study of criminology using the Harvard system.

When the authors are not named directly, they are listed in brackets at the appropriate point in the sentence or at the end of the sentence (as with a single author). In this case their names are separated by an ampersand (&) rather than 'and':

Various sources commonly encountered in the study of criminology may be referenced accurately using the Harvard system (Finch & Fafinski 2012, pp. 165–176).

For sources which have three authors, the same convention is used:

McGurk, McEwan, and Graham (1981) have discovered certain personality traits which are related to criminal behaviour.
Certain personality traits have been discovered which are related to criminal behaviour (McGurk, McEwan & Graham 1981).

For sources with four authors or more, then only the name of the first author is used, followed by 'et al.'. Here et al. is short for the Latin term et alii meaning 'and others'. It is often seen in italics in acknowledgement of its Latin origin, but may also appear in roman (non italic) type:

Wright et al. (2004) found that the deterrent effect of viewing crime as risky was greatest on individuals who were high in self-perceived criminality and low in self-control.

The deterrent effect of viewing crime as risky was greatest on individuals who were high in self-perceived criminality and low in self-control (Wright et al. 2004).

If an author makes or reinforces a point in more than one publication, both should be cited in chronological order (that is, with the earliest publication listed first):

In an American study into the link between mental disorder and crime, Teplin (1984, 1985) observed over 1,000 interactions between citizens and the police.

An American study into the link between mental disorder and crime observed over 1,000 interactions between citizens and the police (Teplin 1984, 1985).

If your piece of work contains references to several works published by the same author in the same year, these are differentiated by adding a lower case letter after the year for each work, starting with 'a' and moving through the alphabet:

Taylor (1993a) commented that the mentally disordered are portrayed as violent on American television almost twice as often as the mentally healthy, but argued (1993b) that psychotics are unlikely to commit serious violent offences.

If these sources are cited at the same point, then the lower case letters should both appear in the brackets:

Taylor (1993 a, b) has conducted research into media constructions of the mentally disordered and their actual propensity to commit serious violent offences.

Contributions to edited collections should cite the name of the author of the chapter, rather than the name of the editor:

> Finch (2007) has considered the issue of stolen identity which has been facilitated by the Internet.

There is nothing in the text that suggests that this is a chapter from an edited collection. However, in the reference list, you must give the details of both the chapter author and the editor of the collection (see section below) so that both can be found if desired.

Secondary references (that is, reference to another's work contained in an original work) are denoted by the words 'cited in'. Look back at the example from earlier in the chapter:

> White supremacist 'White Singles' Internet dating sites are preoccupied with fears of cultural pollution arising from a belief that ethnic minorities are culturally and civilizationally inferior (Back 2002 cited in Ray 2005: 239).

Or, as a direct reference:

> Back (2002 cited in Ray 2005: 239) argued that white supremacist 'White Singles' Internet dating sites are preoccupied with fears of cultural pollution arising from a belief that ethnic minorities are culturally and civilizationally inferior.

In this instance, your list of references must only contain the works that you have read in the original (Ray) and not the works to which they refer (Back).

Compiling a bibliography/list of references

The detail provided in the list of references should enable the reader to find the sources which have been cited in the text itself. If you are providing a bibliography instead, you should ensure that you also list the sources which you consulted in the preparation of your work, even if you did not cite them directly.

There are some variations in layout which are acceptable. In particular, punctuation can vary when using Harvard. Some references may have full stops after each part of the reference and some may not. Equally, the use of commas may vary. Remember to check first to see if there is a house style to which you should adhere and, most importantly, make sure that you are consistent with your style and use of punctuation throughout your work.

All sources should be listed alphabetically by author. The sections which follow will demonstrate the way in which most common sources should be referenced in your bibliography. Remember that any tables of cases or legislation are normally listed separately.

Referencing printed material

Books

The basic elements of a book reference are:

> Author | (date) | Title. | Series title. | Edition. | Place of publication: | Publisher

Author names are given with surname first, followed by a comma and initials (with full stops after each initial). Books with two or three authors should list all authors with the last two being joined by an ampersand (&). For four authors or more, list the first, followed by '*et al.*'.

The title is provided in italics followed by a full stop. Then come the series title (if any) and edition number (if not the first) in regular type. Finally the place of publication and publisher are given, separated by a colon and terminated with a full stop. For example:

- Thompson, K. (1988) *Moral Panics*. London: Routledge.
- Roberts, H., Smith, S. & Bryce, C. (1995) *Children at Risk? Safety as a Social Value*. Buckingham: Open University Press.

Edited collections

For books with an editor, then (ed.) or (eds.) are added after the author's name(s). Note that both abbreviations are terminated with a full stop:

- Jewkes, Y. (ed.) (2007) *Crime Online*. Cullompton: Willan.
- Hale, C., Hayward, K., Wahidin, A. & Wincup, E. (eds.) (2005) *Criminology*. Oxford: OUP.
- Maguire, M., Morgan, R. & Reiner, R. (eds.) (2007) *The Oxford Handbook of Criminology*. 4th Ed. Oxford: OUP.

Journal articles

For journals, the order of the bibliography entry is as follows:

Author | (date) | Title of article. | *Full title of journal*, | Volume number | (issue number), | Page range

The author details are given in the same format as for books. Article titles are in regular type, terminated by a full stop and not enclosed in inverted commas. Journal titles are given in full (no abbreviations) and in italics. Any volume number is also given, followed by any issue information (usually an issue number or date) in round brackets, a comma (a colon may also be used) and the range of page numbers in the article (optionally preceded by pp.).

For example:

- Myers, R. & Berah, E. (1983) Some features of Australian exhibitionists compared with paedophiles. *Archives of Sexual Behavior*, 12, pp. 541–547.
- Farrington, D. (1989) Early predictors of adolescent aggression and adult violence. *Violence and Victims*, 4, 79–100.
- Fritz, N. & Altheide, D. (1987) The mass media and the social construction of the missing children problem. *Sociological Quarterly*, 28(4): 473–492.

Chapters in edited collections

Chapters in edited collections are referenced like this:

Author of chapter | (date) | Title of chapter. | In: Editor (ed./eds.) | *Title of Edited Collection*. | Place of publication: | Publisher, | Page range/Chapter number

The elements of the citation follow the conventions for books and edited collections as before. This form of citation requires either the chapter number or page range of the contribution to be provided:

- Finch, E. (2007) The Problem of Stolen Identity and the Internet. In: Jewkes, Y. (ed.) (2007) *Crime Online*. Cullompton: Willan, Ch. 3.
- Levi, M. & Pithouse, A. (1992) Victims of Fraud. In: Downes, D. (ed.) (1992) *Unravelling Criminal Justice*. London: Macmillan, pp. 229–246.

Newspapers

Newspaper articles are generally referenced like this:

> Author | Year | Title. | *Newspaper*, | Day and month, | Page (if known)

If there is no author identified, or the article is an editorial piece, you should use the title of the newspaper in italics to begin your reference instead:

> *Newspaper* | Year | Title. | Day and month | Page (if known)

For example:

- Milne, S. (1999) Thugs make plans to riot. *Scottish Daily Record*, 16 October.
- Bindel, J. (2005) The life stealers. *Guardian*, 16 April.
- *Daily Mirror* (1973) Scandal of soccer's savages. 20 August.

Magazines

Magazines follow the same sequence as journals:

> Author | (date) | Title of article. | *Full title of magazine*, | Volume number | (issue number) | Page range

For example:

- Cunningham, L. (1982) Love and rage. *Vogue*, July: 60.
- France, D. (1995) Life after death. *Good Housekeeping*, July: 110–113.
- Werner, L. (1986) My husband hit me. *Ladies' Home Journal*, November: 14.

Statistics, graphs, and charts

All material which is directly imported or used to construct statistics, graphs or charts within your work must be referenced back to the source from which it is derived. Where there is more than one source, all should be shown in the citation and listed separately in the list of references. The form of the citation will depend on the type of material from which the data have been gathered.

For example:

Football related arrests in England and Wales 2008–09

League	Attendance	Arrests
Premier League	13,527,815	1,288
Championship	9,877,552	753
League One	4,171,834	458
League Two	2,304,765	252
Total	29,881,966	2,751

(Home Office 2009)

List of references

Home Office (2009) Statistics on football-related arrests and banning orders 2008–09 London: HMSO.

Referencing Government publications

Law Commission Reports

Law Commission Reports are referenced as follows:

Law Commission | (year) | *Title of Report.* | (Law Com number, | Command Paper number) | Place of publication: | Publisher

For example:

- Law Commission (1989) *Criminal Law—Computer Misuse.* (Law Com No. 186, Cm 819) London: HMSO.
- Law Commission (2009) *Intoxication and Criminal Liability.* (Law Com No. 314, Cm 7256) London: HMSO.

Command Papers

Command papers should be referenced as follows:

Author | (year) | *Title of Command Paper.* | (Command Paper number) | Place of publication: | Publisher

For example:

- Secretary of State for the Home Department, Secretary of State for Constitutional Affairs & the Attorney General (2005) *Criminal justice: rebuilding lives—supporting victims of crime.* (Cm 6705) London: HMSO.
- Home Office (2009) *Extending our reach: a comprehensive approach to tackling serious organised crime.* (Cm 7665) London: HMSO.

See chapter 3 on statistics and official publications for more information on the various series of Command Papers.

Parliamentary papers

Parliamentary papers should be referenced like this:

> Committee Name | (year) | *Title of Report*. | (HL/HC | report serial number | of | year of Parliamentary session) | Place of publication: | Publisher

For example:

- European Union Committee (2005–06) *The Criminal Law Competence of the European Community: Report with Evidence*. (HL 227 of 2005–06) London: HMSO.
- Joint Committee on Human Rights (2006–07) *The Council of Europe Convention on the Prevention of Terrorism*. (HL 26 of 2006–07; HC 247 of 2006–07) London: HMSO.

Parliamentary debates (*Hansard* or the Official Report)

Hansard debates are generally referenced as follows:

> *Hansard*, | HL/HC/Parl. Debs. | (series number) | Volume number, | Column number(s) | (date)

Remember that the first four series of *Hansard* contain reports from both the House of Lords and House of Commons bound together. They are referred to collectively as Parliamentary Debates. In the fifth series (from 1909 to date) the reports of the two houses are bound into separate volumes (H.L. Deb and H.C. Deb).

For more information on Hansard see chapter 1 on criminal law and chapter 3 on finding official publications.

For example:

- *Hansard*, HC (series 5) vol. 166, col. 1135 (9 February 1990)
- *Hansard*, HL (series 5) vol. 684, cols. 604–606 (11 July 2006)
- *Hansard*, Parl. Debs. (series 4) vol. 21, col. 849 (20 February 1894).

Referencing legal sources

Cases

Harvard referencing does not seem to have any hard-and-fast rules regarding the referencing of legal cases within the text of an essay. This is probably because Harvard referencing emerged in the social sciences and did not require a standard for citing legal authorities as these were not commonly encountered in those disciplines.

There are two options; first, include only the case name and year in the text (with the year in round brackets) but ensure that a list of cases with full citations is provided at the end of your essay, or, secondly, include the full case citation in the text of your essay.

If you take the latter approach, remember that you should only provide the full citation the first time that the case is mentioned; after that, the case name alone (or its shortened form) will suffice. With this in mind, either of the two approaches shown here is acceptable.

First, with just case years provided in-text:

In *DPP* v. *Baker* (2004), the High Court considered the meaning of 'course of conduct' in relation to criminal harassment.

Table of cases

DPP v. *Baker* [2004] EWHC 2782 (Admin)

Alternatively, with full citations provided in-text:

In *DPP* v. *Baker* [2004] EWHC 2782 (Admin), the High Court considered the meaning of 'course of conduct' in relation to criminal harassment.

Table of cases

DPP v. *Baker* [2004] EWHC 2782 (Admin)

You will find more information regarding conventions used in case citation in chapter 1 on finding and understanding the criminal law.

Legislation

Again, there is no Harvard standard for citing Acts of Parliament. However, there seems to be a general consensus that at least the following information is given for Acts post-1963:

Short Title of Act (including year). | (c. chapter number)

The short title of the Act is given in italics. For example:

- *Dangerous Dogs Act 1991.* (c. 65)
- *Crime and Security Act 2010.* (c. 17)

For Acts prior to 1963 (when the Acts of Parliament Numbering and Citation Act 1962 came into force) the Regnal year citation is given.

Short Title of Act (including year). | (Regnal year, c. chapter number).

For example:

- *Piracy Act 1837.* (1 Vict., c. 88).
- *Indecency with Children Act 1960.* (8 & 9 Eliz. II, c. 33).

See chapter 1 on criminal law for more information on Acts of Parliament, chapter numbers, and the Regnal year numbering system.

Some styles also include the name the place of publication and publisher and/or the country of origin:

- *Indecency with Children Act 1960.* (8 & 9 Eliz. II, c. 33). London: HMSO.
- Great Britain. *Indecency with Children Act 1960.* (8 & 9 Eliz. II, c. 33). London: HMSO.

Opinion seems to be divided as to whether or not statutes in-text should be italicized. You should see if your lecturer has a particular preference.

Statutory instruments are cited in a similar way to legislation, with the year of publication and SI number also provided:

- *Data Protection Act 1998 (Commencement No. 2) Order 2008*. SI 2008/1592
- *Equality Act (Sexual Orientation) Regulations 2007*. SI 2007/1063

Referencing audio-visual sources and interviews

Radio

In general, radio programmes may be cited as follows:

> Radio station | (year) | *Title of programme*. | Day and month.

For instance:

- BBC Radio 4 (2010) *Today*. 20 January.
- BBC World Service (2010) *Home from Home*. 2 July.

If however, the author, presenter or producer is important then you may cite these specifically, like this:

> Author/presenter/producer | (year) | *Title of programme*. | Radio station | Day and month.

If you cite an individual's name, then you should also explain their role in brackets:

- Humphreys, J. (Presenter) (2010) *Today*. BBC Radio 4. 20 January.
- Friction, B. (Presenter) (2010) *Home from Home*. BBC World Service. 2 July.

Television

Television broadcasts may be cited like this:

> *Title of programme* | (year) | Episode: Episode title (if any). | Broadcaster. | Day and month.

For example:

- *South Park* (2003) Episode: Lil' Crime Stoppers. Comedy Central. 23 April.

Similarly to radio programmes, the author, presenter, or producer may also be cited if relevant:

> Author/presenter/producer | (year) | *Title of programme*. | Episode: Episode title (if any) | Broadcaster. | Day and month.

Again, the individual's role should be specified:

- Young, K. (Presenter) (2008) *Crimewatch*. BBC 1. 23 June.

Film

Films may be cited as follows:

> *Title of film* | (year) | [medium] | Country of origin: | Name of studio/distributor.

The medium is that on which the film was seen: this will generally be DVD (or Blu-ray), VHS (for older films), or 'Motion picture' for films seen in the cinema. For instance:

- *Twelve Angry Men* (1957) [Motion picture] USA: MGM Studios.
- *Scum* (1979) [DVD] England: Slam Dunk Media.
- *A Clockwork Orange* (1971) [Blu-ray] USA: Warner Home Video.

Interviews

If you have conducted interviews as part of your research and you want to use these in your work, then you should ensure that you have the consent of your research participants. See chapter 12 on research ethics for further detail.

Interviews may be cited with the following information:

> Name of interviewee | (year) | [Interview] | At | Place of interview | with | Name of interviewer/ author. | Day and month.

You should also ensure that you have copies of the material to which you refer (interview notes, transcripts, completed questionnaires, or recordings) which can be made accessible to others if necessary. For instance:

- Martin, J. (2010) [Interview] At Barry Island with author. 10 July.
- Williams, R. (2010) [Interview] At the University of Surrey with Al-Khalili, J. 2 March.

Referencing electronic sources

Online sources

Online sources are generally referenced like this:

> Author | (Year) | *Title.* | Type of resource | [Online] | Available at: URL. | [Accessed] | date]

You might see some variation in Harvard referencing of online resources: remember the guiding principles that you should provide enough information so that the reader can find the source and that you should be consistent in your approach to citation.

If there is no author name, then use the name of the website instead. The year of the material is given in round brackets as usual. However, you may find that online resources are undated, in which case you should put 'n.d.' (short for 'no date') in the year brackets. After the title of the source (in italics) you should then state [Online] in square brackets, followed by the URL (which is underlined) and the date of access in square brackets.

For example:

- Council of Europe (2007) *Countries worldwide turn to Council of Europe Cybercrime Convention*. (Press release 413(2007)) [Online] Available at: https://wcd.coe.int/ViewDoc.jsp?id=1150107. [Accessed 2 June 2010].
- Duff, R.A. (2002) *Theories of Criminal Law*. (Stanford Encyclopaedia of Philosophy) [Online] Available at: http://plato.stanford.edu/entries/criminal-law/. [Accessed 2 June 2010].
- University of Cardiff (n.d.) 'Avoiding plagiarism' [Online] Available at: https://ilrb.cf.ac.uk/plagiarism/tutorial/index.html. [Accessed 2 June 2010].

Personal e-mails

Personal e-mail correspondence may be referenced, but you should ensure that you obtain permission from the sender and never publish the sender's e-mail address:

Name of sender | (Year) | E-mail to | Name of recipient | re: | Subject | Day and date.

- Finch, E. (2010) E-mail to Fafinski, S. re: Harvard referencing styles in criminology. 1 July.
- Darbishire, A. (2007) E-mail to Fafinski. S. re: Selection of charges in computer misuse offences. 17 April.

Tweets/Blog postings

Messages posted on the Twitter service (known as 'tweets') or items posted on blog sites may also be referenced:

Name (or pseudonym) of poster | (Year) | Tweet message/Blog posting | re: | Subject | Day and date posted | Available at: URL. | [Accessed] | date].

For example:

- Leicestertalk (2010) Tweet message re: News—Leicestershire Police, ASBO for Hinckley schoolboy. 12 July. Available at: http://twitter.com/leicestertalk. [Accessed 12 July 2010].
- Science 2.0 (2009) Blog posting re: Blame for UK Gun Crime. 29 July. Available at: http://www.science20.com/news_articles/whos_blame_uk_gun_crime. [Accessed 12 July 2010].

 CHAPTER SUMMARY

- Plagiarism is a form of academic dishonesty that is readily detected and attracts negative consequences both within your institution and in your future career
- Bear in mind that a thorough and precise approach to references will avoid accusations of inadvertent plagiarism. If in doubt, reference
- Note the situations outlined in this chapter in which a reference should be provided, taking particular care to ensure that ideas are attributed to their source
- Find out whether your institution or department has a 'house style' and, if so, ensure that you follow it

- It is important to be consistent in the way in which you reference. As a general rule of thumb, always check to see that you have given sufficient information for a reader to find the material to which you are referring
- Take particular care with Internet sources
- Always provide a complete bibliography/list of references as required

FURTHER READING

- Staffordshire University has developed a very comprehensive guide to the Harvard referencing system which can be found at http://www.staffs.ac.uk/about_us/university_departments/information_services/learning_support/refzone/harvard/.
- If you are required to use it, more detail on the APA style of referencing can be found in the *Concise rules of APA style* (2009).
- Similarly, further detail on the MLA style can be found in *The MLA handbook for writers of research papers* (2009).
- The OSCOLA style of footnote referencing can be found online at http://www.law.ox.ac.uk/publications/oscola.php.
- The British Standards Institution published several standards covering the Harvard style of referencing. They are not for the faint-hearted, but, should you wish to dig much deeper, they are:
  - *Recommendations for references to published materials* (BS 1629: 1989)
  - *Recommendations for citing and referencing published material* (BS 5605: 1990)
  - *Information and documentation—Guidelines for bibliographic references and citations to information resources* (BS ISO-690–2: 1997).

GLOSSARY

- A **bibliography** appears at the end of a piece of work. It is a list of *all* the materials that you have consulted during the preparation of a piece of work, irrespective of whether or not they are referenced in the body of that work.
- A **list of references** appears at the end of a piece of work. It contains only the materials that you have mentioned in the body of the text and, unlike the bibliography, does not contain materials that you have read in preparing your work but not referenced in the text.
- **Paraphrasing** refers to the practice of rewriting the author's original words in a shortened form but in a way that retains the meaning of the original work.
- **Plagiarism** is a term used to describe all situations in which a person has used the work of another without acknowledgement of the source. Plagiarism may be deliberate, whereby the student has intentionally tried to pass the work off as their own, or inadvertent, as a result of poor referencing.
- **Quoting** refers to the exact reproduction of another's words.
- **Summarizing** is the term used to describe the practice of rewriting an author's words in a shortened form in a way that captures the key points that they made.

REFERENCES

APA (2009) *Concise rules of APA style*. 6th Ed. Washington, DC: American Psychological Association.

Back, L. (2002) Aryans reading Adorno: cyber-culture and twenty-first century racism. *Ethnic and Racial Studies,* 25(4), 628–651.

Chernin, E. (1988) The 'Harvard System': A mystery dispelled. *British Medical Journal,* 297, 1062–1063.

Finch, E. (2007) The Problem of Stolen Identity and the Internet. In: Jewkes, Y. (ed.) (2007) *Crime Online*. Cullompton: Willan, Chapter 3.

Gibbens, T. (1981) Shoplifting. *British Journal of Psychiatry,* 138, 346–347.

Jenkins, P. (1992) *Intimate Enemies: Moral Panics in Contemporary Great Britain*. New York: Aldine de Gruyter.

Laing, R. (1967) *The Politics of Experience*. Harmondsworth: Penguin.

McGurk, B., McEwan A. & Graham F. (1981) Personality types and recidivism among young delinquents. *British Journal of Criminology,* 29, 286–394.

MLA (2009) *The MLA handbook for writers of research papers*. 7th Ed. New York: Modern Language Association of America.

Ray, L. (2005) Violent crime. In: Hale, C., Hayward, K., Wahidin, A. & Wincup, E. (2005) *Criminology*. Oxford: OUP, 223–244.

Stothard, M. (2008) '1 in 2' admit to plagiarism. *Varsity,* 30 October.

Szasz, T. (1970) *The Manufacture of Madness*. New York: Dell.

Taylor, P. (1993a) Mental illness and violence. In: P Taylor (ed.) (1993) *Violence in Society*. London: Royal College of Physicians.

Taylor, P. (1993b) Schizophrenia and crime: Distinctive patterns of association. In: Hodgins, S. (ed.) *Mental Disorder and Crime*. Newbury Park, CA: SAGE.

Teplin, L (1985) The criminality of the mentally ill. *American Journal of Psychiatry,* 142, 593–598.

Teplin, L. (1984) Criminalising mental disorder: The comparative arrest rate of the menally ill. *American Psychologist,* 39, 784–803.

University of Leeds (2010) *Cheating, plagiarism, fraudulent or fabricated coursework and malpractice in University examinations*. Office of Academic Appeals & Regulation. [Online] Available at: http://www.leeds.ac.uk/AAandR/cpff.htm. [Accessed 25 May 2010].

Wall, D.S. (2007) *Cybercrime*. Cambridge: Polity Press.

Wright, B., Caspi, A., Moffitt, T. & Paternoster, R. (2004) Does the perceived risk of punishment deter criminally prone individuals? Rational choice, self-control and crime. *Journal of Research in Crime and Delinquency,* 41, 180–213.

Essay writing

8

The focus of this chapter is essay writing. Earlier sections of this book have outlined techniques for locating and understanding primary and secondary criminology sources. This chapter builds on those skills by exploring the ways that this source material can be used in your coursework. It will also guide you through the stages of planning, researching, and constructing an essay with practical advice on interpreting the question and producing a structured response that demonstrates the required skills and knowledge. It should be read in conjunction with chapter 6, which focuses on writing skills, and chapter 7, for information on referencing. Doing so will ensure that you produce a polished piece of work that is well-expressed and fully referenced in an appropriate style.

The essay is a popular method tool of assessment on criminology courses. Essay questions make frequent appearances on exam papers across a range of modules as well as featuring as the dominant approach for coursework assessment. Given the prevalence of this method of assessment, it is important that you ensure that your essay-writing craftsmanship is of the highest level. Students often make the mistake of thinking that an essay is marked on its content alone but this is not the case: a good essay is a combination of knowledge and skills. In fact, there are a whole package of skills involved in essay writing, all of which need to be demonstrated if your work is to achieve good marks. This chapter will introduce these skills and explain what you need to do to demonstrate them to the person marking your essay.

LEARNING OUTCOMES

After reading this chapter, you will be able to:

- Appreciate the combination of knowledge and skills required to produce a successful piece of written work

- Be able to 'unpick' the question to ensure that you have a clear grasp of its requirements

- Conduct effective research and extract relevant information to enable you to produce a focused and well-supported essay

- Create an effective introduction and conclusion to your essay and structure a cohesive line of argument

- Evaluate the essay that you have written to ensure that it demonstrates the relevant skills and knowledge and that it adheres to the necessary style and referencing requirements

What makes a good essay?

This is an important question as you cannot be expected to produce a good essay until you know what features combine together to create a good essay. In essence, a good essay is one that answers the question and, in doing so, demonstrates a range of written and analytical skills. It is important to emphasize that a good essay requires as much thought to be given to the way that the essay is constructed as is given to its content. In other words, it is not enough that you know the relevant criminological theory and literature; you must also know what to do with it in order to write an effective essay. A good essay should demonstrate the following:

- A foundation of accurate and relevant knowledge about the criminology topic that is the subject of the question.
- Wide-ranging research that identifies a variety of relevant source material appropriate to the subject matter.
- Effective use of source material so that it is integrated into the essay and used to strengthen your arguments in a way that demonstrates your understanding of the material and its role in your work.
- The ability to filter out irrelevant or peripheral points and to maintain a firm and consistent focus on the central issue raised by the question.
- A flowing line of argument set in a clear structure with an effective introduction and conclusion.
- An appropriate balance between description and analysis.
- Good written communication skills in producing a coherent and eloquent piece of work.
- A thorough approach to referencing that ensures that all source material is acknowledged in a complete and appropriate style.

This mix of knowledge and skills can be further illustrated if the process of creating an essay is broken down into stages as illustrated in Figure 8.1.

This chapter will provide a detailed account of the requirements of each of these stages in order to assist you with the production of an essay that answers the question set, demonstrates appropriate skills, and which meets with the approval of your marker. Remember, though, that it may be necessary to move backwards and forwards through the stages: you may, for example, find that you need to do more research once you have moved into the writing stage or that you need to reconsider what the essay means during the research stage, but that is not a problem. This chapter does not intend to suggest that there is a rigid progression through the stages but to ensure that each stage is given adequate attention to help you with the production of your essays.

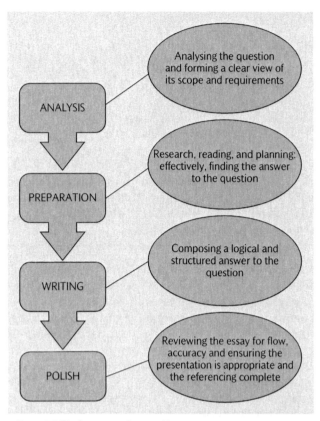

Figure 8.1 The four stages of essay writing

Analysing the question

It is important to take time to analyse the question in order to work out what it requires. This is a fundamental first step although it may have to be combined with some initial research to help you understand the precise requirements of the question. For example, you may be able to identify the subject matter of the question on the basis of its wording and your existing knowledge but a little preliminary investigation in your textbook might be necessary to help you understand the question more fully. However, try to pinpoint the precise requirements of the question as early as possible as this will add focus to your research and enable you to identify relevant material more effectively.

What does the question ask?

It is essential to the effectiveness of every stage of the essay-writing process as well as to the overall success of the essay, in terms of the mark that it is awarded, that you focus on what the essay *asks* rather than the broader issue of what the essay is *about*. This distinction can be described in terms of the particular question (what the essay *asks*) posed about a more general topic (what the essay is *about*).

Practical exercise: topic and question

If you ask someone how to make pizza, you will be annoyed if they respond by telling you where to buy pizza or how many calories there are in the average pizza or if they embark on an account of the history of pizza making. This is because they have not answered your question even though they are talking about the same general topic.

The same principle applies to essay questions in criminology. Take a look at the following question and decide (a) what it is about and (b) what it asks:

Critically assess whether the Sexual Offences Act 2003 has achieved its objectives of simplifying the law and affording greater protection to victims of rape.

The answer to the first question is straightforward: the question is about sexual offences legislation and the offence of rape. However, there are any number of different questions that could be asked about this topic so it would be important that your answer focused on the specific question asked here, which is whether this legislation achieved the two stated objectives.

Far too many students limit their prospects of success by responding to what the essay is about rather than narrowing their focus and providing a response to the specific question. This leads to the inclusion of irrelevant material as there is a vast range of points that could be made about the general topic (sexual offences) that have nothing to do with the specific question (the effectiveness of the legislation). For example, a discussion of grooming—a new offence introduced by the Sexual Offences Act 2003 to deal with those who use the Internet to lure children into sexual activity—has little relevance to the question even though it is covered by the Act mentioned in the question. In other words, you do not have to take too many steps away from the specific question asked in order to stray into the realms of irrelevancy, even if your discussion is still within the same broad topic.

Practical advice: finding and keeping focus

It is essential that you identify what the question asks and keep this to the forefront of your mind at every stage of the research, planning, and writing process to ensure that your essay does not lose its focus.

- Make sure that you isolate the specific question asked about the topic and write this in a prominent place so that it acts as a reminder whilst you are working on your essay.

- Check every point that you find during your research for its relevance to the question (not the topic). You might want to develop a simple ranking system to help you with this.

- Points that do not have immediate relevance can be made relevance if you slant them towards the question. For example, you could include a discussion of grooming in the example above if you used it to illustrate how it criminalizes conduct that might precede a rape.

- When you are drafting your essay, make sure that each paragraph touches base with the specific question. You can use signposting to do this (this is discussed later in this chapter in the *Preparation* section).

Rewording the question

One of the most effective ways to work out what the question asks is to rewrite it in your own words with the aim of discovering one or two clear questions that you understand. For example, the following two questions simplify the sexual offences question and make it far easier to keep its core issues in mind when researching and writing the essay:

- Is the offence of rape easier to understand than it was prior to the introduction of the Sexual Offences Act 2003?

- Has the Sexual Offences Act 2003 improved the protection available for victims of rape?

This approach will enable you to establish and retain a focus on the question posed by the essay and it also offers a starting point for structuring the essay as it is clear that there are two separate issues that need to be addressed.

It can also be helpful to reword an essay question if it is phrased in a way that does not give you much by way of clues as to what is expected. A question that is made up of a quotation followed by the instruction to 'discuss' is an example of this as it puts the onus on the student to work out what it is that needs to be discussed. The way to deal with this is to reword the question yourself using alternative words so that you make a distinction from the start about what aspect of the question needs to be described and what it is that needs to be analysed.

You will find an explanation of how so-called 'process words'—such as 'discuss'—are used in the construction of essay questions and how these can help you to understand what the question requires of you later in this chapter.

Practical exercise: rewording the question

It is a good idea to practice analysing essay titles by rewording them as this will give you the confidence to do it with your own coursework questions. There is an example below followed for some questions for you to try yourself:

It is not possible to determine the true extent of crime. Official statistics do not illuminate the dark figure of crime. Discuss the accuracy of this statement.

This can be reworded using process words to indicate what needs to be described in the question and what part of it should be the focus of analysis:

- Explain the dark figure of crime and consider whether it is possible to know the true extent of crime.

- Assess whether official statistics are able to provide an accurate calculation of the extent of crime.

- This can be made clearer still by breaking this down into a series of questions that need to be answered:

- What is the dark figure of crime?

- Why is the true extent of crime considered to be unknowable?

- What is counted by official statistics?

- Does this provide a measure of the extent of crime?

Try to identify the questions that are asked by the following essay titles. You should be able to make an attempt at this even if you have little prior knowledge of the subject matter.

- It is often said that the media create, rather than report, crime. Consider the validity of this statement, ensuring that your answer includes examples from at least anti-social behaviour and sexual offences against children.

- Criminology is preoccupied with questions about why people deviate rather than why they conform. Discuss.

- Outline the problems posed by the criminal justice system in the policing and prosecution of domestic violence and consider whether there are measures that could improve the situation.

 You will find answers to these questions and an explanation of how they were reached on the Online Resource Centre.

Remember that you are rewording the question to enhance your understanding of what it requires. You must take the utmost care to ensure that you are not rewording it in a way that changes its sense or meaning. When your essay is marked, it will only attract credit for material that is relevant to the question that was asked and not for other points, however interesting or clever, that are not pertinent.

Preparation: research and planning

The preparatory stages of research and planning should take at least as much time as the actual writing of the essay. During this stage you will find different points of interest leading towards a draft conclusion, select material for inclusion in your essay, and engage in some preliminary planning of the structure of your argument. Taking care with these preparatory stages does make the writing of the essay less troublesome, as many of the difficult issues will have already been resolved.

Focus on the question(s)

The aim of the last section was to emphasize the importance of working out the requirements of the question before starting the process of research, planning, and writing that will produce the essay. This is because you cannot answer a question effectively unless you know what it is asking. Students sometimes think that research is the first stage, but you will be so much more effective in your research if you start with a clear idea of what you are trying to find out.

Try to remember that you do not need to know the answer in order to conduct research: after all, that is what research is all about—finding answers. Of course, you are likely to discover information during your research that assists you to reach a more closely informed understanding of the question.

You should be able to identify the general topic from the wording of the question itself and this will enable you to start your research. Remember that each topic has a number of different questions that can be asked about it (see Figure 8.2) and your initial job is to sift through the information on the topic and identify material that is pertinent to the particular question that you have been asked.

Brainstorming

One method of exploring what you already know about a topic is brainstorming. This involves writing down everything that you can think of about a topic in the order it comes into your mind. This technique is useful in essay writing as a way to establish a list of potential topics for inclusion in your essay, so that you can make some preliminary decisions about relevance and thus direct the focus of your research and reading.

Practical example: brainstorming

Brainstorming can be a good way of getting all your possible points about a topic down on paper so that you can look at them and assess their relevance to your essay. You might fine it useful to work with a friend as you can share ideas and discuss the relevance of the different points that you generate.

1. Write the topic at the top of a piece of paper and divide the paper into two columns.

2. Give yourself a set period of time—two minutes should be ample—to make a list of all the points that spring into your mind about that topic. Do not worry about their relevance at this stage – just get all your ideas down on paper.

3. When your time is up, review the points that you have listed and think about their relevance to the particular question that is asked in your essay. Use a ranking system in which 1 = highly relevant, 2 = some relevance, and 3 = irrelevant. You can also add notes that reflect your thoughts about the role of each point that is relevant in your essay.

4. Reorder your points according to their relevance. Alternatively, you might want to start grouping similar points together to create a draft structure for your essay.

This approach may not capture all of the points that you want to include in your essay as you are likely to find new material as your research progresses but it will help to give some direction to your research by identifying potential lines of investigation. You will find an example of a brainstorming exercise on the Online Resource Centre.

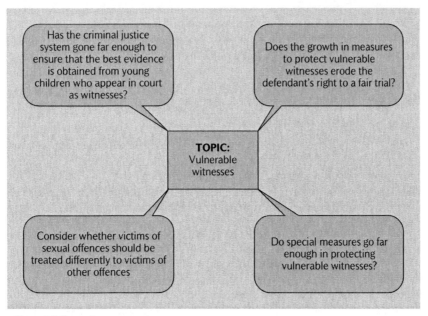

Has the criminal justice system gone far enough to ensure that the best evidence is obtained from young children who appear in court as witnesses?

Does the growth in measures to protect vulnerable witnesses erode the defendant's right to a fair trial?

TOPIC: Vulnerable witnesses

Consider whether victims of sexual offences should be treated differently to victims of other offences

Do special measures go far enough in protecting vulnerable witnesses?

Figure 8.2 One topic, many questions.

Getting started

It can be extremely difficult to make a start on the research and planning of an essay just because it all seems such an immense task, particularly if you feel that you are overwhelmed from the start because you are faced with a topic that you do not understand. This section outlines some of the early steps that can be taken that will help you to make a start on your preparation.

Earlier chapters in this book have provided in-depth coverage of a range of sources, how to find them, and how to make effective use of them. This chapter will not repeat that information but will merely highlight a few key points of particular relevance to conducting research for an essay. You will probably find that you need to make reference to earlier chapters to help you with the research process.

The most sensible starting point for your research is the relevant chapter(s) in a textbook. This is because textbooks are designed to provide exactly what you need at this point in time: a clear and relatively comprehensive explanation of concepts in criminology. It is important that you use textbooks in an appropriate way when conducting research for your coursework. This means that you must use them in a way that is (a) useful to you and (b) acceptable to your lecturers.

- **Start with the set textbook.** Even if you do not like the book and have found an alternative, it would be a mistake not to read it in case you miss out on information that the lecturer expects you to know and that other students on your module will have read.

- **Make sure that you understand the basics of the topic.** If the set textbook does not give you a clear understanding of the important points, make a note of them and find a simpler explanation in an alternative book. You may need to try several textbooks before you find one that explains the issues in a way that makes sense to you but you must persevere with this as it is crucial that you have a grasp of the basics from a source aimed at students before you start to explore the issues in greater depth.

- **Use a range of textbooks.** Each author will explain the key points in criminology in their own way and will use different examples to illustrate their points, so you can gain a broader perspective on the topic by using a several different textbooks.

- **Do not make too many notes at this stage.** You are reading textbooks to gain an overview of the topic and to identify useful source material and lines of investigation relevant to your essay. It is not a good use of your time to copy large chunks out of the textbook so try to use a condensed approach to note-taking in which you describe the points that you want to find again and note the page on which it occurs. For example, you might write 'p. 110 defines rape, p. 112 has a table of rape statistics, p. 129 mentions a useful article by Broome'.

- **Move on to consult a wide range of sources.** Remember that textbooks are written for students. They do all the hard work for you by summarizing the information that you need to understand topics in criminology. You are expected to use this as a starting point to enable you to identify source material such as articles, government reports, and criminal case law that you will then read yourself and use as authority in your essay.

A textbook is a good source of basic information that should be used to give you a solid understanding of the topic. However, quoting from a textbook in your essay or using textbooks as the sole point of reference for your arguments will not impress your lecturers. You need to demonstrate the ability to move beyond a textbook and engage with the sort of analysis that you will find in other sources. There are a range of different types of source material that you can use as shown in Table 8.1 but be sure to think carefully about the value and reliability of the various sources when deciding whether or not to include them in your criminology essay.

Organizing your research

During the course of your research, you will use a variety of sources and you will want to keep a record of the relevant information that you have found. There are two aspects to this: firstly,

Table 8.1 Source materials

Source	Content	Further detail
Monographs	These provide detailed explorations of particular issues that offer greater depth than textbook coverage. The authors are experts on the subject matter who will be offering their own viewpoint on the subject matter as well as an objective analysis of the issues. This is a good source that can be referred to with confidence in your essay.	You will find more detail on this source in chapter 2.
Key readings	These are collections of writings by leading authorities in the field of criminology that are gathered together in a book for ease of reference. Each contribution to the collection can be treated as a source in its own right as if you had read it in its original place of publication rather than encountering it in a book.	Chapter 2
Journal articles	Articles are shorter pieces of writing that tend to focus on quite narrow issues thus offering depth of discussion. As journals are published monthly or bi-monthly, articles will often be the best source of up-to-date discussion and analysis of recent developments. Each contribution to a journal is subject to rigourous review prior to its acceptance for publication so it is a solid authority to use in your essay.	Chapter 2
Official reports and *Hansard*	Publications from government departments tend to be factual rather than analytical and are often long and detailed. They set out of the background to the issue under consideration and may explore different possible solutions to a particular problem. They are a good source to use when you are presenting the official stance on an issue. You may want to supplement this with any relevant discussions in Parliament by consulting *Hansard*.	Chapter 3
Case law	The appellate decisions of the Court of Appeal and Supreme Court in criminal cases can be useful source material in criminology. They set out the decisions of the judges on the interpretation and application of the criminal law or rules of criminal procedure so can be a useful authority to include in your essay. The judges in each case sometimes disagree with each other so can provide useful insight into alternative arguments.	Chapter 1 provides detailed information about finding and using cases in your work.
Media sources	Unless you are specifically discussing media constructions of crime, you should use media sources with caution as they were written with the general public in mind as a consumer rather than as an authoritative source of information on criminology.	Chapter 4 discusses the use of media sources and provides guidance on how they should be used in your work.
Internet sources	As with media sources, you need to be wary about too great a reliance on Internet sources as these may not be produced by a reliable source. In particular, lecturers tend not to be impressed by reference to tertiary sources such as Wikipedia.	See chapter 4 for more detail on the use of Internet sources and methods for determining the reliability of such material.

recording the points from the sources that you want to include in your essay and, secondly, ensuring that you keep a full record of the bibliographic details of each source so that you can reference it appropriately in your work.

The most popular method of recording information is, unfortunately, the least effective as it involves rewriting every textbook, article, and case in a more condensed form. This is labour-intensive and does not produce a very useful set of notes. A less time-consuming alternative is described earlier in this chapter. This involves making a note of the value of the point that you have found rather than writing out the point itself.

Although this method is quicker than writing full notes, it still results in a set of notes that is organized on a source-by-source basis. In other words, you have a set of condensed notes of each article as you read them. There is an alternative approach to organization that will make your notes easier to use when it comes to working out how they fit into your essay which is issue-by-issue.

Practical example: organization by issue

This approach uses the points that you identified during your analysis of the question and brainstorming as the basis for arranging your notes.

1. Identify key words and phrases from your analysis of the question and brainstorming session and write each of these at the top of a separate sheet of paper (or create a document for each if working on a computer).

2. Select a piece of source material and read it carefully, looking out for any points that are relevant to the issues that you have identified. If you are working from a copy, you could highlight these points or annotate the page to indicate that they are important points.

3. Make a descriptive note of the point such as 'explanation of the process of attrition using rape as an example' under the relevant heading. Be sure to include something that identifies the source such as the name of the author or the article and the page on which the point appears.

4. Review your headings from time-to-time. It may be that certain issues need to be amalgamated or a discrete issue may emerge under one of your headings that you decide to treat separately. You may find material during your research that identifies a new issue that you had not originally thought of but which you discover has a place in your essay.

These points will be the building blocks of your essay so it will be useful to have your notes arranged in this way. You will see an example of notes organized by issue in Figure 8.3.

Figure 8.3 illustrates two pages of notes organized by issue. It shows sub-divisions within the page of notes on the left-hand side which have allocated space to note questions that have arisen during the research process and further avenues of investigation to be pursued. These separate sections within each page or document will serve as a useful reminder of thoughts that occurred to you as you were reading and act as a prompt when you are deciding what further research needs to be undertaken.

You may also have noticed that some points in the example are written in full and that the word QUOTE appears in capital letters beside them. You might think that this is unnecessary as the words appear inside quotation marks but it is very good practice to do everything possible to draw your attention to the fact that these words are not yours and must be attributed to their source if used in your essay. It is very easy to forget to add quotation marks or overlook

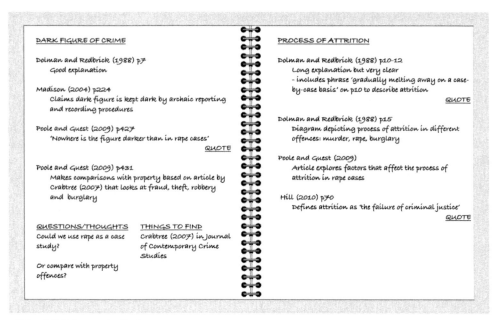

Figure 8.3 Notes organized by issue.

them when reading your notes some time after they were written and think 'what a good point. I've expressed that really well' and include it in your essay without realizing that it was a quotation. As you will see from the discussion in chapter 7, even unintentional replication of the work of others without acknowledgement will contravene the plagiarism/unfair practice rules at your university so it is worth taking extra effort to ensure that you do not make a mistake when using your notes to create your essay.

Whichever approach you use to recording and organizing your material, it is important to remember that you must ensure that you keep full bibliographic details of all your source material. There is nothing more frustrating than having the feeling of success and relief that accompanies finishing your essay replaced by the realization that you still need to track down references for your source material. One useful approach is to start a separate document entitled 'references' as soon as you start working on your essay and add each source to it as you read it. You might also find it useful to keep a separate list of literature that you want to read but have not yet found, just as a reminder.

You will find some information on effective note-taking techniques in chapter 5.

Planning a structure

The structure of the essay is important as it is this that determines the coherence of your argument. Determining the best structure involves deciding which points should be grouped together into a paragraph and the order of these paragraphs in relation to each other. In other words, you need to decide on the content of each paragraph and then fit these paragraphs together so that they present a logical line of argument. It is useful to give at least some thought to this during the research stage so that you have an idea of how your points fit together before you start to write.

As your research progresses and you gather a detailed set of notes, you should develop some idea of the points that you want to make in your essay. If you organized your research by issue as illustrated in Figure 8.3, you should find that your notes are already arranged into categories that can help you to determine the content of each paragraph. This is just a starting point so be prepared to make some adjustments when dividing your points into paragraphs when you come to write your essay.

There is a more detailed discussion of creating structure within a paragraph in the section on writing an essay later in this chapter.

It is a good idea to create a working structure for your essay as you are conducting research as it will give you an idea of how all your ideas fit together and help you to identify any gaps in your argument that can be filled with further research. It will also reduce the amount of work that you have to do at the writing stage as you will have a preliminary structure in mind from the outset. Of course, it is often the case that your structure will change as you write but it is still a good idea to have a tentative idea of the shape of your essay before you start to write. One way to do this is to create a structure using the ideas for each paragraph as illustrated in Figure 8.4.

This structure reminds you that your essay must have an introduction, a conclusion and a line of argument that runs through it whilst giving you space to label each paragraph according to its content or purpose. You can then use each label as a heading on a separate sheet of paper and make a list of the points that you plan to include in that paragraph. Alternatively,

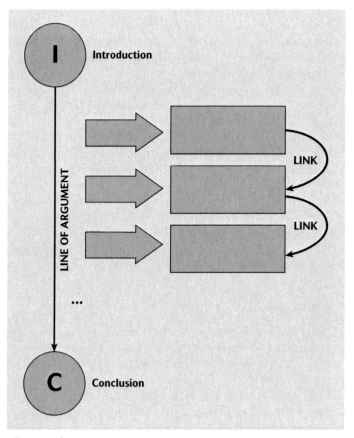

Figure 8.4 Structuring an essay

you might want to start by making a list of all the points that you want to include in your essay and then group them into paragraphs before deciding on a label for the paragraph and putting the paragraphs in order. The presence of the arrows acts as a reminder that each paragraph must be linked to the next and/or back to the question. You might find it helpful to add a few words to your plan to capture the nature of the link.

There is a discussion of the use of signposting words and phrases to create links between paragraphs and between your essay and the question in the next section of this chapter.

Planning and drafting

Activities that you undertake during the preparation stage should make writing a draft of your essay much easier, as you will have your source material to hand and a good idea of how your points will be organized in your essay. However, this does not mean that you should treat preparation and writing as separate activities to be undertaken consecutively—it is actually a good idea to start drafting parts of your essay as soon as you feel able even if you are still following up some lines of research for other parts. Not only will the process of writing help to develop your ideas, it may enable you to identify gaps in your research or even new lines of investigation. Moreover, the sooner you start writing, the more time you will have to redraft your essay and refine your arguments.

Some students delay the start of the writing process and, as a consequence, are left with insufficient time to produce a polished piece of work. There is nothing worse than having to submit work that you know is something less than your best effort because you have run out of time.

There is a discussion of techniques that you can use to get started with writing in the next section on writing the essay.

Writing the essay

Once you have researched the topic, gathered your material, and put together a preliminary plan of your essay, it is time to start writing. This section will discuss the factors that contribute to the construction of a successful essay. It will start by outlining the key components of an effective introduction and set out some strategies for constructing paragraphs before moving to consider the need to achieve an appropriate balance between description and analysis. It will then address techniques for creating a focused and flowing essay before ending with an exploration of the characteristics of a strong conclusion.

Writing an introduction

It should go without saying that the first paragraph of your essay should be an introduction that unpicks the question and explains how it will be tackled, but a great many undergraduate criminology essays simply launch straight into the first substantive point without any attempt at an introduction. This may be an accidental omission by students who do not understand how to create an introduction and who believe that their first paragraph is actually fulfilling the role of an introduction. Alternatively, it may be a deliberate omission by students who have sacrificed the introduction in order to meet the word limit in the belief that it makes no difference to the essay whether or not it has an introduction. This is a mistake. The introduction has a number of functions to fulfil, all of which are important to the overall success of the essay:

- It identifies the central subject matter of the essay.

- It unpicks the question thus demonstrating to the marker that you have understood the requirements of the essay.

- It sets out the issues that will be addressed in the essay in order to answer the question which gives the marker an idea of what to expect in the essay.

- It may give an indication as to the conclusion that is reached in the essay (although opinion is divided on this point).

In essence, then, the introduction gives the marker an instant impression of whether you have understood what the question requires and an indication of the points that you have included in your essay. This is why, from a pragmatic point of view, it is important for you to provide an introduction and to make sure that it is a good one: first impressions count so make sure that the first impression that your marker has of your essay is one that is going to discuss appropriate subject matter in an organized manner. You will find an explanation of how to do this in Table 8.2.

Many students prefer to write the introduction to the essay at the end of the writing process so that they can reflect what is actually in it. This can be a useful approach because the eventual content of your essay may be different to your planned essay as your ideas evolve once you start writing. However, there is no harm in writing a draft of an introduction at the beginning so that it is always taken into account in the overall word limit. You can always amend it once the essay is finished.

Start writing

It is very frustrating to be in a situation in which you know that your essay deadline is approaching but you feel unable to start writing. There can be a number of reasons for this:

- **I don't know enough about the subject matter to start writing.** Be realistic. If you have done a lot of research, you should have sufficient source material to start to write even if there are still a few elusive sources that you have not been able to track down. You cannot expect to find everything that has been written on the subject matter so you may have to start writing on the basis of what you have been able to find. Of course, if you have only read a couple of sources, it is likely that you are right and you are not yet ready to start writing so keep going with your research until you feel better prepared.

- **I don't know where to start.** This is quite common and can be very frustrating. You have done all your research, it is organized into issues, and you have broken it down into paragraphs but still the words will not come. One way around this is to write something that you know will have a place in your essay: it might be a definition of a key concept, a summary of the views of a particular theorist, or an outline of a relevant criminal offence. In other words, write content without context, i.e. without knowing where your words will fit in the essay, just so that you get over the block of staring at a blank sheet of paper or empty computer screen.

- **I can't write because I don't understand it.** Obviously it is not a good idea to start writing an essay if you have not yet understood the subject matter. Try to find a really simple explanation in a basic textbook, perhaps even using one that is not intended to be used at degree

Table 8.2 Structuring an introduction

Line	Role	Example
Your first sentence should grab the marker's attention.	Your marker has to read your essay but you should strive to make him want to do so by making your first sentence one that identifies the theme of the question in a interesting way. Under no circumstances should your essay start with the words 'this essay': it is very dull!	It is often said that 'there are three kinds of lies: lies, damned lies and statistics' due the propensity of statistical data to be manipulated to achieve any desired result.
The next sentence establishes the specific focus of the essay question.	This sentence can start with 'this essay' as its role is to explain to the marker the objective of your essay.	This essay will question whether official statistics are able to provide a true picture of the amount of crime which is committed in England and Wales.
The next sentences should set out how the objective of the essay will be established.	This gives the marker an indication of the content of your essay and the structure that it will take. In essence, this aspect of the introduction tells the marker what to expect in your essay.	In doing so, it will explain the 'dark figure of crime' and the process of attrition which reduces the number of criminal cases reaching court. It will outline the different methods of counting crime and comment upon whether they are able to provide a sufficient insight into how much crime takes place.
Some lecturers like the final sentence of the introduction to give an indication of the conclusion. Be aware that some lecturers really dislike this, believing that the conclusion belongs at the end of the essay only. It would be worth checking with each lecturer to see if they have any strong preferences.	This ensures that the introduction provides a complete snapshot of the essay by giving the marker an insight into your conclusion right from the start.	The essay will conclude that the advent of the victim surveys merely serve to highlight the inadequacies of attempts to count the true extent of crime thus it is likely that the dark figure will remain forever obscured from public view.

level. Once you have got the basic idea, you can revisit the section in your set textbook and see if it makes sense. Alternatively, you may have to ask a lecturer for help but remember that this may not be forthcoming in relation to assessed coursework. You could also try to write the parts of the essay that you do understand—it is sometimes the case that this will make things click in your mind and it will all become clear.

- **I just can't write.** Sometimes, the requirement to write in quite formal language can be off-putting so try writing in a way that is easier for you just to get your ideas flowing. One way of doing this is with free-flow writing.

Practical example: free-flow writing

This approach is very useful for overcoming writer's block.

1. Get a blank sheet of paper or open a fresh document on your computer.

2. Write a trigger word or phrase at the top of the paper or document. This can either be a key term relevant to the essay or some idea that you want to put in it such as:

   - The aim of my essay is to…
   - In the first paragraph, I am going to explain…
   - The main argument that I want to make is…
   - What is it that I'm trying to say?

3. Set yourself a short period of time—one or two minutes is plenty—and start writing. Do not worry about how you express your ideas or the order in which you make them. Just get your thoughts down on paper so you can see them.

4. Make sure that you keep writing for at least the period of time that you have set yourself even if you feel as if you are writing nonsense. However, if you find that you still have points to make when the time is up then be sure to keep writing until you have exhausted your ideas.

When you are finished, review what you have written. You should have produced something that captures your ideas in ordinary language but you can easily reword them into a more appropriate written style. You will probably need to reorganize your ideas too. This is fine. At least you are writing and getting your ideas down on the page.

Creating paragraphs

Paragraphs are the building blocks of your essay. They divide your essay into smaller, easily-digestible chunks with each one containing a separate idea or argument. Each paragraph should follow on logically from its predecessor and lead into the paragraph that follows it. In other words, there should be a sense of logical progression to your essay as your paragraphs are organized in such a way that each one contributes to the construction of a flowing line of argument.

This idea that each paragraph should contain a separate idea or argument does not really give a clear idea of how much detail should be in each paragraph. In fact, one of the commonest questions asked by students on this topic concerns the ideal length of a paragraph. This is a difficult question to answer. On the one hand, a paragraph should be as long as it needs to be in order to explain its argument but, on the other hand, it can be really hard work for the marker to read paragraphs that are pages long so many markers would say that there should be at least two paragraphs on every page of your essay. One technique that is quite widely used to determine the content of a paragraph is the PEE technique (point, elaboration, example) which has been modified here by the addition of a fourth characteristic (link) to create the PEEL technique:

- **Point.** A paragraph should start by outlining its central point.

- **Elaboration.** The sentences that follow should expand on this point to explain it in greater detail.

- **Example.** This provides support for the argument that you are presenting to make it more convincing.

- **Link.** The final sentence should either relate the point made back to the question or provide a link to the next paragraph.

You will find a more detailed discussion of paragraphing in chapter 6.

Signposting

Signposting is the process of making your essay clear to the reader. It refers to the words and phrases in your essay that explain the significance of your points. In essence, signposting words and phrases create focus (by linking your points to the question) and flow (by explaining how each paragraph relates to the next).

One way in which signposting is useful to the reader is in indicating the big ideas and themes in your essay. This is the equivalent of this book stating 'this chapter will deal with coursework' or 'this section explores issues associated with planning your essay'. This sort of signposting involves phrases that give the reader an insight into the overall focus of the whole essay or the next significant section of your essay and creates a strong structure for your work:

- The central focus of this essay is...
- The main theoretical perspectives examined in this essay are...
- The first section of this essay will be a review of the literature that examines...
- Having discussed [insert topic], it is now necessary to consider...
- The main argument that emerges from the case law is...

Signposting is also commonly used to communicate the relationship between different points and ideas to the reader. You might think that this is unnecessary and that the links are obvious but remember that you see your own work with full knowledge of the thinking behind it which gives you an advantage over your reader who has only the words on paper to rely upon. What seems obvious to you is therefore far less obvious to the reader so it is a good idea to add signposting to your essay so that your meaning is clear to the reader.

Practical example: signposting

The importance of signposting to indicate the relationship between points raised in your essay is demonstrated in the following example.

- Richards (2005) states that white collar crime is a product of society's inclination to equate material wealth with success and status. Porlock (2003) sees white collar crime as an inevitable consequence of the growth of entrepreneurialism.

What is the relationship between these sentences? Do Richards and Porlock agree or disagree with each other? Is the essay presenting two opposing views or is it using two viewpoints in conjunction with each other to strengthen the argument? These questions can be answered without difficulty with the insertion of a single word.

- Richards (2005) states that white collar crime is a product of society's inclination to equate material wealth with success and status. Moreover, Porlock (2003) sees white collar crime as an inevitable consequence of the growth of entrepreneurialism.

- Richards (2005) states that white collar crime is a product of society's inclination to equate material wealth with success and status. However, Porlock (2003) sees white collar crime as an inevitable consequence of the growth of entrepreneurialism.

The use of the word 'moreover' indicates that the points are to be read in conjunction with each other with Porlock's point adding support to Richards' view, whereas the use of the word 'however' indicates that the two views are incompatible with each other.

As this example illustrates, a single word can add a great deal of clarity to your writing. Table 8.3 sets out the different roles played by signposting words and phrases in signalling the relationship between the points made in your essay.

Table 8.3 Signposting words

Agreement or similarity	moreover, also, similarly, in addition, furthermore, additionally, as well as, what is more, in the same way, likewise.
Disagreement or contrast	however, nevertheless, on the other hand, conversely, by contrast, but, yet, by comparison, although, alternatively.
Providing exemplification or explanation	because, due to, as a result, owing to, by virtue of, as a consequence of, therefore, thus, particularly, hence, by way of illustration, including, especially.
Reformulating or reiterating an idea	in other words, in essence, that is, in simple terms, to clarify, rather, to paraphrase, to reiterate.
Enumerating and sequencing	there are a number of considerations, firstly, secondly, finally, subsequently, consequently, before, eventually, first and foremost.
Providing examples	to illustrate this point, for example, for instance, this can be demonstrated, such as,
Summarizing	in conclusion, in summary, finally, hence, as an overview.

Description versus analysis

Earlier in this chapter, it was said that a successful essay is one that answers the specific question asked rather than discussing the topic in general terms. In order to answer the question, your essay must be analytical rather than merely descriptive. A descriptive essay is one that explains the key concepts whereas an analytical essay moves beyond this to investigate how those concepts operate or relate to each other, depending on the requirements of the question. For instance, if you were answering the question about crime statistics that has been used as an example in this chapter, a descriptive approach would explain the dark figure of crime and set out the different methods of counting crime but would not do enough to discuss and evaluate whether such methods provide an accurate picture of the amount of crime that takes place.

It is understandable that students often produce very descriptive essays, especially in the early stages of their study of criminology, because it is far easier to describe than it is to analyse. Every textbook on criminology will provide its own descriptions of core concepts so all that is required is that these descriptions are read and reworded in your essay. Textbooks are far less likely to provide inspiration for the analysis part of an essay because it will have been written by your lecturer to test your powers of reasoning and your ability to criticize and appraise issues in criminology. Many students lack the confidence to do this, particularly if they cannot find any source material to rely upon, and so fill their essay with description, often only trying to explain how this answers the question in the final paragraph.

Descriptive essays are limited in the success that they will achieve. It is essential that you create an essay that is a combination of description and analysis. You will be better able to do this once you have a good understanding of the clues provided by the wording of the question that will indicate what concepts need to be described and what direction the analysis should take. You can do this by using the 'do what to what?' technique. This asks 'what does this essay require me to do (skill) with what concept in criminology (description)?' as is illustrated in Figure 8.5.

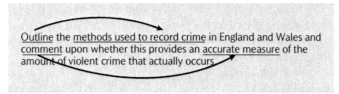

Outline the methods used to record crime in England and Wales and comment upon whether this provides an accurate measure of the amount of violent crime that actually occurs

Figure 8.5 'Do what to what'?

This will give you a clear idea as to what needs to be described and what needs to be analysed:

- Do what? Outline.
- To what? Methods used to record crime in England and Wales.
- Do what? Comment.
- To what? The accuracy of the measurement of violent crime.

Of course, the success of this method rests on your ability to recognize what the words used in the question require you to do in your essay. The words which give you instructions are called **process words** and these are best understood by considering the work of educational psychologist, Benjamin Bloom. He conducted research into the skills demonstrated by students in their essays, divided them into six categories, and arranged them in a hierarchy to demonstrate their importance and complexity as illustrated in Figure 8.6.

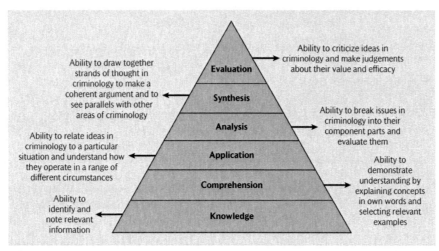

Figure 8.6 Bloom's taxonomy

Bloom described knowledge and comprehension—the two categories of skills at the bottom of the hierarchy—as **lower-order skills** because they are easier to demonstrate. By contrast, the **higher-order skills** of application, analysis, synthesis, and evaluation are harder to master and provide evidence that the student is able to *use* knowledge rather than simply to acquire and repeat it.

To take a very basic example, if you needed to drive to a new area that you had not visited before, you would be able to demonstrate *knowledge* by finding a map of the area and *understanding* by explaining the route to another person, but *application* would be demonstrated by actually reaching your destination. Once there, you might want to *analyse* how useful the route was and, ultimately, decide whether to use it again or to find an alternative.

You can identify the skills that are important within an essay by the process words that are used in the question. Table 8.4 identifies some of the process words commonly associated with each of the categories of skills and provides some elaboration on what each of these requires from the writer of the essay.

Table 8.4 Skills and process words

Skill	Indicated by...	Example
Knowledge	Words that invite a factual or descriptive response or a straightforward statement	describe, define, outline, state, identify, list, what, how, when, which
Comprehension	Words that require an explanation, interpretation, or the ability to extrapolate key information	explain, use examples, summarize, paraphrase, interpret
Application	Words that suggest the need to apply theory to different circumstances or to predict how such theories would react to a new situation	apply, demonstrate, advise, predict
Analysis	Words that indicate that a criminological principle should be broken down into its component parts and subjected to close scrutiny	analyse, assess, consider, measure, quantify, how far
Synthesis	Words that indicate the ability to draw together strands of an argument and to identify similarities and differences	justify, compare, contrast, distinguish
Evaluation	Words that indicate that whether a response to a particular issue is effective, consistent, moral, desirable, better than before, or a useful solution to a particular problem	appraise, criticize, evaluate, comment, reflect, discuss, how effective

Bloom's taxonomy demonstrates the point that a successful essay rests upon more than mere identification and explanation of the relevant theory or literature relating to a particular topic. The lower-order skills are considered to be more straightforward and easier to demonstrate, so an essay which moves beyond knowledge and comprehension to demonstrate higher-order skills is likely to be more successful. That does not mean that the lower-order skills are unimportant or should be omitted, merely that they should be considered the foundation upon which a demonstration of higher-order skills is based. In other words, you need to be able to describe criminological phenomena in order to analyse them.

It is essential that you remember that a successful essay requires an appropriate balance between description and analysis. An essay that is heavily descriptive does not demonstrate sufficient higher-order skills to achieve a high mark whilst an essay which contains insufficient description will also struggle because analysis needs to be based upon a foundation of description in order to make sense. For example, you could not comment on the accuracy of measurement of recorded crime without first describing the methods by which crimes are recorded.

Achieving the right balance between the two is a difficult task as there is no magic formula that sets out the appropriate contribution of each to an essay as this will vary according to the question. The most effective rule to apply is to include sufficient description to support the analysis; in other words, describe things that need to be understood so that the discussion will make sense to the reader.

Writing a conclusion

As with the introduction, the conclusion plays a crucial role in your essay and yet it is often absent thus leaving the marker with the distinct feeling that the student just stopped writing when they ran out of time, inspiration, or words.

Remember, the conclusion is the last thing that your marker reads before he starts deciding what grade to award. Make sure that he is left with a good impression of your work by ensuring that it has a strong conclusion that ties together the strands of the argument that you have outlined in your essay to create a direct response to the question. This should include the following:

- A statement of the aim of the essay.
- A brief reminder of the arguments that you have presented.
- An evaluation of which of any opposing views is to be preferred.
- A direct answer to the question.

Your conclusion should not, as a general rule, introduce any new material that has not been discussed in the body of your essay. It can make reference to a point that has not been discussed if it is simply there to emphasize your conclusion. For example, you might want to say 'so, in relation to the official crime statistics, it seems reasonable to borrow the words of William W. Watt and say that we should not put faith in what statistics say until we have considered carefully what they do not say'.

Remember your assessment criteria

Assessment criteria have an obvious importance to your essay as they are the criteria against which it will be marked. You should therefore make sure that you understand how essays are marked at your institution and what is expected of you. Assessment criteria tend to be agreed on a department-wide basis and identify the factors that your marker will be looking for in your essay. You may find these on an assessment feedback form that may be attached to your work when it is returned to you. It is often the case that the relevant criteria are listed and accompanied by a series of tick boxes in which the marker can indicate your level of achievement in each area as illustrated in Figure 8.7.

By looking at the categories that are listed on the feedback form, you can identify what skills are being evaluated in your work and try to ensure that these are demonstrated. Another approach that is used to communicate the assessment criteria to students is to categorize the level of skills that are expected in work that falls within a particular classification. This is demonstrated in the example shown in Figure 8.8.

There are, therefore, various methods that can be used to ascertain what skills and competences you need to demonstrate to impress your lecturers with the quality of your essay. For

	Weak	Below Average	Satisfactory	Good	Excellent
Critical analysis	☐	☐	☐	☐	☐
Research	☐	☐	☐	☐	☐
Referencing	☐	☐	☐	☐	☐
Written style, grammar, and punctuation	☐	☐	☐	☐	☐

Figure 8.7 Sample assessment criteria

FAIL: Less than 40%
A weak answer that fails to address the question posed and which shows inadequate understanding of the subject area. Little or no evidence of reading or research and reference to irrelevant materials. Significant weakness in presentation and organization as well as numerous errors of grammar and punctuation.

PASS, THIRD CLASS: 40–49%
A fair answer that provides some material of relevance to the question posed and which shows some limited understanding of the subject area. There may be some reference to supporting materials but little, if any, attempt at analysis; a highly descriptive answer with some errors and omissions. Presentation and organization are likely to be poor and there may be significant errors of grammar and punctuation.

LOWER SECOND CLASS: 50–59%
A satisfactory answer that covers a fair degree of the material of relevance to the question albeit in largely descriptive detail. There may be an attempt at analysis that is either ineffective or fails to get to grips with the issue at the heart of the question. There should be evidence of a reasonable level of understanding and an ability to incorporate some supporting materials into the answer. There may be some grammatical and presentational errors but these should not be widespread.

Figure 8.8 Example assessment criteria by classification

some reason, students often fail to take these matters into account and continue to produce essays that comply with their own personal view of a good essay. This can be extremely costly in terms of lost marks if their view does not coincide with what the lecturer considers to be a good essay. Lecturers are looking for a combination of legal knowledge and an ability to use it and thus are likely to consider the following factors to be important:

- The relevance of the material included and the arguments put forward to the question.
- Evidence of comprehension and an ability to analyse the law.
- A strong structure and clear and logical organization of material.

- Evidence of research and incorporation of wider reading into the essay.
- An appropriate written style with good grammar and punctuation.
- Full and accurate referencing including a bibliography.
- Good presentation.

Polish

It is a mistake to think that your essay is finished as soon as you have written the final word: this is just a first draft and there is still work to do to ensure that the work is ready for submission. This section covers a range of activities that should be done at the final stage of the essay-writing process to ensure that you produce a piece of work that is expressed with clarity, that develops a logical line of argument, and that has had sufficient attention paid to all aspects of its presentation. You should allow yourself plenty of time to do these things, so do not leave it until an hour before the submission deadline.

Meeting the word limit

It is usual for each piece of coursework to have a maximum word limit that must not be exceeded. Many universities have a policy of imposing a penalty, usually a deduction of marks, on work that exceeds the word limit. Students often struggle with word limits, viewing them as an annoying restriction that stops them making all the points that they want to make in their essay, but it is important that you ensure that your work does fit within the word limit.

So, what should you do to ensure that your work adheres to the word limit? The first step to take is to ensure that you know what the word limit is and what content counts toward it. The bibliography is usually excluded from the word count but what about the in-text references? You must find out what the regulations are on word counts in your university because an inadvertent contravention of the rules will still attract a penalty.

There is some difference of opinion amongst lecturers and students about whether you should try and work to the word limit as you write or whether it is preferable to get all your ideas down as you want them to be and then redraft your work to fit the word limit. This is a matter of personal preference but each approach has advantages and disadvantages as you will see from Table 8.5.

If you do find that you are over the word limit, you are going to need to find a way to reduce the number of words that you have used. There are two ways to do this: you can either cut whole sentences or paragraphs out of your essay or you can keep all of your content but try to find a way to express it in fewer words. The best approach is a combination of the two methods. Firstly, read your essay to ensure that you have not included any unnecessary points. Perhaps you have used two examples to support your argument when one would have done or maybe you have included a point because it was an interesting aside rather than being strictly relevant to the question. Once you have cut out the unnecessary material, you will have to find a more concise method of expressing the points that remain if you are still over the word limit. Look at each sentence and see if you can reword it using fewer words: even if you only reduce each sentence by a single word, that will be a significant reduction to the overall word count of the essay.

Table 8.5 Condensing text

	Advantages	Disadvantages
Condense as you write	The process of condensing your work as you write it may help you to develop a more concise and precise written style. It may also encourage you to experiment with language to find new words that express the same ideas in fewer words. It will make you really concentrate on what is essential to your essay and conscious of using words wisely.	It can be time-consuming if you find you are constantly redrafting sentences to save words and it may ultimately not be necessary. You may stifle your flow of ideas or even discard whole lines of argument that would have been useful to your essay because you are concentrating on keeping your word count low.
Condense at the end	If you write everything that you want to write as you want to say it, your ideas will all be down on paper just as you wanted to express them. It may be that you find that you do not have a problem with the word limit.	You might end up with a piece of work that is double the word limit. You have to work through it from start to finish to reduce the word count which is almost the equivalent of writing the essay again.

Structure, flow, and focus

Remember that your essay must present a flowing argument that develops in a logical way and which answers the question. This means that you need a strong structure, clear links to be made between each paragraph, and frequent references back to the question. Check that your essay has structure, flow, and focus using the following steps:

- **Structure**. Read each paragraph and describe its content in a few words. Look at the list that this produces and see if it tells a story in a logical order. If, for example, you find that your criticism of crime statistics precedes your description of how crime is counted, then it is likely that changes need to be made. Compare your list with the plan of your essay that you created before you started writing (see Figure 8.4). Departure from this plan is not necessarily a problem as your essay may not have fitted together as you expected before you started writing but it will be a useful reference point if you find that your essay does not seem to have a logical structure.

- **Flow**. Check that the relationship between the end of one paragraph and the beginning of the next is clear. If not, add signposting words and phrases to clarify the connections between your ideas as this will ensure that there is a logical development to your essay. If you find a point or a paragraph that cannot be linked to the ideas around it using signposting, then it does not belong in that part of your essay and must be moved. If you cannot find a new place where it fits, then it is likely that it does not belong in your essay at all.

- **Focus**. Does every paragraph make a contribution to the development of an argument that actually answers the question rather than simply being about the relevant topic? You might find that you need to 'touch base' with the question explicitly to strengthen your focus. You can do this by repeating key words from the question or by relating the point that you have made in your paragraph back to the question. For example, you might write 'the process of attrition makes it clear that there is a great deal more crime committed than is ever reflected in official crime statistics'.

Proof reading

It is tempting to heave a sigh of relief when the final word of your essay is written and think 'that's it done' but you should really not assume that you got everything right in your essay in the first draft. Neither should you rely on the spelling and grammar checking tools on your computer to pick up all your mistakes—there are plenty of common typing errors that the computer will miss.

Practical example: proof reading

Proof reading is an essential part of the process of ensuring that your work is fit for submission. Careless errors suggest lack of care and this is not the impression that you want your marker to have of your work. Many lecturers will deduct marks from work that is strewn with errors so it is worth taking great care to ensure that this does not happen to your essay.

1. Print a copy of your essay. It is much easier to read what you have actually written on paper than it is to spot errors on a computer screen.

2. Read it very carefully and slowly. Remember, you are not reading to find out what you have written but to spot mistakes and that requires that you pay close attention to every word. Some people find that reading out loud helps with this.

3. Circle every error and make a note in the margin as to what is wrong. You might also like to note how you intend to correct the error.

4. Pay particular attention to punctuation. If you are unsure as to whether you have used, say, a semi-colon correctly, reword your sentence so that it does not need one.

5. Use a thesaurus to check the meaning of any words if you are not confident that you have used them correctly.

6. Once you have been through the entire document, make all the necessary changes. Cross each circle made on your printed version so that you have a record of which problems have been addressed.

Ideally, you should carry out this process once again after the errors have been corrected just to be sure that no mistakes remain. Leave it overnight if possible or at least have a break of a few hours and start again with a clean printed copy of your work.

It is often easier to spot mistakes in the work of others because you will read it with fresher eyes. When you read your own work, there is a tendency to skim it because you are so familiar with its content whereas proof reading requires far more detailed attention. As such, you might find it useful to see if someone else will proof read your essay for you. Remember, though, that you must correct any errors that they spot yourself.

Referencing

You should have been adding references to your work as you wrote it so use this final stage of the essay writing process to check that all the necessary references are present, both in the text and in the bibliography. You should also ensure that your references are complete. This means that the reference in the text to specific points and quotations should include a page reference and that you should ensure that you provide full bibliographic information in your list of references.

You will find detailed guidance on when and how to reference in chapter 7.

CHAPTER SUMMARY

Preliminary analysis

- Make sure that you take time at the outset to analyse the essay rather than starting research or, worse still, writing without having identified the focus of the essay
- Rewrite the question(s) at the heart of the essay in your own words to make sure that you have a simple and clear grasp of what is required, taking care not to change the meaning of the essay

Research and planning

- Start by consulting a textbook to ensure that you have a clear understanding of the topic area but make sure that you move on to consider other materials such as monographs and articles; an essay written solely on the basis of textbook research will probably lack depth of analysis and certainly will not demonstrate impressive research skills or width of reading
- Keep careful note of the sources used in your research but try to avoid excessive note-taking that can degenerate into compulsive writing that is not accompanied by sufficient thought. Remember, you are looking for answers to a particular question, not producing a summary of all the material that you locate
- Plan a working structure for your essay that can be used as a framework for your writing. Make sure that you think about the way that your arguments will flow and never forget the importance of keeping a firm focus on the central issue of the question
- Give careful consideration to the selection of supporting materials, remembering that it is important to present a balanced argument that acknowledges different perspectives on the issue at hand

Writing the essay

- Make sure that you give yourself sufficient time to write the essay and bear in mind that the structure you have planned may not work in practice, in which case you may need to start from scratch and reorganize your arguments
- Take care to ensure that every paragraph does something to further your argument and give thought to the balance between description and analysis in your essay
- Keep a firm focus on the question; if you cannot see how a point relates to the question, it may be that it has no place in your essay. Remember, you are answering a specific question rather than merely writing about a particular topic
- The purpose of an essay is to test knowledge and understanding of the topic but also to assess the level of skill that you have in using your sources appropriately. Ensure that your essay strikes an appropriate balance between description and analysis
- Write an effective introduction and conclusion. The introduction is the first impression that your marker receives of the quality of your work whilst the conclusion is the last thing that they read, so may stick in their mind as indicative of the overall quality of your essay whilst they are marking

Polish and presentation

- Allow plenty of time to check your essay for coherence, accuracy, and consistency
- Find out what the requirements are for the presentation of essays and ensure that you adhere to these requirements to the letter. Easy marks can be lost for failing to do so and it gives the marker a poor impression of your essay if you have not troubled to follow the rules regarding the submission of coursework
- Check the presentation of your essay and, in particular, check that the referencing and bibliography are immaculate

9 Dissertations and research reports

INTRODUCTION

Many criminology students will be required to produce a longer piece of work in their final year, either in the form of a dissertation or a research report on a project involving analysis of data. This chapter explains the distinction between these two pieces of work and provides practical advice on the requirements of each. It is important to remember that there are a distinct set of skills involved in the production of these longer pieces of work that are not tested in other forms of assessment. This chapter addresses skills such as selecting a workable research question and developing an effective relationship with your supervisor as well as offering advice on organizing your workload and creating a suitable structure for your dissertation or report. However, some of the skills needed to produce a dissertation or report have already been covered earlier in the book so be sure to look back at chapters on finding source material (chapters 1–4), writing skills (chapter 6) and referencing (chapter 7) and use them to supplement the points made in this chapter.

Some students think that dissertations and reports are just long essays. Although it is true that these longer pieces of work, particularly dissertations, do share some characteristics with essays, there are also significant differences that set these pieces of work apart. In particular, they offer students the opportunity to select their own topic and to decide on an approach to conducting the research that determines the difficulty of the work and hence its potential to achieve high marks. The longer length of these pieces of work presents greater challenges in terms of structure and there is far greater emphasis on independent research involving a range of source materials. Due to the greater demands that they make, dissertations and research reports are often viewed as a real measure of the ability of the student, and the range of skills involved in their production make them a real showcase of your ability that can impress potential employers.

LEARNING OUTCOMES

After reading this chapter, you will be able to:

- Appreciate the benefits of engaging in a large piece of research and understand the distinction between a dissertation and research report
- Select an appropriate topic upon which to focus and generate a suitable research question
- Organize the workload involved in a longer project and manage your time effectively

- Conduct research in a methodical manner and keep accurate and useful records of the research trail

- Understand the contribution of a literature review to a research project

- Select an method of gathering data that is appropriate to your research question

- Produce a piece of work that is well-written, makes reference to relevant literature and takes an analytical approach

Dissertations and research reports

The first point to address is a matter of terminology so that you will be able to select the section of this chapter that is most useful to you depending on the nature of the piece of work that you are about to undertake. This is necessary as there is no consistency across criminology departments in different universities as to the terminology used to describe these longer pieces of work. This means that you might find that your university uses the word 'dissertation' to describe both types of research described in this chapter or that the term 'research report' is used for both. There is no right or wrong approach to this: both are longer pieces of work based upon independent research. It is simply the case that some institutions make a distinction between library-based research (dissertation) and research involving the analysis of data (research report) and others do not make this distinction.

Practical example: terminology

Both examples below focus on the same subject matter—reliability of eyewitness testimony in criminal trials—but differ in the way that the research is carried out and the way that source material is used.

Dissertation

A dissertation on the reliability of eyewitness testimony would use existing literature to explore the role of such evidence in criminal trials and rely on the findings of others to establish the factors that contribute to its lack of accuracy. The skill here lies in finding published sources of information on the relevant subject matter and drawing on these to answer the research question.

Research report

A research report on the reliability of eyewitness testimony would revolve around a question that can only be answered by carrying out some original data analysis: the research report would be the final output from the research project. The data that you gather from the experiment would be analysed and the findings outlined in the research report. Literature is still important to this type of work but it is used in a different way to create a setting for the research question and as a context for the findings. In essence, a question is asked that is answered by analysing data and the importance of the findings is established by reference to existing literature.

This chapter will treat these pieces of work as separate in order to explain the differences between them. There are also some common issues so these will be cross-referenced to avoid repetition in the two sections. Before doing this, the section that follows will outline the benefits of undertaking a longer piece of research-based work.

Benefits of research-based work

Some students have no choice in the matter: a dissertation or a research report may be a mandatory part of the criminology degree at their university. For other students, a dissertation or a research project may be one of the optional modules that can be taken, usually in the final year of undergraduate study. Postgraduate courses are also likely to offer students the opportunity to undertake a longer piece of work.

So, if it is a matter of choice, why might you opt to write a dissertation or carry out a research project?

- To **study an interesting topic.** Unlike most other forms of assessment that you will encounter on your criminology degree, dissertations and research projects give you the opportunity to choose your own subject matter and formulate your own research question (subject to the availability of an appropriate supervisor and approval of your research proposal to ensure that it is a viable piece of work). This means that you can pick an area of criminology that has captured your interest in lectures or tutorials and follow it up in far greater detail. Alternatively, it might be that there is a particular area of criminology of interest to you that was not covered in any of your modules so you might like to take this opportunity to carry out research on it.

- To **develop research skills.** Dissertations offer an opportunity to conduct far more wide-ranging library-based research than other pieces of coursework whilst a research project allows students to do some 'hands on' data analysis and may also involve the collection of original data. You may want to undertake a dissertation or research project in order to improve your research skills or to take advantage of the opportunity to try a different method of research.

- To **impress potential employers.** If you intend to work in a particular area after your studies are complete, you may want to undertake a research project or dissertation that reflects this interest with a view to helping you to gain employment in your chosen field. Remember that these pieces of work will demonstrate your research skills as well as your knowledge of the subject matter so they will also be a good choice if the ability to conduct research or organize larger research projects is one of the skills needed in your future career.

- To **avoid exams.** Some students opt for a dissertation or research project simply because it is a way of reducing the number of exams that they have to take in their final year. If you always perform far better in coursework than you do in examinations, it might be that a dissertation or research project is a good choice as it builds on your strengths.

Dissertations

The sections that follow will address the stages of writing a dissertation from the early issues of the choice of topic and the formulation of a research question through the research process and onto matters such as deciding on a structure and dividing the dissertation into chapters. Remember that, in this chapter, a dissertation is considered to be a piece of library-based research. If you are undertaking a dissertation in your institution that involves the collection and/or analysis of research data, then you should read the section devoted to research projects that you will find later in this chapter.

Preliminary considerations

If you have decided to write a dissertation or are giving it serious consideration then there are other questions that need to be addressed in the early stages. You need to make a decision about your choice of topic and, within this, to isolate a particular research question that will be the focus of your research. You will also need to find a suitable supervisor from amongst the academics in your department and you will need to write a dissertation proposal that sets out what it is that you intend to do and how you plan to do it.

Choosing a topic

For some students, this is a straightforward matter as it was a desire to conduct research into a particular topic that led them to opt to write a dissertation in the first place. However, most students make the more general decision that they want to write a dissertation first and then ponder the question of the topic thereafter.

There are a number of practical considerations to bear in mind when selecting a topic: there must be enough relevant literature accessible to you to enable you to carry out your research, it must be a topic that someone in your department is able and available to supervise, and the topic must be one that is capable of giving rise to a research question that can be explored in sufficient depth in the time available and within the constraints of the dissertation word limit.

A final, and often overlooked, factor is that the topic should be one that you find interesting. This is a long-term project that spans the entirety of the academic year and you will find that it is easier to maintain your enthusiasm and to keep working if the topic is one in which you have a genuine interest.

Practical exercise: finding a dissertation topic

The following are some methods that you might find useful when trying to select a dissertation topic.

1. Make a list of the five most interesting topics that you have encountered during your study of criminology from across all of the modules that you have taken so far. Take each topic and write a sentence that captures what it was that interested you. Is there anything here that could be the focus of your dissertation?

2. Crime and criminality is all around you. Have a look at a few different newspapers and see what stories about crime are being reported or think about any storylines involving crime that have been featured in your favourite television programmes and see if this gives you any inspiration for your dissertation.

3. Browse through some criminology journals and see what articles catch your eye. Not only may this give you inspiration for your dissertation, it will also give you an insight into how much literature is likely to be available on your topic so be sure to take note of any references to other source material on the topic.

4. Ask a lecturer who taught on a module that you particularly enjoyed if they can suggest a good topic. This has the additional advantage of identifying a potential supervisor.

> **5.** Think of a question involving crime, criminal justice, or offending that you would really like to be able to answer. Just let your mind wander on the general topic of crime and see if you hit on a question that starts 'I wonder why...' or 'I wonder how...' as this may identify a viable dissertation topic. You will find an example of this approach leading to a really interesting and original research project later in this chapter.

You might also find it useful when selecting a topic to think about some of the issues raised by questions that are often asked by students:

- **Can my dissertation be about something that we covered in a tutorial or in coursework?** There is no reason not to select a topic that has been covered in lectures or tutorials or that was the focus of coursework. Many students like to select such topics as they already have a foundation of understanding upon which to build and there is often a good range of source material available in the library on topics that are taught and assessed within a module. It is also the case that there will be at least one potential supervisor with expertise on the topic if it was covered in a module. The disadvantage of choosing a topic that has been taught is that you will need to move quite a long way beyond the points covered on the syllabus in order to demonstrate your research skills. The best approach is to take the topic as a starting point and try to find an interesting angle on it that was not covered in lectures or tutorials.

- **Several other students want to write their dissertation on my topic. Does that mean that I can't do it?** There are certain topics that are always a popular choice for criminology dissertations that are chosen by several students each year. That does not mean that you cannot be one of them but you should be aware that you will be in competition for resources in the library and that there is a certain extent to which you will be measured against each other to see who has produced the best dissertation (wider research, more depth of analysis, better written style). Try to avoid a direct comparison by ensuring that your research question is formulated so that you are taking a different slant on the topic to other students.

- **I want to do something completely different that isn't covered on the criminology syllabus at all. Is that going to be a problem?** There are always one or two students each year who have a really original idea for a dissertation topic. This may prove difficult if there is no supervisor available who has expertise in the subject matter but, then again, many universities take the view that the supervisor's role is to provide guidance on the process of writing a dissertation rather than to check as to the accuracy of the content. If you want to research something a bit different, try approaching a few lecturers to seek their views on whether your idea is a good one and ask whether they would be able to supervise it. You may find that your topic does fall within their expertise or that your ideas have provoked their interest and they are happy to supervise you.

Formulating a research question

Once you have chosen a research topic, the next stage is to narrow your focus further by deciding what research question will be at the heart of your dissertation. Just as an essay will have a stronger focus if you concentrate on what the question asks rather than what it is about (see chapter 8), your dissertation is about a particular topic but it must also ask a question that you set out to answer.

Students often find it difficult to identify a research question. However, it is really just a matter of refining your research idea so that you are clear about the particular aspect of the chosen topic that you are focusing on and then rewriting this as a question.

Practical example: finding a research question

Try the following method to see if it helps you to sharpen your focus and identify a research question.

1. Take your dissertation topic and ask what is it about this topic that you are interested in. There might be a number of different aspects so list all that occur to you.

2. Capture each of these ideas in a single sentence.

3. Reformulate this sentence in the form of a question.

4. Check to ensure that your research question is not too broad or too narrow and make any necessary adjustments. You can do this by looking to see how the literature tackles the topic or you can seek guidance from your potential supervisor or personal tutor.

For example, your main topic might be domestic violence but there are a number of different ideas within this topic that could be the focus of your dissertation. You might be interested in how effective the law is at controlling domestic violence or in exploring the impact of domestic violence on the children of the relationship. Perhaps you are interested in domestic violence in same-sex couples or in the setting of particular religions. Any of these issues could be the focus of your dissertation and could lead to the following research questions:

- How effective is the current law at controlling domestic violence?
- Does violence beget violence? Do children of abusive relationships go on to be abusers?
- Is adequate support provided for victims of domestic violence in same-sex relationships?
- What are the particular considerations in policing domestic violence in Muslim relationships?

Choosing a supervisor

In some institutions, students are allocated to an appropriate supervisor on the basis of their expertise in the topic chosen by the student. However, some institutions allow students to choose their own supervisors or at least to express a preference as to their supervisor. If you do have the ability to make a choice, you should talk to all the potential supervisors to see what ideas they have about how your dissertation should be tackled and to get a feel for which of these you would most like to work with on your dissertation. Of course, it may be that you are not successful in getting your first choice supervisor and you should remember that all of the lecturers in your department will be able to offer a good level of support to guide you through your dissertation.

Writing a proposal

Not all universities require that students submit a full dissertation proposal as part of the procedure of signing up to undertake a dissertation: some institutions require nothing more than students stating that they wish write a dissertation and giving a broad indication of the proposed focus of the dissertation. However, in some institutions, places to undertake a dissertation are limited and the selection process involves the students submitting a dissertation proposal.

A detailed proposal will require a fair amount of thought, planning, and research. It is possible that your university will have particular requirements in terms of the points to be covered in the dissertation proposal. Make sure you find out whether this is the case and, if so, ensure that you adhere to the requirements of your particular institution.

If no guidance is provided on the content of the dissertation proposal, you might like to consider including the following points.

- State the research question and explain the scope of your dissertation.

- Explain why the topic that you have selected is interesting and how it raises an important question that is worthy of research. This is your justification for wanting to write a dissertation so it is important that you provide a sound rationale for your choice of subject matter.

- Outline the literature that has been identified on the topic so far and state the steps that will be taken to identify further relevant source material. This could involve listing details of books and journal articles, identifying databases that will be searched, or noting any authors that you have found who seem to be specialists on the topic.

- Provide a preliminary indication of how the dissertation might be organized in terms of the number and content of chapters. This is only an indication of possible content and structure to establish that you have given thought to what material could be included and how it might be organized. It is inevitable that changes will be necessary as your research uncovers points that you had not initially realized would be included and that your structure will alter once writing is under way and you fit the strands of your argument together.

You will find an example of a dissertation proposal that illustrates these points at Figure 9.1. This will provide you with some insight into how a proposal could look but remember that you should find out what points your own university expects to be covered and what its requirements are in terms of the length of the proposal and the level of detail that is expected about source material.

Planning and organization

Your studies can be broken down into a series of activities with deadlines. You have some deadlines every week (seminar preparation) and others a couple of times a term (coursework submission) and one event occurring a fair time after everything else has finished (exams). This gives you a working pattern of regular seminar preparation with intermittent bursts of activity when coursework is due and a final push at the end when the exams are looming. Consider how the process of researching and writing your dissertation will fit into this pattern.

Allocate time and establish milestones

Remember in particular that your dissertation is one of the modules that you are taking and, as such, that you should try to ensure that you do some work on it each week just as you would with your other modules. Some students start their dissertation with a flurry of enthusiasm but this tails off as other pieces of work with a more immediate deadline crop up and then the dissertation seems to get forgotten until its deadline is looming. This is not a good strategy as you might find that problems occur that mean you cannot work effectively in the time remaining: you might be ill, your supervisor might be ill or otherwise away from the university, or you might find that you cannot get hold of the materials that you need. Most importantly, you will find that you have not left yourself enough time to think about the dissertation and to develop your ideas properly. There is also a risk, depending on the date for

---

'I done a bad murder'– Multiple homicides and the media.

Research question

David Sowerbutts, a character in the BBC series *Psychoville*, became embroiled in a series of murders with his mother, Maureen. Katie Price revealed in the *Sun* that she is 'captivated' by the world of serial killers and wants to make a TV series in which she would interview 'Britain's Worst Criminals'. There are a range of lurid true-crime books such as *The Only Living Witness* (Ted Bundy) and *Killer Clown* (John Gacy). There has been an intense public fascination with multiple killers since Jack the Ripper and the Whitechapel murders in the late 1800s, through Ted Bundy, to Dr Harold Shipman, convicted in 2000. This dissertation will explore the extent to which media depictions of multiple killers contribute to their public allure. It will compare and contrast the criminological understanding of multiple homicide with its media image. The question that will be addressed at the heart of this dissertation is 'do media depictions of serial killers contribute to a disproportionate fear within contemporary UK society'?

The importance of the research

The current public interest in true crime, and especially horrific true crime, could contribute to an increasing culture of fear. This research will aim to demonstrate, by way of a content analysis of mediated depictions of multiple killers, the extent to which the public perception of the phenomenon is at odds with the objective statement of its key characteristics. As such, it will shine an important light onto the contribution made by amplified and sensationalized media coverage to societal views of risk.

The literature

There is very little reliable data available on the extent of serial killing; much of that which has been published is based on the data collected from as little as four or five offenders and is largely anecdotal (Ressler & Shachtman, 1992 and Douglas & Olshaker, 1999). Other comparative studies of multiple homicides were conducted throughout the 1980s (Levin & Fox, 1985; Leyton, 1986; Ressler, Burgess & Douglas, 1988) and a typology of multiple homicide was put forward by Holmes and Holmes (1998). Offenders who have been classified as serial murderers (Nelson, 2004) are very limited in numbers and are difficult to study. However, there has been substantial research exploring developmental and motivational factors of these offenders (Ressler, Burgess & Douglas, 1988; Jenkins, 1994; Lester, 1995; Egger, 1998; Schlesinger, 2004). This research will further explore the literature on media construction of criminality in general and of killers, and multiple killers in particular. It is expected that the majority of this literature will be US based, but the general findings should be equally applicable to the UK within which social context the comparison with the media depictions will be undertaken.

Proposed structure

Introduction

Chapter 1: A history of multiple killers and public interest

Chapter 2: Literature review: the criminology of multiple homicide

Chapter 3: A content analysis of UK television and newspaper coverage of multiple killers

Chapter 4: An evaluation of media depictions versus criminological studies

Conclusion

Figure 9.1 Example of a dissertation proposal

submission of dissertations at your university, that you will have to spend time writing your dissertation when you should be revising for your exams.

You might find the following suggestions useful to help you to organize and manage your time:

- **Allocate regular time to your dissertation.** This might be two one-hour slots a week, a whole day every fortnight or one full weekend each month depending on your other commitments and whether you prefer to work in frequent short bursts or in more concentrated periods of time. You should review the amount of time allocated on a regular basis and make adjustments if you (or your supervisor) feel that you are not making sufficient progress.

- **Put it on your timetable.** This will help you to be disciplined in your approach to your dissertation and ensure that you get into the habit of working on it regularly. Once it is on your timetable, treat it as an immovable obligation in the same way that you would a tutorial.

- **Set yourself milestones.** Decide at the start of your dissertation what you want to achieve each month. Make sure that you set realistic targets as it can be very disappointing not to achieve the objectives that you set for yourself—students who plan to finish their dissertations before Christmas very rarely do so! Each month, look at the milestones that you need to achieve and break this down into a series of smaller tasks. Decide when you will do each of these and add it to your timetable.

Practical example: setting milestones

Try to think about the different activities involved in each of the tasks that you set yourself as part of your dissertation planning.

October: conduct research for chapters 1 and 2.

- Search databases, Internet, and textbooks to create a list of relevant literature.
- Browse through journals in the library looking for useful source material.
- Borrow relevant books, print or copy journal articles.
- Order literature using inter-library loan.
- Make a note of how source material might be relevant to each chapter.
- Start a bibliography.

By breaking the task of research down into a series of smaller tasks, you will have a clearer idea as to what you need to do during this month and you will be able to estimate how long this will take and add it to your timetable.

Bear in mind that your university may impose a certain structure on your dissertation by establishing a timetable of meetings with your supervisor and milestones that have to be met by certain dates. Check your course information to see if there are is a compulsory meeting structure or specific milestones that you need to meet. You will find an example in Figure 9.2.

Organizing your research

A dissertation is a much longer piece of work than you are used to producing and it is carried out over a longer period of time. This means that you should conduct far more research and generate many more notes than would usually be the case when preparing a piece of coursework. It is important that you find a way to keep a track of searches that you have carried out in particular databases and the literature that it uncovered or you will end up replicating work that you have already done. It might be a good idea to keep a list that details the database searched, the search terms used and the literature that it uncovered. This should include any refinements that you needed to make to broaden or narrow your search. You should also note whether each piece of source material seems relevant to your dissertation and, if so, whether

Schedule of Dissertation Meetings

A failure to attend the compulsory meetings or adhere to the deadlines specified will be penalized by a deduction of 5 marks when the final mark for the dissertation is awarded.

Week 1	Students taking a dissertation module <u>must attend</u> the lecture given by Dr Harris.
Week 2	First compulsory meeting with supervisor to discuss aims of dissertation.
Week 4	Draft breakdown of chapters to be sent to supervisor.
Week 5	Second compulsory meeting with supervisor to discuss chapter breakdown and progress.
Week 9	Draft of first chapter to be sent to supervisor.
Week 10	Third compulsory meeting with supervisor to discuss draft chapter.
Week 20	Fourth compulsory meeting with supervisor to discuss progress.
Week 24	Dissertation submission deadline (May 3rd by 12 noon).

Students should note that it may be possible to see their supervisor at other times by arrangement.

Figure 9.2 Schedule of dissertation meetings

you have obtained it. A spreadsheet or table would be a good way to record this information as illustrated in Table 9.1.

You will find further information on planning a search strategy in chapter 2.

Another aspect of organization of your research relates to the way that you deal with source material once you have obtained it. Do you make notes about each article that you find? This can make you feel as if you are working hard but, as discussed in chapter 6, it is not necessarily a very effective use of your time as you often end up with a shortened version of the article written out by hand. You might find the following technique to be a more effective way of identifying and recording points that are relevant to your dissertation.

Table 9.1 Research trail

Database	Search Terms	Articles Found	Found
PsycARTICLES	Expert Witness in keyword field	More than 50	
		Narrow search	
	Expert Witness and Child Witnesses in keyword field	None	
		Broaden search	
	Expert Witness in keyword field and Child Witness in all text field	1 only	Yes
		Allen (1995) Expert as Educator	
	Child Witnesses in all keyword field and suggestibility in all text field	30	
		Narrow search	
	As above with NOT false memory in all text	4 found, 1 relevant	Not yet
		Nikonova (2005) Juror Perceptions of Child Witnesses	

Practical example: effective note-taking

This method of note-taking will ensure that you read each piece of source material with a purpose, with a view to identifying the parts of it that have a role to play in your dissertation.

1. Identify themes that are likely to occur in your dissertation. For example, if your research is about the role of vulnerable witnesses in the criminal justice system, one theme might be the emergence of concerns about vulnerable witnesses, another might be the developments in law to protect vulnerable witnesses, and a third might be concerns about the impact of special measures on a defendant's right to a fair trial.

2. Read the article through once to get an idea of the arguments that it makes. As you read, highlight key passages or make notes in the margin when you encounter points that are useful to your dissertation. This will be even more efficient if you develop a system of colour coding or abbreviations that categorizes the points according to the themes that you have identified.

3. Make notes about each theme on a separate page. Instead of copying points out of the article, simply write the author's name and date, the page number of the article on which the point can be found, and a brief description of the point as illustrated below.

Fairness to the Defendant

Osk (1999, p. 43) argues that every change in the way that witnesses give evidence has the potential to erode the defendant's presumption of innocence that is an integral part of his right to a fair trial.

Osk (1999, p. 55) useful quotation from *R* v. *C (a child)* about the potentially prejudicial effect of special measures. Need to read this case.

Gartree and Bosworth (2003, pp 149–150) summarize other cases that have criticized special measures for interfering with the defendant's right to a fair trial.

Vernon (2010, p. 7) suggests that the use of screens prejudices the jury who assume that the victim needs to be protected from the defendant. References to other studies by Vernon that I need to find.

Vernon (2010, p. 11) useful quotation that begins 'There is no longer any scope' and ends 'dismal failure'.

Research and writing

The success (or otherwise!) of your dissertation rests on a combination of the quality of your research and the way that your understanding of the subject matter of your dissertation is expressed in writing. The skills involved in identifying and locating relevant source material were covered in chapters 1–4 whilst you will find useful information about writing and referencing in chapters 6 and 7. The remainder of this section will focus on points about research and writing that have particular relevance to your dissertation and is based around common questions asked by dissertation students.

- **I've been told to use 'a wide range of source material' but I've only found articles.** Research is the foundation of a successful dissertation so it is essential that you demonstrate your ability to identify a good range of source material. This might involve a variety of different types of source material, such as books, monographs, articles, official publications, case law, and web resources, or a quantity of a narrower range of materials. There is certainly no numerical requirement that you must use seven different types of source material or 50 different articles to get a good mark but your marker is looking for evidence that you have researched widely and thoroughly.

- **What can I include other than books and articles?** There are chapters that outline the different types of source material that you might use when conducting research in criminology earlier in this book (see chapters 1–4). You might want to include sources of law such as statutes and cases, media output such as films and television programmes, debates in Parliament, or material produced on the Internet by interest groups. Remember, though, that you should only include material because it makes a relevant contribution to your dissertation and not simply for the sake of increasing the range of source material used.

- **A lot of my articles are in psychology journals. Does it matter?** Remember that criminology draws on a diverse range of disciplines such as psychology, law, economics, and sociology. If the subject matter of your dissertation is covered in psychology journals then you should use these articles but be sure that you understand what you are reading and remember to search in other disciplines for material too.

- **I've done a lot of research but I haven't started writing yet and everyone else I know has written at least a chapter.** Some students get really immersed in the research process and are determined to track down every piece of information on their topic before they start writing. Thorough research is important but it is counterproductive if you do not leave yourself sufficient time to dedicate to the writing process. Avoid this problem by starting to write at an early stage of your dissertation so that you combine the research and writing processes. It might also be the case that 'everyone else you know' is in the same position as you, but trying to make themselves feel better by claiming to have written a lot—students are not always truthful creatures!

- **When should I start writing?** You should start writing as soon as possible: the longer you delay, the harder it can be to start writing. There is no need to complete your research on the first chapter in order to start writing it. Start with something that you know that you are going to include in your dissertation—a definition of a central concept or an explanation of the core subject matter—and write it. You should feel more confident about the whole dissertation process once you start writing and you will then have something to show your supervisor who can comment on whether your written style and approach to referencing is appropriate.

- **I don't know how to divide my dissertation into chapters.** This is a common problem. One technique that can be helpful is to break your dissertation down into three, four, or five separate questions that need to be answered and create separate chapters around these questions. It might also help to identify the first and last chapters (which are usually easier to spot) and then see how you might divide up what is left. A chronological approach can also be useful: how did things used to be, how are they now, and how might they be in the future? It might be useful to discuss the different possible structures and chapter divisions with your supervisor.

- **Shall I use sub-headings in my chapters?** With a piece of work of this length, it is perfectly permissible to use headings and sub-headings providing the rules relating to dissertations at your university do not prohibit this. Have a look at any guidelines that you have been given on presenting your dissertation to see what they say on this point. Remember, though, that headings are no substitute for structure so make sure that your points are still in a logical order and that the direction of your argument is clearly signposted.

- **Some of my references are missing or incomplete.** This is a problem as you will be expected to provide complete references and full bibliographic details for all your source material. The answer is to ensure that you capture all the necessary information about each of your sources right from the start by creating a separate bibliography file and ensuring that you update it every time you find a new source, or by using a bibliographic software package. You should also make sure that you make a note of page references for quotations and specific points (see chapter 7 for further guidance on referencing).

- **My supervisor won't help me with my structure/writing/content.** Problems arise in the supervisor–student relationship if there is a misunderstanding about what sort of support will be provided. If your supervisor has refused to help you with a particular aspect of your dissertation, it is likely to be because of constraints on permissible assistance imposed by the regulations at your university. Check the regulations to make sure that you are not making unrealistic demands on your supervisor. If necessary, you could email your supervisor and explain (politely) that you are stuck on something that you think they should be able to help you with and ask for an appointment. Alternatively, you could seek guidance from a study support advisor or your personal tutor.

- **I'm worried that there might be mistakes in my dissertation.** This is a cause for concern. Inaccurate or incomplete content will have an adverse effect on your mark as will errors in referencing or grammar, spelling, and punctuation. Make sure that your research is thorough and that your information is up-to-date. If you are struggling to understand a concept that needs to be included, make sure that you take the time to puzzle it out rather than ignoring it and hoping that your markers will not notice. In terms of presentational errors, aim to finish your dissertation a week before the deadline so that you can proof read it thoroughly. It can be hard to notice your own errors so you might find it useful to offer to swap with another student and proof read for each other. Careless errors suggest lack of care so it is worth taking the time to make sure that your work is perfect before it is submitted.

Research reports

This part of the chapter deals with the production of a research report that outlines the findings of a research project. A research project is taken to be a piece of work that involves some analysis of data that may or may not have been gathered by the student. In other words, there must be some data analysis, but the data may have been provided by the university for students to use in their projects rather than requiring them to gather data for themselves.

The approach that you take to the research project will depend upon whether it is exploratory or experimental in nature.

- **Exploratory research** aims to find out more information about a particular topic. It uses inductive reasoning—sometimes called a 'bottom up' approach—to identify patterns in the data and create a theory that explains the observed data. An example of exploratory research in criminology would be an investigation of public perceptions of the fairness of sentencing in burglary cases.

- **Experimental research** is a deductive method of research that reflects a 'top down' approach as it starts with a theory from which a hypothesis is formed that predicts that a certain relationship will exist between variables. For example, you could design research to test the hypothesis that people under the age of 25 are more likely than older people to use the Internet to research the background of a case if they were serving on a jury.

The differences between these approaches are illustrated in Figure 9.3.

It seems to be the case that exploratory research is viewed as a safer option by students as its aim is to find out more about a topic whereas experimental research puts forward a hypothesis

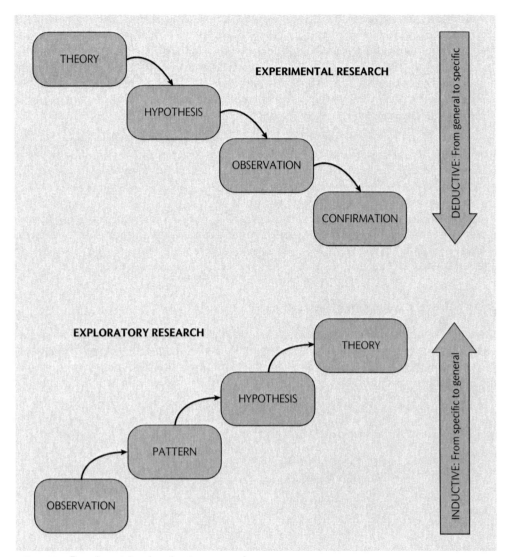

Figure 9.3 Experimental and exploratory research

which may or may not be supported by the data that is gathered. Some students fear that their research will have no value and, as a consequence, will receive a low mark if the hypothesis is not supported. It is true that it is not possible to predict whether or not your hypothesis will be supported by the data that you collect; however, it is not the case that a finding that the hypothesis not supported makes your research worthless. If your hypothesis is not supported, there are only two other options:

- **Your hypothesis is incorrect**. This is still a valuable finding and one that furthers the over-all store of understanding of the subject matter. This is because you have eliminated one potential relationship between two variables thus leaving future research to explore other possibilities. For example, using the example about jurors and the Internet, perhaps the age parameters need to be altered to see if there is an age group that is more likely to research a case online if they were called for jury service.

- **Your results are inconclusive.** This suggests a flaw in your experimental design—perhaps you did not use the best method of gathering data to provide an answer to the question—but all is not lost because you can explore the reasons for this outcome in your discussion session and suggest ways in which the research design could have been altered to produce more conclusive results. This shows your reflective awareness of the limitations of your research and suggests a more productive approach thus offering something to researchers who explore the same hypothesis in the future.

In essence, try not to be deterred from undertaking experimental research because you fear that your findings will not be useful: a negative finding is just as valuable a contribution to the body of knowledge as a positive finding and the risk of inconclusive results can be minimized by taking a careful and thorough approach to research design, particularly in terms of choosing a method of data collection.

The sections that follow will outline the stages of carrying out research, drawing a distinction between the approach taken in exploratory and experimental research where necessary. You will also find it useful to look at the discussion on organizing and writing a large piece of research that can be found earlier in this chapter in the section on Dissertations.

Formulating a research question

The most important element of a research project is the research question. The aim of the project is to answer the question so it is crucial that every aspect of the project maintains a strong focus on the question and every decision about the way that the project is conducted is made with the research question at the forefront of your mind (see Figure 9.4).

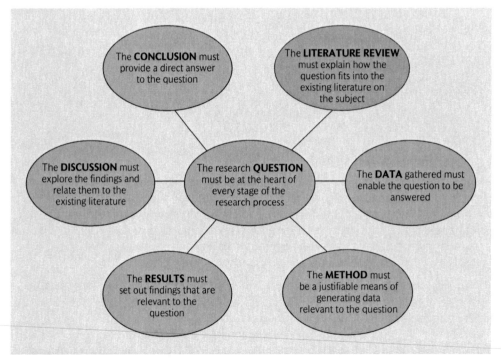

The **CONCLUSION** must provide a direct answer to the question

The **LITERATURE REVIEW** must explain how the question fits into the existing literature on the subject

The **DISCUSSION** must explore the findings and relate them to the existing literature

The research **QUESTION** must be at the heart of every stage of the research process

The **DATA** gathered must enable the question to be answered

The **RESULTS** must set out findings that are relevant to the question

The **METHOD** must be a justifiable means of generating data relevant to the question

Figure 9.4 Question at the heart of the research

Irrespective of whether the research that you plan to undertake is exploratory or experimental, it is important that you formulate a question that is clear and unambiguous. If your question is not clear, the person marking your report will not be able to see whether your research has achieved its objective. It will also be harder for you to keep a focus if the boundaries of your research are not set out with clarity. Your question must also be viable in the sense that it is possible for you to conduct the research necessary to answer the question within the time available and with the resources at your disposal. The question should also not be too wide or too narrow.

Practical example: refining a research question

Consider the following research question. Do you think that the question gives a sufficiently clear insight into the issue at the heart of the research?

- Are community penalties a better way of dealing with young offenders?

The main difficulty concerns the use of the word 'better'. It suggests a comparison between community penalties and some other unidentified method of disposal. The question can be clarified by specifying the alternative method in the question.

- Are community penalties better than incarceration at dealing with young offenders?

This question is still too vague as there is no clue as to the way in which one system could be considered better than the other. This is not helped by the generality of the words 'dealing with young offenders'. The comparison could be undertaken from a number of perspectives, all of which would fit within the question. It could be an investigation of which approach is a more effective method of punishment, which is the most cost-effective solution for the criminal justice system, or which offers the most satisfying outcome for victims of young offenders. As such, further elaboration is needed in order to pinpoint the focus of the research.

- Are community penalties more successful than incarceration in reducing re-offending rates in young offenders?

However, although the question is now far clearer, it may still be too wide as the factors that influence re-offending may vary enormously according to the nature of the offence committed. A further narrowing of the focus of the research would make this a more manageable project.

- Are community penalties more successful than incarceration in reducing re-offending rates in young offenders who commit alcohol-related property offences?

It is also a good idea to try and formulate a question in which you have a genuine interest in the answer. Criminology is a vast discipline that covers a wide range of subject matter so you ought to be able to find at least one question that you would really like to answer. This can be difficult—it is far easier to identify a general area of criminology in which you want to research than it is to formulate a particular question. Look at the suggestions for finding a research topic in the dissertations section above or try the following activity with some friends.

> **Practical exercise: finding a research question**
>
> 1. Work with at least two other students. Each student should identify two general topics in criminology on which they would consider carrying out research and write them on a slip of paper. The papers are placed in the centre of the table.
>
> 2. Each student takes a slip of paper and, without any discussion, writes at least one interesting question on the topic on a separate piece of paper. Repeat this until each topic has been circulated to all the students present.
>
> 3. Compile a list of all the questions relating to each topic and, through discussion, try to generate a preferred question that may be one of those listed, a combination of several questions, or an entirely new idea that emerges from the discussion.
>
> *You will find the results of such an exercise on the Online Resource Centre along with a note of the questions that the students concerned used in their projects.*

Alternatively, you could just think of a question that interests you that relates to some aspect of criminology, perhaps based upon some situation you have encountered in everyday life. For example, a student supervised by one of the authors gained inspiration from an accident that he witnessed on his way to a tutorial. He came in late, interrupting a discussion of the difficulties of formulating a research question, and said 'why do cyclists think they don't have to stop at red lights?' and another student responded 'you should research it'. The project that resulted was based on questionnaires and interviews with cyclists and was entitled 'Selective Compliance: Cyclists' Perceptions of Road Traffic Law'.

Writing a literature review

The literature review is an essential component of a research report. Its role is to justify the existence of your research project by showing how it fills a gap in the existing knowledge. It also demonstrates that you have read widely when researching for your project and that you have an up-to-date and comprehensive knowledge of the subject matter. Finally, it also serves a very practical purpose of ensuring that you are familiar with the research that has already been done in your area of interest thus ensuring that you do not duplicate work that is already in existence.

It is not just a summary or description of the literature. It gives an overview of the literature on the topic of your research, outlining the findings and arguments of key authors, and emphasizing areas of consensus and pointing out issues upon which there is disagreement. It should identify the main theories and hypotheses and highlight the questions that have been asked about the topic. It should also establish what methods have been used to conduct research thus far and draw attention to any gaps that this identifies. By doing this, you will be able to show how your study builds on previous research and will therefore contribute something new to the literature.

One of the challenges of creating a literature review involves a decision as to how to organize its content. It should start with an introduction that defines the parameters of the topic and conclude by summarizing the current state of knowledge on the topic and emphasizing any flaws in the methods used and/or gaps and contradictions in the existing research in order to highlight areas for further study. It is the organization of the analysis of the literature that goes in between the introduction and conclusion that is more complex. There are various possible approaches:

- **Chronologically**. This is quite a straightforward approach that starts with the earliest research and works through to the current day. It is a useful method of organizing your literature review if there is clear evidence that thinking on the topic has evolved over a period of time but it would be a poor choice in the absence of any historical pattern to trends in the research.

- **Theoretically.** It may be the case that research on the topic can be divided into two or more theoretical perspectives. Perhaps there is a dominant theoretical viewpoint on the subject matter and evidence of criticism of that position or, alternatively, there may be several strong opposing viewpoints. It is a good choice if you intend to approach the topic from a different theoretical perspective to that covered in the existing literature. Obviously, this would not be a sensible approach in relation to research that does not fit into clear categories of criminological theory.

- **Methodologically.** The review could be organized according to the methods used in the literature. A basic delineation into qualitative and quantitative methods could be further sub-divided according to the statistical tests used or the methods used to generate data. This is the most useful approach if there is evidence to suggest that any lack of agreement in findings in the research could be attributable to the use of different methods or if there is a gap in the literature arising from the absence of a particular method that you intend to use in your research.

- **Thematically.** Thematic organization groups the literature together according to particular approaches to the topic or lines or argument. You will need to survey the literature carefully in order to identify the relevant themes. If the literature does not present a chronological pattern and there is no obvious way to group it according to theory or method then you will need to identify themes within your source material in order to organize your literature review. Of course, you may choose a thematic approach to organization even if one of the other methods is available as it can be a really powerful way of emphasizing the key debates and perspectives on a topic.

Practical exercise: organizing the literature review

 Take a look at the two extracts from literature reviews provided here. Make a note of the differences between them. Which do you think offers a more useful approach? Compare your thoughts with the commentary provided on the Online Resource Centre.

Extract 1

There is very little reliable data available on the extent of serial killing. Much of the literature that has been published is based on data collected from as little as four or five offenders which is largely anecdotal (Ressler & Shachtman 1992 and Douglas & Olshaker 1999). Other comparative studies of multiple homicides were conducted throughout the 1980s (Levin & Fox 1985; Leyton 1986; Ressler, Burgess, & Douglas 1988) and a typology of multiple homicide was put forward by Holmes and Holmes (1998). Offenders who have been classified as serial murderers (Nelson 2004) are very limited in numbers and are difficult to study.

Extract 2

Whoever Fights Monsters (Ressler and Shachtmann 1992) recounts interviews with such murderers as Edmund Kemper, Charles Manson, John Wayne Gacy, William Heirens, and Ted Bundy. It corrects the misleading, romanticized criminal profiles found in the novels of Thomas Harris and Mary Higgins Clark, discusses how Ressler compiled his profiles of actual criminals who were later apprehended, and tells how he worked with mental-health professionals to explore killers' personality traits.

Douglas and Olshaker (1999) consider the motivations behind serial, mass, and spree killings in *The Anatomy of Motive* (1999), considering cases such as Dunblane, the Chicago Tylenol poisonings, and the Unabomber, Ted Kaczynski.

Irrespective of the method of organization used, it is always essential that you remember that your literature review must centre on your research question. Its aim is to provide a justification for your research project so it is important that you situate your research within the literature by highlighting the gap that it will fill or the way in which it will use a different method to supplement existing knowledge.

Practical exercise: analysing the literature

It can be difficult to decide what information to include in the literature review. There has to be sufficient detail to ensure that a clear picture is presented of previous research but not so much detail that your review becomes too descriptive. You might find it useful to use the following questions to help you to extrapolate useful information from each piece of source material.

1. What is the focus of the author's work?

2. What is the author's main argument? Is it persuasive, objective, and well grounded?

3. What weaknesses or omissions could be made about the author's work?

4. Do other commentators agree or disagree with the author?

5. What has the author contributed to the field of knowledge on the topic?

6. How does the author's work relate to your study?

 Have a look at the articles on white-collar crime that you will find on the Online Resource Centre. Use these questions to identify the key points that you would want to include in your literature review and think about which method you would use to organize your review.

Selecting a method

A research project requires a great deal of planning so it is a good idea to decide what method of data collection will be used in your project as early as possible, preferably when you formulate your research question. Of course, your initial decision may change once you read the literature as you may find that your method has already been used or you may find inspiration in the literature that prompts you to select a different method of gathering data. Some students find that they reach a preliminary decision by a process of elimination. In other words, they rule out methods that they do not want to use and keep an open mind about those remaining until they have surveyed the literature. This is not necessarily a bad approach but do bear in mind that some methods of data collection are more time-consuming than others—either in terms of preparation, administration, or analysis—so it is important that you have a clear idea of what needs to be done at as early a stage as possible so that you can make sensible decisions about how to plan your time.

There is a detailed discussion of methods of data collection in chapter 13 but Table 9.2 summarizes these methods and sets out factors to take into account when making a decision about which method to use.

Table 9.2 Research methods summary

	Considerations	Advantages	Disadvantages
Interviews	• Tend to give rise to qualitative data. Ethical clearance will be needed. • Content or discourse analysis are common methods of analysis. • Generally used in exploratory rather than experimental research.	• May provide original insights into the topic that have not previously been explored. • Flexible method that allows diversion from planned discussion to pursue interesting points raised by participant.	• Time-consuming to arrange, conduct, and transcribe. • May involve expense if travelling is involved. • Participants may not say what you expect them to say.
Questionnaires	• Predominantly quantitative data. • Can use descriptive and inferential statistics. • Can be used for exploratory or experimental research depending on the questions asked.	• A useful method of eliciting information from a large number of participants. • Can be used to gather quantitative and qualitative data.	• Design is complicated and may involve several drafts and pilots before the wording and question order is correct. • Completion rates tend to be quite low so it may be hard to get as much data as you would like.
Experiments	• Predominantly quantitative data. • Used for experimental research. • Statistical tests are used to explore the relationship between the dependant and independent variables.	• Can be replicated by others using the same method so is often seen as giving rise to more reliable and scientific findings. • Provides potential to test relationships between variables in innovative ways.	• It can be tricky to get the design right. • It may be difficult to find participants for long or onerous experiments unless payment or some other incentive is offered.
Focus groups	• Predominantly qualitative data. • Used for exploratory research. • Data is analysed by content or discourse analysis.	• Group discussion may lead to richer data than interviews. • Participant interactions may lead discussion thus minimizing risk of researcher bias.	• Can be difficult to keep the discussion on track. • Dominant participants may skew the data.
Observations	• Qualitative or quantitative data. • Used mainly for exploratory research.	• Provides the opportunity to gather data in a natural setting. • Offers the potential for original insights that could not be gained by any other manner.	• Covert observation is controversial as it precludes the possibility of obtaining consent. • Difficult to control the environment so data may be diluted or incomplete.

It is also important to remember that all of these methods will require ethical approval from your university. This is discussed in detail in chapter 12. In terms of planning, remember that the process of getting a favourable ethical opinion can be quite time-consuming, particularly if you need to respond to particular concerns raised by the reviewers. It is therefore sensible to begin the ethical review procedure as early as possible.

Structure of a research report

In the following sections, the structure of a typical research report is outlined. There may be some differences between institutions in terms of the names given to the headings but the basic structure should be similar. It is usual for a research report to start with an abstract that summarizes the report and for this to be followed by an explanation of the question at the heart of the research and a section that sets this question in context by outlining relevant literature. The method used to gather data is then explained and the findings set out. This is followed by a general discussion of the implications of the findings in light of the existing literature and some comment on directions for future research. Each of these components of a research report will be outlined in the sections that follow.

Abstract

Although the abstract is the first part of a research report, it is usually the last part of the report that you would write. This is because the abstract is a summary of the report that is placed at the beginning to give the reader an overview of the content of the report.

The abstract should not be too long and it should be expressed in a concise manner. Make sure that you do not include points that should be included in other parts of the report: it is quite common for students to include material that should be in the introduction or the discussion section. It is fine to touch on points that are included in these sections but make sure that you are not too detailed in doing so.

The overall length of the abstract may be determined by your university as it is sometimes the case that students are given a word limit for each element of the report. If this is not the case, you will have to decide how much detail to include but remember that it should never exceed 10% of the overall length of the report.

The abstract should summarize your research, focusing on the results and significant conclusions. It should be a stand-alone statement of the content of the report so should not make reference to any other part of the report, so do not use the abstract to steer the reader to particular sections. It should also not include any figures, tables, or diagrams. If you think of your report as a film that tells a particular story, then your abstract is the trailer for that film: it gives you an insight into what it is going to be about with a few key highlights, but without revealing so much detail that 'watching' it (that is, reading the report) is unnecessary.

Introduction

This section of the report sets out the focus of the research and provides a statement of the research question. It should explain the relevance of this question to its broader topic and to the discipline of criminology. In doing so, however, you should take care not to encroach on the literature review section of the report.

There should be an explanation of your hypothesis and an outline of how the method deployed is suitable as a means of generating data to answer that question. The objectives of the research should be set out and the anticipated results stated.

Literature review

The literature review provides a context for the research by setting out the background against which the research question is asked. It draws upon literature associated with the subject matter of the research to explain what knowledge already exists and how the research that you have conducted fits into this body of knowledge.

This is an important section of the report as it is by establishing that there is a gap in the existing literature that you justify your decision to carry out your piece of research to fill that gap. As such, it is essential that your investigation of the existing literature is comprehensive to ensure that you are not, through incomplete exploration of the literature, seeking to fill a gap that does not actually exist.

Method

This section should set out what you did to generate data. If you used more than one method of collecting data, you should explain here how these methods complemented each other and why this approach has more to offer than the use of one of the methods alone. If, with hindsight, you feel that your method was not the most effective one that you could have used, this section is not the place to set this out. Any limitations on the effectiveness of the research should be addressed in the discussion or conclusion sections.

There are a number of issues to address in this section:

- **Sampling**. You should also outline the size and composition of your sample and explain your sampling strategy (see chapter 13). Again, if you feel that your sample was too small or unrepresentative, this should not be addressed in this section but raised in the discussion or conclusion section. In essence, the method section is an account of what you did and how you did it: it is not the place to comment on the weaknesses of your approach.

- **Variables**. If your research was experimental in nature, you should use the method section to identify the dependant and independent variables and explain how these were manipulated.

- **Method of analysis**. Although there is a separate analysis section in your report, it should be used to outline the results of your analysis rather than to describe the method of analysis itself. The approach taken to analysis is part of the method used to generate data so should be included in the methods section of your report.

- **Ethics**. This section is also the place to address the ethical issues raised by your research and to explain how these were addressed. You will find a detailed account of the ethical considerations relevant to criminological research in chapter 12.

This section should be detailed and it should provide a very clear explanation of how the research was carried out so that another criminologist could replicate the research. It can be useful to bear this in mind when selecting information to include in this section of the report. Ask yourself whether someone else would be able to carry out the research in exactly the same way on the basis of the information that you have provided or whether they would need to ask you questions for clarification or to elicit key details.

Analysis

This section sets out the results of your research. The form that this takes will depend upon whether you have used qualitative or quantitative methods of analysis.

If your data was quantitative and has been subjected to statistical analysis, you should include the results of descriptive and inferential tests in this section. You should not include the raw data in this section—it belongs in the appendix if it is to be included at all. The purpose of this section is for you to set out your findings after the analysis has been completed so that you are presenting the converted data.

It may be that your results can be depicted as a figure or table rather than as a narrative: these can be generated by SPSS (Statistical Package for the Social Sciences) (see chapter 14). This is often a far more effective way of communicating information to the reader as it provides an instant snapshot of your findings. Remember, though, that the findings depicted in diagrams should always be explained so use words and diagrams to complement each other rather than using one as a substitute for the other. In other words, rather than leaving a figure to speak for itself, you should follow it up with a section of explanation that describes its relevance to your study. This should be a short explanatory statement only and should not impinge on the interpretation section of the report.

If your research generated qualitative data, you should set out the results of your analysis in this section by identifying the themes that emerged from your analysis and giving an indication of whether these are major themes that reflect the views of a significant proportion of participants or whether they emerged from a minority of participants. You can comment here on any interesting features of these themes: perhaps they were prevalent amongst participants who shared some common socio-demographic characteristic or perhaps there was strong polarity with all participants holding one or the other of conflicting views about some aspect of the subject matter of the research. Again, remember that this section of the report should only state your findings: the discussion of their significance should be reserved for the interpretation section.

Interpretation and discussion

This part of the report explores the significance of your findings. It should take each of the findings that were detailed in the analysis section and consider whether and to what extent they answer the research question and support your hypothesis.

In essence, this is the section of the report in which you take the data that you have gathered and analysed and use it to answer the question that you set out to answer. You should spend time planning this part of the report and think about the order in which to present your conclusions. Are you going to start with the points that offer the greatest support for your hypothesis or is some other order more appropriate? Think about how the different points that you want to make relate to each other so that your discussion presents a logical chain of reasoning.

Irrespective of the order in which you present your points, make sure that you relate each point to the research question and explain what it contributes towards answering that question. Make sure that you explain the reasoning behind your conclusions rather than just stating them: this will help the reader to understanding your interpretation of your findings and may persuade them to agree with you. If any part of your findings do not support your hypothesis, make sure that you address this head on rather than skirting around it or, worse still, omitting it from your discussion. Think about why it is that your findings do not support the hypothesis and consider the implications of this. If your results were inconclusive, you should consider why this has occurred: was it a problem with the design of your research or is some other factor responsible?

Your discussion should incorporate references to the work of others and explain how your findings relate to it. For example, you might write 'Gardener (1978) found that witness memory was affected by the presence of distracting events occurring at the same time as the central event. The findings of the current study are in line with this as participants whose attention was redirected to a distraction gave descriptions that were significantly less detailed than participants whose attention was devoted to the central event'.

The most important point to remember about this part of the report is that it should not simply restate your findings but should explain why the results are as they are and how they relate to the research question.

Conclusions

This section of the report should have a summary of its key findings expressed in a concise manner that emphasizes the way in which your findings have answered the research question. There should be some comment on how this fits in with the existing literature and some suggestions for directions for future research. Consider whether there are any questions that remain unanswered, either because your results were inconclusive on a particular point or because there are further questions to be asked that flow from your research.

It is also a good idea to discuss the limitations of your study in this section. If your results were inconclusive, think about the reasons for this and offer suggestions as to how the research design could be improved. Do not be afraid to draw attention to any shortcomings; your marker will have identified them in any case and, by highlighting problems and explaining how they could be remedied, you are demonstrating that you have learned something of value from the experience that will make you better able to carry out research in the future.

References

The references section should provide full bibliographic details of all the literature cited in your report. It should be organized alphabetically by first author. You will find guidance on referencing in chapter 7.

Appendices

The appendix is the place to include any material that does not belong in any of its main sections that would be useful to the reader to help them understand your report. For example, you might include a copy of a questionnaire that was administered to participants, a copy of the instructions or stimulus material that participants received, or details of your raw data. The appendix is also the place to include copies of a consent form or other documents relating to the ethical conduct of your research.

CHAPTER SUMMARY

Dissertation topic and research question

- Select several alternative topics that you might like to cover for your dissertation and conduct some preliminary research to identify those that could form the basis of your dissertation
- Make sure that you select a topic that you find interesting as you will be working on it for a significant period of time
- Once you have decided on a topic, formulate a question that needs to be answered that can form the basis of your dissertation

Dissertation proposals

- Check to see whether your university requires you to write a dissertation proposal. If you have to write one check also to see if there are any stipulations as to length, the level of detail that is required, and any particular points that must be addressed within the proposal

- If there are no guidelines, it would be sensible to cover: (1) the research question; (2) the importance/interest of the proposed research; (3) an outline of the literature that you have found and/or where you plan to search for literature, and (4) a preliminary indication of how the dissertation could break down into chapters

Planning and organizing

- Consider carefully how best to fit the process of researching and writing your dissertation into your other study commitments (lectures, seminars, coursework, and exams)
- Allocate sufficient time to your dissertation and try to work steadily on it in the time available rather than leaving it until a few weeks before the submission deadline to begin in earnest
- Consider different ways of dividing up the work and managing your time that suit your own study preferences
- Try to combine research and writing as much as possible rather than seeing them as separate stages of the dissertation process
- Find a way to keep track of searches that you have carried out in particular databases and the literature that you find throughout the process
- Work on your technique for note-taking so that you capture key points from the literature rather than writing an extended summary of everything that you have read

Research and writing

- Thorough research is the backbone of your dissertation. Remember that you are trying to impress your marker with the breadth and depth of your research
- Although you should consider including a range of different sources, you should only include material that makes a relevant contribution to your dissertation
- If the subject matter of your dissertation is also considered in other disciplines, such as law, psychology, economics, or sociology, you should consider using relevant materials from those disciplines
- Make sure that you know how to reference the materials that you find and keep a complete and accurate record of all sources to ensure that you can compile a comprehensive bibliography
- Refer to the chapters on writing skills, referencing, and essay writing to refresh your understanding of the requirements of good academic writing
- Leave yourself enough time to proof read your dissertation to ensure that it is free of errors

Research reports

- The approach that you take to your research project will depend on whether it is exploratory or experimental in nature—but in either approach, the most important element of the project is the research question
- It is important that the research question is clear and unambiguous—this will help your marker to evaluate the report and help you to keep focus. It should also be viable within the time and resources available

Literature reviews

- The literature review exists to justify your research by showing how it fills a gap in the existing body of knowledge. It also helps you to demonstrate that you have read widely

- The literature review is not a summary or description of the literature: it should be an organized and analytical coverage of the literature including (where appropriate) the findings of key authors, areas of agreement and contention, key theories, and methods used
- There are various possible approaches to organizing a literature review: chronologically, theoretically, methodologically, and thematically. Regardless of the organization you choose, remember that you must stay focused on your research question

Selecting a method

- It is a good idea to decide what method of data collection you will use as early as possible. These methods are set out in detail in chapter 13
- You may wish to consider interviews, questionnaires, experiments, focus groups, or observations—remember that all of these methods will require ethical approval and you should start the process of ethical review as soon as you can

Structure of a research report

- A typical research report takes the structure: abstract | introduction | literature review | method | analysis | interpretation and discussion | conclusion | references | appendices
- The abstract is a summary of the report that gives the reader an overview of its content: the 'trailer for your film'
- The introduction sets out the focus of the research, states the question and explains its relevance, gives an outline of hypothesis and method, and establishes the research objectives
- The literature review provides context and the background against which the research question is asked
- The method section sets out how you went about gathering data—it should include issues of sampling, variables, methods of analysis, and research ethics. It should be sufficiently detailed for another criminologist to be able to replicate your research
- The section on analysis gives the results of your research and the qualitative or quantitative tests that you used to reach them. It should only state the findings, rather than discussing or interpreting them
- The discussion/interpretation section takes the data that you have gathered and analysed and uses it to answer the research question that you set out to answer. It explains why the results are as they are and how they relate to the question
- The conclusion provides a summary of the key findings, a commentary on how this fits with the literature, suggests future avenues for research, and comments on any limitations of the study
- The references section provides full bibliographic detail of all your sources
- Appendices can be used to include useful supplementary material that does not belong in the main report

10 Presentations

INTRODUCTION

In some respects, a presentation could be said to be the oral equivalent of an essay or a research report: it is a way of disseminating the findings of a piece of research into a particular topic. Of course, the crucial distinguishing factor is that a presentation is delivered to a larger audience and the oral nature of the communication requires a different skill set to a piece of written work. This chapter will draw upon some of the material covered in previous sections of the book concerned with formulating and carrying out research into a particular topic. It will discuss the stages of preparation for a presentation such as selecting a topic and making decisions about the use of supplementary materials such as handouts and PowerPoint slides. The chapter will then move to consider issues relating to the actual delivery of the presentation including matters such as timing, combating nerves, and engaging the interest of the audience.

Many students are reluctant to give an oral presentation. This is entirely natural; an oral presentation focuses the attention of many people on a single person which makes it a very nerve-wracking situation even for otherwise confident students. However, the ability to present information orally is important in many professions so it is a valuable skill to develop. Like anything else, the prospect of giving a presentation is daunting only until you know that you can do it proficiently. Many people are not natural speakers and will quail at the thought of addressing even a small audience but the fear does recede with practice so the experience would be extremely valuable. This is particularly important given the growing tendency amongst prospective employers to require a presentation from job applicants. This chapter aims to equip you to prepare and deliver an easy-to-follow and engaging presentation.

LEARNING OUTCOMES

After reading this chapter, you will be able to:

- Select an appropriate topic that fits within the constraints of your course

- Conduct effective research into your presentation topic

- Construct an organized and flowing presentation

- Prepare some appropriate visual aids and use them effectively

- Understand the importance of practising the presentation

- Deal with common problems associated with nerves

- Deliver a comprehensive and engaging presentation

- Take questions from the audience with confidence

- Reflect upon your performance in order to strengthen future presentations

The presentation process

For most people faced with the need to give a presentation, the focus is on the actual delivery of the material. It is usual to think of 'the presentation' as the time-slot in which the material is communicated to the audience. Whilst this is clearly an important time, most of the work required for an effective presentation will be complete before you get to your feet in front of your audience. Planning and preparation are essential pre-requisites of a good presentation and yet this 'behind the scenes' activity tends to receive very little attention.

Most students accept that they have to do *something* before standing up and speaking but there seems to be general uncertainty as to what form this preparation might take and how exactly it prepares you to speak for the required amount of time. The central problem seems to be that students omit an essential stage of presentation preparation treating it as a two-stage process:

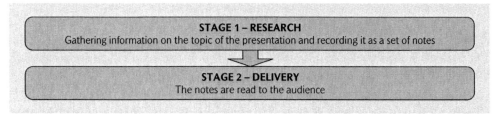

Figure 10.1 Two-stage presentation process

Although this approach does serve the purpose of transmitting the information to the audience, this is not necessarily packaged in a particularly palatable form. In fact, many student presentations are extremely boring because of the way in which the material is delivered: listening to someone read their notes for ten minutes is not in the least engaging for the audience and it can be very off-putting for the presenter to look around and see a distracted and bored audience. To overcome these problems, it is valuable to insert a further stage in between research and delivery:

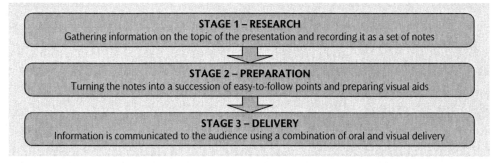

Figure 10.2 Three-stage presentation process

As you will see, by inserting a middle step in the process, the end stage is also different and the presentation is far more engaging for the audience as a result.

It is important to consider a fourth stage that takes place after the presentation is complete. This stage involves a period of review in which the presenter takes stock of the way in which the presentation was received and seeks to identify examples of good and bad practice. The reflection stage maximizes the learning impact of the presentation and should enable you to strengthen future performances.

> **STAGE 4 – REFLECTION**
> Critical evaluation of the performance in order to improve future presentations

Figure 10.3 The reflection stage

Each of these stages will now be considered in turn to guide you through the process of preparing, constructing, and delivering a presentation as well as providing comment on the reflection stage.

The research stage

It is always tempting to see the delivery of the presentation—the end product—as being of primary importance. After all, it is the delivery of the presentation that seems to determine its success (or, if it does not go well, its lack of success), irrespective of whether success is measured in terms of the response of the audience or, in the case of an assessed presentation, the mark awarded. However, an effective end product is only possible if the groundwork has been done properly. In the sections that follow, we will be addressing two of the important preliminary issues: topic choice and the research process.

Choosing a topic

In some instances, particularly if the presentation is part of assessed coursework or is a compulsory non-assessed part of a course, the topic of the presentation will be allocated to you. Although this gives you no scope to choose your subject matter, it does ensure that you have a workable presentation topic which gives you a clear direction for your research. This means the topic 'fits' within the time allocated (or is capable of 'fitting' within it), that there is sufficient material available for you to research the topic, and that it is sufficiently linked to the relevant course material.

In the absence of a predetermined topic, you will have to choose an area of criminology upon which to base your presentation. This can be a tricky business as the success or otherwise of your presentation may depend upon the choice of subject matter, so give it some serious thought and take the following factors into account.

How long is the presentation?

Many presentations are spoilt by content overload as the presenter tries to cram too much material into the time available. The opposite problem arises if a topic is too narrow for the time available; here, the presenter ends up running out of things to say and having to fall back on repetition to fill the time available. Avoid these problems by selecting a topic that can be covered within the time available: obviously, more detail is expected in a 45-minute presentation than is the case in a ten-minute slot at the start of a tutorial.

What are the assessment criteria?

If the presentation is assessed, you should check the assessment criteria to discover what attributes are regarded as important to ensure that you select a topic that allows you to cover all the relevant skills. For example, it is usual for credit to be given for independent research so this might steer you away from topics that are covered in detail in textbooks. It may help to make a list of the desirable characteristics of a successful presentation from the assessment criteria and note how your topic will satisfy these characteristics.

What is your aim?

Make sure that you are clear about what you are trying to achieve in your presentation as this will help you to select a research topic with a purpose. You might aim to compare two different theoretical perspectives on the causes of violent crime or to present the findings of your own empirical research project. Perhaps you want to summarize the literature on a particular topic or to compare how a particular offence is treated in three different countries. Are you going to pose a question and then answer it for your audience? Try to make sure that your presentation has a purpose and make sure that this is communicated to the audience at the outset.

Who are your audience?

It is likely that you will have your own aims in mind when delivering a presentation such as obtaining a good mark, not looking foolish in front of your friends, or impressing a prospective employer but the predominant aim of any presentation is to communicate something of value to the audience. In order to achieve this, you need to have some idea of what the audience wants, needs, or expects from your presentation. In other words, in order to choose an appropriate topic and select content at a suitable level, you need to understand how much your audience already knows about the subject matter.

Practical advice: what does the audience know?

As the person organizing the presentation, what level of prior knowledge can you assume is possessed by your audience? If you are presenting to other students, are you supposed to treat them as criminology undergraduates or are you to treat them as some other audience who either has less or more advanced knowledge?

   For example, some lecturers create hypothetical scenarios to encourage you to pitch your presentation at a particular level. You might be told that your presentation is to a group of schoolchildren so you would need to ensure that you provided simple explanations of basic principles that you would not need to explain at all to fellow criminology students. Conversely, you might be told to imagine that you are trying to convince a potential sponsor to fund your research in which case you would need to demonstrate how your proposed research fits within the existing literature.

What material is available?

Imagine that you have had an idea for a comparison of the treatment of female prisoners in mother-and-baby units in Britain and China. You have two weeks to prepare your presentation and the 400-page report that you need is being sent to you by post from China and will need to be translated when it arrives. It is unlikely that you will be ready in time.

The most brilliant presentation topic will only become a brilliant presentation if there is sufficient source material to enable you to research the topic thoroughly. You must be able to identify a range of source books, articles, and reports on your chosen topic and be able to obtain them in good time to prepare for your presentation. The increasing availability of online resources may help here but remember the importance of ensuring that material that you encounter online comes from a reputable academic or professional source.

You will find some valuable guidance on evaluating the source of online materials contained in chapter 4. Remember that anyone can post anything on the Internet so you should not rely on material for academic purposes unless it comes from a reputable source.

Is the topic interesting?

If you have free choice, it is also useful to take into account any interests of your own within the subject as it is always easier to research something that interests you and your enthusiasm for the topic will communicate to the audience making your presentation more engaging.

You should also consider whether the topic will be interesting for your audience. One important factor to take into account here is whether other students have also presented on the same topic. It will be more challenging for you to engage and hold the audience's interest if they have already heard ten presentations on the same subject matter. It is not impossible, of course, as you might find a different way of exploring the same topic but you should bear in mind that replicating a topic that has already been covered by others carries a risk that your presentation will seem uninteresting and uninspired to the audience even if it is actually the result of a great deal of hard work and independent research.

Researching the topic

Once you have an idea of a topic that could form the focus of your presentation, you can start to carry out your research. The process of identifying and locating books, articles, and other sources for a presentation is no different to that which is involved in any other piece of work in criminology so that chapters on finding source material in chapters 1–4 of this book will be useful here.

There are some general points to consider:

- **Start early.** Students often leave insufficient time to carry out research for a presentation, perhaps because a presentation feels like a much smaller piece of work than a 2,000 word essay. However, even a ten-minute presentation can contain a lot of material and requires a great deal of detailed research so be sure that you give yourself enough time to research your topic thoroughly.

- **Be focused yet flexible.** Achieve a good balance between keeping your focus and being receptive to new material that may alter your research topic. Do not stick rigidly to your original topic (unless you have to do so) if you find a more interesting or original slant on it. Remember, your original choice of topic should be the starting point of your research but not necessarily your final destination.

- **Be effective in note-taking.** Remember that there is nothing to be gained from copying large reams of material word-for-word from books and journals unless you plan to use precise quotations in your presentation. Note key points and ensure that you know where to find them. You may find it useful to devise a note-taking strategy that allows you to differentiate between factual information that you find during the course of research and your ideas about how this could be useful in your research, perhaps by dividing your notes into two columns or by using different fonts or colours.

- **Keep a list of all your sources.** Although you are presenting material orally, you may still need to provide a bibliography to demonstrate the extent of your research to your lecturer or to detail further reading for your audience.

- **Consider how points will be presented.** Your presentation should be a combination of oral and visual communication. When you are carrying out your research, bear this in mind and think about the best way to present information. Can you use a graph to depict complex information that you then supplement with an oral explanation? Can you use video or sound clips? Will a picture help to demonstrate your point? Make sure that you cast your net widely when carrying out your research to ensure that you have access to all the possible types of sources that you need to create an engaging presentation.

- **Stop researching in good time.** Remember that you are engaged in a three-stage process: research, preparation, and presentation. You need to leave sufficient time to take the material that you have found and prepare a presentation with it. This takes time and it will need refinement. Moreover, you may find, once you start to put your presentation together, that you need to come back and do a little more research.

The preparation stage

Once you have conducted your research into your presentation topic, you will probably feel somewhat overwhelmed (a) by the volume of material that you have gathered and (b) by the prospect of turning it into a presentation. This is not unusual. However, this situation can result in two of the key limitations on the effectiveness of student presentations.

- Trying to cover too much information in the time available; and,
- Reading from a set of notes that are not suited to oral delivery.

Both of these problems can be avoided by judicious selection of material and by planning a structured presentation that is not exclusively reliant on oral delivery but which makes effective use of visual aids.

Creating a presentation

If you think about the best presentations that you have attended (some of your lectures should spring to mind), you should realize that a good presentation tells a story. This is your aim in your presentation. You have to present some complex information to your audience so it is essential that it flows in a logical order and does not divert off into tributaries of interesting yet irrelevant detail. You can do this by taking care with the selection and organization of your material.

Selection of material

It is always tempting, having devoted time and effort to conducting research, to try to make use of all the interesting facts that you have discovered. However, it is important to ensure that you do not exceed the time allocated for your presentation: in fact, if the presentation is assessed, you may actually lose marks for failing to work within the timeframe stipulated.

Equally, a hurried presentation that skims over a great deal of material is very difficult for the audience to follow and is likely to be a negative factor if your presentation is assessed.

Formulating a question that you will answer in your presentation is a good way to identify your focus and select relevant material as it tends to identify the 'job' that the presentation is trying to do. Once you are clear about what you are trying to achieve, you can sift through all the material that you have gathered to eliminate that which is not relevant. As with essay writing, remember to judge the relevance of material in relation to the issue not the topic: in other words, try not to think 'is this about jury decision-making?' or even 'is this about jury decision-making and false confessions?' but rather 'does this help me to explain how juries are influenced by a retracted false confession?'. The more specific you are in framing your issue, the easier you will find it to decide whether material is relevant.

Practical exercise: determining relevance

Try the following technique to help you to determine the relevance of material to your presentation.

1. Write the title of your presentation at the top of a blank piece of paper (or at the start of a new document if you are using a computer).

2. Make a list of all the points that you found during the course of your research that you could include in your presentation.

3. Once it is complete, review the list. Group similar points together and eliminate any repetition or overlap.

4. Draw three columns headed 'essential', 'peripheral', and 'irrelevant' and allocate each of your points to one of these three columns, remembering that relevance is determined by reference to the specific title of your presentation and not to the general topic.

5. Dealing only with the point in the essential column, try to organize them so that they tell a story (there is more on this in the next section). Do you need any of the peripheral points to link the essential points together or to elaborate on them? If you have too much material, repeat the exercise again but this time divide only your essential points into the three columns.

 This can be a really effective way of filtering out material that is interesting but which is not really needed in your presentation. You will find a worked example of this technique on the Online Resource Centre. You might find it useful to look at this example and read the accompanying note to ensure that you have a good understanding of how to select material for your presentation.

Organization of material

Once you have made a preliminary selection of the material to include in the presentation, you need to consider the order in which your points will be made. Bear in mind that your presentation should follow a logical progression; it should 'tell a story' and, like all good essays, it should have a beginning (introduction), middle (the bulk of the presentation, divided into a series of issues), and an end (conclusion) as illustrated in Figure 10.4.

Introduction

The introduction should be succinct, clear, and straightforward. It should outline the topic to be discussed, explain the structure and duration of the presentation (including any time at the end for questions), and it should tell the audience why the topic is important and/or interesting. In essence, the introduction should give the audience an understanding of what

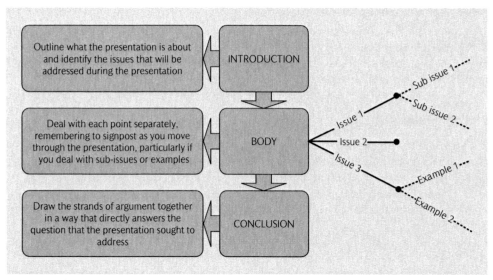

Figure 10.4 Organizing the material

is to follow and give them a clear and concise account of the question that the presentation will address and the reason that this is important.

Main body

The body of the presentation can be more complicated to organize so keep in mind the argument that you are going to advance and break this down into a series of issues and sub-issues. Bear in mind that one point leads into another and that you should take care to select examples that demonstrate the point that you are making and do not distract from the flow of your presentation.

You might want to experiment with more than one potential structure to ensure that you find the most effective way to organize your material. Try making a list of all the points that you want to make and varying this to see which order seems to flow most smoothly. Remember that it is your words that create the flow between points so give some thought to what you will say as well as looking at the order of points on paper. You could jot down some notes about this but do try to avoid the temptation to write a script. If you write a script, you will read it and that tends to lead to very stilted delivery.

For the audience listening to the presentation, there are two tasks that need to be carried out simultaneously. Firstly, they have to digest the point that you are making and, secondly, they have to slot this into the bigger picture of the topic as a whole. This can be difficult so it is essential that you help your audience to follow the structure of the presentation with clear signposting: phrases that indicate to the listener how each point fits into the overall structure of the presentation, such as:

- The starting point for this discussion is . . .
- There are three points of importance here and I shall discuss each in turn. Firstly . . .
- This is a strong argument but there is a powerful counterargument that we must now consider.
- In conclusion . . .

Conclusion

The conclusion should provide a brief summary of the material covered and a direct answer to the question addressed in the presentation. Try to think of a way to make the central message of the presentation stick in the mind of the audience by identifying a maximum of three points that you want them to remember and highlighting these.

Using visual aids

Research into the psychology of effective communication has indicated that people take in more information from visual images than they do from listening. Therefore, it is a good idea to ensure that your presentation engages the eyes as well as the ears of the audience by using visual aids whether this is in the form of a handout, use of an overhead projector or a PowerPoint presentation or by writing/drawing on a whiteboard or flipchart as the presentation progresses.

Effective use of visual aids can achieve the following four objectives:

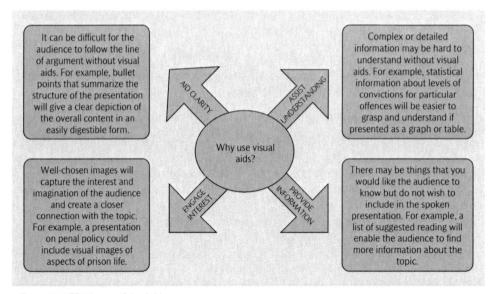

Figure 10.5 Effective use of visual aids

Although there are clear benefits to using visual aids, there are some pitfalls associated with their use that can cause difficulties and may distract or disengage the audience. Follow these tips to help you to avoid these problems when producing visual aids:

- **Take care with their production.** Shoddy and ill-prepared visual aids give a negative impression to the audience so make sure that your visual aids look like they are the product of care and effort rather than something that was thrown together at the last minute.

- **Make sure you can use the technology.** If you are going to use PowerPoint, you will need to be able to use the software to create a presentation and be able to use it during your presentation. Your presentation will be spoilt if you are always fiddling with the computer and losing the order of their slides.

- **Do not overload visual aids.** A lot of type in a small font is very hard to read on a handout or a PowerPoint slide. With slides in particular, the audience will be annoyed and feel that they are missing something important if they cannot read them.

- **Be selective in your use of colour.** Just because it is possible to use many different fonts and colours of text does not mean that this is a good idea. Visuals aids that are too busy or colourful are not easy for the audience to use. Aim for simple use of colour to enhance the appearance of your visual aids and to assist the audience by using a colour to highlight points of particular importance.

- **Do not read from your visual aids.** If material is provided in written form, the audience can read it for themselves. Reading during your presentation will interfere with the manner of delivery and the audience will wonder why you are bothering to present at all if all the information is written down for them. If you have provided a quotation, for example, on a handout or PowerPoint slide, do not read it to the audience: draw their attention to it so that they can read it and then talk about it.

- **Do not use visual aids as a dumping ground.** As time is limited, there is a temptation to add all the information that you would like to cover on visual aids. A few additional points or suggestions for follow-up reading is fine but the inclusion of a vast amount of additional information suggests that you were not wise in your selection of material for inclusion in the presentation. Remember that visual aids are supposed to supplement, not replace, your oral presentation and that the presentation should be complete in itself.

- **Choose images with care.** A well-chosen image can be an effective way of communicating with the audience and engaging their interest but make sure that the relationship between any images is either clear or explained to the audience. You want the audience to be listening to you, not wondering why you have displayed a picture of a bird when you are discussing penal theory (you might be picking up on the slang 'doing bird' for prison but your audience may be unaware of this).

The following section will outline the main types of visual aids that you may wish to use in your presentation and comment on how they can be used to good effect. Further on in the chapter, you will find suggestions on how to use these aids during the delivery of the presentation.

Handouts

A handout used to be an essential accompaniment to every presentation but they tend to be less common since the use of PowerPoint has become widespread. However, even if you are using PowerPoint, there is no reason not to provide a handout to supplement this. The advantage that a handout has over a PowerPoint slide is that it is available for constant reference by the audience throughout the presentation whereas information on slides will change as the presentation progresses and one slide replaces another. As such, a handout can be a useful reference guide for the audience as it can help them to understand the structure of the presentation and to see how different points made fit into the overall picture of the presentation.

A further advantage of the handout is that it can be taken away by the audience at the end of the presentation; therefore, it can be a means of ensuring that they are provided with core pieces of information relevant to the presentation, particularly in relation to material where accuracy of wording is important such as definitions, quotations, and statutory provisions. For example, if your presentation topic was corporate crime, you might want to discuss the implications of the Corporate Manslaughter and Corporate Homicide Act 2007, in which case giving the audience the wording of the statute might be useful. If you put this on a slide, it cannot be referred to throughout the presentation or taken away afterwards and if you read it to the audience they will have to write very quickly to note it all down. The other advantage of a handout, of course, is that the audience can add their own notes during the presentation.

A handout is a guide for the audience and a source of essential information. It should not be overloaded with detail and it should never be a word-for-word copy of your presentation: why would the audience bother to listen to you if you are providing them with a transcript of your presentation? An audience who is paying no attention when you speak is very off-putting for a presenter, so make sure that you use your visual aids to increase engagement with the audience rather than to distract them or give them an excuse not to listen. Remember, visual aids supplement, rather than replace, the spoken word.

PowerPoint

Microsoft Office PowerPoint, like its Mac equivalent Keynote, is slide-based presentation software that can be used to display words, images, graphs, and video clips to the audience. It is quite simple to create a presentation using this software (your university will probably have training sessions available if you would like some help) as you type text or insert images into the template provided and these are turned into a slideshow. The range of features makes PowerPoint an excellent visual aid that can enhance your presentation for the audience and, of course, by using it you are expanding your computer literacy skills.

You should construct a slideshow that reflects the structure of your presentation. In doing so, the following types of slide are likely to feature:

- **Title slide.** This tells the audience who you are and the title of your presentation.
- **Presentation outline.** This should be used during your introduction as you tell the audience what points you are going to cover and in what order.
- **Content slides.** These slides will form the bulk of your presentation. The general rule is that there should be one slide for each major concept or idea that you introduce to the audience. Remember to be relatively sparing with the amount of words used on each slide and keep the font size large: visual aids are not useful if they cannot be read by the audience.
- **Summary slide/s.** This is the conclusion to your presentation and it should pick out the key points as you explain how they fit together. This can be a single slide or spread over several slides as necessary. Remember that there was a purpose to your presentation—an issue to be explained or a question to be answered—so make sure that your summary deals with this head on.
- **Any questions?** However much you might hope that nobody asks any questions, it is usual to allow the audience an opportunity to do so. In an assessed presentation, it is likely that the lecturer will ask a question even if nobody else does.

When it comes to deciding on the content of your slides, the PowerPoint template offers a range of options of full and divided slides allowing you to incorporate text, diagrams, and images in a variety of different configurations. Take time to look at what options are available and experiment with different ways of setting out your material to decide which slides are most suitable.

A combination of text and image as illustrated in Figure 10.6 can be an engaging design for the audience. Notice that the text is limited to key words that encapsulate each point that you will discuss rather than setting out the point in full. Remember, the purpose of PowerPoint is to make the presentation easier to follow for the audience so cramming on too much text will not achieve this.

Carefully crafted slides should avoid the risk that you will subject your audience to what has become known as 'Death by PowerPoint'. This is a phrase used to describe the bore-

Figure 10.6 A PowerPoint slide

dom and weariness experienced by an audience as a result of information overload during a presentation arising from these common faults:

- Too much detail, especially text, contained on each slide.
- Too many slides which are passed through too quickly.
- Overuse of PowerPoint features such as flashing and moving text.
- The presenter looking at and talking to the slideshow rather than the audience.
- The presenter reading the text of the slides to the audience.

Practice

The most important element of the preparation stage is practice. Most people are not used to speaking in public so it is inevitably something that is going to need a little bit of practice.

Why practise?

You must practise your presentation several times over to ensure that:

- The presentation fits within the time allocated to it.
- The order of the material is appropriate and one point runs smoothly into another.
- There are no tricky words or phrases that trip up your tongue.
- You familiarize yourself with the appropriate pace at which to speak.
- You become accustomed to hearing your own voice.
- You know how and when to use any visual aids.
- You identify and eliminate any distracting habits.

Many of these points will be more readily addressed if you practise in front of an audience. For example, you may think that your pace of delivery is appropriate but only someone who is listening can tell you whether that is the case. Equally, if you have any odd habits, such as fiddling with a pen or flicking your hair, you are likely to be unaware of this unless it is pointed out to you. Finally, a third party can give you feedback on the most important element of all: whether your presentation makes sense to the audience. If you cannot persuade anyone to watch you practise, find out whether your university has a video suite that you can use to record your practice session so that you can observe yourself in action.

What to practise?

Although the obvious answer to this question would seem to be 'the presentation', it is not necessarily useful to devote too much practice time to the actual presentation. There are two separate facets to a good presentation: (1) the subject matter and (2) the presentation style.

Although you will want to practise the actual presentation for the reasons noted in the preceding section, you should not neglect to practise in order to strengthen your presentation style. Until you are a seasoned public speaker, it might be an idea to practise the two separately, particularly if you are asking an audience of your peers to comment on your presentation as they may get tied up with commenting on the content rather than style.

Practical exercise

The following exercise can be used to help you to practise your presentation style. You will find that it will also help you to work on issues such as the organization of the content of the presentation and incorporating signposting.

1. Choose something that you know extremely well as the topic for a ten minute presentation. There is no need for it to have any academic merit as the essence of a good presentation is the communication of information irrespective of the nature of that information. Suitable topics could be (1) good pubs in your home town, (2) favourite sporting activities, or (3) your first term as an undergraduate student.

2. Prepare a presentation on the topic. The idea of the exercise is to evaluate your presentation style but this will not work if you treat it as a freeflow speaking activity in which you spill forth thoughts without structure. Use some of the techniques suggested in this chapter to help you to structure and organize your presentation.

3. Ask a couple of friends to observe your presentation and comment upon your style. Try to emphasize to them that you want honest and constructive feedback: it is much easier for your friends to say 'that was great' as they do not want to upset you so you may need to convince them that you want to hear an objective review of the strengths and weaknesses of your technique. It can help to give them a feedback table and ask them to write comments as they may find this easier than voicing any negative views to you in person.

4. Make a list of the strengths and weaknesses that your audience noted. Ask them for suggestions as to what they think would improve on areas of weakness. Reflect upon your own experience as a presenter: how did it feel when you were delivering the material? What things would you change in future presentations?

5. Rework the presentation taking these observations on board and ask your friends to watch it again or present to a different group of friends. The aim is to determine whether you have improved on your previous performance.

Once you have some general insight into your presentation style, it would be useful to practise the actual presentation to work on issues associated with the content. Remember to practise with the visual aids that you plan to use to make sure that you can use these without interrupting the flow of your presentation.

Having considered the mechanics of putting together a presentation, all that remains is to consider how to deliver it to the audience with clarity and confidence.

The delivery stage

This is the stage of the process that you probably think of as *the* presentation. Having followed the steps outlined in relation to preparation, you should have a presentation in a clear and accessible form which is supplemented by carefully constructed visual aids. This section will go through some of the factors which will influence the success of the actual delivery of the presentation.

Delivery style

Your main objective in giving a presentation is to communicate an idea to the audience. This means that they need to be able to understand you. It is your job to make sure that you deliver your presentation in such a way that it is capable of being understood and, more than that, that it is packaged so that the audience want to listen. As such, there are a number of points to take into account.

- **Do not read from a script.** People who read from a script tend to speak too quickly and in too flat a tone without making eye contact with the audience. This is not engaging. It can also create problems because good written language and good spoken language are very different so reading from a script tends to feel very stilted and unnatural for the audience.

- **Take care with timing, pace, and volume.** Presentation speech tends to be slightly slower than normal speech and to involve more pauses and more repetition. It is important to enunciate words clearly and to use a slightly louder volume than usual to ensure that the audience do not have to strain to hear you.

- **Use plenty of signposting.** Telling the audience what you are doing makes it easier for them to follow the development of your argument. Your audience should always be clear whether the point you are making is an elaboration of something you have already mentioned, one in a line of examples or an entirely new part of the discussion. You can do this in conjunction with your visual aids: for example, you could say 'this slide sets out the three theories that I will be discussing' or 'you can find these four points listed at the top of the second page of the handout'.

In essence, you should aim to adapt your natural style of speech to suit the task of making a presentation. If you know that you are going to give a presentation, start to really listen to the way that lecturers speak when they give lectures: focus on their style rather than content for a short period of time. You should notice the differences between this and their ordinary speech.

Combating nerves

Nerves are a problem for many students who are faced with the prospect of making a presentation. Even students who are confident at speaking out during group discussion in tutorials tend to find the prospect of standing in front of the group and speaking somewhat daunting. One of the best ways of overcoming nerves is to try and isolate what it is that is causing anxiety—knowing what the problem is takes you halfway towards overcoming it. The following sections identify some common fears and make suggestions as to how they can be combated.

Presenting inaccurate material

This is a common worry but it should not be an issue provided you have carried out your research thoroughly. Even if you do make some inaccurate points, it is unlikely that other students will notice. Your lecturer will notice but will not interrupt the presentation to correct you and should not comment on any inaccuracy in front of other students. As such, it is a matter for the lecturer to raise with you in the feedback that you receive for your presentation so it will be no different to finding out that you made a mistake in a piece of written coursework.

If you find that you are very concerned about a particular point in your presentation that you are struggling to understand, it might be worth approaching your lecturer about this. If the presentation is assessed, there may be a limit to how much the lecturer will help you with the content but you can at least make them aware of the problem so that they can reassure you that they will not draw attention to any errors in front of other students. Some lecturers may be prepared to give you a little assistance if you are struggling with the material, perhaps pointing you towards some source material that will be easier for you to understand.

Forgetting what to say

Students who express this concern generally mean one of two things: either they will be so nervous that they cannot speak at all or they will forget the particular forms of words that they want to use in their presentation.

The first of these would be an exceptionally rare occurrence. You may feel nervous about speaking and your mouth will feel dry but it is highly unlikely that you will open your mouth and no words will come out. The trick to overcoming this fear is to make sure that you take some water to sip to deal with your dry mouth and to practise your first sentence over and over again. This is because students who experience presentation nerves report that the first sentence—actually starting to speak—is the most nerve-wracking part and that once the first sentence is out of their mouths, the rest followed on without any difficulty.

As to problems with remembering a particular form of words, this should not be an issue because, provided your presentation is clear and people can understand you, it does not matter what words you use so there is no need to memorize a particular form of words. Students often like to have particular phrases incorporated into their presentation because they look impressive on paper but remember that none of us speak in the same style that we write: written and spoken language are entirely different.

Practical exercise

The following exercise should demonstrate the difference between spoken and written words and persuade you that you do not need any particular form of words to communicate your ideas to the audience.

Select one point that you want to make in your presentation and write a script for it in your usual written style. Put this to one side. Now find a method of recording yourself speaking and explain the same point without planning and using ordinary language. Transcribe the recording and compare it with your script. Hopefully, you will find that you have made the same points but in different language.

You can take this a step further by recording yourself explaining an idea in ordinary language and then reading your script and listening to the difference between the two versions. This may convince you that your less formal, natural spoken language is actually a better way to communicate in your presentation.

Being visible and feeling judged

A presentation focuses uninterrupted attention on one person for a protracted period of time. This visibility and focus renders the speaker vulnerable to the criticisms of their peers and it is this that is the most commonly expressed fear associated with giving a presentation. In fact, you could say that all feelings of nervousness stem from a common concern about looking foolish in front of others.

There are a couple of points that you should note here. Firstly, do not imagine that every member of the audience is paying attention to your presentation. The only person that you can guarantee is listening is the lecturer. Secondly, if the people are paying attention then this is because they are interested in what you are saying, not because they want to criticize you. In fact, most people will be willing you on to succeed, knowing that they have either survived the experience or have their own presentation to give later that term so it is really a mistake to assume that there is any negative judgement being directed towards you.

Ultimately, most students undertaking a presentation will not have much experience of speaking in front of others so it is only natural to feel nervous about it. Try to minimize this prior to the presentation by increasing the frequency of your contributions to tutorial discussion to get more and more used to sharing your opinions with other students. There are all sorts of techniques to help people overcome nerves. Some students find that the best way to feel confident is to pretend to be confident; they watch those who they consider to be confident when giving presentations and emulate their behaviour. For others, a more forthright approach is useful and they start their presentation by confessing to the audience that they feel nervous. Overall, though, try to remember that it is unlikely that anything will go wrong during your presentation and, even if it does, there is no need to feel foolish.

Practical exercise

The following exercise might help you to overcome any nerves that you are experiencing as the day of your presentation approaches.

1. Think about what aspect of the presentation makes you feel nervous. What is it that you think might go wrong? Try to be as specific as possible and write a numbered list.

2. Take each point in turn and ask yourself (a) why you think this will happen and (b) what the consequence will be if it does happen. For example, you might be worried that you will run out of time and not be able to finish your presentation. If the presentation is assessed, this could lead to a deduction of marks.

3. Think of at least two ways that you could prevent the problem from arising. For example, you could practise your presentation several times to make sure it fits within the time allocation and you could

review your content to identify any points that could be omitted or condensed if you find you are short of time on the day.

4. Consider how you will deal with the outcome of your feared situation; in other words, address not just the consequence but the consequence of the consequence! For example, if you run out of time then you will lose marks as a consequence but this is unlikely to make a difference between a pass and a fail as it is only one factor that the marker will take into account. Moreover, if the presentation is only part of the assessment for the course, you can work hard to make up for the lost marks in the other pieces of coursework or the examination.

By identifying your fears, you should be able to reduce the possibility that they will occur and devise ways to cope if they do happen. Hopefully, this will help you to realize that there is very little that could go wrong in your presentation and, even if the worst happens, it will be something that you can survive.

Dealing with questions

Most presentations conclude with a period of time for the audience to ask questions. It is probably fair to say that even the most confident presenter has some qualms about dealing with questions. This is because it is actually the only part of the presentation that you cannot control. If the presentation is assessed, the ability to deal with questions assumes a particular importance because it gives the marker an indication of the depth of the speaker's background knowledge. Try to take into account the following points to help you deal with questions:

- **Listen to the question.** Concentrate on what the person asking the question is saying rather than worrying that you will not know the answer. Ask them to repeat the question if you did not follow it.

- **Take time to think about an answer.** Try not to be afraid of silence. It is better to take a few moments to ponder so that you can say something sensible rather than saying the first thing that pops into your head just to fill the silence. If you do not know the answer, say so rather than trying to bluff.

- **Do not talk for too long.** Think about your answer and make a couple of succinct points. Long rambling answers will detract from the overall impression of your presentation skills.

The reflection stage

You may think that your task is complete as soon as the final question has been answered and you have taken your seat with a sense of relief and achievement but there is another stage of the process which is frequently overlooked in its importance and that is the post-presentation reflection.

Why reflect?

You should reflect upon your performance to ensure that you gain something from the experience that will make you a more effective and confident presenter in the future. Try to formalize the reflection process by making notes so that you have a record of your thoughts while they are still fresh in your mind. Make a note of things that went well and what, if anything, you would do differently if you were giving a presentation next week.

Presentation skills are important and it may impress an employer if you can demonstrate that you reflected upon your performance and made changes to your approach to preparation or delivery as a result. It may also help you to fulfil any PDP requirements at your institution (see chapter 5 on study skills).

Seek feedback

The process of reflection need not take long and you can make use of any feedback that you have been given by your lecturer and by the audience. If the presentation was assessed, you may have a written feedback form. If not, and you are struggling to remember any comments that the lecturer made at the time, drop them an email asking for more feedback. Remember that a specific answer often requires a specific question so rather than asking for feedback in general terms, perhaps you could ask the lecturer to list three things that were good about your presentation and three areas where improvement was needed.

You could also ask for feedback from the audience. If you are really keen to find out what people think, you could create a feedback form to distribute to the audience, asking them to note positive and negative features of the presentation. Make sure you do not ask for too much feedback from the audience; they are there to listen to your presentation not to provide you with a detailed commentary on your presentation technique.

CHAPTER SUMMARY

The research stage

- Take care to formulate a presentation topic that takes account of the timeframe within which the presentation must be delivered, the availability of material, the aim of the presentation, and the requirements of the assessment criteria
- Start your research as early as possible to ensure you have time to identify and obtain relevant material and make sure that your note-taking is effective
- Strive to find an original or interesting slant on the material to ensure that the presentation is interesting, particularly if you are aware that other students are covering the same topic

Preparing the presentation

- Content overload is a major problem for many presentations. Select your topic and the content of the presentation carefully to ensure that you do not try to cram too much material into the time available
- If you are having difficulties in making a decision about the content, try ranking each point on the basis of its relevance to the question that your presentation is seeking to answer
- Make sure that your presentation tells a story by giving it a clear introduction, a series of inter-related points within the body of the presentation and a conclusion that draws together the issues raised and provides a succinct answer to the question posed by the presentation
- Give careful thought to the selection and presentation of visual aids to ensure that they complement, rather than replace or distract from, the presentation

- Practise, preferably in front of an audience. Present on everyday topics to practise your delivery style and then practise the actual presentation to ensure that it fits within the timeframe and that everything flows smoothly

Delivering the presentation

- Try to adopt a style of delivery that is engaging for the audience to listen to and follow. Take particular care with the timing, pace, and volume of your presentation and remember that good spoken English differs enormously from good written English
- Signposting is essential to enable your audience to follow the line of your argument and to understand how each point relates to others in the presentation. Use a signposting phrase in relation to each new point raised
- Anticipate issues that will cause you to feel nervous and try to formulate a means of pre-empting any problems that you fear may arise. Remember that most people suffer from presentation nerves
- Be prepared to answer questions from the audience. Listen carefully to what is being asked and take a moment to think about the answer before launching into a response

Review and reflection

- Presentations are increasingly required as part of the job application process so take advantage of this opportunity to become a more accomplished presenter by reflecting upon your performance. Try to be honest with yourself about your limitations as a presenter and find ways to strengthen areas in which there is room from improvement
- Be active and precise in seeking feedback from others about your qualities as a presenter and remember that asking precise questions tends to elicit precise answers. Consider circulating a short feedback sheet to the audience

Revision and examinations

INTRODUCTION

The earlier chapters in this part of the book have been aimed at helping you to develop the skills that you need to study effectively and to succeed in coursework. Chapter 5 outlined a range of study skills whilst chapters 6 and 7 contained guidance on the technicalities associated with the production of a good piece of written work. Chapters 8 and 9 built upon this by considering in detail the requirements of essays, dissertations, literature reviews, and research reports. This chapter covers the skills that will help you to ensure that your revision is effective and productive. Unlike many other resources that abandon students at the door of the exam room, this chapter will not only guide you through the revision process but also provide you with various strategies that can be employed in the exam itself.

The marks that you gain in examinations make a significant contribution to your overall degree classification so it is essential that you enter the exam room fully prepared and equipped with the skills that will enable you to perform to the best of your ability. However, revision and exam skills are not always covered by lecturers or study skills textbooks. Perhaps this omission is due to an assumption that students who have worked steadily thought the course will have all that they need to succeed in the exams without any additional advice on revision techniques and exam skills. This is a misconception as the skill set relevant to revision and exams differs from that required for day-to-day study. Without the acquisition of these skills, student could be left ill-equipped to succeed in the exams, especially as the approach to revision that is favoured by students—re-reading and re-writing notes—is not particularly effective. This chapter provides a range of practical tips on formulating an effective revision strategy from issues of planning through to suggestions for practical tasks that can be undertaken alone or in groups.

LEARNING OUTCOMES

After reading this chapter, you will be able to:

- Formulate a realistic plan of revision appropriate to your circumstances

- Review your syllabus to identify appropriate topics for revision

- Use a range of different strategies to engage in active revision

- Acknowledge the value of practice answers and incorporate these into your revision strategy

- Plan and produce focused and successful answers to exam questions

- Avoid some of the common problems that limit exam success

Preparing to revise

Planning and preparation are the key to successful revision. Too many students dive straight into the revision process without any clear idea of what they are trying to achieve. It is worth taking time at the start of the revision period to formulate an organized and structured approach to revision that will enable you to work steadily and effectively towards the exams.

Preliminary matters

Before you can start to revise, you should ensure that you have a clear idea of what you are working towards. This requires more than knowing the date and time of the first exam; you should have a more precise objective, which is to ensure that you have the knowledge and skills to be able to answer the required number of questions on each exam paper. In order to achieve this objective, you have to know a little more about what it involves so you should be able to answer the following questions in relation to each of your modules:

- What is the date of the exam?
- How long is the exam?
- How many questions are there on each exam paper?
- How many questions do you have to answer on each paper?
- Are there any compulsory questions?
- Do you have any information about the topics that will (or will not) be examined?
- Are any materials permitted in the exam room?

If you cannot answer these questions at the start of the revision period, make it your first task to track down this information so that you have a precise picture of the task ahead. You might find it useful to enter the information into a table so that it can be referred to with ease during the revision period.

As you can see from Table 11.1, a table provides a useful reference point that can be used to make decisions about the topics and skills that are to be the focus of the revision period. For example, a student taking the exams detailed in Table 11.1 could take the following into account when planning their revision:

- Revision topics must include policing and PACE as well as focusing on the tutorial topics in Penology and the case studies covered in Social Problems. There is no need to revise sexual offences.
- The time available to answer each question is 45 minutes for one paper and one hour for the others so the revision period should include writing practice answers within those two timeframes. Consideration should also be given to the difference of depth of discussion that will be required in an answer as a result of the shorter time per question in the Criminal Law exam.
- There are three different types of question that will need to be answered: essays, problem scenario questions, and an analysis of a case study. Each of these types of question will require different preparation and differing skills in its production.
- The revision period should include any preparation work that needs to be done with regards to materials to be taken into the exam room.

Table 11.1 Exam overview

	Criminal Justice System	Criminal Law	Penology	Social Problems
Date of exam	1st June	3rd June	5th June	10th June
Length of exam	3 hours	3 hours	3 hours	2 hours
Total number of questions	6	8	8	6
Number of questions to be answered	3	4	3	2
Time per question	1 hour	45 minutes	1 hour	1 hour
Compulsory questions?	Yes	No but must answer one question from each part. Part 1 is essays and Part 2 is problem questions.	No	Yes (a critical analysis of one of the case studies covered in the module).
Topics covered or not covered	Compulsory question is on policing and PACE procedures.	There will be no questions on the coursework topic (sexual offences).	There is one question on each tutorial topic.	No info on topics.
Materials permitted?	No	A criminal law statute book (with no writing or highlighting).	No	One side of A4 with notes on the case studies.

Gathering materials

Part of the preparation process should include gathering together all the materials that you will need during the revision period. It can be very disruptive to have to break off part way through a revision topic to track down some missing notes or find an article that you need to read. Check that you have all the relevant materials from the following list:

- **A complete set of notes for each subject.** Did you miss any lectures or fail to make notes for seminars? Gaps in your notes are often a sign of gaps in knowledge so think carefully about whether you need to fill in the gaps or whether your time would be better spent consolidating your understanding of topics that you have already covered.

- **A textbook that writes in a way that you find accessible.** It is sometimes the case that the set text that you bought at the beginning of the academic year just does not work for you. Perhaps it is a bit simplistic and you would like more depth or perhaps it is heavy going and you would prefer something a little easier to read. Your revision can be made so much easier if you are working with books that suit you so explore what the library has to offer, making sure that the books that you choose are sufficiently up-to-date.

- **Past exam papers for each of your subjects.** These are an invaluable revision resource because they give you information about the way that the exam is organized and the sorts of questions that you might encounter, which you can use for practice answers. You should check with a lecturer to ensure that the format of the exam has not changed, though.

- **Any materials that you are permitted to take into the exam room.** Make sure that you have all the necessary materials and that they comply with the rules of your institution; for example, it is usually the case that any books that are permitted must not be annotated in any way.

- **A selection of relevant articles and other materials such as statutes or cases.** These will help you to gain a greater depth of understanding of the topics that you revise and the ability to incorporate these sources in your answer will impress your examiners.

Working environment

Where do you do your revision? For many students, their revision takes place at the same location as the majority of their work during the course of their studies. This can be positive; for some people, having a set place to work means that they can slip easily into study mode as soon as they sit down. However, do bear in mind that revision may require far more concentration than the rest of your studying activities so make sure that it is a quiet environment that is free from distractions.

You may also want to consider taking your revision to other locations. Memory is triggered by association so it can really help the effectiveness of your revision if you create a link between a topic and a particular location. Once the link is established, you may find that it is easier to recall the information needed on a particular topic in the exam if you visualize being back at the place where you committed it to memory. This need not involve dramatic location changes; some students have reported using this technique successfully simply by sitting in different places in the same room.

Revision planning

One of the most common problems that students encounter with regards to revision is covering enough material in the time available. One of the reasons for this seems to be that many students start revision without any clear plan of work. If you start to revise your first topic without any idea of how long it will take then it will be difficult for you to judge whether you are working at an appropriate pace so that you know when to move on to the next topic. At the start of the revision period, there can be a sense that there is plenty of time before the exams start which tends to lead to quite a leisurely approach to revision that is then followed by last-minute panic once the first exam looms and there is still material left to be covered. This can be a particular problem for students who have not moved on from revision for the first exam and who are relying on the days between exams to revise other subjects.

Avoid this problem by taking time to plan out a programme of work to ensure that you make steady progress and cover all the subjects evenly before the start of the first exam. In this way, you will feel in control of your revision, which can help alleviate feelings of stress, and you will avoid having to cram in last minute revision on the day before the exam.

Constructing a revision timetable

A revision timetable provides a visual reminder of your planned schedule of work so that you know what you are supposed to be doing and you can keep an eye on your progress. In order to construct a revision timetable, you need to take into account the following factors:

- **Days until the first exam.** Pick a day to start your revision and count how many days there are from then until the first exam. Aim to complete your revision by the date of the first exam so that you can use the days in between the exams to refresh your memory of revision you have already done. Of course, you can fall back on these 'in-between' days if you need to but you are likely to feel less pressured if you can avoid this. Remember to deduct some days from your calculation so that they can be designated as rest days. If you feel anxious at the thought of taking too many days off during the revision period, try factoring in some half-days for rest.

- **Working hours each day.** Decide how many hours you want to study each day. Try not to set yourself an unrealistic workload; if you become too tired from working long days, you will find that you become progressively less effective and less able to commit material to memory.

- **Preferred pattern of work.** Everybody has their own preferences when it comes to working patterns. Some people like to start very early whereas others feel that they cannot concentrate until mid-morning or even later in the day. Also consider how long you can concentrate at a single sitting to determine the length of your revision sessions. Some students can concentrate for four hours without a break whilst others feel restless unless they have a short break every hour. It is important to tailor your timetable to suit your preferences as you will revise more effectively this way than if you force yourself into uncomfortable working patterns.

- **Order of subjects.** You could either organize your revision time according to subjects so that you spend a period of days working on topics from one particular subject before moving on, or you could mix the subjects up so that you spend one day revising, say, a topic from Criminal Law and the next on Criminal Justice System revision.

Once you have made some decisions about these issues, you can start to draw up a revision timetable. The example shown in Figure 11.1 has allocated one week to each subject and has allocated one or two topics to each day. Each week has at least one rest day. Notice that the subjects are studied in reverse order; Criminal Justice Systems is the first exam but the last revision topic. This may seem counter-intuitive. Most students start by revising for their first exam but the reverse approach means that the subject matter of the first exam is fresh in your mind and the days between exams can be used to revisit the other topics and refresh your memory.

It is a good idea to break each day down into a series of revision sessions, each of which has a specific task allocated to it. This ensures that you are revising with a purpose, especially— as the example in Table 11.1 that shows Monday 22nd in detail illustrates—if you combine periods in which material is digested with activities that test your memory and practise the application of your knowledge. You will find some suggestions for revision activities later in this chapter.

Choosing revision topics

You will notice in Figure 11.1 that each subject has been divided into revision topics. For example, Criminal Justice Systems has been broken down into six topics: the jury system, court structure, appeals process, police procedures, PACE Codes, and the prison system. Each

Monday	Tuesday	Wednesday	Thursday	Friday	Saturday	Sunday
1 Case study	2 Case study	3 Rest Case study	4 Drugs and alcohol	5 Anti-social behaviour	6 Poverty and crime	7 Rest
8 Drugs and prison	9 Release and resettlement	10 Sex offenders	11 Community sentences	12 Female offenders	13 Electronic monitoring	14 Rest
15 Homicide	16 Non-fatal offences	17 Property offences	18 Rest	19 Self-defence Duress	20 Insanity Intoxication	21 Rest
22 Jury system	23 Court structure	24 Appeals process	25 Police procedure	26 PACE codes	27 Prison system	28 Rest

Monday 22nd	
11 - 12	Jury eligibility and selection
12 - 1	Criticisms of jury system
1 - 1.30	Lunch
1.30 - 2.30	Practice question on juries
2.30 - 3.30	Review and correct practice Q
3.30 - 4	Break
4 - 5	Jury decision- making
5 - 6	Make memory test materials
6 - 7.30	Break
7.30 - 8.30	Tests and review topic

Figure 11.1 A revision timetable

of these has been allocated a particular day on the revision timetable (that is not to say that you would always deal with each topic in one day: a complex topic may require more time and a short or simple topic may require less).

If you look back at the details of each subject in the table at the beginning of the chapter, you will see that the Criminal Justice System exam requires that three questions are answered from a choice of six and that there is a compulsory question on police procedures and PACE Codes. Once the compulsory question is taken out, the student taking this exam must answer two questions from a choice of seven so a revision program that covers the two compulsory topics plus four more topics should leave the student well-prepared for the exam.

It is essential that you do not limit your revision to the same number of topics as there are questions to be answered, as this will cause enormous problems if one (or more) of your topics does not appear on the exam paper or if a topic that you have revised is combined with other topics or you feel that you do not understand the question that is asked about a particular topic. In essence, limiting the number of topics that you revise limits your choice in the exam and may leave you struggling to complete the required number of questions.

Practical exercise: test your topic selection

Taking into account the advice given in this section of the book, make a decision about how many topics you will revise for one of your modules and then make a list of the topics that you would select for revision.

Using the resources available at your university, find a past paper from the previous year and analyse it to see whether or not you would have been able to answer the required number of questions on the basis of the topics that you had planned to revise. Repeat this for more than one past paper to allow for variation in the topics covered.

This should give you some insight into whether or not you have chosen enough topics and selected a good range of topics.

You will also see in Figure 11.1 that each revision session breaks the topic down further into more specific issues. This is a good idea as it suggests that you have considered what particular aspects of a topic are likely to give rise to questions that could appear on the exam paper and can focus your revision accordingly.

You can gain a useful appreciation of the way in which topics can be assessed by looking back at past exam papers. However, be wary of falling into the trap of question spotting. This occurs when students assume that a particular question will be asked about a topic or that a topic will definitely make an appearance on an exam paper just because it has done in the past. Certainly, it can be the case that some areas of a topic are popular with examiners and make regular appearances on an exam paper but that is no guarantee that it will continue to be so. If you work to an assumption based upon question spotting, you will again be narrowing the focus of your revision and limiting the choices available to you when answering questions in the exam.

Revision activities

It is not only the division of the revision into manageable chunks that can cause difficulties; once the structure for revision is established, it can often be hard for students to know what to do to revise effectively within that structure.

In other words, whilst everyone knows that they must revise, not everyone is clear on what exactly this involves. This lack of certainty leads many students to read and re-read their notes in the hope that the information contained therein will stick in their minds whilst other students take this further and write and re-write their notes. These strategies may lead to a greater familiarity with the relevant information but it is not nearly as effective as some other revision techniques that involve more active engagement with the material.

Rather than viewing the purpose of revision as to fix information in your mind, it is preferable to see it as a process that prepares you for the exam. This involves recollection of information and the ability to use it in an effective manner. Simply re-reading or re-writing notes is not sufficient in isolation to achieve the first aim and does nothing whatsoever towards the second. An active approach to revision is far more effective in achieving both of these aims.

Condensed notes

Although note-making alone is not an effective revision strategy, a good set of notes is the foundation of successful revision. Ideally, these will have been produced incrementally as the course has progressed; it is not useful to start the revision process with a blank sheet of paper and nothing to revise. You should aim to take the notes that you have made during lectures, in preparation for seminars, and as part of your private study and condense them into a more concise and memorable set of key points.

Condensing your notes is an important part of the revision process. Not only does it produce a set of concise points that can be committed to memory, the actual process of filtering and recording information will contribute to your understanding of the material as you make decisions about the significance of different points and the relationship between them.

Recorded notes

Making a recording of your notes that you can play back can be a good way of adding variety to the way in which your mind receives information and can help you to make effective use of spare periods of time such as travelling by car or train, sitting in the bath, or lying in bed at night (although the merits of playing recordings through the night are hotly debated—do make sure that you get proper rest during the busy revision period).

A variation upon this theme is to record a group of friends discussing a revision topic and listen to this, bearing in mind that you have less control over the accuracy of the content.

Memory and recall

It is essential that you find a way to make the material memorable.

The first point to note is that it is much easier to recall things that you have understood. This is why it is useful to review the syllabus and weed out topics that have never made any sense to you. If you have not grasped them by the time that the revision period starts, it will probably require far too great an investment in time to get to grips with them now. In fact, you should only really try to incorporate topics that have always mystified you into your revision if it is absolutely necessary, e.g. the topic is the subject of a compulsory question or you have been puzzled by so much of the course that dealing with some difficult topics is essential.

Although it is easier to remember things that you understand, do not assume that just because you understand something you will automatically remember it. During the revision period, you are trying to commit a large amount of information to memory so you might like to try some of the following strategies that can improve your ability to recall information when it is needed.

Association with places

As mentioned earlier in this chapter, it can be easier to recall information if there is an association between the memory and a particular place. This is because it is easy to remember familiar places so you can help yourself to remember other information if you create a link between it and a particular place. There are various ways of doing this, for example:

- **Revise each topic in a different place.** In this way, when you are trying to remember facts about, say, the prison system, you will be able to differentiate this from all the other information milling about in your mind by focusing on the kitchen table which was where your revision for this topic took place. Take yourself back there in your mind, visualize the situation, and you may find that the information itself comes flooding back.

- **Create a concept journey.** This involves visualizing a particular journey—around your parent's garden, for example, or from your front door to the local shop—and mentally placing a particular name or concept at a certain spot on the way. This can be especially useful if you have to remember a series of points in order.

You will find an excellent discussion of this technique and other ways of improving your memory at http://www.mindtools.com/memory.html.

Working with others

In the same way that it is possible to improve recall by linking a topic with a particular place, you can create a link between a topic and a person. This can be particularly effective as collaborative study involves talking and listening as well as reading and writing. Not only does this provide your brain with alternative forms of information, it is also the case that people are more used to processing, storing, and retrieving complex information when it is heard rather than seen.

It may be that you can collaborate with a group of friends so that you divide into different pairs to work on each topic. Alternatively, ask family members and friends from outside of the course to test you on a particular topic or to listen to you explain the finer points of penal theory to them.

There is a further discussion of the value of working with others as well as suggestions for collaborative revision activities later in this chapter.

Making use of images

Images can be easier to recall than written information as they tend to be simpler and they communicate structure as well as content. A further advantage is that the process of creating memorable images will itself help to lodge information in your brain as you select key points for inclusion and make decisions about how to represent particular information and how it links to other points.

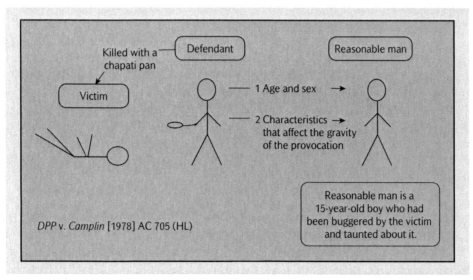

Figure 11.2 Using pictures to remember case law

Pictures

Try to create simple pictures that capture the essence of a piece of information so that it triggers a memory of all the associated facts. Pictures are a particularly good way of capturing the facts of any case law that you may encounter (see Figure 11.2).

Practical exercise: create memorable images

Get together with a small group of other students and draw up a list of cases or concepts that you want to remember. Divide the list between the group and see who can create the most memorable images.

If this seems a bit too much like 'messing about' to include in the serious business of revision, try to look beyond the bad drawings to the skills behind the activity. You will be picking out the most memorable aspects of a case or concept in order to make it recognizable to others. You will be discussing the material with others and you will be creating an image which will stick in your mind and assist with recall in the exam.

Diagrams, flow charts, and mindmaps

Visual representations of information can be a great asset during revision in terms of enabling you to see the entirety of a large topic at a glance. This can be useful in helping you to understand and remember the relationships between sets of criminal offences, the structure of the criminal appeal process, or the development of a theoretical concept. The preparation of a flow chart or diagram will make you really think about these relationships and you should be able to visualize the diagram once in the exam room, which is an excellent way of jogging your memory as to its contents, and you could scribble the diagram down from memory in the rough notes areas of your exam booklet. You will see an example in Figure 11.3.

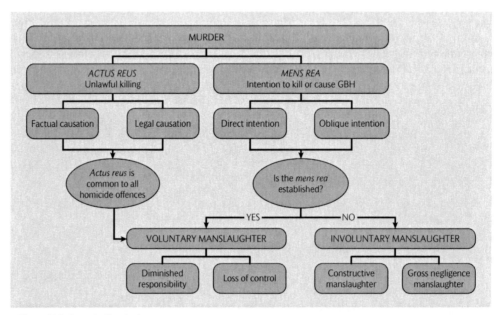

Figure 11.3 A murder flowchart

Testing recall

Activities which test your recollection are a particularly valuable part of revision as they enable you to assess how much you do know and how much work you still have remaining. Try to incorporate at least one of the memory-testing activities detailed below into each day of revision. You might like to do this at the end of the day to see how much you have committed to memory or at the start of the following day to determine how much you have retained. Remember that the process of constructing these materials is also a valuable part of revision as it involves identifying the important aspects of the topic that need to be committed to memory.

Quizzes

Try breaking a topic down into a series of crucial questions that you must be able to answer. Make a note of these questions (and the answers) and use this to test your memory at the end of the revision session. You might find it useful to work with other students. Not only can you test your knowledge by answering another person's quiz questions but you will also be able to see from the questions what the other student considered were the key points of the topic. If there is an enormous difference then it is likely that one of you has misunderstood the topic so you can then work together to strengthen your grasp of the material in question.

Revision flashcards

In essence, revision flashcards are a portable quiz. They are small cards that have room for limited amounts of information to be recorded which should help you to condense your points thus making them easier to remember. Create these by writing a question on the front and the answer on the back. The alternative is to write a key word or phrase on the front and a definition on the back.

Create a set of flashcards for each of your revision topics and carry them with you so that you can revise in spare moments. As they have the answer on the back, they make it easy for you to recruit friends and family who have no knowledge of criminology to test you as part of your revision.

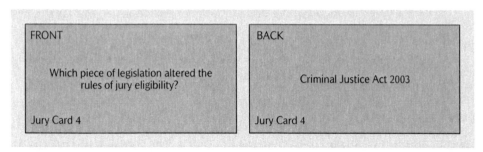

Figure 11.4 A revision flashcard

Templates

A template is a way of testing your recall of key pieces of information. It involves the preparation of a paragraph of text with key words and phrases omitted. You will find an example in Figure 11.5 of a template that outlines the essential elements of the offence of murder.

Alternatively, you could create templates by producing blank versions of diagrams, flow charts, or mindmaps that you have created.

Free-flow writing

Not all activities that test your memory require preparation. Free-flow writing is an excellent way to test your recollection of a topic that requires no preparation whatsoever. Simply select a word, phrase, or concept and write it at the top of a blank piece of paper, and allocate a set

Murder is a _____ offence that carries a _____ penalty of life imprisonment this means that the trial judge has no _____ in sentencing. Prior to the _____ Act 1965, the sentence for murder was the _____. A person who is liable for murder may seek to avoid life imprisonment by entering a plea of _____ or _____. These are known as _____ defences as they do not allow the defendant to avoid liability altogether but impose liability for _____ which gives the trial judge discretion to impose any sentence. These defences, initially introduced to mitigate the harshness of the death penalty, are described as a _____.

Figure 11.5 A template for criminal law revision

period of time in which you will write everything that comes to mind about that topic without any concern for structure, order, or grammatical sense. Any period of time from one minute to five minutes will work well for revision and it might be an idea to start short and build up to longer periods of time as your knowledge increases. It can be a useful starting point for revision so that you can identify what you know and, more importantly, what you do not know by comparing your free-flowing writing with your notes.

Remember that, although free-flow writing can be a useful way of unlocking information stored in your brain, it is not necessarily a useful technique to use if you get stuck in the exam itself as this could encourage you to include all sorts or irrelevant or peripheral material when what is required is that you provide a focused answer to the question. It is a good technique to use for revision and could help if your mind goes blank during the exam provided that you did this as part of your rough work and extrapolated relevant points to use in your actual answer.

Practice answers

Writing practice answers is the most important part of revision. This involves finding questions from past papers or from tutorials, for example, and writing an answer in the same constraints as would apply during the exam. This means that answers should be hand-written within the timeframe that is available in the exam and produced without reference to notes.

Students are often disinclined to write practice answers as part of their revision. Two main reasons are given for this and are discussed in the sections that follow.

The question will be different in the exam

Students often fail to see the value of writing practice answers because they see no point to being able to answer a question that is not on the exam paper. However, the value of the activities lies not in finding the perfect answer to the question but in honing the skills needed to tackle any question that you encounter in the exam.

It is essential that you remember that exams do not only test what you know but also what you are able to do with the knowledge. In other words, you could have a memory full of knowledge of criminology but you still need to demonstrate skills such as the ability to construct a reasoned argument and to engage in critical analysis of the relevant concepts. These are inherently practical skills which require practice to get them right. You would not expect to be able to drive a car simply because you had read about driving in a book; you need to practise driving on the road. The same applies to the skills that you need to produce effective and successful answers in the exam so you should not expect to be able to do this without practice.

Even if you feel that you have the requisite skills that you have developed as a result of producing coursework, you should acknowledge that there is a difference between producing an essay over a period of days or weeks in electronic format, so that changes to the structure and organization are easy to make with reference materials nearby, and writing an answer by hand in a short time and without notes. Writing practice answers, in conditions that are as close to those that you will encounter in the exam as possible, enables you to test, review, and refine your technique and is the key to producing effective and successful answers in the exam room. They enable you to become familiar with the amount that you can write in the given timeframe and get you used to producing focused and structured answers under pressure.

No feedback on the accuracy of the answer

Some students question the value of the exercise if there is no means of determining whether the content is correct or of receiving comment on the quality of the answer and what needs to be improved. In other words, it does not seem to be a useful exercise unless the end result is marked.

As explained in the preceding section, practice answers facilitate the development of the skills needed in an exam. Moreover, it is not the case that there is no feedback available on the content and quality of your answers. You might find that your lecturers are prepared to read practice answers and offer feedback upon them. Even if you cannot find a lecturer who will do this (and it does vary), you should be able to evaluate your own work to a certain extent:

- Compare your answer with your notes and see if you have omitted any key points or made any errors.
- Look at the structure of your answer and consider whether it could have been arranged in a more coherent way to produce a more logical argument.
- Assess the balance between description and analysis. Excessive description and insufficient analysis is a common weakness in exam answers.
- Read your answer, or parts of it, out loud and consider whether you expressed your ideas with sufficient clarity.

Although this may not seem as useful as obtaining feedback from a lecturer, the ability to engage in critical evaluation of your own work is a key skills that you should strive to develop. You could also work with other students to produce practice answers and evaluate each other's work. This could be especially useful as a revision strategy if it generates discussion of the criminological issues relevant to the question; for example, you can use other students to shed light on points that you found difficult in your answer or to clarify how particular theories could have been used more effectively to support your answer. Never underestimate the contribution that is made to the improvement of your own essay writing skills that is made by engaging in constructive criticism of the work of others or by gaining comment on your own work.

Overall, then, the benefits of writing practice answers are:

- You get the feel of how much you can write within 45 minutes or one hour (or however much time is available per question in your exams).

- You will test how much information you are able to recall about a particular topic.

- They offer an opportunity to practise the skills that are necessary to produce an effective essay in exam conditions.

- You can enhance your knowledge and understanding of a topic by reviewing answers written by others and by gaining comment on your own work.

Practice answers not model answers

Writing practice answers is a very useful revision activity but it should not be confused with the practice of creating model answers. Some students produce model answers to past exam questions in the expectation or hope that the same question will be asked in their exam (remember the perils of question spotting covered earlier in the chapter). Model answers are carefully crafted pieces of work that are the result of many hours of work. The aim is to create the perfect answer to the question which can then be memorized and reproduced in the exam room.

This is not a good strategy and it is not an effective way to use your revision time. The chances of the exact question that has been asked in the past arising on your exam paper are extremely slim. Even if you encounter a similar question on the same topic, it will raise different issues so reproducing a memorized answer to a different question is not a sensible idea. Try to remember that the most important rule to follow in the exam is that you must answer the question that has been asked and not the question that you had hoped to find. A model answer prevents you from doing this and will limit the success of your answer.

Collaborative revision

One of the best ways to make revision more effective and more enjoyable is to work with others. There are a range of ways that have already been mentioned earlier in this chapter that you can involve others in your revision but the following are a few more suggestions of things that other students have found particularly useful.

If you form a study group with other students, you will be able to share the workload of evision amongst the members of the group. This could include any of the following activities:

- **Share revision notes.** You can decide on a set of revision topics and distribute these amongst the group. With four people in a group, you would have notes on eight topics even though you had only prepared two yourself. Of course, this means that you are somewhat dependent on the work of others so do try to collaborate with students whose work you trust.

- **Record a group discussion.** Decide on a task to complete as a group and either record the discussion or nominate someone to take notes so that you have a record of what was discussed. For example, you could agree to spend an hour discussing what points to include and how you would tackle a question on alcohol-related crime.

- **Prepare test activities.** Each member of the group could compile twenty quiz questions on a different topic for the others to complete. One group of students came up with the idea of using Trivial Pursuit as a way of testing their knowledge of the criminology modules that were being examined in their second year that was so good that other students offered to pay to take part! This shows that revision can be made enjoyable as well as productive but be wary of devising activities that take too long to create or organize. The students who created a criminology version of Trivial Pursuit started writing questions in October so spread the preparation across two terms of the academic year.

- **Give a lecture.** It is often said that you can only be sure that you understand something properly if you are able to explain it to other people. Revise a topic in criminology and then give a lecture on it to someone else. It can be other criminology students or people who know nothing about the subject; it does not matter whether they understand the topic because it is your job to explain it to them. If you do so in a way that makes sense to them, then you will know that you have understood the topic and can set it out with clarity. Allow your audience to ask questions as this will flag up any points that were not explained with sufficient clarity or that you did not remember to include. At the end of your lecture, ask your audience to explain the topic back to you. If they provide a clear, accurate, and relatively detailed account of the topic then you will know that you explained it well.

In the exam room

It is probably true to say that however much revision you have done and however diligently you have followed the advice in the earlier sections of this chapter, you will probably still quail at the thought of the exam itself. Most people dislike exams and suffer from varying degrees of nerves. The following sections are designed to address a range of issues related to the exam with a view to ensuring that you are able to put in a good performance that makes the most of your hard work during the revision period and throughout the year.

It is important that you realize that there is not an expectation that you will produce coursework quality answers during exam conditions. Naturally, you will be able to produce less detailed answers during the exam but that does not mean that there should be any sacrifice of the other elements that contribute towards the final answer. Although the primary purpose of the exam is to test knowledge and understanding, it also assesses your ability to use your knowledge of criminology to produce structured and discursive essays so it is important to use the exam as an opportunity to demonstrate your skills as well as your knowledge.

Be prepared

Make sure that you have everything that you need to take into the exam room collected together the day before the exam. Most students feel quite stressed on the day so you may feel less flustered if you know that all you have to do is pick up your things and go rather than rushing round looking for spare pens. Work out what you are likely to need (pen, pencil, ruler, highlighter to mark key points on the question paper, calculator if necessary) and ensure that you have spares in case anything breaks or runs out of ink during the exam. Check to see if your institution has a list of prohibited items such as correction fluid.

Ensure that you have remembered any materials that you are permitted to take into the exam room and that they comply with any regulations about the use of such materials. If it is an open book exam, do you have free choice or is there a specific book that is permitted? If statute books are allowed in the exam, there are likely to be rules prohibiting annotation so you will need to check to make sure that nothing is written in your book. If you are allowed to prepare materials to take into the exam, check that they are easy to use: there is no point in cramming copious notes onto a single side of A4 if you cannot find the information you need because the writing is too small and cramped. It is essential that you find out what the rules are regarding materials that can be taken into the exam as checks will be made in the room and anything that does not comply with the regulations will be removed. Not only will you then be without the book or notes, which will place you at a disadvantage compared to the other students, but the removal of your materials will be quite a disruption that may interfere with your concentration.

Follow the rubric

The rubric is the explanatory notes or instructions that accompany the exam and is generally found on the front of the paper, giving instructions about the format of the paper, the number of questions that must be answered, and the timing of the exam.

Once in the exam room, it will be important to take a few moments to check the rubric on the exam paper to ensure that you are clear about what is expected from you in the exam. Do not assume that the requirements of this exam will be the same as any other that you have sat previously unless you are absolutely certain that there is a uniform format for all exams in your department or institution. It is important to check the rubric as it will draw your attention to any compulsory questions or any requirements to answer questions for a particular part of the paper.

Analyse the paper

Some institutions give you a short period of reading time at the beginning of the exam during which you can read the paper but you cannot start writing your answers. If your institution does not have this policy, make sure that you take a few minutes to read the paper carefully anyway; it does not matter if everyone else has started writing straight away. A few minutes spent analysing the paper and thinking about the requirements of each question and whether or not you would be able to answer it will save you time overall. You will see an example of this in Figure 11.6.

It can be useful to make notes about the questions, either on the paper itself (if this is permitted), or on rough paper (if it is provided), or at the back of your answer booklet, to ensure that you have a clear idea of the scope of the questions. This will enable you to make an informed decision about which questions to answer. You may find these steps useful to help you analyse the paper:

1. On a sheet of spare paper or the first page of your exam booklet, write a list of the question numbers and note the main topic of the question.

2. On the basis of the list of topics, eliminate any questions that you feel that you could not answer. For example, if there is an essay question on miscarriages of justice in the Criminal Justice System and you did not revise this topic then you can rule it out as a potential question to answer right from the start.

3. Look at the questions that remain and read them carefully. Note a few more details that might help you appreciate what they require and whether you want to tackle them. Do bear in mind that it is not enough that you know a lot about a topic: you must be able to answer the particular question that is asked about the topic.

4. If you are not sure whether or not you would be able to answer a particular question, try making a quick list of the issues that you think are raised by the question to see how much information you can generate.

5. Make a note of the questions that you feel that you could definitely answer. Hopefully this will be sufficient to tackle the paper. If you have ticked more questions than are needed, you will have to make a judgement about which of these to tackle based upon your preferences for the subject matter. If you have not ticked sufficient questions to

complete the paper, you will have to revisit some of those that you have crossed off and reconsider whether you could attempt an answer.

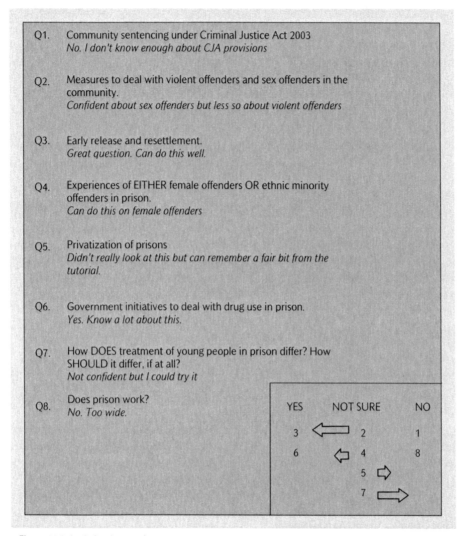

Figure 11.6 Analysing the question paper

Plan each answer

It does not take a great deal of time out of the overall time available to write an answer plan and this investment of time tends to pay immense dividends as it leads to stronger and more focused answers. It is important that you realize that it is not just knowledge that attracts marks in the exams but the way that this knowledge is deployed in response to the question. As with any form of assessment, exams assess not just what you know but what you do with that knowledge so it is crucial to your success that your answers reflect a range of skills, such as the construction of a structured essay and the logical development of an argument, as well as your knowledge of criminology. A plan should help to ensure that your answers have structure and are focused on the question.

Structure

Students who start writing straight away without making a plan often produce a poorly structured essay that is peppered with asterisks and arrows denoting paragraphs that need to be inserted. Unplanned answers also tend to lack logical progression as the student raises different points as they come to mind and this impedes clarity of expression and limits the possibility for depth of analysis and carries a real risk that important material will be omitted.

Focus

It is imperative that you answer the question that has been asked and not the question that you had hoped would be asked. It is all too easy to focus on the overall topic of an essay question and to include all sorts of points that are relevant to the topic but have no bearing whatsoever on the specific question.

As there is no credit available for material that is included in the answer that does not answer the question, a failure to filter out information that is relevant to the topic but not the question can have a detrimental impact on the success of the answer. If you take a little time to create a plan of your answer, make sure that you check every point that you intend to include to ensure that it is relevant to the question rather than relevant only to the topic. This should help you to avoid falling into the 'writing everything you know about the topic' trap.

Writing the answer

This final section will address a range of factors that you need to take into account when writing your exam answers and will conclude with a list of 'top tips' for success in exams.

Timing

It is relatively common for students to run out of time and fail to complete the requisite number of questions. Avoid this by dividing the time available by the number of questions to determine how much time is available to answer each question. Factor into this the five minutes that is needed to plan each answer and make yourself a time plan for the exam. Write this down and note the time at which you need to start a fresh question and make sure that you stick to it. In a three-hour paper that requires that you answer four questions, your time plan might look something like this:

Question	Plan	Answer	Finish
7	2pm	2.05	2.45
5	2.45	2.50	3.30
2	3.30	3.35	4.15
3	4.15	4.20	5pm

Figure 11.7 Planning your time

It can also help to write the starting time alongside the relevant question on the exam paper as this might help you to keep to it. It is important that you allocate equal amounts of time for each question (unless there is not an equal weighting between them). There is always a temptation to devote more time to the questions that you feel that you can answer more proficiently but this is not a good practice.

In this example, there are four questions to be answered in three hours. Each carries equal marks so it would be a mistake to spend the first hour-and-a-half answering your first question, the next hour answering the second, twenty minutes on the third, and then having a frantic scribble for the last ten minutes to try to get something down for the final question and yet this is exactly how many students end up allocating their time. Some students try and avoid doing this by answering the question that they feel will be their weakest first on the basis that it will probably not take up so much of their time. This can be a useful strategy but it can also be dispiriting if you are disappointed with the quality of your answer. It is preferable to start with a presumption that each question will take the same amount of time and move on as soon as your chunk of time for a question has finished irrespective of whether or not your answer is complete. You can always go back and complete the answer if you have time spare at the end.

Stick to the plan

If you have taken the time to write a plan, you should try to stick to it. If a fresh idea occurs to you whilst you are writing, rather than putting it straight into your answer, make a note of it in your rough work area and then take a moment to consider where this additional point fits within your plan, what that will do to the structure of your essay and how it will impact on the other points that you had planned to raise. There is nothing wrong with finding fresh points to include as your answer progresses—sometimes writing out one point jogs your memory about another—but do bear in mind the need for an organized and flowing answer. You should also remember to test every fresh point for its relevance to the question and not just the topic of the question.

Incorporate authority

The use of authority in the exam is an issue that tends to trouble students. It is true that your answer will appear more polished and knowledgeable if you are able to incorporate some reference to authority into your answer but it is important that the use of authority demonstrates understanding rather than appearing as if a random selection of names of theorists and academic commentators have been sprinkled over your exam paper.

The following are types of authority that you should strive to include in your answers where appropriate:

- Key theorists whose work has provided a foundation for criminological study.
- Work of academic commentators that is published in monographs, edited collections, and refereed articles.
- Statutory provisions and case law that establish important principles.
- Official reports and studies.

You might find it useful to refer back to chapters 1, 2, and 3 that explain where each of these sources can be found.

Top tips for exam success

Finally, here are some general pointers that should help to strengthen your exam performance.

- **Answer the correct number of questions.** Some students tackle an extra question if they have done the required number and there is time remaining but you would be better advised to use that time to improve one of your existing answers as you cannot have credit for five questions if the exam requires that you answer four. Equally, some students find that they are struggling to find a question to answer and give up without completing the required number of questions. Always try a last question, even if you feel that your answer will be weak. You will know something of relevance to the question—perhaps more than you realize —and it will at least attract some marks whereas making no attempt will attract no marks at all.

- **Mark sure that your script is legible.** You cannot get credit for work that cannot be deciphered. There are various policies on illegibility so it is impossible to make a generalization about what will happen if your writing cannot be read by the examiners but options include discounting illegible material altogether or requiring the student to pay for the script to be typed out so that it can be read.

- **Stay until the end of the exam.** If you think that you have finished but there is an hour of the exam remaining, it is likely that you have not written enough so it is important to revisit each of your answers and read them through carefully to see if anything can be added to improve their quality. Have you missed out a key issue or have you dealt with a central point in too little detail? If you can spend that hour adding material to your answers that increases the grade of each question by two marks, that will give your paper an additional eight marks which is almost a whole classification.

- **Follow the instructions.** There is no credit available for material that is outside the scope of the question so it is essential that you read the question carefully and do exactly what it asks. For example, if an essay asks you to discuss a particular issue in relation to **either** female **or** ethnic minority offenders then there is no point in covering both. Irrelevant material attracts no credit and takes up time that could be spent writing material that would gain marks.

- **Keep calm.** Many students find exams stressful and get into such a keyed-up state that they are not functioning properly in the exam. This is counter-productive as it interferes with their performance and this leads to a self-perpetuating cycle as they receive poor exam results so become even more anxious in the next set of exams. If you are aware that you suffer in this way, take steps to deal with this prior to the exam. There are some excellent courses on dealing with exam nerves and it may be that some are on offer at your institution. Investigate what help is available and take advantage of it.

Practical exercise: reviewing exam answers

One of the drawbacks of exams is the lack of feedback on your performance; you get your results but there is no comment on what you did well and where there was room for improvement. One way to evaluate your performance is to write practice answers but another way in which to get insight into the characteristics of a good answer and the problems that give rise to a weak answer is to look at the work of others.

Visit the Online Resource Centre to find answers that were produced in criminology exams by students. Read them and make a list of their strengths and weaknesses: you can even award them a mark. Compare this with the comments made and the mark given by experienced markers. Make a note of good practice that you can adopt to strengthen your own performance and also of common errors to avoid.

CHAPTER SUMMARY

Preliminary matters

- Take time to find out information about the exams so that you will be able to make informed decisions about the timing, structure, and content of your revision
- Make sure that you have all the materials that you need to hand before you start to revise
- It is important to create a good working environment free of distractions where you will be able to concentrate on your revision. You may want to vary the location of your revision

Revision planning

- Count the number of days before the first exam and decide how many hours you want to work each day. Take into account your preferences in terms of the timing and duration of revision sessions
- Select an appropriate number of revision topics from across the syllabus in each module. You should cover sufficient material to ensure that you have a choice of questions to answer in the exam
- Create a timetable to organize your revision time

Revision activities

- Try to avoid using exclusive reliance on reading and re-writing notes as a revision strategy as this is a passive approach which does not test your ability to use the material effectively
- Vary the activities that you use as part of your revision. This is to help you to remain engaged and interested in the process and it will aid recollection in the exam
- Consider using a range of methods to record information: written notes, diagrams, pictures, and tape recordings all engage the brain in a different way
- Involving others in your revision distributes the workload and enriches the revision process
- Writing sample answers is the most effective revision activity as it orientates you to the amount of writing that can be done in the timeframe and enables you to make your mistakes prior to the exam and learn from them in order to strengthen your exam performance

Exam technique

- Make sure you are fully equipped for the exam with writing equipment, any materials that you are entitled to take into the exam room, and a clear knowledge of where and when the exam will take place

- Read the question paper carefully, including the rubric, and analyse each question to determine its requirements so that you can make decisions about which questions to answer at the outset
- Allocate your time equally between the questions and remember to include a five-minute period of planning and, preferably, time at the end to read through your answers, making any necessary amendments
- Do not forget that the ordinary requirements of structure, language, analysis, and application relevant to essay writing are still needed in the exam. Answers that demonstrate skills as well as knowledge tend to be more successful
- Remember to include reference to authority to support your answer
- Answer the required number of questions—no more and no less—in legible handwriting using all of the time available. Pay particular attention to any instructions that accompany the question as there are no marks available for moving outside the requirements of the question

FURTHER READING

- Buzan, T. (2006) *The Study Skills Handbook: The Shortcut to Success in Your Studies with Mind Mapping, Speed Reading and Winning Memory Techniques.* London: BBC Active. Tony Buzan invented the notion of mind-mapping and has written many books on the subject. This one is particularly useful as it is aimed at students and contains a great many helpful tips for exam preparation.
- Mindtools is an online resource: http://www.mindtools.com/memory.html. It has a good discussion of the way that memory works and provides a range of methods to improve your memory.

GLOSSARY

- **Model answers** are answers which have been prepared by students in anticipation that they will appear on the exam paper.
- **Practice answers** are answers which are written by hand without notes and within a limited timeframe to simulate exam conditions. They are one of the most valuable revision activities as they enable students to practise the skills that they need in the exam.
- **Question spotting** refers to the tendency of students to make predictions about what questions will appear on this year's exam paper on the basis of questions that have been asked on previous papers.
- **A rubric** is the set of rules that govern the exam. It is found on the front of the exam paper and will include matters such as the duration of the exam and the number of questions to be answered.

PART III
Research skills in criminology

The final part of *Criminology Skills* covers the research skills that you will need to plan and undertake your own research and to make sense of the research of others.

The first chapter considers research ethics which are fundamental to all criminological research: it will equip you with the skills to identify ethical issues that might arise and the knowledge of how to deal with them. Subsequent chapters deal with the business of gathering data and, once gathered, how to analyse both quantitative and qualitative data.

Each of the chapters provides simple practical advice to assist you throughout the various stages of a research project—from idea to analysis.

Research ethics

INTRODUCTION

This chapter will explain the importance of an ethical approach to research in criminology with emphasis on ethical issues arising from research using human participants. It starts by considering the value of ethical approaches to research and moves on to address the particular issues raised by criminological research. The chapter focuses on the British Society of Criminology (BSC) *Code of Ethics* and will use this to explore in detail core ethical principles of confidentiality, anonymity, consent and the avoidance of harm. The final section of the chapter provides guidance on identifying and addressing ethical issues raised by your own research with some suggestions on points to consider when formulating an application for approval for a Research Ethics Committee.

An understanding of research ethics is a valuable asset for anyone studying criminology irrespective of whether or not they plan to conduct their own research. This is because the ability to identify ethical issues and assess the way in which they have been addressed will enable you to take a more critical approach to evaluation of published research. Of course, if you do undertake original research, the ability to recognize and resolve the ethical issues that it raises is a necessity, particularly as it is likely that you will be required to apply for ethical approval prior to commencing research. Moreover, it is only right and proper that you carry out research in a way that adheres to the ethical principles of your discipline both out of concern for your research participants and as a demonstration of your professionalism as a criminologist.

LEARNING OUTCOMES

By the end of this chapter you will:

- Be aware of relevant Codes of Ethics and have an understanding of the principles contained within them

- Have an appreciation of the ethical considerations surrounding research with human participants and understand the value of core principles such as informed consent

- Be able to identify the ethical issues arising from published research and to engage in critical consideration of whether or not the researchers took sufficient steps to address them

- Have developed the ability to identify ethical issues raised by your own research and to formulate a research plan that takes into account these issues

What are research ethics?

When criminologists talk about research ethics, they are referring to the principles that govern the research that they carry out: the 'rules of fair play' of criminological research. These principles are set out in various **Codes of Practice** and Research Statements by organizations such as funding bodies, professional associations, and universities. These different sets of guidelines on research ethics tend to cover broadly the same considerations but are tailored to the objectives and priorities of the particular institution or discipline. Research ethics are particularly associated with **empirical research**—that is, research that involves the use of experiments or observation to gather data—but some key ethical principles are just as relevant to theoretical or library-based research.

According to the Economic and Social Research Council (ESRC), research ethics are 'the moral principles guiding research, from its inception through to completion and publication of results and beyond' (ESRC 2010: 7). It is possible to pick out two key points from the ESRC definition. Firstly, the definition describes research ethics as moral principles. Normally, morality is used as a basis to differentiate between right and wrong so this suggests that there is a right way and a wrong way to behave when carrying out research. Secondly, the definition makes it clear that research ethics apply to *every stage* of the research. It is important to remember this as it is often the case that discussions of research ethics focus exclusively on the processes and procedures used to gather data. The ESRC definition highlights the importance of ensuring that the way in which the research is carried out is acceptable within the ethical parameters of the discipline (procedures) and that there is contemplation of the consequences that the findings of the research might have on others (effects). It also stresses the need to ensure that the results of the research are valid and reported with integrity (output and dissemination).

Research ethics can be difficult to understand in abstract terms so before we start to explain the individual principles involved, we will look at a real example of research carried out in the late 1960s and early 1970s. Read through the details of the project and make a note of any aspects of the research that you think raise problems in terms of research ethics.

Practical example: the tearoom trade

Laud Humphreys conducted a study of homosexual behaviour in public toilets (known colloquially as 'the tearoom trade') as part of his research into human sexual behaviour. He was interested in discovering what sort of people engaged in such behaviour and what their reasons were for doing so.

He gathered data by posing as a 'watch queen' (a voyeuristic lookout who is present at homosexual encounters and who warns the men of potential interruptions or police presence). Humphreys noted the car registration details of the men involved and used these to obtain their names and addresses (via a contact in the police). A year later, with his appearance changed, Humphreys visited the men in their homes under the guise of conducting a public health survey. In this way, he was able to discover that more than 50% of the men who had taken part in homosexual activity were married and leading ostensibly heterosexual lives.

Humphreys' findings dispelled stereotypical views about men who engaged in homosexual activities in public places and was a valuable contribution to knowledge about human sexual behaviour. However, his research is better known for the ethical issues raised by the way he gathered his data. These are some of the points that you could have listed about the research:

- Humphreys deceived research participants on two occasions: first by acting as a watch queen and again when he posed as a researcher conducting a public health survey.

- As a result of the deception, none of the participants were aware that they were taking part in research so could not be said to have given consent.

- It was unlawful to commit a homosexual act in a public place at the time that the research was carried out; thus Humphreys may have been committing a criminal offence by acting as lookout.

- Humphreys used car registration details to obtain names and addresses of participants via 'a friendly policeman' (1975: 193) which may be a breach of rules concerning access to confidential information.

- The research created a risk that the men engaged in unlawful activities could be identified and prosecuted for their offences and that they might be exposed to their families.

There is no need to worry if you did not spot all of these ethical issues: you will be better equipped to do so by the time you have read to the end of the chapter as you will find discussion of the issues raised by Humphreys' research in the sections that follow.

Why are research ethics important?

In some respects, we should not need to ask why research ethics are important. If there is a right way or a wrong way to carry out research or a choice between conducting research in a way that is ethical or unethical then we would like to think that all researchers would select the right way and the ethical approach. However, in order to understand the value of research ethics, it is useful to consider some reasons why an ethical approach to research is beneficial:

- **Adherence to ethical principles ensures that research is carried out with integrity and its results have validity.** Israel and Hay (2006: 10) observe that nobody is watching when research is carried out so there is potential for researchers to use improper methods to gather information, to fabricate data, or interpret findings selectively to suit the research hypothesis. A shared set of ethical principles creates confidence that all criminologists are conducting their research properly and that their results are accurate and reliable. This means that we can rely on research conducted by others rather than repeating it to check its validity and accuracy, thus criminological knowledge can advance at a faster pace. For example, if you wanted to conduct research on binge drinking, you need not replicate the fieldwork carried out by Measham and Brain (2005) that explored levels and patterns of intoxication but could build upon it, safe in the knowledge that their findings are valid as their research was conducted properly in accordance with a Code of Ethics.

- **Collective values minimize the risk of variable standards arising from the application of individual approaches to ethical issues.** In the absence of a Code of Ethics, researchers would be left to apply their own moral judgement to decisions regarding research. This creates potential for different researchers to reach divergent conclusions about the ethical acceptability of a particular piece of research. For example, one researcher might decide that deception of participants is never ethical whereas another might consider some deception to be justifiable if it generated valuable data that would not be forthcoming in the absence of deception. However, it is important to remember that Codes of Ethics offer guidance, not hard and fast rules, so there still may be scope for a difference of opinion with both views representing a sound ethical approach.

- **An established Code of Ethics provides guidance for researchers faced with new situations.** It may be that you want to research a topic that has not been addressed before or you want to use a new and different method of collecting data. For example, technological advances can give rise to new ways to gather data such as analysis of chat room exchanges and recordings taken from CCTV footage. Each new method raises its own ethical consid-erations so it is useful to have an established set of ethical principles that can be applied and, if necessary, developed to suit new situations.

• **Codes of Ethics emphasize the need to protect participants from harm so may encour-age people to take part in research.** Much criminological research would not be possible without the involvement of human participants from whom data can be collected and it is important that they should not suffer harm as a result of their involvement. Ethical principles concerning autonomy, anonymity, and confidentiality exist to protect partici-pants from harm and awareness of this may be an important factor that encourages people to take part in criminology research. Such principles also contribute to the creation of an environment of trust in which participants feel able to make frank disclosures about sensi-tive subject matter thus improving the quality of the data that is gathered. For example, it is unlikely senior figures within professional bodies would be interviewed about institutional racism (Phillips 2005) if they feared that their views would be misrepresented or sensa-tionalized or that burglars would discuss their methods (Nee and Meenaghan 2006) if they thought their details would be passed to the police.

These points demonstrate that ethical principles are pivotal in securing participation, protect-ing participants from harm, and ensuring quality of data.

Research ethics in criminology

Research ethics are important in all disciplines and each major field of research has its own Code of Ethics. Despite the differences between the disciplines, there are core ethical princi-ples such as respect for a participant's autonomy, confidentiality, and anonymity which are common across all fields of study. Even though these core principles are the same, the issues raised by them differ: for example, the protection of research participants from harm is likely to involve different considerations in biomedical research, where participants may be taking part in clinical trials of a new drug, than it does in criminology.

One of the main issues raised by criminological research that distinguishes it from other fields of study stems from its focus on crime which, by its very nature, involves conduct which is harmful and undesirable. The commission of a criminal offence involves at least one offender and one victim (with the exception of so-called 'victimless crimes'). Offenders and victims are both a legitimate focus for research in criminology but both raise complex ethical considerations; the victim has already suffered harm and may re-live this if they are the sub-ject of research whilst the offender risks apprehension if he talks about his misdeeds.

Criminological research may also focus on the personnel of criminal justice: police officers, judges, court officials, prison officers, probation officers, coroners, and youth justice workers to name but a few. Although there is less potential for their involvement to lead to harmful consequences to them as individuals, there might be a conflict between their personal views and their professional roles or participants may fear reprisals if they expose questionable work practices or express negative views.

Research with offenders

Research with offenders may take many forms. It may look at their early life with a view to establishing causal factors leading to their offending, it could focus on their experiences of arrest, prosecution, and imprisonment, or it may explore their perceptions of proposed crime reduction measures or new legislation aimed at curtailing their offending in order to anticipate the likely success of such strategies. Another area of research concentrates on the methods and motivation of offenders (how they commit crime and why they do it) and this can have a valuable role in the formation of policies and practices to reduce crime. For example, Copes and Cherbonneau (2006) found that technological advances in anti-theft devices had halted traditional methods of car theft but that offenders had adapted by resorting to burglary or fraud in order to obtain keys for vehicles. Such findings enable the authorities to tackle the problem by educating car owners about the risk of 'vamoose' burglary (burglary committed with the sole purpose of obtaining car keys) such as the KEYP Safe campaign developed by Buckinghamshire Community Safety Partnership.

Research with offenders raises challenging ethical issues. Foremost of these concerns the very real possibility that the offender will provide details of past offences for which he was not apprehended or that he will make reference to planned future offences. What is the researcher to do with such information? He may consider it unconscionable that past offences are not brought to the attention of the police or that potential victims are not warned about the possibility of future offences. This personal view has to be balanced with the ethical requirements that information provided by participants is kept confidential and that participants should not be harmed as a result of their involvement in research (as exposing a person to the risk of arrest, prosecution, and imprisonment would certainly amount to harm). These issues are explored in greater detail later on in this chapter but, for now, consider the following situation:

Thinking Point

Imagine that you are carrying out research interviews with drug users as part of your research into the effectiveness of Drug Treatment and Testing Orders that were introduced as a community penalty by section 61 of the Crime and Disorder Act 1998. The interviews were conducted in accordance with the British Society of Criminology Code of Ethics and you were at pains to emphasize that all disclosures will be absolutely confidential. In doing so, you were aware that drug users may disclose details of offences committed under the Misuse of Drugs Act 1971 and you also contemplated that they may reveal details of property offences such as theft and burglary committed in order to fund drug purchases.

However, during the interview with one drug user, he claims to be the person responsible for a series of muggings that have taken place locally. You have seen the reports of this detailed in the local paper and know that most of the victims were elderly and that some were badly injured. Two days after this interview, you read that one of the victims died in hospital as a result of her injuries.

▶ What could you have done differently to avoid this situation?

▶ What can you do about it now that this has happened?

 You will find some suggestions on the Online Resource Centre. The discussion of confidentiality and 'heinous discovery' later in this chapter may help to shape your thinking.

There are a number of other ethical issues that are particular to research that involves offenders:

- Offenders may pose a risk to the researcher, particularly if they are apprehended shortly after they take part in research and erroneously assume that the researcher has told the police about their offending.

- Remorseful offenders may be ashamed of their behaviour and experience negative emotions as a result of taking part in research.

- Imprisoned offenders may feel that they lack freedom to choose to refuse to take part in research or may participate to break the boredom of prison routine. Alternatively, they may experience anxiety concerning possible reprisals such as loss of privileges if they criticize the prison or prison officers.

- The police may become aware of the research and demand that you disclose your notes or details of the participants. Concerns about the ability to honour assurances of confidentiality and anonymity caused research into drug-taking to be suspended at the University of Melbourne (Fitzgerald and Hamilton 1996).

- It is usual for participants to be paid a nominal sum to compensate for the time they spend involved in the research. Is it ethical to pay an offender to talk about his criminal activity?

Research with victims

Research into the experiences of crime victims can increase understanding of the impact of particular offences which could, in turn, lead to the development of more effective policing practices, an increase in the severity with which the offence is viewed, and the introduction of support mechanisms tailored to the needs of victims of a particular offence. Research may focus on victims of a particular offence (for example, Gale and Coupe (2005) conducted research on the impact of street robbery on victims) or explore the impact of a crimes on a community (such as Mawby's (2004) exploration of perceptions of crime and disorder in Cornwall).

The main difficulty to consider when contemplating research with individual victims of crime is that their involvement in the research may increase the harm that they have already suffered by causing them to revisit painful events. This may lead to the re-emergence of feelings of anxiety, shame, fear, or guilt and they may experience the return of physical symptoms such as panic attacks. However, for some victims, the opportunity to contribute to research may be a positive experience: they find that talking about their experiences after the lapse of time is cathartic or they may feel as if they are helping others to avoid the same situation by contributing to research. As it is difficult to anticipate how victims will react, it is important to ensure that they have a clear understanding of what the research is likely to involve so that they can make an informed choice about whether to participant and to remind them that they are free to withdraw at any time. This issue will be discussed in greater detail in the section dealing with informed consent. It is also common practice to ensure that a list of sources of help and support are available for participants.

When considering the impact of involvement in research on victims, it is also relevant to contemplate the effect of participation on potential crime victims. All people are potential future victims of crime and research may be conducted with the general population in order to explore their perceptions of a particular crime or their concerns about their risk of falling victim to crime in general. For example, Nellis (2009) conducted interviews with 532 people in order to explore the differences in perceptions of risk of terrorism between men and women. The issue in relation to such research that needs consideration is whether it could cause anxiety amongst research participants by increasing their belief that they might fall victim to an offence.

Thinking Point

Imagine that you are conducting research that explores whether fear of violent crime is greater in elderly people living in rural areas than it is in those living in urban areas. Selected participants across twenty different areas are sent questionnaires with an accompanying letter that sets out the purpose of the study.

You receive a telephone call from an elderly lady, Maggie, who has received your questionnaire. She tells you that she had not realized that her village was at risk of crime. She reports that she is afraid to go out to collect her pension in case she is mugged (there were five questions about mugging on the questionnaire). Several days later, you receive an email from the Police Liaison Officer attached to the Community Centre in Maggie's village. He tells you that Maggie has called the police 17 times in the past three days because she thought she heard an intruder in her home.

▶ What could you have done differently to avoid this situation?

▶ Can you do anything to resolve it now that it has arisen?

 Have a look at the Online Resource Centre where you will find some further discussion of this scenario that outlines how the problem could be avoided and remedied.

Criminal justice professionals

Research with criminal justice professionals can provide valuable insights into the operation of the criminal justice system. It has been argued that public officials talking about their public role should be a matter of public record (Israel and Hay 2006: 79) but it is important to appreciate that ethical considerations must apply equally to all participants. Those working in the criminal justice system may not be willing to participate or offer frank views in the absence of assurances of anonymity and confidentiality. For example, Kibble (2005) interviewed 78 judges to explore their views regarding the admissibility of previous sexual history in rape trials and found that some judges considered the law unjust so sought to circumvent it. It is highly unlikely that such controversial disclosures would have been made if the participants were not granted anonymity.

Accordingly, it is probably advisable to start from a position in which anonymity will be offered to all participants, modifying this only if it seems appropriate in view of the nature of the topic under discussion, the status of the participant, and their willingness to take part without remaining anonymous.

Ethical principles

The previous section outlined the importance of an ethical approach to research and highlighted some of the ethical dilemmas have can arise in criminology. This section will introduce Codes of Ethics as the source of the principles that may resolve those dilemmas and then take a more detailed look at some of the core ethical principles of relevance to research in criminology.

Codes of Ethics

The most appropriate reference point for information about the ethical principles that guide a piece of research is the relevant Code of Ethics. These are compiled by different organizations and are tailored to the needs of the discipline that they govern. Organizations such as funding bodies and professional bodies may issue Codes of Ethics and some departments within universities also produce their own Codes, usually mapping the provisions of the Code issued by the relevant professional body but tailored to the needs of the student body and the sort of research that is likely to be conducted within the department.

The aim of such Codes is to set out the parameters of accepted practice and to provide guidance for researchers to ensure a uniform high standard of practice amongst members of the discipline. In essence, it is a framework of moral principles that guides the conduct of research by members of a particular profession or organization.

The section that follows looks at the approach taken in the British Society of Criminology *Code of Ethics*. As the British Society of Criminology states that its *Code* should be read in light of any other professional body's ethical guidelines, you may find it useful to look at the following Codes as well as that of your own university or department:

- **Economic and Social Research Council**, *Framework for Research Ethics* (2010) http://www.esrc.ac.uk/_images/Framework_for_Research_Ethics_tcm8-4586.pdf
- **British Psychological Society**, *Code of Ethics and Conduct* (2009) http://www.bps.org.uk/sites/default/files/documents/code_of_ethics_and_conduct.pdf
- **British Sociological Association**, *Statement of Ethical Practice* (2002) www.britsoc.co.uk/equality/Statement+Ethical+Practice.htm
- **Socio-Legal Studies Association**, *Statement of Principles of Ethical Research Practice* (2009) http://www.slsa.ac.uk/images/slsadownloads/ethicalstatement/slsa%20ethics%20statement%20_final_%5B1%5D.pdf.

British Society of Criminology Code of Ethics

The most recent Code of Ethics for Researchers in the Field of Criminology was published by the British Society of Criminology (BSC) in February 2006. It can be accessed on the BSC website: http://www.britsoccrim.org/codeofethics.htm.

The BSC Code starts by identifying the general responsibilities involved with criminological research (Section 1) and then sets out four sections based upon the researcher's responsibilities to other parties who are involved in the research process as Figure 12.1 illustrates.

General responsibilities

Section 1 of the BSC *Code of Ethics* is concerned with over-arching principles relating to the competence, expertise, and qualifications of researchers. It also emphasizes the importance of keeping up-to-date with developments in relation to ethical and methodological issues and of ensuring that sources of information used are reliable, especially Internet sources.

Key Principle: ensure that you have sufficient knowledge, skills, and competence to carry out your research.

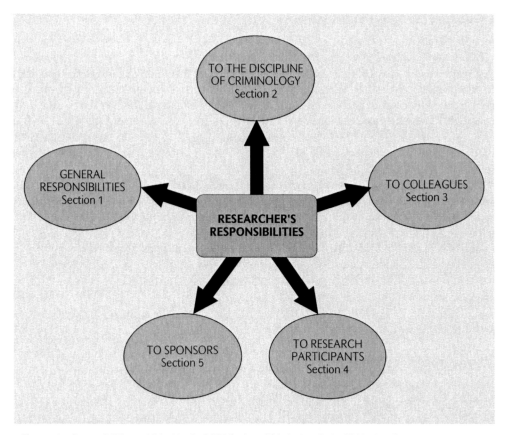

Figure 12.1 Responsibilities established by the British Society of Criminology Code of Ethics (2006)

The discipline of criminology

This section of the *Code of Ethics* states that researchers have a responsibility to advance and disseminate knowledge within the field of criminology and, as such, should cultivate professional relationships and promote open discussion of research findings and research methods. It also emphasizes the importance of avoiding contractual conditions that limit academic freedom to research or disseminate without restriction.

Key principle: seek to further the boundaries of knowledge within criminology.

Responsibility to colleagues

The *Code of Ethics* emphasizes the importance of dealing with colleagues with integrity by acknowledging any contribution made by others to research and ensuring that research assistants receive proper training and support. This section also addresses the importance of referencing to acknowledge the use of others' research and ideas.

Key principle: respect the work of others.

Responsibility to research participants

Section 4 is the most detailed section of the *Code of Ethics* and it covers what many people consider to be the most fundamental feature of ethical research: the responsibility to ensure that research participants do not suffer **harm** as a result of their involvement in the research. In paragraph (i), there is an explanation that this means that 'the physical, social and psychological well-being' of participants must not be adversely affected. It goes on to say that consideration must be given to participants who are vulnerable by virtue of age, social status, or powerlessness and it suggests that it may be appropriate to provide information about support services to participants who may be disturbed as a result of their participation in the research.

This section also deals with important matters such as **informed consent**, the right of participants to withdraw at any point during the research, and the closely related issues of **anonymity** and **confidentiality**. More detailed consideration of these matters can be found in the sections that follow.

Finally, this section draws attention to the particular problems that may exist when using the Internet to conduct research and when otherwise engaging in comparative or cross-national research. The importance of ensuring compliance with the relevant law and taking account of cultural differences is highlighted.

Key principle: protect research participants.

Relationships with sponsors

This section sets out considerations that should be taken into account when dealing with sponsors and funding bodies. It suggests that the obligations of both the funding body and the researcher should be clarified prior to the commencement of the research and that sponsors/funding bodies should be notified of any proposed departure from the original agreement. The *Code of Ethics* reminds researchers that funding arrangements should not jeopardize the integrity of the research by placing unrealistic time constraints upon the researcher or by imposing restrictions on dissemination.

Key principle: develop effective and appropriate relationships with funding bodies and sponsors.

Anonymity

Principles of anonymity and confidentiality are closely related to each other as both concern restrictions on publication of the information provided by research participants. Anonymity refers to the protection of the identity of participants. This is achieved by ensuring that the participant's name and any other personal information that would enable a third party to make the link between the data provided and the person who provided it is not made known. Confidentiality is concerned with the extent to which the data itself that is provided by research participants is shared with others or published.

The word 'anonymity' stems from the Greek *anōnumos* meaning 'nameless' (from *an-* 'without' + *onoma* 'name'). The idea of namelessness can be quite a useful way of thinking about this ethical principle, as one of the main things that researchers do in order to protect anonymity is to ensure that participants are given a pseudonym or a reference number so that they can be referred to in the research without the use of their name:

- In Auburn's work on sex offender treatment, he assigns each offender a pseudonym, denoting this by the use of inverted commas on first usage: 'Richard' is the offender in the 'hot seat'. He is explaining to the group how he came to develop an abusive relationship with his daughter (2010: 114).

- By contrast, Finch (2011) allocates reference numbers to the offenders interviewed in her study of plastic card fraud: Participant D2/32 had also predicted that chip and PIN would not interfere with his involvement in fraud; at his first interview in May 2005, he stated 'I enjoy it too much to stop'.

The subject matter of these two examples highlights the value of anonymity as it is difficult to imagine fraudsters and sex offenders agreeing to discuss their offences if they were going to be identified by name in published research. Not only would this expose them to the risk of arrest for any offences which were previously undetected but there would also be the possibility of other negative consequences if their identity and offences were widely known. The same considerations apply to victims of crime: they can disclose painful or embarrassing details knowing that it will not be linked with them and, as a result, nobody will know whose experiences are being detailed. The promise of anonymity allows participants to discuss controversial or sensitive subject matter without being connected with it, thus it is likely to be instrumental in facilitating the disclosure of more detailed data: participants do not need to protect themselves by withholding material from the researcher as their privacy is protected by the preservation of their anonymity.

Practical advice: protecting anonymity

Names
Make sure that you formulate a list of pseudonyms in advance to ensure that the allocation of a name to a participant is random rather than the result of word association that could disclose the participant's real name. A prepared list should avoid the situation in which Peter is called 'Paul' and George is called 'Michael'. Alternatively, you could allow participants to select their own pseudonym; this could reassure them that the promise of anonymity is one that you take seriously.

Reference numbers
You can either invent a wholly random reference system or formulate something more systematic based upon certain characteristics of the participant and the research. For example, 1LS32M might be the first interview (1) carried out in Leeds (LS) and involve a 32-year-old (32) male (M) participant. This latter approach can be useful to help the researcher remember which participant is which without repeated reference to a key but care should be exercised to ensure that the code cannot be unravelled by others in a way that enables them to identify the participant. The alternative is to create meaningless reference codes and allocate one to each participant:

Option 1	Option 2	Option 3
Participant A50	Participant 001	Participant MW7
Participant B49	Participant 002	Participant GN5
Participant C48	Participant 003	Participant BL1
Participant D47	Participant 004	Participant TR3

In essence, it does not matter what you call a participant provided that it enables you to match them with a single set of data and it does not allow them to be identified.

A final point to note is that it is not only the publication of a person's name that enables them to be identified. A person can be given a pseudonym but will not be anonymous if other bibliographic detail is provided, particularly if the class is small. For example, if you describe a participant as a 35-year-old Australian woman with three children who is studying criminology at postgraduate level at Portsmouth University then this will be sufficient information to ensure that this person can be identified by at least some people.

Confidentiality

Israel and Hay (2006: 78–79) offer three arguments in support of the value of the preservation of confidentiality within the research relationship:

- **Consequence-based.** Without assurance of confidentiality, participants would be reluctant to divulge information, particular on sensitive topics or where disclosure could have damaging consequences for them.
- **Rights-based.** People have the right to impose limits on what information they provide and what happens to that information once it is disclosed in the interests of respect for privacy and autonomy.
- **Fidelity-based.** A promise of confidentiality given should be honoured out of respect for the integrity of the research relationship.

The most significant debate within criminology (and other disciplines) regarding confidentiality is whether it is absolute and, if it is not, in what circumstances it should not be maintained. It is this issue that is at the heart of the example earlier in this chapter where, during the course of interviews about the effectiveness of Drug Treatment and Testing Orders, a participant reveals that he is responsible for a series of muggings, one of which had fatal consequences.

Should this information be kept confidential?

Absolute confidentiality

There are those who argue that all information disclosed should be protected by the promise of confidentiality even if it relates to the commission of serious criminal offences or the threats of serious future (and therefore preventable) harm to an identifiable person. Various different justifications exist in defence of absolute confidentiality:

- Offences committed in the past cannot be undone and may well be detected by the authorities without any assistance from the researcher whilst a threat of harm in the future may not occur for a whole range of reasons.
- There is a distinction between the role of a researcher (to observe, explain, and understand criminal behaviour) and a police officer (to investigate crime and arrest criminals) and a researcher should not encroach upon the police officer's role (Schwartz 1976: xii). Moreover, such disclosures may be boastful and it would waste police time to pass on information that is not supported by evidence.
- If researchers breached confidentiality and passed information on to the police, people would refuse to take part in research and criminologists would be denied these valuable sources of information (Van Maanen 1983: 236–7). Alternatively, participants would simply omit incriminating information and research data would be incomplete and less valuable as a result.
- The disclosure would not have been made if it had not been initiated by the researcher so no adverse effects should be visited upon a participant for something that would not have happened without the researcher's interference (Lowman and Palys 1999: 30).

Limited confidentiality

Despite these arguments, some researchers feel unhappy at offering absolute confidentiality as there is always a possibility that participants will disclose something that they feel cannot be kept confidential such as plans to commit offences in the future or to cause harm to identifiable individuals. For example, Barter and Renold (2003) conducted research interviews with over 70 children in residential care under the auspices of limited confidentiality as they were not prepared to maintain confidentiality if a child disclosed that they were being physically or sexually abused.

The BSC *Code of Ethics* recognizes that it may not always be possible or desirable to promise absolute confidentiality as it states that '[r]esearch participants should be informed about how far they will be afforded anonymity and confidentiality' (2006: para. 4(iii)). The *Code of Ethics* does not set out situations in which it is appropriate to offer only limited confidentiality but leaves that to the discretion of the researcher to decide what information they could not bear to keep confidential. This means that it is not unethical to place limitations on confidentiality but it is unethical not to tell participants about these limitations.

Thinking Point

Reflect on your own views about the extent of confidentiality. Would you agree with Barter and Renold (2003) that certain disclosures are too damaging to be protected by confidentiality or are you persuaded that there are good reasons to promise absolute confidentiality? Would it depend on the nature of the information that was disclosed?

Dealing with a 'heinous discovery'

So far, we have contemplated two possible situations:

- The researcher decides that he will keep all disclosures confidential irrespective of their nature (absolute confidentiality).
- The researcher realizes that there are certain types of disclosure that he would not be prepared to keep confidential and warns the participant in advance that confidentiality is limited and will not cover certain specific types of disclosure (limited confidentiality).

Whichever of these positions is preferred, it should be the product of considered reflection; in other words, the researcher should think about the sorts of disclosures that are likely to be made, in light of the subject matter of the research, and reach a decision as to whether to offer absolute or limited confidentiality. However, even after careful contemplation of the sorts of disclosure that are likely to be made, a researcher could be faced with a 'heinous discovery' in which 'a researcher obtains unanticipated information about a prospective harm that a research participant intends to inflict upon himself or a third party' (Palys and Lowman 2001: 262).

Thinking Point

The example earlier in this chapter concerning the research into Drug Treatment and Testing Orders involves a heinous discovery. The researcher has thought about the sorts of disclosures that are likely to be made and concluded that it is likely to be drugs offences and property offences committed in order to pay for drugs. The researcher did not consider that a participant may have caused someone's death. Would you have thought of this if you had been conducting this piece of research?

Think about the following scenario and work out how you would deal with confidentiality.

Research with Young Offenders

You are conducting interviews with young offenders who are serving their first custodial sentence to determine whether incarceration has deterred them from carrying out further offences. Each participant will be interviewed on three occasions:

1. At an early stage of his sentence when he is trying to adjust to custody.

2. Just before the end of his sentence when he is anticipating his life upon release.

3. Six months after his release to see whether he has committed any offences.

The participant in question is a 16-year-old boy (Paul) who is serving a three-month sentence for repeated offences involving the theft of motor vehicles. At your first interview, it is clear that he is finding life in prison difficult.

▶ What disclosures do you think would be made?

▶ Would you be prepared to offer absolute confidentiality to Paul?

▶ If not, in what way would you limit confidentiality?

 Have a look at the Online Resource Centre where you will find some further discussion of the issues raised by this scenario and some other similar exercises that you can complete.

Most students that complete this exercise focus on the possibility that Paul will admit to other offences for which he has not been convicted or that he will state that he plans to commit theft or motoring offences when he is released. However, as he is finding prison life difficult, there are all sorts of other possible heinous disclosures: he may be harming himself or being harmed by other prisoners or prison officers, he may be contemplating suicide, or planning to escape. Did you think about these possibilities? Would you feel able to keep such disclosures confidential?

The examples set out in Table 12.1 opposite demonstrate two extreme positions taken by researchers in similar situations.

Leibling did not anticipate disclosures about self-harm and had made a promise of absolute confidentiality that she felt compelled to keep whereas Zinger had avoided any possibility of a heinous discovery by offering such limited confidentiality that the very information that he sought was unlikely to be disclosed. Ideally, you want to avoid being in either position so give thought to the following issues before embarking on a piece of research:

1 Start by thinking about the sorts of disclosures that could be made taking into account the subject matter of your research and the nature and position of the person who will be taking part in your research. Expect violent people to be violent, dishonest people to steal things, and people in desperate situations to do desperate things. If you are prepared to keep these disclosures confidential then you can offer absolute confidentiality but remember that this may create an ethical dilemma if you are faced with a heinous discovery.

2 If you are not prepared to offer absolute confidentiality, consider whether the sorts of things that you would want to disclose are at the heart of your research. Try to avoid conducting research on topics that are going to give rise to information that you will not want to keep confidential as this is rather unfair to participants. It would be rather odd to embark on research with perpetrators of domestic violence if you were not prepared to extend

confidentiality to offences of violence committed against their partners, as this is exactly the sort of information that you want participants to tell you.

3   If you want to limit confidentiality in relation to things that are not at the heart of the research but which might occur, think about how to word this so that the participant is clear about what is covered but is not deterred from taking part in the research. It would be appropriate to issue warnings to the participant if you think that he is heading towards a disclosure that is not covered by confidentiality. For example, you could say 'I think that you are giving me a bit too much detailed information about offences you are planning to commit in the future. Can you speak in general terms only? Remember, if I know of an offence that you are going to commit in detail, I have to pass that information on to the police'.

4   If faced with a heinous discovery, it would be appropriate to stop the participant as soon as you can and warn him that you may not be able to keep this information confidential. Seek the advice of your supervisor and other experienced researchers and be guided by them. Remember, though, that a moral dilemma can only be resolved by reference to your own sense of what is right and wrong. Codes of Ethics and the views of others may offer guidance but the decision will ultimately be yours which is why the situation is best avoided wherever possible.

Table 12.1 Two approaches to disclosures made by prisoners

Very limited confidentiality	Preservation of confidentiality
Zinger and Wichmann (1999) studied the effects of long-term segregation on prisoners. They believed that long periods of solitary confinement would cause prisoners to become aggressive and to harm themselves or others. They advised participants that confidentiality was limited and that they would have to disclose any information that they received that related to the safety of the prisoner or the institution including suicide plans, plans of escape, injury to others and the general security of the institution.	Leibling (1992) conducted research on suicide and self-harm in prison. During the course of her research, a female prisoner with a history of self-harm admitted that she had been able to smuggle a piece of glass into her cell. She stated that she wanted to have the glass 'just in case' she felt the urge to cut herself. Leibling had not specified limited confidentiality prior to commencing the interview and ultimately decided not to disclose the information to the prison authorities. Fortunately, the participant did not harm herself.
This approach was criticized as it excludes from confidentiality the very information that the researcher expects to receive and that is at the heart of the study. Palys and Lowman argue that it is unacceptable to limit confidentiality in relation to core subject matter of the research as this is tantamount to asking participants to incriminate themselves: '[r]esearchers effectively said to prisoners 'We want to know about your aggressive tendencies towards yourself and others in order to reveal the truth about solitary confinement but if you tell us about any we must report you' (2001: 257).	Leibling does not elaborate on the factors that influenced her decision not to disclose the information. It may have been that she felt that the participant's history of self-harm would have led to the glass being discovered by prison officers or that breach of confidentiality would damage her relationship with the woman and jeopardize the research. Perhaps she felt that the participant should have the right to decide whether or not to harm herself. Leibling visited the woman after the disclosure to ensure she had not harmed herself but questions whether she made the right decision (1992: 123).

> **Practical advice: Data Protection Act 1988**
>
> In addition to the ethical issues raised by the collection and storage of data from participants, there are also legal obligations imposed by the Data Protection Act 1988. You will either have to comply with the requirements of this legislation or ensure that your data is completely anonymized so that it falls outside the Data Protection Act. This latter option requires that it must not be possible to link the data to the person who provided it. For example, if you assign each participant a code but keep a key that reminds you of their identity then this is not sufficient to take the data outside of the Act. If your research falls within the Act, you should find that your university provides detailed guidance on the rules on dealing with data; many institutions have a dedicated records management officer who will be able to advise you. The most relevant Data Protection Principles for research in criminology are:
>
> - First Data Protection Principle: informed consent (see below).
> - Third Data Protection Principle: collect no more information than you need for your research.
> - Fourth Data Protection Principle: ensure your information is accurate and up-to-date.
> - Sixth Data Protection Principle: protect the rights of participants.
> - Seventh Data Protection Principle: ensure that data is stored securely.

Consent

It is regarded as a fundamental aspect of ethical research practice that consent is obtained from participants. For the purposes of criminological research, consent has three characteristics (BSC 2006: para. 4iii) so it must be:

- **Informed**. Potential participants should be given enough detail about the nature and purpose of the research and what is expected from them to enable them to make a reasoned decision about whether they want to take part. The BSC *Code of Ethics* also suggests that participants should be told who is undertaking the research and who, if anyone, is financing it. Participants should be told why it is being undertaken and how the findings will be disseminated (2006, para. 4iii). In essence, participants should know what they are agreeing to so that their consent is meaningful. However, there are some situations (discussed below) in which it is possible to give less detailed or even misleading information.

- **Voluntary**. As a researcher, you will want people to take part in your research but remember that they may not want to do so. You must not coerce or bribe people to take part and you must ensure that those who do agree have the freedom and capacity to make the decision. Particular care must be taken with children and other vulnerable people, such as those with mental illness or prisoners, to ensure that they are truly willing to take part. The BSC *Code of Ethics* states that it is unwise to rely exclusively on consent given on behalf of such participants (by a parent or custodial institution) and that the consent of the participants themselves should be sought (2006, para. 4iii). Make sure that the circumstances in which people are told about the research leave them free to decline to participate. For example, if an employer asks employees to co-operate, they may feel that they cannot refuse. Equally, if a lecturer distributes a questionnaire in a lecture, students may feel compelled to complete it, particularly if everyone else is doing so.

- **Continuing**. The BSC *Code of Ethics* makes it clear that 'research participants have the right to withdraw from the research at any time and for any reason without adverse consequences' (2006: para. 4iii). Participants should be made aware from the outset that they are free to change their mind and withdraw from the research after it has started. There are some situations in which it would be appropriate to check during the research if the participant is happy to continue: for example, if distressing topics are covered during interview.

Informed consent

The essence of informed consent is that comprehensive and honest information will be provided to potential participants to enable them to make a decision about whether or not to participate in the research. However, there might be circumstances in which the provision of information about the project would have a negative impact on the research. Consider the following scenario and imagine the impact that obtaining informed consent would have on the research findings.

Thinking Point

Imagine you want to conduct research to build on Corbett and Caramlau's (2006) findings regarding the difference in responses of male and female drivers to speed cameras. You decide that the best way to do this is to recruit a sample of drivers of both sexes and accompany them on a short journey in order to observe their behaviour on a route that passes several speed cameras. In order to obtain informed consent, you explain to your participants that the purpose of the study is to explore how aware drivers of different sexes are of speed cameras and how this affects their driving behaviour.

How do you think that this explanation will affect your participants? Do you expect that you will be able to observe their normal driving behaviour? If not, what affect will this have upon the validity of your data and the value of your research?

It is likely that awareness of the purpose of the study will make participants drive differently. They will certainly be looking out for speed cameras and it is likely that they will alter their driving behaviour. Many people, not wishing to be seen as bad drivers or as people who break the speed limit, will decide to adhere to the speed limit for the entirety of the journey whilst others may decide to drive more recklessly than usual, perhaps speeding up to a camera and braking sharply just before reaching it. What will this tell you about their normal driving behaviour? Nothing. As such, the results of your research are meaningless. Your efforts to obtain informed consent have negated the value of your research.

What can be done to overcome these problems? One solution would be carry out the research in a different way but this can be troublesome if you are certain that your chosen method will provide the most reliable and informative data. The other options are to deceive the participants so that they are either unaware that they are taking part in research at all (thus you would be studying natural behaviour) or so that they think that the research is about something else (so that they are distracted from the main purpose of the research and cannot respond to it). Both of these possibilities are explored in the following sections.

Observation of natural behaviour

One way to ensure that people do not modify their behaviour as a result of their knowledge of the nature of the research is to prevent them from becoming aware that they are taking part in a research project at all. The advantage of this is that it enables you to observe people behaving in a natural manner but the disadvantage is that it precludes any possibility of obtaining any consent at all. Consider the following example:

Practical example: on being sane in insane places

Rosenhan (1973) conducted research to explore the accuracy of psychiatric evaluation and diagnosis. Each member of his research team attended a different psychiatric hospital and reported suffering from auditory hallucinations: namely, that they could hear a voice in their head repeat words like 'empty', 'hollow', and 'thud'. All researchers were admitted to hospital and all but one were diagnosed as suffering from schizophrenia. They reported no further symptoms after admission and behaved normally at all times but took an average of 19 days to be discharged. Rosenhan's study revealed that psychiatric patients were not well treated as polite requests for information about their illness and treatment were ignored and ordinary behaviour was treated as a pathological symptom (for example, one nurse wrote 'patient exhibits writing behaviour' to describe the researcher's practice of writing a diary whilst another researcher was described as 'nervous' because he was pacing the corridor when he was simply exercising to relieve his boredom).

Rosenhan's research involved deception of medical staff as the institutions and individuals concerned were unaware of his research and were not asked for their consent. Was this unethical? Rosenhan believed the deception was necessary as the research would have been meaningless without it: hospitals were unlikely to allow such research to take place and, even if they did, medical staff would not have behaved naturally with the researchers. This captures the criticism of much research carried out in natural settings: it is carried out without the knowledge, let alone the consent, of those who are studied and who might well have refused to take part if they had been asked.

Despite the value of the data that can be obtained in this way, the current position of most Codes of Ethics does not favour this level of deception. The BSC *Code of Ethics* does not mention deception at all but states that informed consent should be obtained in all but exceptional circumstances and that this relates to the importance of the research rather than the difficulty of obtaining access (2006: para. 4iii). The British Psychological Society *Code of Ethics and Conduct* provides more specific guidance, acknowledging that some deception may be necessary to preserve the integrity of the research but that, in the absence of informed consent, a person should only be observed for the purposes of research in places where they would ordinarily expect to be observed by strangers (2009: 13).

Thinking Point

How would the approach outlined in the BPS *Code of Ethics and Conduct* assist you in devising an approach to studying the reactions of male and female drivers to speed cameras? Do you think that a car would be a place where a person would ordinarily expect to be observed by strangers?

▶ You could argue that cars are driven on public roads so it is reasonable to observe a person's driving habits without notifying them of the research or obtaining informed consent.

▶ However, drivers are usually observed by strangers from outside their cars so it is arguable that the inside of a car is personal space where they would not expect to be observed by strangers.

▶ Perhaps the best alternative would be to position yourself on the road near a speed camera and note the behaviour of drivers as this is something that would ordinarily be observed by strangers.

There are some situations in which a person would reasonably expect to be observed by strangers that might be of particular interest in criminology research:

- Most criminal courts are open to the public and are often reported in the newspapers so observations might be carried out of court proceedings.

- Observation of large scale public events would seem to be covered so this could be a useful way to research the policing of public protests, for example, or the nature and prevalence of football violence.

- There is growing interest in internet research but some lack of clarity about how ethical principles should operate in cyberspace. It is possible that this principle could be extended to cover, for example, discussions in a forum or messages posted in a chatroom.

Observation of people in places where they would expect to be observed by strangers does enable you to research people without their knowledge or consent but is of limited value if you want participants to discuss a particular topic or carry out a particular task because the behaviour of people in a natural setting is outside of your control. The alternative approach is to recruit people to take part in research but not to tell them the complete truth about the nature of the research.

Deception as to the nature of the research

This approach strikes a balance between the ethical principle of informed consent and the need to produce meaningful and valid research data which might not be forthcoming if participants were aware of the purpose of the research. Participants are aware that they are taking part in research and give their consent to doing so but they are not given accurate or complete information about the research. This is a very useful approach when such information would make people behave differently (as in the driving example used earlier). Read the description of a famous piece of research carried out by Stanley Milgram in the practical example below and think about why it would not have worked unless the researcher had deceived participants.

The purpose of Milgram's research was to discover whether ordinary people would inflict harm on others if ordered to do so. If participants were told the truth—that is, that the other 'participant' was a researcher who was only presenting to feel pain because he was not really receiving electric shocks—then the experiment would have become meaningless. Telling the truth would have made it impossible to test what Milgram wanted to test so deception was necessary to ensure the success of the experiment. However, Milgram's experiment was subject to heavy criticism, not just because of the level of deception but also because of the level of distress suffered by the participants once they became aware of the true nature of the experiment.

Although it is unlikely that Milgram's research would get ethical approval today, the general approach of offering less than full information to participants to ensure that the purpose of the research is not thwarted is acceptable provided that the deception does not go beyond what is necessary to protect the integrity of the research.

Practical example: obedience and authority

Following the atrocities of the Second World War and the Holocaust, Milgram (1963) conducted research to explore the extent to which ordinary people would inflict suffering on others in a way that was contrary to their own morality if they were ordered to do so by someone in authority.

He advertised for participants to take part in a study of memory and learning (deception: the study was about authority and obedience).

Milgram's advertisement

Public Announcement

WE WILL PAY YOU $4.00 FOR ONE HOUR OF YOUR TIME

Persons Needed for a Study of Memory

•We will pay five hundred New Haven men to help us complete a scientific study of memory and learning. The study is being done at Yale University.

•Each person who participates will be paid $4.00 (plus 50c carfare) for approximately 1 hour's time. We need you for only one hour: there are no further obligations. You may choose the time you would like to come (evenings, weekdays, or weekends).

•No special training, education, or experience is needed. We want:

Factory workers	Businessmen	Construction workers
City employees	Clerks	Salespeople
Laborers	Professional people	White-collar workers
Barbers	Telephone workers	Others

All persons must be between the ages of 20 and 50. High school and college students cannot be used.

•If you meet these qualifications, fill out the coupon below and mail it now to Professor Stanley Milgram, Department of Psychology, Yale University, New Haven. You will be notified later of the specific time and place of the study. We reserve the right to decline any application.

•You will be paid $4.00 (plus 50c carfare) as soon as you arrive at the laboratory.

- -

TO:
PROF. STANLEY MILGRAM, DEPARTMENT OF PSYCHOLOGY, YALE UNIVERSITY, NEW HAVEN, CONN. I want to take part in this study of memory and learning. I am between the ages of 20 and 50. I will be paid $4.00 (plus 50c carfare) if I participate.

From the book *Obedience to Authority: An Experimental View* by Stanley Milgram.

Participants were told they would be working with one other volunteer (deception: this 'volunteer' was a research assistant named Wallace) and that they would draw lots to allocate the role of teacher and learner (deception: the draw was fixed to ensure that the participant was the teacher and Wallace was the learner).

The participant was seated in front of equipment that administered electric shocks and through a window could see Wallace strapped into a chair and covered in electrodes (see photograph below). Participants were instructed to teach Wallace pairs of words and administer electric shocks of increasing intensity when errors were made. The dial was labelled to show the intensity of the shock with words such as 'strong', 'intense' 'danger', and 'severe' (deception: the equipment was fake).

Milgram's experiment

From the film *Obedience* copyright ©1968 by Stanley Milgram, copyright renewed 1993 by Alexandra Milgram and distributed by Penn State Media Sales.

Wallace pretended to react to the shocks with his reaction increasing in line with the strength of the shock (deception: he received no shocks). He screamed, banged on the wall and asked to leave the experiment, collapsed on the floor complaining of chest pains, and ultimately appeared to lose consciousness. Participants continued to administer shocks although they protested about doing so and some became very distressed. The researcher instructed the participant to continue with a series of commands:

- Please go on.
- The experiment requires that you continue.
- It is absolutely essential that you continue.
- You have no other choice. You must go on.

Milgram was astounded by the results of the experiment as 65% of participants (26 out of 40) administered shocks at the highest possible level despite witnessing Wallace's seeming distress and suffering. Prior to the experiment, Milgram had predicted that only one person in one thousand would go all the way to 450 volts. Even participants who did not continue to the maximum level mostly carried on until they reached 300 volts.

Thinking Point

Does this approach of recruiting participants to take part in a research study but deceiving them as to the nature of the research provide a solution to the difficulties outlined in the study of male and female reactions to speed cameras?

Can you think of a way that the research could be explained to participants so that they would not modify their driving behaviour whilst not deceiving them any more than is necessary to ensure that the data produced is valid?

▶ You could tell participants that the research was about some other driving behaviour so that they would not look out for speed cameras. For example, you could say that the research was to test whether listening to the radio affected their standard of driving. Of course, they might then focus on driving performance so much that they failed to notice speed cameras they would otherwise have noticed!

▶ This is one of the pitfalls of deceiving participants—even the deception might make them act differently. One solution would be to focus their attention on something unconnected with driving performance that will happen at the end of their journey. Perhaps you could tell participants that you were interested in the factors that they take into account when selecting a parking place as part of research on how fear of crime affects every day decisions such as what areas of a town to visit. In that way, you would still have cause to be in the car with participants so as to observe their driving and their response to speed cameras but it is less likely that the standard of their driving will be altered.

When formulating an approach to consent in relation to your own research, it will be important to give careful thought to whether or not the validity of your data will be compromised by giving participants full and accurate details of the research and their role. Your starting point should always be the provision of full and complete information so as to obtain informed consent but remember that there is scope for omission of key details or deception if this is necessary to ensure that the research produces valid results.

Practical advice: constructing a consent form

Many institutions have templates for researchers to use to help them to create a consent form that covers all the key information that is needed. In the absence of this, the following points should be included:

1. Formulate a brief statement that captures the nature and purpose of the research and the procedure that will be used to collect data.

2. If the project is funded or otherwise supported, ensure that the relevant bodies are identified on the consent form.

3. Ensure that the name of the principal researcher is stated and contact details are provided. It may be appropriate to name others involved in the research, such as the person who is carrying out interviews or facilitating focus groups, and if the research is conducted under supervision, the name and contact details of the supervisor should be included.

4. Identify the relevant Code of Ethics that governs the research and advise participants of where they can obtain a copy. State whether ethical approach has been obtained for the research and, if so, from whom it was obtained.

5. Include express statements about the extent of anonymity and confidentiality and any exceptions to these principles that may exist. Make a brief statement of the procedure that will be followed to ensure that anonymity and confidentiality will be preserved.

6. Explain what will be required from the participant, including details such as the duration, timing, and location of their participation. Draw attention to the possibility of withdrawal at any point and without any negative consequences.

7. If payment is to be made to participants or expenses covered, ensure that details of this are provided.

8. If participants are to be offered any material such as a transcript of their interview, a summary of the findings of the research, or a copy of the final report, include details of this including whether this is provided automatically or if they need to register to receive it.

 You will find some examples of consent forms and associated information sheets to be given to participants on the Online Resource Centre.

Prevention of harm

The principle that no person should be harmed by taking part in research is the most fundamental ethical principle. Indeed, some researchers believe that other principles such as anonymity, confidentiality, and the need for informed consent are merely parts of the overriding need to protect participants from harm. However, even with adherence to these other ethical principles, there is still the potential for participants to be harmed by taking part in research as this example demonstrates.

Practical example: the Stanford Prison experiment

Zimbardo (1973) set up a complex simulation of the prison environment with a view to exploring the effects of a harsh prison regime on prisoners. He recruited 24 participants to take the role of guard and prisoner in a mock prison in an experiment that was designed to last for two weeks. There was a random allocation of the roles of prisoner and guard with both being given uniforms appropriate to their allocated role.

The guards were given freedom to formulate their own rules and practice for dealing with prisoners and were also given the ability to impose punishments. The experiment was abandoned after only six days as those assigned the roles of guard became increasingly brutal and those participants in the role of prisoner were seen to suffer extreme stress and depression as a result of their incarceration and the treatment meted out by the guards.

Zimbardo noted 'By the end of the study, the prisoners were disintegrated, both as a group and as individuals. There was no longer any group unity; just a bunch of isolated individuals hanging on, much like prisoners of war or hospitalised mental patients. The guards had won total control of the prison, and they commanded the blind obedience of each prisoner'.

This experiment was organized by experienced researchers at a reputable university with input from a range of experts with knowledge of the custodial system. Participants were aware of the nature of the experiment and the hardships associated with the role of prisoner so had given informed consent to taking part. Despite this, participants suffered such harm that the experiment had to be abandoned. You may like to watch the film, *The Experiment* (2010), which is based on these events.

The obligation to protect participants from harm is wide-ranging as the *Code of Ethics* states that participants should be protected from physical, social, and psychological harm whilst Israel and Hay state that participants should not be exposed to even a risk of harm (2006: 97). This means that researchers must contemplate all possible harmful consequences of the research and eliminate them or, at the very least, warn participants that they exist. This can be difficult. Zimbardo did not anticipate such extreme behaviour in his prison simulation and, thinking back to an earlier example regarding Maggie and the crime questionnaire, you probably would not have anticipated this to give rise to such a high level of anxiety.

Just as careful contemplation does not prevent a researcher from encountering a heinous disclosure, it is also true that researchers sometimes fail to anticipate all possible manifestations of harm that participants might suffer. People are unpredictable and unique. They come to the research with all sorts of experiences that might mean that they react in an unexpected way to the subject matter. Researchers can only do so much to anticipate and address potential harm so must remain alert for signs that the participants are unhappy as the research progresses. It is for this reason that it is essential that participants are told that they are free to withdraw at any stage of the research.

Finding an ethical approach

This final section of the chapter draws together the strands of discussion into a series of practical recommendations to help you to find a way to carry out your chosen research in a way that complies with the ethical requirements of the discipline of criminology and of your institution.

Things to consider

The best way to deal with an ethical dilemma is to avoid it from occurring in the first place. The following points will help you to anticipate and address ethical issues that could arise in your research.

1. **Find out what steps you have to take in order to obtain ethical clearance to start your research.** Does your institution set out milestones in the research planning

process that you have to reach by a particular point in time? Is there a cut-off date for applications to the Ethics Committee? Does your supervisor have to approve your application prior to its submission to the Committee? It would be a good idea to create a timeline of tasks so that you are in no doubt about what has to be achieved and when it has to be done.

2. **Identify the ethical framework that is applicable to your work.** Does your institution require that you adhere to the BSC *Code of Ethics* or has it created its own set of ethical considerations that you need to take into account. It is essential that you know from the outset what is required of you in order to ensure that your research is tailored to the particular demands of your institution. Extract the key principles and requirements and list these. You are then ready to think about how they apply to your research.

3. **Think about the ethical issues raised by the research topic and the potential participants.** Are you looking at some particular type of unlawful activity? Do you want to consider an issue from the perspective of offenders or victims of crime? Remember that research into unlawful activities tends to raise more complex ethical issues, especially in relation to anonymity and confidentiality, and that victims of crime will need particular consideration to ensure that they are not harmed by their involvement in your research, remembering that this covers physical, psychological, and social harm. Are you planning to talk to criminal justice officials? What issues does this raise?

4. **In light of this, will you be offering absolute or limited confidentiality to participants?** Take care to contemplate all possible disclosures that could be made and decide whether there are some things that you would not be prepared to keep confidential. Remember that you will need to make participants aware of any limits to confidentiality prior to commencing your research. Think also about how you will deal with a heinous discovery.

5. **Consider whether there is any risk of harm involved in your proposed method of data collection.** Try to identify all possible risks and consider how you can guard against them. If a risk of some particular harm will still exist, you must either warn participants about this as part of the process of obtaining informed consent or change your method so that the risk is removed. This should include a consideration of any potential for harm to come to you in the course of the research. This means that you should take sensible precautions such as alerting your supervisor to the dates, times, and locations of any interviews or other meetings with participants and adopting a system for checking in with the supervisor when the interview is concluded.

6. **Identify information that needs to be included on a consent form.** There is guidance earlier in the chapter on this. Give particular consideration to the interests of vulnerable participants such as children, prisoners, or people suffering from mental illness. Are you planning to deceive your participants? If so, how will you deal with this in relation to the need for informed consent? Make sure that you tell partipants that they are free to change their mind even after the research has started.

7. **Assess whether there are alternative ways to carry out the research.** Make sure that you do not adopt the first method that you think of without considering alternatives. An Ethics Committee may want to know why you have chosen a particular approach or method so you need to be prepared to defend your decision by explaining what different approaches you considered and why they are less appropriate than that which you decided upon. In the earlier example of comparing male and female drivers' reactions to speed cameras, we looked at different ways that this data could be gathered and balanced the ethical issues

against the quality of the data that would be produced. This sort of evaluation will be useful as a way of justifying your chosen approach.

8. **Seek advice from others on your proposed research.** Your supervisor or another lecturer on your course is an obvious source of advice but remember that research ethics involve moral decisions so you may find that other people, who may know nothing about criminology, are able to spot an ethical issue that you have not identified simply by applying their own standards of right and wrong.

Dealing with the Ethics Committee

If you have followed these steps then you should be ready to complete the paperwork associated with an application for ethical approval. The composition of the relevant Ethics Committee will vary depending upon whether it is within your department, in which case it is likely to be composed wholly or mainly of criminologists, or it is a university committee, in which case it will have members from a whole range of science and social science disciplines.

It is often the case that an application to an Ethics Committee will be returned to the applicant with further questions that need to be asked. Depending on the procedure in place at your university, this will either require a written response or you will need to appear before the Ethics Committee to answer questions in person. Try not to be daunted by this and remember that the Ethics Committee is not trying to obstruct your research; they are trying to ensure that you adopt the most ethical approach possible to carrying out your research.

It can help if you include examples of research that has used a similar method in your application, particularly if the membership of the Ethics Committee is taken from a range of disciplines; these people who are experts in other fields may not understand how criminology research 'works' so be prepared to explain this to them and to support your explanation with examples so that they do not think that you are the only person who has ever wanted to interview convicted murderers serving life sentences in prison.

Finally, be prepared to adapt your research in order to obtain approval from the Ethics Committee. If the only way that the Ethics Committee will permit you to carry out research on imprisoned murderers is by administering a questionnaire or by conducting a telephone interview then this may be a change that you have to make in order to go ahead with your research even if you would have preferred to have conducted face-to-face interviews. Alternatively you may feel that you cannot proceed with the research in light of the modifications to the focus or method required by the Ethics Committee in which case you will have to reformulate your research and make a fresh application.

Practical example: data gathering in internet forums

Kate wanted to carry out research on homophobic bullying as part of her final year project on the effectiveness of university anti-bullying campaigns. She tried administering a questionnaire but found that the response rate was very low and the information provided on those questionnaires that were returned did not reveal information that was useful for her project. She approached the President of the LGBT (lesbian, gay, bisexual, transgender) Society for permission to interview its members but this was refused. Kate then decided to make use of internet forums to gather data.

 Visit the Online Resource Centre to find out more about Kate's research project and see if you can put into practice the knowledge that you have gained from this chapter by identifying the ethical issues and suggesting how they can be resolved.

CHAPTER SUMMARY

- Research ethics are based upon morality so are principles that provide guidance on the right way to carry out research
- Find out which Code of Ethics is used in your institution and ensure that you become familiar with its requirements
- Bear in mind that a Code of Ethics provides guidance only, not hard and fast rules, so there will still be situations in which there is more than only one way to behave in an ethical manner
- Think about ethical dilemmas that could arise in relation to your research and seek to avoid them
- Get into the habit of scrutinizing the methods used in published research to see if you can identify the ethical issues and then consider whether you agree with the approach taken by the researcher
- Make a decision prior to commencing your research as to whether you will be able to offer absolute confidentiality or whether you will limit it so that certain disclosures are not covered
- Seek informed consent from participants and, wherever possible, avoid deception
- Always assess your research to ensure that it does not carry a risk of causing harm to research participants or, by virtue of its findings, to the wider community
- Take a reasoned approach to the process of applying for ethical approval that strikes a balance between defending your decision to carry out research in a particular way whilst acknowledging the expertise of the Ethics Committee and responding to any recommendations that they may make

FURTHER READING

- Feenan, D. (2002) Legal Issues in Acquiring Information about Illegal Behaviour Through Criminological Research. *British Journal of Criminology*, 42, 762–782. This article provides a detailed discussion of the issues surrounding the preservation of anonymity and confidentiality in the light of disclosures of unlawful activities and draws on a wide range of studies to illustrate how researchers have dealt with the difficulties encountered. It engages in a more detailed debate of the issues covered within this chapter so may help you to develop your thinking in this area.

- Westmarland, L. (2001) Blowing the Whistle on Police Violence: Gender, Ethnography and Ethics. *British Journal of Criminology*, 41, 523–545. This is a thoughtful account of the ethical issues that arose in the course of the author's research into police culture that draws on a range of literature and examples to explain how the issues were resolved.

- Israel, M. & Hay, I. (2006) *Research Ethics for Social Scientists*. London: SAGE. This book provides a critical assessment to the current approach to research ethics in the social sciences. It has a good level of theoretical content and combines this with practical guidelines on dealing with ethical dilemmas. It provides a wide selection of examples and case studies.

- *Ethics Review* is an international journal that publishes articles that focus on a whole host of issues associated with research ethics including theoretical discussion, practical advice, and case studies. It can be found online at http://www.research-ethics-review.com/electronic/.

abc GLOSSARY

Anonymity is offered to research participants to assure them that they will not be identified either directly (by name) or indirectly (by virtue of disclosure of information that will enable others to connect them with the research). Research participants are often assigned an alias or code number to protect their identity. Anonymity is closely associated with confidentiality.

Confidentiality refers to the assurance given to participants that the information that they share with the researcher will be used only in agreed circumstances, usually relating to a particular piece of academic work. It is often a problematic concept in criminological research if a research participant discloses unexpected information relating to criminal wrongdoing or which poses a real threat of harm to others.

Consent (see also **informed consent**) relates to the agreement given by the participant to their involvement in the research project.

Consent forms are the paper manifestation of the participant's agreement to take part in the research and usually outline the terms upon which their participation has been secured. There can be a conflict between the requirement to sign a consent form and the assurance of anonymity.

Deception in criminological research occurs if the researcher is less than honest about their identity or the nature and purpose of the research. Some deception is regarded as acceptable if the value of the research would be negated if the participants were told the complete truth about the research.

Empirical research is research which generates data as a result of direct observation or experimentation.

Ethical approval should be sought from the Ethics Committee within your university before the research commences. It is a statement of agreement that your research can go ahead using the method that you have proposed. It is granted after you have identified the ethical issues raised by your research and explained how they will be addressed.

Ethics in research refers to the moral code that guides the researcher to ensure that the research is carried out in a manner that is acceptable within their discipline.

Ethics Committees are bodies which monitor research to ensure that it complies with the required practices of the discipline and which exist to promote ethical research. In many instances, research cannot go ahead unless it is approved by the Ethics Committee of a particular institution or funding body.

Harm is broadly defined in relation to research ethics to cover adverse consequences of a physical, psychological, economic, social, or emotional nature.

Informed consent describes the situation in which participants have been given sufficient information about a research project and their role within it to make an informed decision about whether or not to take part.

Participants are the subject matter of research. They are the people who are studied or who provide the data that is analysed.

REFERENCES

Auburn, T. (2010) Cognitive Distortions as Social Practices: an Examination of Cognitive Distortions in Sex Offender Treatment from a Discursive Psychology Perspective. *Psychology, Crime and Law*, 16(1), 103–123.

Barter, C. & Renold, E. (2003) Dilemmas of Control: Methodological Implications and Reflections of Foregrounding Children's Perspectives on Violence. In: Lee, R. & Stanko, E. (eds.) *Researching Victims: Essays on Methodology and Measurement*. London: Routledge: 88–106.

British Psychological Society (2009) *Code of Ethics and Conduct* [Online] Available at: http://www.bps.org.uk/sites/default/files/documents/code_of_ethics_and_conduct.pdf.

British Society of Criminology (2006) *British Society of Criminology Code of Ethics* [Online] Available at: http://www.britsoccrim.org/codeofethics.htm.

Copes, H. & Cherbonneau, M. (2006) The key to auto theft: emerging methods of auto theft from the offenders' perspective. *British Journal of Criminology*, 46(5), 917–934.

Corbett, C. & Caramlau, I. (2006) Gender differences in responses to speed cameras: typology findings and implications for road safety. *Criminology and Criminal Justice*, 6(4), 411–433.

ESRC (2010) *Framework for Research Ethics.* [Online] Available at: http://www.esrc.ac.uk/_images/Framework_for_Research_Ethics_tcm8-4586.pdf [Accessed 28 October 2011].

Finch, E. (2011) Strategies of adaptation and diversification: The impact of chip and PIN technology on the activities of fraudsters. *Security Journal*, 24, 251–268.

Fitzgerald, J. & Hamilton, M. (1996) The consequences of knowing: ethical and legal liabilities in illicit drug research. *Social Science & Medicine*, 43, 1591–1600.

Gale, J. & Coupe, T. (2005) The Behavioural, Emotional and Psychological Effects of Street Robbery on Victims. *International Review of Victimology*, 12(1), 1–22.

Humphreys, L. (1975) *Tearoom Trade: Impersonal Sex in Public Places*. Chicago: Aldine Publishing.

Israel, M. & Hay, I. (2006) *Research Ethics for Social Scientists: Between Ethical Conduct and Regulatory Compliance*. London: SAGE.

Kibble, N. (2005) Judicial Discretion, and the Admissibility of Prior Sexual History under Section 41 of the Youth Justice and Criminal Evidence Act 1999: Sometimes Sticking to your Guns means Shooting yourself in the Foot. *Criminal Law Review*, 263–274.

Leibling, A. (1992) *Suicides in Prison*. London: Routledge.

Lowman, J. & Palys, T. (1999) *Going the Distance: Lessons for Researchers from Jurisprudence on Privilege*. A third submission to the SFU research ethics policy revision task force. [Online] Available at: http://www.sfu.ca/~palys/Distance.pdf [Accessed 28 October 2011].

Mawby, R. (2004) Crime and Disorder: Perceptions of Business People in Cornwall. *International Review of Victimology*, 11(2–3), 313–332.

Measham, F. & Brain, K. (2005) 'Binge' drinking, British alcohol policy and the new culture of intoxication. *Crime, Media, Culture*, 1(3), 263–284.

Milgram S. (1963) Behavioral Study of Obedience. *Journal of Abnormal Social Psychology*, 67, 371–378.

Nee, C. & Meenaghan, A. (2006) Expert decision making in burglars. *British Journal of Criminology*, 46, 935–949.

Nellis, A. (2009) Gender Differences in Fear of Terrorism. *Journal of Contemporary Criminal Justice*, 25(3), 322–340.

Phillips, C. (2005) Facing Inwards and Outwards: Institutional Racism, Race Equality and the Role of Black and Asian Professional Associations. *Criminology and Criminal Justice*, 5(4), 357–377.

Rosenhan, D. (1973) On Being Sane in Insane Places. *Science*, 179(4070), 250–258.

Schwartz, R. (1976) Preface. In: Nejelski, P. (ed.) (1976) *Social Research in Conflict with Law and Ethics.* Cambridge, MA: Ballinger.

Van Mannen, J. (1983) On the ethics of fieldwork. In: Smith, R. (ed.) (1983) *A handbook of social science methods: volume 1: An introduction to social research.* Cambridge, MA: Ballinger, 227–51.

Zimbardo, P. (1973) On the ethics of intervention in human psychological research: with special reference to the Stanford prison experiment. *Cognition*, 2, 243–256.

Zinger, I. & Wichmann, C. (1999) The psychological effects of 60 days in administrative segregation (Research Report R-#85). Ottawa: Correctional Services of Canada.

13 Gathering data

INTRODUCTION

Criminological research uses a range of different methods to generate data about crime, criminality, and the criminal justice system. This chapter outlines the dominant methods used by criminologists and explains how each method can be used to generate particular kinds of data. It will also explain the strengths and weaknesses of each method. The methods discussed in this chapter all involve the use of human participants as a source of data; these might be victims, offenders, witnesses, criminal justice professionals, or ordinary people who have no involvement with crime but whose experiences reflect the view of the general public. The use of human participants necessitates a discussion of the different approaches to sampling that are used to select participants. There are also ethical concerns about the use of human participants in research so you may wish to consult relevant sections of chapter 12 to ensure that you have grasped the ethical considerations associated with each method of generating data.

Data collection is a time-consuming task and, for that reason, it is not always possible for undergraduate students to undertake research involving the collection of original data during their studies. However, this does not mean that this chapter is of no relevance. An awareness of the different ways that criminologists go about collecting data is an essential component of understanding the published research of others that you will encounter in academic journals and other publications. You will be better able to engage in critical evaluation of published research if you can assess the suitability of the method of data collection used. In essence, every student of criminology needs to understand the issues associated with the various approaches to generating data irrespective of whether or not they engage in any data collection because it will equip you to understand the research of others.

LEARNING OUTCOMES

After reading this chapter, you will be able to:

- Understand different methods of generating data and the role of these methods in criminological research

- Differentiate between methods of sampling and select a method that is most suited to a particular research study

- Appreciate the strengths and weaknesses of each method of data collection

Approaches to criminological research

Research in criminology exists with the aim of finding out the answer to a particular question that is in some way related to crime. It is inevitable that you will carry out *some* research during the course of your studies: every time you read a section of a textbook in preparation for a tutorial or find an article that is relevant to a piece of coursework, you are carrying out basic criminological research because you are finding the answer to a question, albeit a question set by somebody else.

Of course, reading about a topic in a textbook is a very basic form of research. It is possible to carry out more sophisticated research involving documentary analysis of, for example, case law, official documents, media sources, and newspapers as has been discussed in earlier chapters in this book. However, the focus in this chapter is research that involves generating new data by using people as a data source by asking them for information, observing their behaviour, or testing their responses in controlled situations. Before considering these methods of gathering data, there will be a discussion of the methods used to determine which people will be selected as research participants.

Sampling

Whatever form of survey you decide to undertake when gathering data, unless you are able to survey each and every possible respondent in your target group of respondents, then you will need to consider which subset of these respondents you will use. For example, if your research involved seeking the attitudes of 16-year-old juvenile offenders in England and Wales to carrying knives by way of interview, it would be impossible for you to be able to interview all such juvenile offenders within the limits of the time and resources that you have available. Equally, if you decided instead to survey each of these offenders by a questionnaire, you would probably still not be able to send a copy to each of them. Therefore you will need to decide to survey a smaller number of juvenile offenders from the pool of all possible respondents.

There is quite a lot of terminology associated with sampling, and so it will be helpful to establish a few pieces of key terminology throughout the discussion that follows.

A **unit** is the individual 'thing' that is being surveyed.

In criminological surveys, the unit is usually a person, although it does not have to be—units could equally well be things such as towns, companies, police forces, or regions. In the example, the unit is 'a juvenile offender aged 16 in England and Wales'.

A **population** is the entire set of units from which the sample is to be selected.

The population would be *all* juvenile offenders aged 16 in England and Wales.

A **sample** is the part of the population that is selected for investigation.

So, in order to conduct your survey, you need to select a sample from your population. The question then becomes how you go about selecting them. The answer to this question will depend upon whether you want to be able to generalize the findings that you reach from the sample to the entire population. In other words, do you want the results from the sample to be the same as they would have been if you had somehow been able to get a response from the whole population? If so, you will need to ensure that the sample reflects the characteristics of the population from which it is drawn.

A **representative sample** is a sample that reflects the characteristics of the population accurately.

A closely related concept to the representativeness of a sample is that of the sampling error.

The **sampling error** is a measurement of the error caused by observing a sample instead of the whole population.

Therefore, the higher the sampling error, the less reliable it is that your sample is representative of the population as a whole.

Sampling methods can be divided into two main types: probability sampling and non-probability sampling.

Probability sampling

Probability sampling methods are those which use some form of random selection. In order to have a random selection method, you must have a process or procedure that means that each unit in your population has an equal chance of being chosen. For large surveys, computers are used to generate a random sample of units from the population: the principle is no different to that of picking names out of a hat.

A **probability sample** is a sample in which each unit in the population has a known chance of being selected.

There are different forms of probability sampling that you may wish to consider:

- random sampling
- systematic sampling
- stratified sampling
- cluster sampling
- multi-stage sampling.

Random sampling

Random sampling is the most basic form of probability sampling. In a random sample each population unit has an equal chance of being included. Imagine that you have the resources to survey 100 of your population of 2,000 16-year-old offenders. On a random basis, then, this means that the probability of any particular offender being included in the sample is:

$$100 / 2,000 = 0.05 \text{ (that is, 5\% or 1 in 20)}$$

Assuming that you had a list of each individual in your target population, you would then need to pick your random 100 from that list. One of the easiest ways to do this is via a computer spreadsheet. Assign a random number from 0 to 1 in the column next to each name: in both Microsoft Excel and Numbers for Mac, this is done by the = RAND() function:

Deana Chew	0.681733491
Lynna Wedel	0.122391528
Danette Gean	0.715532688
Bart Arredondo	0.852235304
Roseline Marchand	0.228047409
Chantal Mattioli	0.914560138
Gayla Mcmillen	0.035494255
Jose Diggs	0.540716578
Georgene Mcgaughey	0.439592362

Then simply order both columns in ascending order of random number:

Claud Whiting	0.018236151
Rena Galindez	0.031741108
Gayla Mcmillen	0.035494255
Theda Hayles	0.063548954
Denyse Wimer	0.070068728
Kayleen Bosco	0.085658357
Lynna Wedel	0.122391528
Shannon Ulery	0.127678576
Pura Beauchamp	0.130790194

This has given you a random ordering of your population—you can then simply take the first 100 names in this list and use those as your sample. This method is done without human bias or intervention and also without the knowledge of any of the participants.

Systematic sampling

Systematic sampling is similar to random sampling, but avoids the need to assign random numbers. Here, you would create a list of each member of the population as before. Given that you need to select one name in 20, you would begin by selecting one name from the first twenty on the list at random—say the fifth name on the list. You then select every twentieth name thereafter, so your sample is comprised of those in positions 5, 25, 45, 65, etc. This is a good method provided that there is no ordering of the list of names before you start. If there is, then it would be advisable to rearrange it before you begin.

Stratified sampling

Stratified sampling involves dividing the population into homogeneous subgroups and then taking a simple random sample in each subgroup. This is useful when you want to ensure that your sample is proportionately representative of some other characteristics of the population. For example, the population of juvenile offenders could be split along gender lines so that it is 75% male and 25% female. It is possible that the sample derived from simple random sampling would give a sample that was 60% male and 40% female which may not give results that could be confidently generalized to the population as a whole. Therefore you could divide the overall population of 2,000 into 1,500 males and 500 females and sample 5% of each category—75 males and 25 females. This gives a total sample size of 100 as before, but ensures that it is representative along gender lines of the population as a whole. This idea works for any number of known strata within the population—providing of course that the data by which you categorize the units are available.

Cluster sampling

Having undertaken a random, systematic, or stratified approach to selecting your survey of juvenile offenders, you could still find that you ended up with a widely geographically dispersed sample. This would mean that you would have to visit a large number of detention facilities all over England and Wales—adding time, costs, and burdensome travel to the project. You could minimize this by using cluster sampling. Cluster sampling works best when there are natural groupings within the population.

With cluster sampling, every member of the population is assigned to one, and only one, group, known as a cluster. You then choose a sample of clusters (usually by simple random sampling) and then surveying only those within those clusters. Since each of your juvenile offenders will only be held at one facility, you could first choose some of the facilities at random and then sample offenders within each facility.

Note the difference between cluster sampling and stratified sampling. With stratified sampling, the sample includes units from each of the strata. With cluster sampling, in contrast, the sample includes elements only from sampled clusters. The main disadvantage of cluster sampling is that the sampling error is larger than in other forms of probability sampling.

Multi-stage sampling

In most real-world criminological research, you would combine the methods described so far in order to come up with a sample with an acceptable sampling error that allows you to perform your research as efficiently and effectively as possible. Multi-stage sampling is the term used to describe samples that are chosen using a mixture of sampling methods. For instance, the British Crime Survey uses a stratified multi-stage cluster sample: in order to reduce sampling error for a given level of expenditure. Although clustering tends to increase sampling error, the reduction in field work costs permits a larger sample size, thus reducing the likely sampling error. This leads on to the perennial question in survey research—how big should my sample be?

Sample size

The sample size question involves a delicate balancing act between precision (or reliability—that is, minimizing sampling error) and the resources (time and cost) to perform the survey. However, there are two key points that you should note:

- **It is the absolute size of the sample that is important, not the relative size.** In other words, the bigger the number of units sampled, the lower the sampling error. This may well seem counterintuitive, but a probability sample of 1,000 individuals in the Thames Valley has as much statistical validity as a probability sample of 1,000 individuals across the UK, even though the UK has a much greater overall population than the Thames Valley.

- **There is a law of diminishing returns.** There comes a point where increasing the sample size has a relatively low overall effect on the precision of the sample and so the survey ceases to become cost-efficient.

There is a survey size calculator that is available online at http://www.surveysystem.com/sscalc.htm. This will require you to understand the statistical terms *confidence level* (how sure you can be) and *confidence interval* (margin of error).

See chapter 14 for more detail on quantitative statistics.

Non-probability sampling

Non-probability sampling is a broad term for samples that are not selected using probability sampling (random) methods. There is always a chance that a non-probability sample may not represent the population well, and it will often be difficult to calculate the extent to which the sample is representative. However, in criminological research there may be circumstances where it is not feasible or practical to take a probability sample. This section will deal with two main types of non-probability sampling methods used in criminology—convenience sampling and snowball sampling.

Convenience sampling

As its name suggests, convenience sampling involves you taking a sample that is readily accessible to you. For example, if you wanted to survey the experiences of football supporters in relation to the police, you might decide to stand outside one of the turnstiles at your local football club on a match day and administer a questionnaire to each supporter that came along. However, it is unlikely that your sample would be representative of the population as a whole: your local club might be one which prides itself on its family-friendly atmosphere (in which case, involvement with the police might be minimal) or one with a reputation for disorder (in which case, there might well be a disproportionate amount of negative views of the police). Since the sample is not chosen at random, the inherent bias in convenience sampling means that the sample is unlikely to be representative of the population being studied. This means that you cannot make generalizations from your sample to the population you are studying.

However, convenience sampling is very easy to carry out and the relative costs and time required to perform a survey of convenience are small compared to probability samples. Convenience sampling is certainly useful for piloting a survey which will allow you to iron out any flaws in your method before launching it on a larger sample.

Snowball sampling

Snowball sampling can be considered to be a form of convenience sampling, in that it selects a sample based on availability and accessibility.

In snowball sampling, you begin by identifying a participant who meets the criteria for inclusion in your study and then ask them to recommend others who they may know who also meet the criteria.

Snowball sampling, like convenience sampling, would be very unlikely to lead to a representative sample. It is impossible to determine the sampling error and make generalizations from the snowball sample to the population. That said, there are times when it may be the best method available. Snowball sampling is especially useful when you are trying to survey a population that is difficult to access: this may often be the case in criminology.

For instance, if you are studying prostitution, you will not be able to find a directory of prostitutes in a particular area. However, if you go to that area and identify one, they may be able to tell you of other prostitutes in that area and how you might find them, or they may offer to facilitate an introduction. Snowball sampling is useful for research subjects that are less willing to identify themselves and take part in research. Indeed, in such cases, there may be no other viable way of accessing your sample.

There will be further discussion of sampling in relation to each of the methods of generating data that follow.

Questionnaires

Questionnaires are a popular method of eliciting information from people. A questionnaire is a series of questions designed to gather data about a particular topic and, in some instances, socio-demographic data about the respondents.

The process of using a questionnaire to gather data can be broken down into three stages:

- **Design**: what questions are you going to ask, who are you going to ask and how does this contribute to your research?

- **Distribution**: how are you going to get the questionnaire to the participants and how will they complete they survey?

- **Analysis**: how do you go about working out what the responses mean and using them in your research?

Questionnaire design

There are a number of important factors to take into account when designing a questionnaire. These really do require careful thought because a badly designed questionnaire will not elicit the data that you want and it carries a risk that it will provide partial, misleading, or incomplete data that will make your research findings inaccurate or unreliable.

What is the purpose of the research?

This is the first question that you must ask yourself before you start to even think about formulating questions for inclusion on your questionnaire. Your research has (or should have) a clear goal and your questionnaire must be designed in such a way that it facilitates the collection of relevant data in furtherance of that goal. You should keep this goal at the forefront of your mind when you are creating your questionnaire, to ensure that you do not overlook important issues and that you do not create a questionnaire that is overly long due to the inclusion of questions that are peripheral or irrelevant to the purpose of your research.

What sort of data do you want to generate?

It is important to consider whether a questionnaire is the most appropriate method of collecting the sort of data that you want to obtain. Think about what it is that you want to know, what sort of questions you anticipate that you will ask to elicit this information, and what sort of answers you would expect to receive in response to your questions. As a general rule, questionnaires are most appropriate for generating data that can be coded and analysed using quantitative methods (see chapter 14). If you were hoping to obtain qualitative data then you may want to consider alternative methods of collection such as interviews or focus groups.

Most questionnaires will generate a combination of different types of data:

- **Personal factual data** about the participant such as their age, gender, ethnicity, religion, marital status, occupation, income, etc. Think carefully about whether you need to capture this data, remembering that participants may refuse to complete the questionnaire if they feel that it contains intrusive questions. Remember also that you will have to take into account provisions of the Data Protection Act 1998 if you collect personal data (see chapter 12).

- **Other factual data** relevant to the study. For example, in a study about driving behaviour, a questionnaire might ask how long the participant has held a driving licence, what sort of car they drive, whether they have ever been involved in an accident, and whether they have any convictions for motoring offences.
- **Knowledge-based data** relates to the extent and accuracy of the participant's knowledge on a particular subject. For example, you might want to ask questions to explore whether drivers are aware of the penalties for particular offences.
- **Attitudinal data** based upon the participant's opinions and beliefs. Such questions are often asked as in the form of statements and the participant is asked to indicate the extent of their agreement by selecting one of the stated responses as illustrated in Figure 13.1.

I believe that the sentences imposed for domestic burglary are too lenient:

STRONGLY AGREE	AGREE	NEITHER AGREE NOR DISAGREE	DISAGREE	STRONGLY DISAGREE
☐	☐	☐	☐	☐

Figure 13.1 Attitudinal data response form

Question type

Questions may be open or closed. A **closed question** is one that has a limited range of answers. This may be because there are only a limited range of possible answers (such as 'are you male or female?' or 'have you been arrested in the past twelve months?') or because the questionnaire creates an artificial limitation on the range of answers by asking participants to select a response from those listed as Figure 13.2 demonstrates.

How did you feel when you were arrested? Tick one box that most closely reflects how you felt:

Angry	☐
Anxious	☐
Embarassed	☐
Frightened	☐
Frustrated	☐

Figure 13.2 Closed question response form

An **open question** is one that has a wide range of possible responses, and where no limitations are placed upon the way in which the participant answers the question. For example, the question presented as a closed question in Figure 13.2 could be rephrased as an open question: 'explain how you felt when you were arrested'.

Open questions allow participants to express their views in their own words. This may be advantageous in encouraging participants to engage with the questionnaire by formulating a response that reflects their views rather than simply ticking boxes. It may also elicit a more accurate response than if the participant has to select from a range of pre-determined answers and, as such, may provide more valuable data particularly if the response is unexpected. For example, a participant may have written that they were proud to be arrested in response to an open question; an answer that would not have been possible if using the tick boxes illustrated in Figure 13.2.

Although open questions have the potential to elicit rich data and may open up a whole new avenue of research, closed questions are more commonly used in questionnaires as they are easier for the participants and more straightforward to analyse. That is not to say that closed questions sacrifice depth of data in return for convenience; there is no reason why a questionnaire composed of closed questions cannot give rise to equally rich and insightful data provided careful thought is given to the range of responses made available. Moreover, a combination of closed and open questions is perfectly acceptable. However, if you find that your questionnaire will only elicit the data that you desire using mostly open questions, it may be that an interview would be a more suitable method of data collection.

Question order

The order in which the questions are presented should be such that there is a logical progression to the questionnaire. Try to ensure that one question flows from the previous question. Remember that your questionnaire can include instructions to the participant or information to help them understand what is expected of them and this can help to explain the order of the questions. For example, if the questionnaire has several questions on different topics, headings could be used to indicate the change of topic or you could include an explanation such as 'That concludes the questions on your driving experience. The next section of the questionnaire focuses on any accidents that you have had in the past five years'.

This approach will also help participants to navigate the questionnaire if there are sections that only need to be answered by certain participants. It is likely that all but the simplest questionnaire will involve **sequencing** of questions whereby the answer to one question determines whether the participant answers the following question or jumps to another part of the questionnaire. Clear instructions will help participants understand what questions they are expected to answer as Figure 13.3 illustrates.

Q. 10

Have you been convicted of a motoring offence in the past 5 years?

Yes ☐

No ☐

If yes, go to Q. 11. If no, go to Q.20.

Figure 13.3 Sequencing instructions

Formulating questions

It is not straightforward to construct questions. It is all too easy to assume that everyone will interpret the question in the way that you intended or to formulate questions that are ambiguous or that do not elicit the desired data.

Practical exercise: assessing questions

Read the questions listed below and see if you can identify the problems that could arise if they were included on a questionnaire administered to drivers to explore attitudes to motoring offences. If you are a driver, try answering them yourself as it may help you to identify the problems. Each of the issues raised by the questions will be addressed in the discussion that follows.

1. What is the make and model of your car?

2. Do you drive regularly?

3. Are you a good driver?

4. Do you agree that speeding is dangerous?

5. How many times in the past year have you exceeded the speed limit?

6. Have you ever driven after consuming large quantities of alcohol or recreational drugs?

7. Do you believe that it is not acceptable for drivers not to be required to retake a driving test after a period of disqualification?

8. What would your priorities be if you were Minister for Road Safety?

Irrelevant questions

It is not fair to participants to take up their time with unnecessary questions so be sure to limit your questions to those that need to be asked in order to elicit the data that is necessary if your research is to achieve its purpose. For example, if you had included a question about the make and model of car simply because the questionnaire was about driving then it would be irrelevant as the data that you would obtain will not be used in any way. However, if you had asked the question because you thought that drivers of high-performance cars would have a more tolerant attitude towards speeding offences then the data is of direct relevance to the purpose of the research.

Wide, vague, or ambiguous questions

Try to formulate questions that are capable of being understood without difficulty and which can be answered with precision as this will improve the chances that you will elicit clear and relevant data in response. Think about the question 'do you drive regularly?' and consider the different interpretations of it: it could mean 'do you drive your car often?' or 'do you drive your car at regular intervals?' or 'is your manner of driving regular in the sense that it is like the way that most other people drive?'. Even the interpretation that is most likely—'do you drive your car often'—could elicit a range of different responses: for example, 'yes', 'twice a day', and 'very often' are all reasonable responses. Of course, some of this ambiguity can be cured by providing participants with a selection of possible answers and allowing them to select the most appropriate response.

Prestige bias

Questions carry a risk of prestige bias if they are likely to be answered in particular way to avoid embarrassment or to impress the researcher. For example, it is unlikely that many people would answer 'no' to the question 'are you a good driver?' or 'do you think speeding is dangerous?' or 'yes' to the question concerning excess alcohol and recreational drugs because they are socially unacceptable answers. However, the anonymity offered by a self-administration survey may lead people to provide honest answers but it would be difficult to be sure of this, so the data collected is potentially unreliable. Test questions for prestige bias by considering whether there is a possible answer to the question that you would feel awkward giving if you were in a face-to-face situation.

Leading questions

Imagine that you met the authors of this book and were asked: 'do you agree that *Criminology Skills* is the best textbook that you have used during your degree?'. It is obvious from the way that the question is phrased that the desired answer is 'yes' so this is a leading question. Any question that starts with 'do you agree...' has the potential to influence participants towards one particular response more than another so you would expect participants in the motoring offences survey to agree that speeding is dangerous.

Try to word questions so that they are objective. For example, you could make a statement and ask participants to select the response that indicates the extent of their agreement as illustrated in Figure 13.1. Alternatively, you could create an open question that invites participants to provide a word or phrase that encapsulates their opinion: 'write one word that describes your opinion about speeding' or 'which book has been most useful to you during your degree?'. This approach will elicit a wider range of responses but the data will have greater validity as a result of the objectivity of the question.

Double barrelled questions

A double barrelled question is one that asks two questions at the same time which can leave the respondent unsure about how to respond, particularly if their answers to the two questions would be different. In the example above, participants are asked if they have driven after consuming large quantities of alcohol or recreational drugs. If the required response is 'yes' or 'no' then how is someone to answer if they have driven after consuming large quantities of alcohol but not after taking recreational drugs? If they have answered 'yes', how will you know whether they mean yes to alcohol, yes to drugs, or yes to both? The question that asks how many times participants have exceeded the speed limit is also a double barrelled question as it effectively asks whether participants have exceeded the speed limit and assumes that the answer is 'yes' before asking how many times.

Complicated wording

Did you understand this question?

> 7. Do you believe that it is not acceptable for drivers not to be required to retake a driving test after a period of disqualification?

It is not phrased with sufficient clarity as it contains a double negative ('not acceptable' and 'not to be required') which makes it hard to work out its meaning. If the wording of a question is complicated or ambiguous, there is a risk that participants may misunderstand the question. This question could be asking whether participants think that disqualified drivers *should* retake their driving test or that they *should not* have to do so. As the two meanings are so contradictory, the data that the question elicits will not be reliable as it will not be possible to determine how many responses were based on a misunderstanding of the question.

Other problems with wording that can lead to misunderstanding include the use of unusual words or jargon. Try to ensure that questions are worded in clear and simple language and use relatively short and uncomplicated sentence structure.

Hypothetical questions

A hypothetical question is one that asks the participant to put themselves in some imaginary situation and speculate about what they would do. Responses are based upon conjecture and do not represent useful or meaningful data. The question that asks what participants would do to if they were Minister for Road Safety is such a question. It is likely that most participants have never given this any prior consideration and have little insight into what the role involves so can say little by way of meaningful response. If you want to know what participants think should be a priority for new policies or practices then ask that question in a straightforward way without resorting to hypothetical situations.

Practical exercise: phrasing questions

Revisit the practical exercise on assessing questions earlier in the chapter and reword the questions in light of the foregoing discussion. You can omit questions if you feel that they are irrelevant, or split questions into two or more different questions, but be sure to note your reasons for doing so.

 You will find further comment on how the questionnaire could be strengthened on the Online Resource Centre.

Formulating responses

Unless you are asking open questions, you will need to consider what form of responses you are going to offer to participants in relation to each question. There are a range of options and the most appropriate choice will depend upon the nature of the question, the range of possible responses, and the way that the question is worded.

Response selection

If there are a relatively small range of possible answers, you can state these in the questionnaire and ask the respondent to underline, circle, or otherwise indicate which response answers the question. For example, the question 'do you have a full UK driving licence' (see Figure 13.4) has only two possible responses —yes or no—so these are set out in the questionnaire and the participant is asked to circle that which is applicable.

Text entry

Some factual answers can be entered by the participant. For example, you can ask participants to write their age at their last birthday. This type of response can be seen in Q2 in Figure 13.4.

Tick boxes

This type of response requires that the participant place a tick (or a cross) in the relevant box to indicate which of the possible answers has been selected. Your instructions must be clear: is the participant expected to tick one box only (Q3 in Figure 13.4) or to tick all answers that are relevant (Q4 in Figure 13.4). This type of response elicits quite straightforward data as you are asking participants to indicate for each possible answer whether or not it applies to them.

Ranked answers

If you are trying to gain insight into the relative significance of different factors, you can ask participants to rank the factors listed in order of importance. This can either involve participants ranking all the factors that are listed or selecting the most important three (or however many) factors and ranking these in order. This approach is illustrated in Figure 13.4 in Q5 in which the participant is asked to indicate which of the listed consequences of loss of a driving licence had the greatest impact.

| Q1. | Do you have a full UK driving licence? | | YES | NO |
| | *Please circle the correct answer.* | | | |

Q2.   At what age did you obtain a full driving licence?
      Please write in the box.

Q3.   Are you, or have you ever been, disqualified from driving?
      Please tick one box only.

      No, I have never been disqualified from driving .

      Yes, I have been disqualified from driving in the past.

      Yes, I am currently disqualified from driving.

Q4.   If you are, or have been, disqualified from driving, what offence(s) led to the ban?
      Please tick all that apply.

      Speeding offences

      Offences relating to drugs or alcohol

      Other offences related to the quality of driving

      Driving without licence, insurance or MOT

      Offences relating to vehicle defects

      Other *(please give details in box below)*

Q5.   If you are, or have been, disqualified from driving, which three of the following
      consequences were most significant during your period of disqualification?

      Please rank 1, 2, 3 where 1 is the most significant.

      Stigma of disqualification

      Inconvenience

      Cost of alternative transport

      Loss of job

      Missing out on social events

      Relationship difficulties (spouse)

      Relationship difficulties (other family and friends)

Q5.   For each of the following statements, tick the box that reflects your viewpoint.

	Strongly agree	Agree	Neither agree nor disagree	Disagree	Strongly disagree
I would not want to lose my licence again.					
I will not repeat the offence that led to my disqualification.					
I have greater awareness of road traffic laws.					

Figure 13.4 Questionnaire with differing response types

Scales

Scales can be used to elicit attitudinal data. The most commonly used scale is the Likert scale which asks participants to indicate the extent to which they agree or disagree with a particular statement. You can see an example of this in Figure 13.1 and also in Q6 in Figure 13.4.

Piloting the questionnaire

It is important to carry out a pilot study to test whether or not the questionnaire that you have created works properly and elicits the sort of data that you need. This is part of the design process as changes will need to be made if the pilot study reveals problems with the questionnaire. A pilot can be useful in the following ways:

- If all participants answer a particular questions in the same way, it could indicate that there will be too little variance to give rise to interesting results. It may be that the focus of the questionnaire or the research itself should be shifted.

- If particular questions are left unanswered or are not answered in the way expected, it could indicate a problem with the phrasing of the question or the instructions provided to participants.

- If only the first half of the questionnaire is answered, it may be too long and questions should be omitted to ensure that participants do not lose interest or feel overburdened.

- If 'other' is the most frequently selected response, it may be that changes need to be made to the list of responses offered. If participants have been asked to provide details when they have answered 'other' then these responses may be used to formulate a more appropriate list.

Distribution

Once issues of design and sampling are finalized, arrangements will need to be made to distribute the questionnaire. There are a number of possible methods of distribution:

- Researchers could wait in strategic places and intercept potential participants.

- Potential participants could be contacted by telephone and asked the questions by the researcher.

- Questionnaires could be left in appropriate places for participants to collect and complete.

- A postal survey could be used in which the questionnaires are posted to participants who complete the survey and return it by post.

- Increasingly, questionnaires are distributed and returned by email or completed online. There are some excellent survey support websites such as Survey Monkey (http://www.surveymonkey.com) that facilitate the creation and distribution of surveys via the Internet at a relatively low cost (or free for short questionnaires).

The method of distribution chosen will depend upon who the participants are and how many participants are needed (see earlier in the chapter for guidance on sampling strategies). If your participants are ordinary members of the public, then it will be quite straightforward to identify potential participants and distribute the questionnaire to them. However, if your research requires that participants possess particular characteristics (such as falling within a particular age range, being employed in a particular industry, or having experienced a specific event) then you will need to ensure that your method of distribution is suitable for people with those characteristics. For example, it would be unrealistic to expect to conduct

SurveyMonkey website

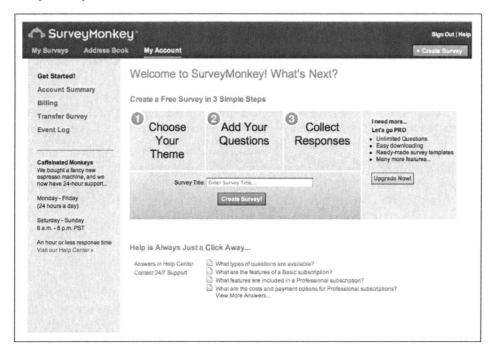

a telephone survey with prisoners or to use a self-complete questionnaire to explore the link between illiteracy and offending. Remember that it is not enough that you want to administer a questionnaire; it has to be a practical and effective method of gathering data. One particular issue of relevance here is whether you will be able to identify potential participants: for example, if you wanted to use a questionnaire to explore the extent to which householder's lives have been altered by burglary, how would you identify burglary victims in order to administer a questionnaire? Different approaches to sampling were discussed earlier in this chapter.

Analysis

The analysis of the data generated by the questionnaire can be a complex matter, particularly if the questionnaire as long and contained questions with a large number of potential responses. It also depends upon the nature of the questions asked and what you hope to prove by analysing them. If you simply want to count the number of people who fall into particularly categories then analysis will be quite straightforward. However, if you want to explore the relationship between different factors and to draw inferences from your data then the process of analysis will be rather more involved.

You will find a detailed explanation of the use of descriptive and inferential statistics in chapter 15. You may also want to read chapter 14 if your questionnaire has gathered qualitative data.

Coding

The first step in analysis of the data is to code it. This involves categorizing data and assigning a number to each category. The purpose of this is to translate non-numeric data into a numeric form so that it can be subjected to quantitative analysis. If you are using closed questions in which the participants select responses from those listed, you can pre-code your question-naire. This involves allocating codes to each possible response for each variable. If you are including open questions then these will have to be post-coded once the completed question-naires are returned, as you cannot allocate a code to an unknown response.

In simple terms, the process of coding involves allocating a number to each possible response to each question. This can be illustrated using a simple example.

Practical example: analysing questionnaire data

Imagine that you have used a questionnaire to explore the differences between attitudes of male and female drivers to a period of disqualification. Every question creates a variable as each question has at least two possible responses or, in other words, two ways in which the answer to the question can vary. For example, one variable could be the sex of the driver, a second could be the reason that they were disqualified, and a third could be whether they intend to avoid repeating the offence that led to their disqualification.

The first variable has two categories so two codes are needed: male = 1, female = 2. The second category has six variables: speeding = 1, alcohol/drugs = 2, quality of driving = 3, document offences = 4, and vehicle defect offences = 5. The final category is 'other' so you would need to wait and see what responses were given here and either allocate them to an existing category or create new categories to accommodate them. The third variable is the extent to which the participant agrees or disagrees with the statement 'I will not repeat the offence(s) that led to my disqualification' with the responses being strongly agree, agree, neither agree nor disagree, disagree, and strongly disagree. Each of these could have a separate code (1–5) or you could categorize those as agreement = 1 (counting 'strongly agree' and 'agree' as a single category), no opinion = 2, and disagreement = 3.

With this coding in place, each participant will have a line of entry into the database that looks like this:

1	1	1
1	4	3
2	2	1

This is a coded way of presenting the following information:

- A male driver who was disqualified for speeding and who agrees that he will not repeat this offence.

- A male driver who was disqualified for not having a licence, insurance or MOT who has disagreed with the statement.

- A female driver who was disqualified for driving under the influence of alcohol or drugs and who agrees that she will not repeat the offence.

Once the data is coded in this way, you can use descriptive statistics to summarize your findings and use inferential tests to explore the relationship between variables. This would enable you to answer the following questions:

- Do more male drivers who are disqualified for speeding agree that they will not repeat the offence than female drivers who are disqualified for speeding?

- Do drivers who are disqualified for speeding seem more deterred from repeating the offence than drivers disqualified for driving under the influence of drugs/alcohol?

- Are male drivers or female drivers most likely to be deterred from future offending by a period of disqualification?

This is a simple example to demonstrate how the process of coding is used in relation to data gathered by questionnaire. There is a more detailed explanation of the allocation of codes and the use of statistics to analyse quantitative data in chapters 14 and 15.

Interviews

Interviews are another method that is widely used in criminological research to gather data from individuals. Interviews can be conducted by telephone or video-link but are usually carried out face-to-face with the interviewer asking questions and the participant providing responses. This method of data gathering tends to be used when the research requires depth of information that could not be elicited using questionnaires.

Interviews may be:

- **Highly structured interviews**. The interviewer will ask questions from a prepared list in a pre-arranged order. There is no flexibility to depart from the interview schedule. The interviewer has a clear idea of the purpose of the interview and the nature of the data that will be elicited from the outset.

- **Semi-structured interviews**. The interviewer works from an interview schedule that contains a list of topics to be covered and key questions that need to be asked but has flexibility as to how the questions are asked and the order in which they are presented to the participant. There is also flexibility to follow up on issues raised during the interview.

- **Unstructured interviews**. The interviewer has no real agenda in mind prior to the interview. A starting question will be asked by the interviewer and subsequent questions formulated as a response to the answers given by the participant. This sort of interview is far more speculative and exploratory in nature.

This chapter will focus on semi-structured interviews as these are most commonly used in criminology research. Before exploring the process of planning and conducting the interview, it is necessary to consider how you will go about selecting participants to interview.

Selecting participants

The discussion of sampling at the beginning of this chapter has outlined different methods of obtaining a sample of participants. Obviously, the method adopted must be one that is suitable to elicit data that is relevant to your research. For example, you could post a questionnaire to every household in a particular town. This would be a valid approach to gathering data if the aim of your research was to elicit information about experiences of violent crime within that geographic area, as it is clear that every recipient of the questionnaire has the potential to contribute something of value to your study. However, this would be an unwise approach if your research aimed to explore recent immigrants' experiences of racially-motivated crime as many of the households would not contain people who fell into your target category.

Practical exercise: selecting an interview sample

Think about the information provided on sampling techniques provided earlier in this chapter and consider which approach you would use in the following situations:

- Interviews with former army personnel who have committed serious offences after entering civilian life, to explore their experiences of imprisonment.
- Interviews with senior police officers to investigate their views about racism within the police force.
- Interviews with female university students to discover whether they feel vulnerable to crime on the campus.
- Interviews with pensioners as part of research into elder abuse.
- Interviews with regular Internet users to find out about whether they are victims of online crime.

 You will find some comment on possible approaches to creating a sample in these situations on the Online Resource Centre.

Interview schedule

The interview schedule for a semi-structured interview contains far less detail and is less pre-scriptive than an interview schedule for a structured interview. An example of an interview schedule can be seen in Figure 13.5.

It is usual for an interview schedule to include the following:

- **Introductory material.** It is useful to have a note of the points that you want to make at the beginning of the interview so that the participant knows what to expect. This could include the duration of the interview, the process for recording the interview, and a summary of the ethical issues raised by this method of data gathering (see chapter 12). These are all matters that should have been covered when the initial arrangements for the interview were made but there is no harm in reiterating this at the start of the interview.

- **List of topics.** The schedule should be divided up according to the themes that you want to pursue in the interview with any particular questions that you want to ask in relation to that theme noted. A list of prompts should be made in relation to each theme to help you to remember all the points that you wanted to ask. Remember, though, that a semi-structured interview is flexible so it may be that not all of these points will turn out to be relevant.

- **Closing remarks.** The schedule can also contain the points that you wish to make in closing to aid your memory. This may include a reminder that a transcript of the interview can be provided for comment or the provision of contact details for the researcher. It could also contain a reminder to check that whether the participant has any questions or comments.

It will be necessary to give careful thought to the choice of themes for the interview. These should be closely related to the purpose of your research so make a list of the things that you need to know in order to answer your research question. Lofland and Lofland (1995: 78) suggest that contemplation of the question 'just what about this thing puzzles me?' as a good way for identifying useful themes to pursue in interview. In other words, you should try to identify

Thank you for agreeing to take part in this interview. As I explained previously, my research focuses on the experiences of disqualified drivers and whether or not the imposition of a driving ban has changed the way that they drive or their attitudes towards motoring laws. You have indicated that you are happy to discuss your experiences of disqualification: is that still the case?

The interview should take about an hour of your time. I have already explained that you have the right to withdraw from the research at any time including during the interview and that the interview will be recorded. Are you still happy with this?

Theme 1 - Driving Experience

* Learning to drive
* Driving test
* Years of driving experience
* Accidents

Theme 2 - Driving Offences

* Sorts of offences
* Frequency
* Penalties - fixed, fines, endorsements, disqualification
* Number of disqualifications

Theme 3 - Court Appearances

* Number and nature
* Feelings about attending court
* Offences admitted or denied?
* Compliance with penalties imposed - fines paid etc.

Theme 4 - Views on Policing

* Perception of policing
* Experiences with police
* Affect of interactions with police

Theme 5 - Attitude to Disqualification

* Compliance with ban?
* Feelings about disqualification
* Negative experiences
* Any positive aspects?
* Future attitudes towards driving offences

Thank you. That ends the questions that I would like to ask you.

Do you have anything that you would like to add about your views of driving or your experiences of disqualification?

Do you have any questions about the interview or how it will be used or my research in general that you would like to ask?

Figure 13.5 Interview schedule

the burning questions that you have about your research topic and categorize these together into themes. Remember, though, that it is not only your perceptions of what is important about your research topic that are relevant here: ensure that participants are given sufficient opportunity to raise issues that relate to the research topic that you may not have considered. This can be an excellent source of inspiration for different avenues of research.

Conducting the interview

There are a number of practical issues to consider in relation to carrying out the interview. Where will you do it? How long will it take? How will you keep a record of what is said? What will you do if the participant keeps veering off point? How will you manage if the participant is not very forthcoming with information?

Some of these issues can be addressed during the planning stages. Practical considerations concerning the duration and location of the interview should be decided at an early stage of the planning process. Remember that the venue should be one that does not compromise your safety and which is relatively free from distractions and the interview should not be too lengthy and overtax the participants. Equally, the method of recording the interview should be determined at an early stage. A small recording device is perfect but remember that the participant may not agree to the interview being recorded, in which case you will need to keep written notes (if the participant agrees) or rely on your memory. Obviously, it would be unacceptable to record the interview without the express permission of the participant.

Issues about over- or under-talkative participants are more difficult to resolve. The phrasing of questions can be useful here. For example, closed questions that start with 'who, 'when', and 'where' tend to elicit shorter and more factual responses than open questions that start with 'how' and 'why'. Use closed questions to keep an over-enthusiastic participant focused and to draw specific information out of a quieter participant and add in more open questions once the interview is back on track or the participant has gained confidence and found their voice. Remember that prompts such as 'go on' or 'anything else?' can be useful in encouraging participants to continue their response and that maintaining silence will indicate to participants that you would like them to amplify on what they have said.

Practical exercises: questioning techniques

1. Enlist a couple of friends to role-play an interview, asking them either to be very talkative or very quiet. Tell them the topic of the interview—you could either use the driving offences example used in this chapter or select something relevant to your research—and allow them time to invent experiences relevant to the scenario. Carry out the interview as you would with a real participant and experiment with different approaches to questioning to see how effective they are in keeping your talkative participant focused and in encouraging your quieter participant to divulge information.

2. ⊙ Watch the video clips of interviews that you will find on the Online Resource Centre and make some practical suggestions about how the researcher could have used different types of questions to better effect. Compare your answers on how the interviews could have been improved with those provided.

Transcribing and coding data

Once an interview is complete, it can be transcribed and coded. There is no need to wait until all the interviews have been carried out in order to do this; certainly, the transcription and some preliminary coding can be done on an interview-by-interview basis.

Transcription

Although the ability to record interviews is beneficial in terms of providing an accurate account of what has been discussed, the disadvantage of recording is that it will usually be necessary to transcribe the recording into written format in order for it to be coded and analysed. This is a very time-consuming process. As a general rule, it takes approximately six hours to type up one hour of recorded speech. You may encounter problems where parts of the interview are undecipherable and spend a great deal of time listening and re-listening to the same sentence to try and work out what has been said. Although persistence can pay off, there will inevitably be some situations in which you have to give up and simply type [indecipherable] in the transcript.

Even though transcription is time-consuming and can be quite tedious to do, avoid any temptation to attempt analysis direct from the recording. Transcription is important because:

- **It facilitates a more thorough examination of what has been said.** It is far easier to scrutinize the text for meaning once it has been typed and printed, as you have a continuous record of the interview in front of you which allows you to see how any particular words fit into the overall context of the interview. When you listen to the recording, you can only concentrate on what is being said at the time.

- **Copies of the transcript can be distributed to other researchers.** The interpretation of qualitative data is vulnerable to accusations of bias by a researcher who is, consciously or unconsciously, looking for data that supports their theory. This can be countered by involving others in the process of coding and analysis or at least sharing the transcript so that other researchers can see that your interpretation of the data is valid and objective.

- **The process of coding is easier if the words can be seen.** Irrespective of whether you code data manually or using computer software, it is useful to be able to see what text has been coded and how it has been coded.

Coding

As explained in relation to questionnaires (above), coding is the process of categorizing data and assigning labels to those categories so that it can be subjected to analysis. However, it is generally the case that questionnaires generate data that is coded so as to be subjected to quantitative analysis (see chapter 15) whereas it is usual to use qualitative analysis in relation to data generated by interviews. All this means in practice, in relation to the process of coding, is that the labels given to questionnaire data are numeric whereas the labels given to interview data are thematic and described in words. In essence, the process of coding involves identifying and naming common themes within the interview data, across all of the interviews.

A further distinction in the coding of questionnaire and interview data concerns the time at which codes are generated. By and large, questionnaires can be pre-coded as the responses are known prior to the questionnaires being administered. By contrast, interview data tends to be post-coded—that is, codes are allocated after the data is collected—because it is not until the interviews are complete that themes can be picked out from them (although, obviously, predictions can be made). In other words, as you do not know what participants will say in interview, it is not possible to know what categories of data will emerge.

The process of coding interview data is cumulative. In other words, the researcher reads the first interview and identifies potential themes. This can be done manually (using, for example, different colours to mark each theme on the transcript) or by using software such as N-Vivo (see chapter 14). Each theme is named and each fresh transcript is analysed to highlight the existing themes and to identify new themes. When new themes are identified, previously analysed transcripts will be re-examined to see if the new themes can be identified. It will also be necessary to engage in constant assessment of the parameters of the chosen categories; in other words, themes may split or merge as the process of coding progresses. For example, you might start with a category that was labelled 'concerns about going to court as a witness in court' but then realize that this breaks down into several, quite separate concerns and so split this into different themes: concerns about giving evidence, meeting the defendant, and not knowing what to do or where to go.

The process of coding is covered in detail in chapter 14.

Focus groups

Focus groups are sometimes described as group interviews but this it not strictly accurate. Group interviews, as the name suggests, involve an interviewer asking the same series of questions to a group of people at the same time. By contrast, focus groups are more akin to a group discussion that is led by a moderator who guides the direction of the discussion to ensure that areas relevant to the research are explored. Participants in a focus group interact with each other and build on each other's contributions to the discussion: it is the interaction between participants that differentiates focus groups from other methods and which creates the potential for generating greater depth of data, particularly pertaining to participants' attitudes, beliefs, and perceptions. However, there are mixed views in existence about the value of focus groups as a means of generating data and some of these strengths and weaknesses are summed up in Table 13.1.

Table 13.1 Strengths and weaknesses of focus group research

Strengths of focus groups	Weaknesses of focus groups
Group discussion generates data that would not be forthcoming in an individual interview setting, as the input of one participant triggers memories or prompts associated contributions from other participants.	Group discussion is harder to control and direct than a one-to-one discussion so the researcher may find it difficult or impossible to keep the discussion on track. As such, the data generated may have no relevance to the research topic.
Focus groups can encourage discussion of difficult or sensitive topics, as participants feel that shared experience creates a safe and reassuring environment in which difficult disclosures can be made.	Participants may feel self-conscious in a group setting, particularly if the focus of discussion is a personal or sensitive topic and hold back from making disclosures that they might have made in a one-to-one interview.
The interaction between group members gives the researcher an opportunity to observe the negotiations between participants who, with little intervention, create shared meanings and discover commonalities. As such, it can be quite a naturalistic method of gathering data.	The discussion takes place in the presence of the researcher and is usually recorded so the setting is not unconditionally natural. Contributions may be aimed at impressing or pleasing the researcher rather than representing the participant's genuine viewpoint.

Conducting focus group research

There are a number of practical consideration to bear in mind when carrying out focus group research. First and foremost, you should be certain that this method will generate data that makes a useful contribution to your research. You should be sure that focus groups will provide data that cannot easily be generated by any other method. Remember that focus groups are particularly useful for exploring attitudes and perceptions.

> ### Practical example: using focus groups
>
> Finch and Munro (2008) used focus groups for two inter-related purposes in their research on jury decision-making in rape trials involving intoxicated consent. Firstly, the data generated from the focus groups was of interest in its own right as it gave insights into attitudes towards drink-spiking, drunken consent, and intoxicated intercourse. Secondly, it enabled the researchers to identify situations where opinion was divided as to whether consent to intercourse was or was not valid as a result of intoxication that could be used in the next stage of the research, which involved trial simulations and mock jury deliberations.

Once you have decided that focus groups are a suitable method to generate data for your research, there are some practical decisions to be made regarding the size, number, and composition of groups as well as the nature and extent of the moderator's involvement.

You will find detailed information of different approaches to sampling earlier in this chapter that may be useful when considering the composition of the groups.

Size of groups

It is generally accepted that a focus group should have at least six and no more than 12 members with eight to ten being the usual size: any smaller and the group atmosphere might be lost and participants may feel too visible to make contributions, whereas participants may 'get lost' in larger groups and not have sufficient opportunity to join in with the discussion.

The main difficulty in controlling group sizes lies in the unpredictability of participants who have been recruited to the study. It is not unusual for participants to fail to turn up to the focus group which can have an adverse impact on the viability of the group if you have only recruited the desired number of participants. It is sometimes suggested that deliberate over-recruitment is a solution to the problem but, of course, this causes its own difficulties in relation to how to deal with the excess participants if all do show up.

Number of groups

One of the criticisms that is sometimes made about focus group research is that it does not produce findings that are capable of generalization; in other words, it is possible to find out what the people who take part in the groups think but no conclusions can be drawn from this about the opinions of the general population.

In order to counter this criticism, researchers tend to repeat focus groups until it is possible to predict the points that will be raised and opinions that will be expressed. This is called saturation point, to indicate that no new themes or ideas will be discovered however many more times the focus groups are repeated.

In practice, it is useful to repeat focus groups as many times as resources (in terms of time and money) will permit in order to ensure that a wide spectrum of attitudinal data is gathered.

Composition of groups

The key consideration when deciding on the composition of the groups relates back to the data that you need for your research as it is important to consider whose attitudes are needed. Are you interested in the opinions of people in general (in which case, recruitment will be relatively straightforward) or does your research require data that relates to the attitudes of particular people? For example, Smith *et al* (2008) used focus groups to explore experiences of cyber-bullying in schoolchildren aged 11–16 so there were age parameters that needed to be taken into account when recruiting participants, whereas Ratcliffe and McCullagh (2001) carried out focus group research with police officers to gain insight into how perceptions of the level of crime in a particular neighbourhood affected policing decisions. If participants need to have particular socio-demographic characteristics, occupations, or experiences in order to fit within the focus of your research, a purposive approach to recruitment and sampling will be necessary.

Of course, there is no requirement that the composition of all the focus groups must be the same. It is possible to determine the composition of focus groups by reference to particular characteristics in order to compare the data that emerges. For example, you could explore perceptions about policing from the perspective of gender, race, age, or social status by engineering the composition of the groups accordingly.

Practical example: exploring diversity

Kitzinger used focus groups to explore perceptions of HIV. Some groups had general membership whilst others were composed of particular types of participant. She explained the process of determining group membership: '[t]he same included so-called "general population" groups...[i]t also included some groups who might be expected to have particular perspectives on AIDS—groups such as prison officers, male prostitutes, [intravenous] drug users and lesbians' as the research aimed 'to explore diversity' rather than to establish representativeness or consensus across groups (1994: 105).

Moderator involvement

How much involvement should the moderator have in the focus groups?

Given that the aim of focus group research is to gain insight into the attitudes and beliefs of the participants, it follows that the moderator should not intervene too greatly into the discussion. However, it is also important that the discussion takes and maintains a line that is relevant to the research, or the data that emerges will have no value to the researcher. It may also be necessary for the moderator to intervene in the following situations:

- Quiet participants may need to be drawn into the discussion so the moderator may direct a question directly to them or address them by name to elicit their opinion.

- It can be the case that two or three participants dominant the group, leaving the less assertive participants unable to break into the discussion. The moderator may wish to intervene to ensure that all participants have an opportunity to express their opinions.

- Participants may ask a question of the moderator. This may be to elicit further information about the topic or to seek confirmation that a particular viewpoint is correct or valid.

- Kitzinger (1994) noted that interactions between focus group participants may be either complementary, drawing out shared understanding and consensus, or argumentative, highlighting areas of difference and disagreement. Either interaction has the potential to elicit valuable data but the moderator must be careful to ensure that argumentative interaction does not become hostile, so intervention may be necessary to quell disagreement.

Other than this, it is the role of the moderator to introduce the focus group session, explain the purpose of the research, and get the discussion started either by posing a preliminary question or introducing the group to material for discussion. The moderator may also prompt debate if it wanes or direct discussion if it strays too far away from its central purpose. The moderator will also bring the session to a close.

There will always be a temptation for the researcher to take the role of moderator but there are advantages to having this role filled by a third party so that you can observe the focus group in operation, noting your thoughts as they occur, without having to think about acting as moderator. Of course, the presence of an objective moderator circumvents any suggestion that the researcher, consciously or unconsciously, influenced the discussion so as to support the research hypothesis.

Recording, transcribing, and coding

In most respects, the issues raised by recording, transcribing, and coding focus groups mirror those discussed in relation to interviews. However, there is one important distinction that arises from the presence of multiple participants and the desirability of attributing comments to their contributor. In other words, it is useful if the method of recording facilitates the creation of transcripts that indicate not only what was said but who said what during the focus groups. For this reason, although it can be more expensive and raises additional ethical issues (see chapter 12), it is worth considering video recording as an alternative to, or in conjunction with, audio recording. In this way, it will be easier to determine which participant made a particular contribution to the discussion. This enables you to analyse the data gathered from each participant as well as data based on the interactions of the group as a whole. In this way, a clearer picture of individual opinions can be obtained. Once this data is transcribed, it can be coded and analysed as described in relation to interview data.

Practical example: transcription of focus groups

Participant A: I think that it's difficult to have a hard and fast rule about it. I mean, there are all sorts of different situations that can come up.

Participant E: I agree. There's a difference between someone who goes out to get plastered and doesn't care if that means they have sex with someone they don't know and someone whose drink is spiked.

Participant B: But is there though? Both of those women—I say women because that's how I think of it, as something a man does to a woman—both of those women were too drunk to give consent so does it matter how they came to be that drunk?

Participant E: Of course there's a difference. It comes down to personal responsibility.

Participant G: What do you mean?

Participant E: Well, if your drink is spiked then it's not your fault that you're drunk and can't consent whereas…

Participant A: Whereas someone who gets themselves that drunk did it to themselves?

Participant G: But does that make it their fault that it happened? Isn't that like blaming someone for getting raped?

Participant D: Yeah, I'm not happy with that.

Participant B: That's what I meant. I don't think it should be about whether it's someone's fault for how they got drunk. The thing is that in both instances a man has sex with a woman who is too drunk to consent. It doesn't matter how they came to be that drunk. If there's any fault at all then it's the man who has sex with a woman who's that drunk.

Participant E: Well that's right, of course, but shouldn't women take some responsibility here? Do we really want a situation where women who get so drunk that they don't know what they're doing and have sex with a stranger get to call it rape just because they regret it in the morning?

Even in this short extract, it is clear that some participants have strong opposing views. This is only apparent because it is possible to attribute each contribution to the person who made it.

Observations and participation

All the methods of gathering data that have been discussed in this chapter so far have involved asking participants for information. There is always a risk that participants will behave unnaturally because they are taking part in research, perhaps tailoring their information to fit the purpose of the research as they believe it to be or exaggerating or falsifying information to impress or shock the researcher. The artificiality of the situation creates a risk that the data will be unreliable. Observation research is a method of gathering data that overcomes some of these limitations as it involves watching participants in their natural setting.

Practical examples: participation and observation

Gaskew used participant observation to gain insight into the daily experiences of American Muslims after 9/11 and the enactment of the Patriot Act. Using this method, he was able to conclude that 'participants perceive law enforcement agencies as oppressors of human rights, with every personal contact centred on targeting them as potential terrorists' (2009: 365).

Williams (2007) explores the expansion of participant observation into the virtual environment in his research as he gathered data based upon his 'pseudo presence' in online communities and the 'simulation of corporeal immediacy' by the creation of an avatar that can interact with other users.

Buckle and Farrington (1984) used psychologists trained in observing adult and child behaviour to pose as shoppers in a department store in order to determine the nature and extent of shoplifting.

There are four variations of this method based upon whether the researcher observes or participates and upon whether this is overt or covert:

- **Overt observation** is a method of gathering data in which the researcher advises participants that research is taking place and asks them to go about their business as if they were not being watched. This gives the researcher some insight into the phenomenon under consideration but there is still a risk that knowledge of the observation will lead participants to modify their behaviour.

- **Covert observation** also involves the researcher watching participants in their natural setting but here the participants are unaware that they are being observed so there should be no changes to their normal behaviour. There are, however, ethical issues related to covert observation as participants are not asked to consent or made aware of their role in the research.

- **Overt participation** occurs if, rather than simply observing, the researcher takes an active part in what is occurring. Participants are aware that research is taking place and are in agreement with the researcher's involvement in the activity that is being researched. This approach gives the researcher first-hand experience of the phenomenon that is being examined but, again, raises the possibility of behaviour modification.

- **Covert participation** also involves participation by the researcher but this time it is without the knowledge or consent of participants. Again, there is likely to be an improvement in the validity of the data obtained as participants are unaware of the researcher's presence but this is counterbalanced by the ethical issues raised by the deception of the participants involved in this method of gathering data.

There is a detailed discussion of the ethical considerations surrounding consent and deception in chapter 12.

Practical considerations

Although participation or observation can be useful in generating data that may not be available by any other means, there are practical considerations to take into account before adopting these methods.

What data are observable?

The first question to consider is whether it is possible to gather the required data by observation. There will be some research questions that cannot be explored using this method simply because they do not give rise to data that can be gathered by observation. For example, if the focus of your research is how victims deal with the aftermath of burglary, participant observation would have little to offer as a method of data collection as it would be impossible for you to predict where burglaries were going to take place and, in any case, much of the victim's reaction would take place in the private domain of their home where observation would not be possible.

Similarly, even if events are observable, there are limitations to the information that they provide. Observation facilitates the recording of events, interactions, and conversations—things that happen—but does not readily provide insight into the motivations or thoughts of those involved. For example, if you wanted to gather data on factors that influenced sentencing in burglary cases and the impact on the defendant and the victim by observing sentencing in burglary cases, you could sit in the public gallery of the Crown Court. You would hear the comments made by the sentencing judge and observe the reaction of the defendant and, if he is present and identifiable, the victim but you would not be party to the reasoning process of the judge nor to the thoughts and emotions of the defendant and victim. Of course, you could always use observation in conjunction with interviews to pursue these other issues.

Practical exercise: observations in a public place

This simple exercise should help you to understand the challenges of observation as a method of gathering data.

Imagine that you are carrying out research on the social function served by coffee shops (obviously, this is not a very good area to research as a criminologist but it is a very useful exercise to give you insight into participant observation).

Find a seat in a coffee shop where you can observe other tables. In order to focus your attention on one particular aspect of the social world around you, focus your attention on one particular table with a view to recording all the customers who use it within a one-hour period, noting how long they are present and the apparent purpose of their visit. At the end of the period of observation, make a note of how effective you feel your observation has been as a method of gathering data.

Here are some comments made by students who have tried this exercise that express their different views on the experience:

- I thought it would be really easy but it was surprising how difficult it was to focus on one table and not get distracted by other things going on.

- It was really hard to keep concentrating rather than drifting off into my own thoughts.

- I couldn't stop myself making deductions about people and why they were there. I'd written 'colleagues discussing work' about two people in suits who were referring to papers and writing notes but then they were holding hands when they left the coffee shop.

- You can see what people are doing but that doesn't really tell you very much.

- I thought it was surprising how much you can work out just from watching people.

Problems of recording and interpreting data

Data that is gathered by observation exists irrespective of whether or not it is studied. In other words, it is something that is happening in the ordinary course of events in the social world and it becomes research data because it is observed by an interested researcher.

The process of recording data that is observed can be problematic. It is generally desirable to record observations in some way as the researcher will otherwise be reliant on memory which can be unreliable, particularly if the observation spans several hours or involves complicated interactions. However, the method of recording may require some careful thought as there may be situations in which writing notes or speaking into a recording device is not advisable, as it may alert those observed to the researcher's presence. This may either place the researcher in danger (you can imagine that those involved in drug transactions or other such unlawful activity may be unimpressed to find that their activities were being observed) or may compromise the validity of the data as people may alter their behaviour as a consequence. It may be that surreptitious recording is possible or it may be that the researcher needs to leave the observation area at regular intervals to make notes of what has occurred.

A further difficulty arises due to the researcher's role in the data gathering process. The researcher must record what is observed but it is all too easy to move beyond this into an interpretation of events that occur by attributing meaning to observed behaviour and interaction. This gives rise to potential for misinterpretation. It is important to ensure, as far as possible, that observations are objective and limited to the facts that are observed. Researchers using this method often refer to the possibility of bias (seeing what they want to see) and misinterpretation when commenting on the process of data collection.

Safety and legality

The final practical consideration is of particular importance within the field of criminology given its focus on crime and criminals. It is essential that the safety of the researcher is not threatened by their presence in the research environment nor must the researcher, by virtue of his activities or the information that he possesses, be in a position where he could incur criminal liability.

Experimental methods

Experimental methods are a very scientific approach to generating data in criminology. The central idea is that the ability of the researcher to control all aspects of the experiment ensures that the experiment is able to explore the relationship between particular variables that are of interest. This is done by the manipulation of one variable (independent variable) to see if it alters another variable (called the dependant variable because its measurement depends upon the independent variable). If the manipulation of the independent variable causes changes in the dependant variable, then this suggests that there is a relationship of cause and effect between them. These ideas can be hard to grasp so the example below may help you to understand the basic nature of experimental methods.

Practical example: dependant and independent variables

Morgan *et al* (2004) formulated an experiment to test whether the ability to recall the face of an attacker was affected by stress. The setting of the experiment was a simulation of a prisoner-of-war interrogation that the participants, all active military personnel, experienced as part of a survival training course. The participants were subjected to either low-stress (questioning only) or high-stress (questioning and physical confrontation) interrogation techniques. The following day, participants were asked to identify those involved in the interrogation using photographs and line-ups. In all cases, the accuracy of identification was greater in the low-stress conditions.

Can you identify the dependant and independent variable? Remember, the independent variable is the thing that is varied by the researcher whilst the dependant variable is the thing that changes as a result of the independent variable.

Here, the level of stress to which participants were exposed was the independent variable as the researcher was in control of this and determined whether each particular was exposed to low- or high-stress interrogation techniques. The level of stress affected the accuracy of identification so it is this which is the dependant variable: accuracy of identification was *dependant* on the level of stress to which the participant was exposed during interrogation.

It is important that only the independent variable changes otherwise there may be some other factor that is responsible for the response of the dependant variable. For this reason, the researcher will control all other variables and strive to keep them constant so that nothing is different except the independent variable. It is also usual to use a control group in which the independent variable is absent to provide a baseline against which to measure the response of the experimental group (that is, the group that is exposed to the independent variable). The control group and the experimental group should be matched in all *relevant* characteristics (such as age or gender).

Table 13.2 Strengths and weaknesses of experimental methods

Strengths of experimental methods	Weaknesses of experimental methods
Experiments offer the greatest precision in exploring cause and effect, as the manipulation of the independent variable and the control of all other variables tends to lead to the conclusion that change in the dependant variable can be attributed to the independent variable.	The level of control exercised creates a very artificial situation in that it is different to ordinary life. This low ecological validity can distort participants' behaviour and make it difficult to make generalizations based upon experimental findings.
A very high level of control can be exercised by the researcher, thus isolating the independent variable. If this does not seem to have altered the dependant variable, the experiment can be repeated with a different independent variable until a causal effect is observed.	Experimental methods are vulnerable to the influence of demand characteristics. This means that participants are aware that they are part of an experiment and may, consciously or unconsciously, adapt their responses to fit with their predictions about what the experiment is trying to test.
Experiments can be replicated, thus their findings can be tested and re-tested to strengthen the conclusion that the findings of the experiment are correct.	There are ethical issues involved in experiments, particularly surrounding deception as it is often the case that the experiment would not work if the participant knew what was being tested.
It is usually the case that quantitative data is generated by experiments and inferential statistics can be used to analyse this data, thus facilitating a calculation of how likely it is that the results were obtained by chance.	Experimental methods assume that the researcher is in control of all the variables that could affect the outcome but there may be variables of which the researcher is unaware, which he cannot control, particularly in relation to the past experiences and mental processes of the participants.

CHAPTER SUMMARY

Sampling

- There are two main types of sampling methods—probability sampling and non-probability sampling
- Probability samples are more likely to be representative of the population as a whole and give results that can be generalized to that population
- Probability sampling involves some form of random selection; this can be undertaken in random, systematic, stratified, or cluster methods. However, in practice, some combination of these methods is likely to form a multi-stage sampling method
- The findings from non-probability samples cannot be generalized to a whole population but convenience sampling can be useful when time and cost are factors, particularly as part of a pilot study
- Snowball sampling is useful when trying to survey a population that is difficult to access

Questionnaires

- Give careful consideration to the design of questionnaires, taking into account the sorts of data that you want to gather, and ensure that your questions are worded in a way that will do this effectively
- Think about who you want to complete the questionnaire and how you are going to administer it to them
- Test the questionnaire to ensure that it does the job that you want it to do by administering it to a small group of participants to see how they answer the questions
- Make sure that the questions are pre-coded as far as possible, as this makes the task for processing the questionnaires for analysis much easier

Interviews

- Plan your interviews by producing a schedule that sets out the points that you want to cover and the order in which you expect to address them. You may need to be flexible with this so that the interview flows
- Consider how you are going to capture the data that is elicited during the interview, particularly if the participant is not willing to be recorded
- Be aware of ethical considerations of anonymity and confidentiality and think about how you will protect these, particularly with a small sample with distinctive participants

Focus groups

- Focus groups can be a really good method of collecting attitudinal data but its success is dependant upon your ability to facilitate a focused and animated discussion. Give some thought to how you are going to get people talking and how you are going to make sure that they stick to the topics that you want them to discuss
- Each focus group should contain at least six participants. Think about where you are going to find your participants and how you are going to reward them for their time
- It can be difficult to keep track of which contributions to the discussion were made by each participant, especially if the group is lively and people speak over each other. Consider using video recording as well as audio recording to maximize accuracy

Observations

- Although observation can be a good method of obtaining data that would not otherwise be available, it can provide quite limited insights as observation enables behaviour but not thoughts or motivations to be recorded
- There is often an ethical dilemma involved with this method as it generally involves observations of people who have not consented to take part in your research
- It is important to ensure that you do not put yourself in danger and that you do not break the law in using this method to generate data

GLOSSARY

A **population** is the entire set of units from which the sample is to be selected.

A **probability sample** is a sample in which each unit in the population has a known chance of being selected.

A **representative sample** is a sample that reflects the characteristics of the population accurately.

A **sample** is the part of the population that is selected for investigation.

The **sampling error** is a measurement of the error caused by observing a sample instead of the whole population.

A **unit** is the individual 'thing' that is being surveyed.

REFERENCES

Buckle, A. & Farrington, D. (1984) An observational study of shoplifting. *British Journal of Criminology*, 24(1), 63–73.

Finch, E. & Munro, V. (2008) Lifting the Veil? The Use of Focus Groups and Trial Simulations in Legal Research. *Journal of Law and Society*, 35, 30–51.

Gaskew, T. (2009) Peacemaking Criminology and Counterterrorism: Muslim Americans and the War on Terror. *Contemporary Justice Review*, 12(3), 345–366.

Kitzinger, J (1994) The methodology of focus groups: The importance of interaction between research participants. *Sociology of Health and Illness*, 16, 103–21.

Lofland, J & Lofland, L. (1995) *Analyzing Social Settings: A Guide to Qualitative Observation and Analysis*. Belmont, CA: Wadsworth.

Morgan, C., Hazlett, G., Doran, A., Garrett, S., Hoyt, G., Thomas, P., Baronoski, M. & Southwick, S. (2004) Accuracy of eyewitness memory for persons encountered during exposure to highly intense stress. *International Journal of Law and Psychiatry*, 27, 265–279.

Ratcliffe, J. & McCullagh, M. (2001) Chasing Ghosts? Police Perception of High Crime Areas. *British Journal of Criminology*, 41, 330–41.

Smith, P., Mahdavi, J. Carvalho, M., Fisher, S., Russell, S. & Tippett, N. (2008) Cyberbullying: its nature and impact in secondary school pupils. *Journal of Child Psychology and Psychiatry*, 49(4), 376–385.

Williams, M. (2007) Avatar Watching: Participant Observation in Graphical Online Environments. *Qualitative Research*, 7(1), 5–24.

Quantitative analysis

INTRODUCTION

The earlier chapters in this part of the book have concentrated on the earlier stages of the research process, particularly in discussing how to gather data (chapter 13) in an ethical manner (chapter 12). The remaining chapters in this part of the book focus on the next stage of the research process: analysing the data that has been generated. This chapter deals with quantitative methods of analysis in which statistical tests are used to describe data and to draw inferences from the data.

Quantitative analysis is a significant feature of criminological research so the ability to understand when and how statistical tests are used is a crucial skill for criminology students. Different degree programs vary in the extent of 'hands on' work that students are expected to carry out: some institutions require that students generate their own data whereas others provide students with a data set for analysis. In either situation, you will need to be able to identify an appropriate statistical test to describe the data or draw inferences from it and carry out that analysis so the step-by-step instructions provided in this chapter will provide valuable guidance. Even if your course does not involve carrying out quantitative analysis, this chapter will still be important to you, as it will provide a foundation of knowledge of statistical analysis which will enable you to understand published work that is based upon quantitative analysis.

LEARNING OUTCOMES

After reading this chapter, you will be able to:

- Identify the different types of variable generated in criminological research

- Appreciate the role of univariate, bivariate, and multivariate analysis and select an appropriate test to analyse particular data

- Enter data into SPSS and carry out some straightforward statistical analysis

- Interpret the results of different statistical tests and appreciate the inferences that can be drawn from them

- Understand and evaluate published research based upon quantitative analysis

The nature of quantitative data

There is a tendency to make a delineation between quantitative and qualitative data on the basis of numerical data (quantitative) and everything else (qualitative) but, in order to understand the distinction between the two types of data, it is important to understand why this distinction exists. Quantitative methods of analysis deal with absolute data or, in other words, data that are amenable to precise measurement. As measurement involves counting, quantitative data are numerical. For example, when looking at how many robberies are committed by offenders with previous convictions and/or drug or alcohol addiction, you are counting several things:

- How many robberies have been committed?
- How many offenders committed those robberies?
- How many offenders have previous convictions?
- How many offenders have problems with drug addiction?
- How many offenders have problems with alcohol addiction?

Once numerical data exists that answers these questions, statistical analysis can be carried out to test whether there are links between them. By contrast, qualitative analysis is concerned with data that describes meaning and experience. As such, it deals with nuances rather than numbers. For example, qualitative research may explore what factors motivate an offender with convictions for robbery to continue to offend.

Types of variable

Before looking at some of the ways in which quantitative data can be analysed, it is first important to understand the different sorts of variables which are commonly generated in criminological research.

- **Ratio variables** are based on a consistent unit of measurement in which the categories are equally spaced and can be ranked from a zero point. For example, 'age in years' is such a variable, since the categories (in this case, years) are equally spaced (with an interval of one year). Similarly, 'annual household income in £000s' would give rise to equally spaced intervals of £1,000. Ratio variables contain numeric data. These are further categorized into **discrete data** (which are expressed in whole numbers only) and **continuous data** (which can include decimal fractions).
- **Interval variables** are similar to ratio variables, but do not have a fixed zero point, such as time or temperature. For practical purposes, since most ratio variables encountered in criminology have a fixed zero, there is no need to differentiate between ratio and interval variables further.
- **Nominal variables** (also known as **categorical variables**) are variables which have no inherent order and therefore cannot be put into a ranking. They can contain any number of mutually-exclusive categories. The most commonly encountered nominal variable in criminological studies is gender (male/female). However, criminological research can give rise to many other sorts of nominal variables. For instance a study on convictions for property offences may include 'offence' as a nominal variable with possible categories being 'theft',

'robbery', 'burglary', 'criminal damage', 'handling', or 'arson'. If there are only two possible categories which a variable can take, the variable is referred to as **binary** or **dichotomous**.

- **Ordinal variables** are those which may be ranked into some sort of order. For instance a response to an attitudinal questionnaire may take the form 'strongly agree', 'agree', 'neither agree nor disagree', 'disagree', and 'strongly disagree'; or a survey may categorize the ages of respondents as 'under 30', '31–40', '41–50', '51–60', and '61 or over'. Ordinal variables are similar to ratio variables in that they are capable of being ordered, but the distances between the categories are not equal.

You may find the flowchart in Figure 14.1 helpful in differentiating between different types of variable.

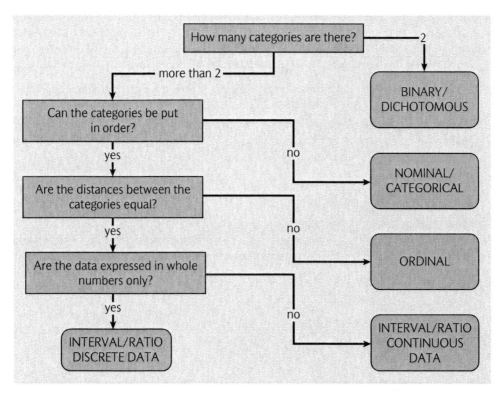

Figure 14.1 Different types of variable

Practical exercise: identifying types of variable

Using the flowchart in Figure 14.1 to assist you, decide the type of variable for each of the following:

1. Ethnic origin: 'White', 'Black', 'Asian', 'Mixed', 'Other', 'Did not answer'.
2. Length of sentence following conviction (in years).
3. University educated: 'Yes', 'No'.
4. Number of times arrested: '0', '1–3', '4–10', '11–20', 'more than 20'.
5. Blood alcohol level as measured at the roadside (in milligrams per 100 ml).

 You will find answers to these questions on the Online Resource Centre.

Having dealt with some of the terminology, we will move on to consider some of the more common forms of quantitative analysis:

- **Univariate analysis** which considers one variable;
- **Bivariate analysis** which looks at two variables;
- **Multivariate analysis** which considers three or more variables.

Univariate analysis

When analysing a single interval/ratio variable, such as the number of convictions, the length of a sentence or the number of units of alcohol consumed per week, there are a number of **descriptive statistics** that can be used to give a general indication about the data themselves. In particular, descriptive statistical analysis looks at two key indicators:

- **Measures of centrality**: that is, describing where the centre of a particular distribution lies: this indicates a 'typical' value for the distribution.
- **Measures of dispersion**: that is, the amount of variation from the centre of the distribution: it is useful in comparing sets of data which may have the same centre point but a different spread of values.

Measures of centrality

There are three measures of centrality which give an average figure that represents a typical value within a distribution. In everyday terms, the word average is commonly understood as the value obtained when adding up a particular set of values and dividing the total by the number of values. However, within quantitative analysis there are three different forms of average:

- The (arithmetic) mean
- The median
- The mode.

Arithmetic mean

The arithmetic mean (or, simply, just the **mean**) of a set of values is more commonly known as the 'average' in everyday usage: that is, the total sum of all the values divided by the number of values. Although the mean is a very frequently used descriptive statistic, it does suffer from the limitation that a few extreme values will have a big effect on it.

Practical exercise: arithmetic mean

The following set of data represents the length of sentence (in months) imposed following conviction for burglary:

14, 16, 18, 15, 16, 17, 16

1. What is the mean length of sentence?

Imagine now that a particular burglary came before the court. The court's view was that the circumstances of the offence were such that the sentence imposed should reflect the gravity of the offence. The court imposed a sentence of five years' imprisonment.

2. Adding this sentence to those above, what is the mean length of sentence now? Does this accurately reflect the distribution of data?

 You will find the answers to this exercise on the Online Resource Centre.

Median

The median of a set of values is the mid-point of that set. In other words, it is the figure above which half the values lie and below which the other half lie. It is found by ordering all the values from the smallest to the largest and then finding the mid-point. If there is an even number of values in the distribution then the median is calculated as the arithmetic mean of the two middle numbers in the distribution.

Practical exercise: median

1. Calculate the median of the set of data from part one of the previous practical exercise.

2. Now add the five-year sentence to the data set and re-calculate the median. How does this differ from the mean previously calculated? Is this a more representative view of the overall characteristics of the distribution?

 You will find the answers to this exercise on the Online Resource Centre.

Mode

The mode of a set of values is simply the value which occurs most frequently. Although it is not especially useful, it does at least show where the most common value in the distribution lies.

Presenting univariate data

A **frequency table** is a very common way of displaying quantitative data. A frequency table lists the possible values that a variable might take and the number of times in which those values occurred within the sample. For instance, you might undertake a survey of a sample of 90 victims of credit card fraud to see which types of fraud were most common. These could be shown as in Table 14.1, which lists:

- the type of fraud;
- the number of victims of each type of fraud;
- the percentage of victims of each type of fraud.

Frequency information is often presented diagrammatically as a **bar chart** or a **pie chart**. A bar chart depicts category values along the x (horizontal) axis, and frequencies (count) along the y (vertical) axis.

Table 14.1 Survey of card fraud victims

Type of fraud	Number of victims (n)	Percentage (%)
Cardholder not present	49	54.4
Lost or stolen card	8	8.9
Card ID theft	7	7.8
Mail non-receipt	2	2.2
Counterfeit fraud	24	26.7
Total	90	100.0

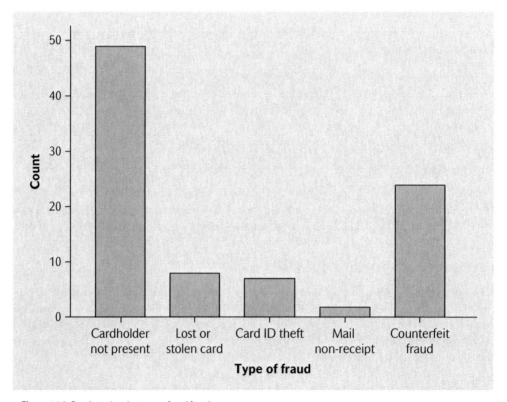

Figure 14.2 Bar chart showing types of card fraud

Alternatively, the slices in a pie chart show the sizes of the different categories and their proportion of the sample as a whole:

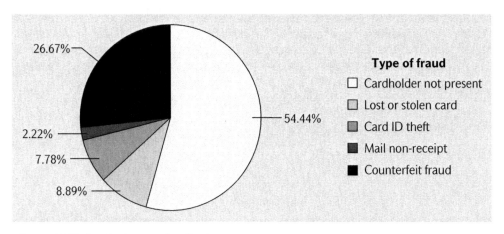

Figure 14.3 Pie chart showing types of card fraud

Measures of dispersion

While the measures of central tendency are useful means of indicating a typical value at the centre of a distribution, it is often interesting to look at the amount of variation in a sample; that is, the way in which the values are distributed.

For instance, say that you measured the IQ of 10,000 people and produced a bar chart of your results. It would probably look something like this:

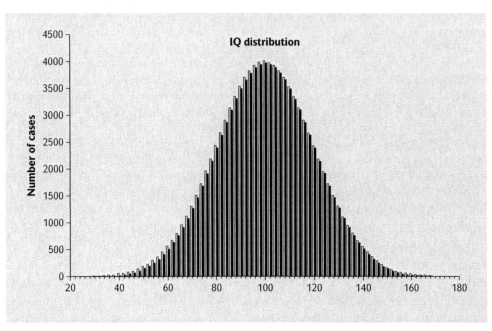

Figure 14.4 Distribution of IQ measurements

This distribution has a bell-shaped curve with a single peak at the mean (in this example, an IQ value of 100) and is symmetrical about the mean. It is an example of a **normal distribution**. A normal distribution is a theoretical frequency distribution for a set of variable data. It is associated with Johann Gauss, a German mathematician and scientist, and is sometimes referred to as a Gaussian curve. When plotted with the values along the horizontal axis and their frequencies along the vertical axis, it takes the form shown in Figure 14.5.

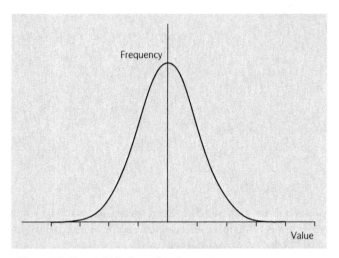

Figure 14.5 Normal distribution or Gaussian curve

In a perfect normal distribution, such as that shown in Figure 14.5, the mean, mode, and median will be the same. The normal distribution is important in statistics because its attributes can be used as a basis for making comparisons between different distributions.

In cases where the mean, mode, and median are different, then the distribution is said to be **skewed**.

If most of the values are to the left of the mean, then the distribution is described as **positively skewed**. As seen in Figure 14.6, the right tail is longer and the bulk of the distribution is concentrated to the left of the figure. For instance, if you were studying the amounts of money acquired in fraudulent transactions and the distribution was positively skewed, then this would tell you that most fraud cases involved relatively low sums.

Conversely, if most of the values are to the right of the mean, then the distribution is described as **negatively skewed**. In this instance, as seen in Figure 14.7, the left tail is longer and the bulk of the distribution is concentrated to the right of the figure. An example of a negatively skewed distribution would be age (in years) of retirement.

When measuring the dispersion of a distribution, two common descriptive statistics are:

- The range
- The standard deviation.

Range

The **range** is a very simple way of measuring dispersion. It is simply the difference between the maximum and minimum values measured. While this is simple to calculate, it does suffer from the same limitation as the mean, in that it is heavily influenced by a single high or low value. For instance, using the same data from the earlier practical exercise on sentence lengths for burglary, the range would be four months (18 minus 14) for the first set of data but 46 months (60 minus 14) once a single five-year sentence had been included.

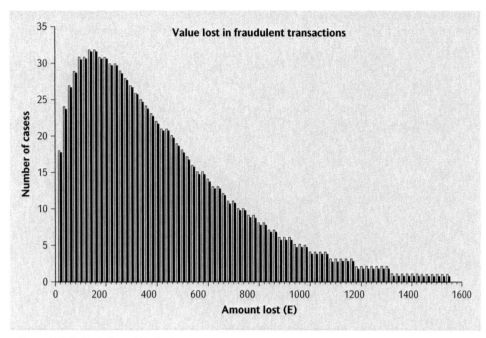

Figure 14.6 Positively skewed distribution

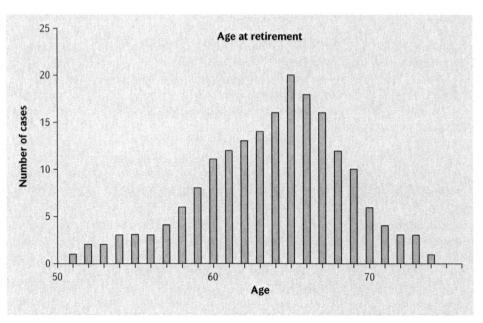

Figure 14.7 Negatively skewed distribution

Standard deviation

The **standard deviation** is another frequently used method of measuring dispersion. It is a measurement which represents the degree of variation there is from the mean. A low standard deviation indicates that the data points tend to be very close to the mean, whereas a high standard deviation indicates that the data is spread out over a large range of values. Figure 14.8 shows a distribution with a low standard deviation; its values are clustered around the mean:

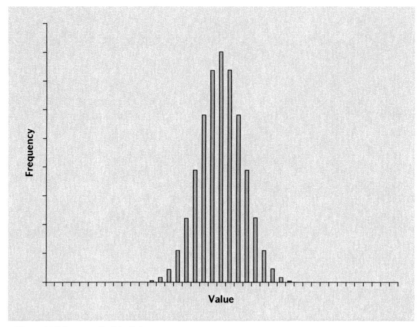

Figure 14.8 Low standard deviation

By contrast, Figure 14.9 shows a distribution with a high standard deviation, where the values are much more widely dispersed.

The standard deviation is less affected by single extreme values than the range.

In a normal distribution, around two-thirds (68.3%) of cases are found within one standard deviation of the mean and approximately 95% (95.44%) of cases are within two standard deviations of the mean.

Manual calculation versus computer-aided calculation

As you should appreciate by now, the underlying formulae for determining the mean, mode, and median are quite straightforward. Sum the values and divide by the total number for the mean, find the mid-point for the median, and work out which value occurs most frequently for the mode.

Even though the arithmetic involved should not be particularly daunting, it is still laborious (and prone to some error) to calculate these simple statistics where there are large volumes of data requiring analysis. The practical exercises so far have introduced you to the idea of manual calculation and demonstrated the effectiveness of the mean, median, and mode as single descriptors of a set of seven or eight values. Criminological studies involve much larger sets of data than those in the examples given and it would be much less fun to calculate the same statistics for a set of seven thousand data items manually.

The standard deviation and other statistics that will be covered in the remainder of this chapter require the use of more complicated formulae for their calculation. While you could

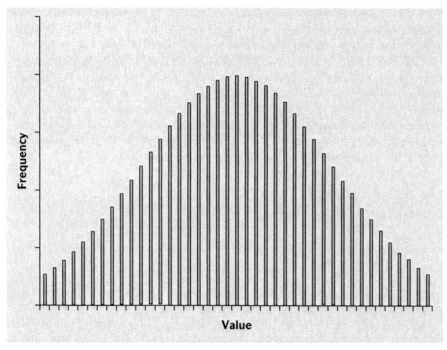

Figure 14.9 High standard deviation

learn these formulae and then apply them to your data, remember that you are studying criminology and not statistics. In practice, quantitative data analysis is carried out using computer software which performs the various calculations for you. It requires no knowledge of the underlying formulae, but you do need to grasp what the various results mean. The most widely used software for quantitative data analysis in the social sciences is IBM SPSS (Statistical Package for the Social Sciences). This was first released as SPSS in 1968. The current version (at the time of writing) is version 20, which was released in August 2011.

Note that between 2009 and 2010, version 18 of the software was called PASW Statistics (with PASW standing for Predictive Analytics SoftWare), so if your institution is using that particular version, you will see PASW rather than SPSS, but the core product is the same. The package will simply be referred to as SPSS from now on (which is how everyone refers to it in everyday use).

Remember, though, that SPSS is simply a tool for researchers to use to help analyse their data: it presents a blank canvas which requires you to tell the package the description and parameters for each variable. It does not provide a general analysis of all your data: it only performs the tests that it is told to perform using the data and descriptions of the data that you provide. As such, it is extremely powerful and flexible, but its use is only as good as the instructions with which you provide it. It has a huge range of capabilities, but does require a certain amount of tuition and guidance. It is not the intention of this section of the chapter to provide a 'standalone' user guide to SPSS, but instead to give you a feel for some of its capabilities and get you used to working with it. You should certainly investigate whether your institution offers any courses or additional support in learning to use SPSS; at the very least you should look at the SPSS online tutorial (accessible from within the program itself) which will show you how to use many of the available features. It is designed to provide a step-by-step, hands-on guide. There is also a comprehensive help facility, a wealth of reference material, and various case studies with sample data sets.

In addition to the help that is available from within SPSS itself, there is an excellent text by Andy Field (2009) *Discovering Statistics Using SPSS*, published by SAGE. It is extremely clear, sharp, and makes a difficult subject accessible, as well as charting its author's life story in a compelling, engaging, and humorous fashion. If you need to engage with SPSS in any depth, you should think seriously about acquiring a copy. It is a particular favourite of the authors, who are not too proud to say that they often use it to help with their own data analysis.

The remainder of this chapter will not dwell on the formulae for calculating particular statistics, but will instead show how to compute them using SPSS.

Univariate analysis with SPSS

This section will demonstrate how to use SPSS to generate the descriptive statistics for a set of data.

The sample data for this section are available on the Online Resource Centre as an Excel spreadsheet and also as a list of data elements in a PDF file. An animated walkthrough of this example is also available on the Online Resource Centre. The screenshots used in this chapter are from version 20 of SPSS. If you only have access to an earlier version there may be some slight differences in appearance, but the fundamental principles remain unchanged.

When you start SPSS, you may be presented with an opening dialogue box which asks you 'What would you like to do?'.

SPSS welcome page

If this is the case, select **Cancel** to move to the SPSS Data Editor (or select the option to run the tutorial if you wish). Alternatively, if this dialogue box has been disabled, then SPSS will open directly into the Data Editor.

SPSS data view

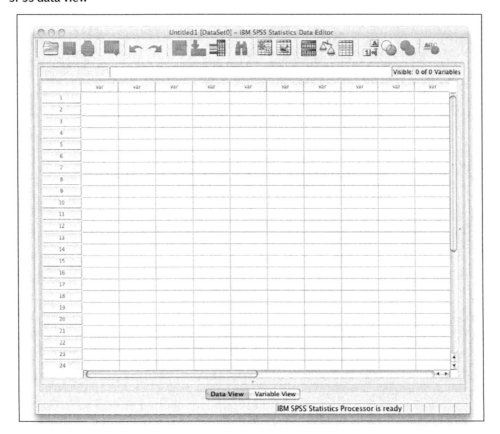

This has two views: **Data View** and **Variable View** which are selected by the tabs at the bottom of the screen. Data View is (as shown above) similar to a spreadsheet in which you enter data. Each **column** (vertical) represents a variable: all are labelled 'var' to start with, but this can be changed to something more meaningful later. Each **row** (horizontal) represents a case: a unit of analysis. The intersection between each row and column is referred to as a **cell**.

Entering data

The sample data in this exercise represent the marks of 100 students in their end-of-year Youth Justice examination.

If you are able to open the data set in Excel, then you can simply cut and paste the marks directly from the Excel spreadsheet into the Data Viewer. Otherwise, you will have to type in each mark individually.

In either case, you should start in the top left-hand cell. If this is not highlighted, then you will need to select it by clicking with your mouse in that cell. To enter the data manually, simply type the first number (42) and then press Enter. The highlight will then move down to the next row.

You should end up with a list of 100 marks in the first column of the Data Viewer (the first 20 are shown here).

SPSS data view—data entered

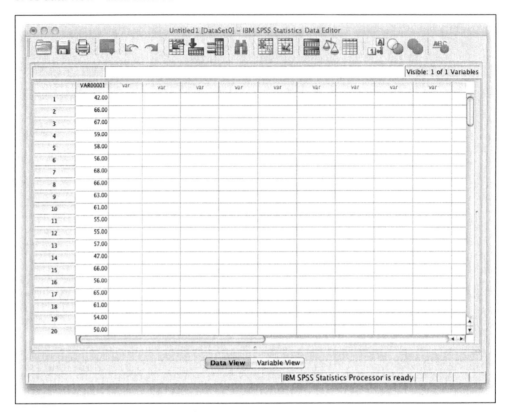

Defining variables

Having entered the data, you can now define your variable in the Variable View.

SPSS variable view

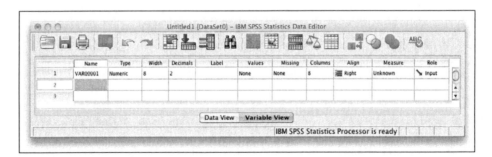

To give the variable a meaningful name, click in the name column (which will contain the default name of 'VAR00001') and type in the name you wish to use (in this case 'Marks'). You will also have noticed when entering your data that each mark was shown to two decimal places (.00). As this is not meaningful in the context of student marks (which are discrete data), then you should also edit the 'Decimals' column to replace its default of two decimal places to zero.

SPSS variable view with data

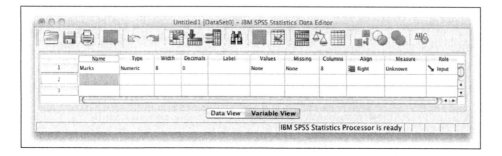

If you switch back to Data View, you will see that the column heading has become 'Marks' and that the marks are now shown in whole numbers.

SPSS formatted data

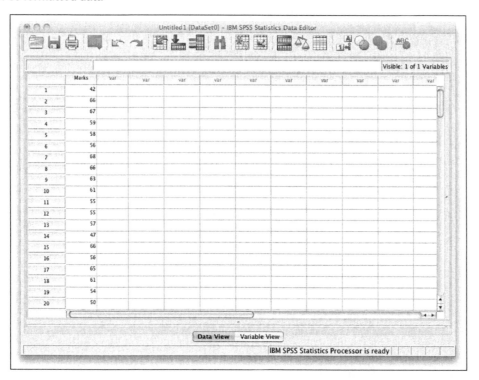

Generating statistics

To generate the statistics we have encountered thus far, select the **Analyze** menu, followed by **Descriptive Statistics**, then **Frequencies**... The Frequencies dialogue box will appear:

SPSS frequencies dialogue

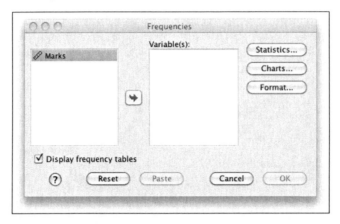

This shows a list of the possible variables in the left hand list. In this example there is only one. The right hand list contains the variables selected for analysis. Move 'Marks' into this list by clicking on the arrow button between the lists. Then click on **Statistics**…which will open a new dialogue so that you can select the particular statistics that you want SPSS to calculate for you. Select the descriptive statistics covered so far: mean, mode, median, skewness, range, minimum, maximum, and standard deviation:

SPSS frequencies—statistics dialogue

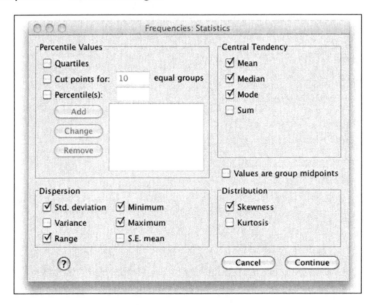

Select **Continue** to return to the previous dialogue.

Then click **Charts**…and select **Histogram**. Make sure that the '**Show normal curve on histogram**' box is ticked:

SPSS frequencies—charts dialogue

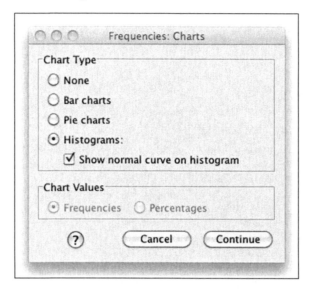

Select **Continue** to return to the previous dialogue and then click **OK**. SPSS should generate various statistics in the Output Viewer:

Statistics

Marks		
N	Valid	100
	Missing	0
Mean		57.37
Median		58.00
Mode		56[a]
Std. Deviation		8.705
Skewness		−.263
Std. Error of Skewness		.241
Range		43
Minimum		33
Maximum		76

[a] Multiple modes exist. The smallest value is shown

This table gives us key information about the distribution of marks in this sample from which we can make the following observations:

- The arithmetic mean mark is 57.37.
- The median mark is 58.

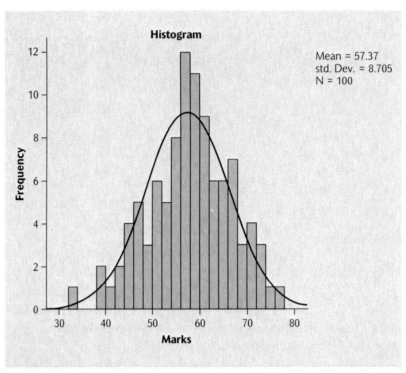

Figure 14.10 SPSS histogram

- There is more than one modal mark, the smallest of which is 56.
- The standard deviation of marks is 8.7. Remember that around two-thirds of the sample will lie one standard deviation each side of the mean, so we can say that two-thirds of students (most students) scored between 48 and 66 marks. Similarly, since around 95% of the sample lie between two standard deviations of the mean, we can say that 95% of students (almost all students) scored between 40 and 74 marks.
- The distribution has a negative skew (– 0.263) which means that it has a tendency to lean towards the higher marks being more common. This can be seen in the histogram produced by SPSS (Figure 14.10).

Standard error and confidence interval

When you are describing a set of sample data drawn from a broader population, it is useful to know about the characteristics of the population as a whole as well as the descriptive statistics of the sample itself.

If you have a set of statistics based on a sample there is always some uncertainty involved in making inferences about that population based on that sample. Therefore, it is important to ascertain whether the mean of a data sample accurately describes the population from which it is drawn. The question to answer is the extent to which another sample drawn from the same population would give the same or a similar result and how similar those results would be.

Say, for instance, that you were undertaking a study to determine the prevalence of repeat burglary across the UK based on surveying a sample of 200 households to ask how many times they had been burgled. You determined these results:

Number of burglaries	Number of households
0	186
1	10
2	3
3	1

Here, the arithmetic mean is 0.095 burglaries per household.

However, if you were to draw several samples of 200 households from the same population, it would be extremely unlikely for them all to have the same characteristics, even if those samples were drawn at random. This is simply a matter of chance. A second sample may have had these results:

Number of burglaries	Number of households
0	183
1	12
2	4
3	1

In this case the arithmetic mean is 0.115 burglaries per household.

Similarly, if you took a third sample, it would be surprising if the mean was exactly the same as either of the first two, but you might reasonably expect it to be close.

Now suppose that you took 5,000 samples of 200 respondents per sample, which would involve a million responses overall. This would give you 5,000 means which you would expect to fall into a normal distribution: the variations from the centre of a very large number of results would be likely to be equally distributed higher and lower. Therefore there would be no skew and the mean, mode, and median would coincide at the highest point on the frequency curve.

You can then apply the same measures of central tendency and dispersion to describe this distribution of sample means.

Although the actual mean of the whole population is not known with absolute certainty, the average of the means obtained from very large numbers of samples will be very close to the mean of the entire population as a whole. The larger the number of samples, the closer the average of their means will be to the mean of the whole population. This principle is known as the **central limit theorem**.

The standard deviation of this set of hypothetical means is referred to as the **standard error** (to differentiate it from the standard deviation of a sample, even though the calculation is the same). The bigger the sample size, the less the standard error. As you would also expect, the standard error is less than the standard deviation of a sample.

A closely related term to the standard error is that of the **confidence interval**. Remember that, in a normal distribution, approximately 95% of cases are within two standard deviations of the mean. Similarly, 99% of cases will be within around two-and-a-half standard deviations of the mean. In the set of hypothetical means, you can say that 95% of sample means (that is a **confidence level** of 95%) lie within two standard errors of the actual population mean, and that 99% of sample means lie within two-and-a-half standard errors of the actual population mean.

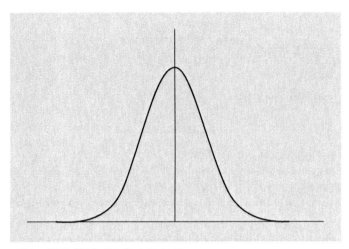

Figure 14.11 Distribution of sample means

Therefore, although you cannot say with absolute certainty what the mean of an actual population is, you can describe a range of values that attempts to measure the uncertainty inherent in relying on information from a sample. This is your confidence interval. It can be thought of as a range of plausible values.

You should be able to see that the confidence interval is closely linked with precision of measurement:

- A narrow confidence interval implies high precision: the range of plausible values is very small;

- A large confidence interval implies low precision: in this case the data may be too broad to be meaningfully informative.

Unsurprisingly, SPSS is also able to calculate the standard error in a sample mean. You can select this from **Statistics** dialogue box as before:

SPSS standard error mean dialogue

Frequencies: Statistics

Percentile Values
- ☐ Quartiles
- ☐ Cut points for: 10 equal groups
- ☐ Percentile(s):
  - (Add)
  - (Change)
  - (Remove)

Central Tendency
- ☐ Mean
- ☐ Median
- ☐ Mode
- ☐ Sum

☐ Values are group midpoints

Dispersion
- ☐ Std. deviation ☐ Minimum
- ☐ Variance ☐ Maximum
- ☐ Range ☑ S.E. mean

Distribution
- ☐ Skewness
- ☐ Kurtosis

(?)   (Cancel) (Continue)

This yields the following result, showing the standard error of the mean to be 0.870.

Statistics

Marks		
N	Valid	100
	Missing	0
Std. Error of Mean		.870
Skewness		−.263
Std. Error of Skewness		.241

The ideas of confidence level and confidence interval are relevant to sampling: see chapter 13.

Practical exercise: confidence intervals

 Go to the Online Resource Centre where you will find a set of data relating to alcohol consumption (in units per week) based on a sample of 500 UK adult women.

1. Load the data into SPSS and calculate the mean, standard deviation, and standard error of the sample.

2. What is the average alcohol consumption of the female population in units per week to 95% confidence and to 99% confidence?

 You will find the answers to this exercise on the Online Resource Centre together with a video walkthrough of using SPSS to calculate the descriptive statistics required.

Bivariate analysis

It is often interesting to investigate the relationship between two variables to see if variation in one coincides with variation in another. Note, though, that there is a distinction between relationship and causation. While there may be a relationship between two variables it does not follow that variation in one causes variation in the other. There may be a whole range of causal influences at play. For example, suppose there was a positive correlation between playing violent video games and violent behaviour in adolescents. It could be that the cause of both of these is something else, such as being a victim of abuse in the home, and that playing violent games and violent behaviour are a result of this.

The ways in which bivariate analysis is performed depends on the types of variable involved.

Cross-tabulation

One of the most adaptable methods of analysing relationships between pairs of variables is a **cross-table** (sometimes referred to as a **contingency table**). These are easily produced within SPSS.

As before, the sample data set for this section is available on the Online Resource Centre as an Excel spreadsheet and also as a list of data in a PDF file. An animated walkthrough of this example is also available on the Online Resource Centre.

The sample data in this exercise represent the types of sentence given to men and women aged 21 or over who were convicted of indictable offences. As with the previous example, if you are able to open the data in Excel, then you can simply cut and paste the values directly from the Excel spreadsheet into the Data Viewer. Otherwise, you will have to type in each case individually. You should end up with a data viewer looking like this:

SPSS data view—two variables

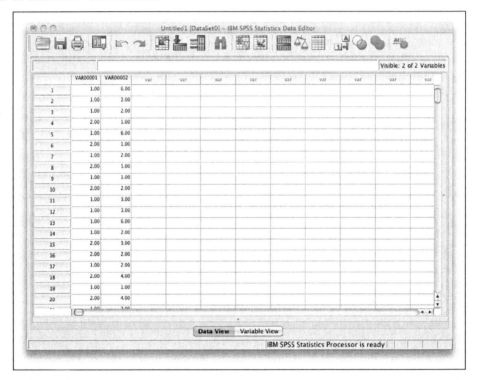

However, the variables here are nominal, so you need to set them up as such in the Variable View. Setting up nominal variables is slightly more complex than the numeric values from the last walkthrough.

Go to the Variable View as before, give variable VAR00001 the name 'Gender' and variable VAR00002 the name 'Sentence'. Also, set the decimal value to zero.

SPSS variable view—two variables

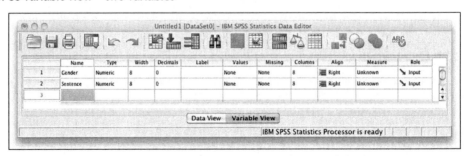

You now need to assign labels to each of the values associated with each variable. In essence, this involves giving SPSS the key, so that it knows that for gender 1 = male, 2 = female, and for sentence 1 = absolute or conditional discharge, 2 = fine, and so forth. This is done by opening the Values cell for each variable.

First of all, click in the Values cell for Gender and then on the '...' button which is displayed in the cell as you click. The Value Labels dialogue box will appear. Type '1' in Value and 'Male' in Label, then click 'Add' to save this assignment to the values list:

SPSS value labels—one

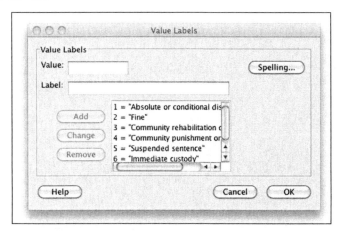

Add 'Female' to correspond to '2' in the same way and then click OK to confirm.

Do the same to add value labels corresponding to the key for the Sentence variable:

SPSS value labels—six

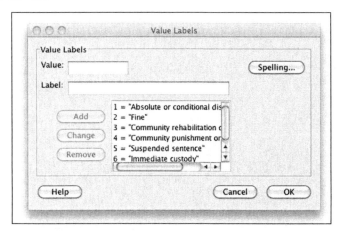

If you then return to Data View, you will see that the values have changed into their descriptive equivalents. If numbers are still showing, check under the View menu and make sure that 'Value Labels' is ticked. You will probably also need to drag the columns to make them wide enough to see the text:

SPSS data view—two categoricals

Now that the sample data has been entered, you can generate the cross-table. Select the **Analyze** menu, followed by **Descriptive Statistics** and **Crosstabs…** This will open the Crosstabs dialogue box. You want to produce a cross-table with Gender in columns and Sentence in rows. Select Gender from the list of variables and click the arrow to move it into the Column(s) list. Next, select Sentence and click the other arrow to move it into the Row(s) list:

SPSS crosstabs dialogue

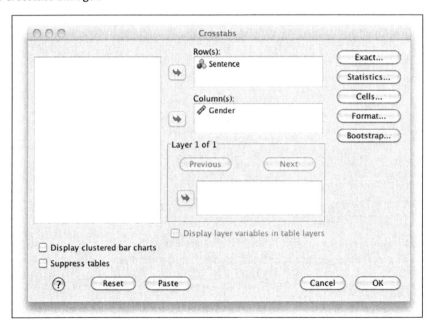

If you then click OK, SPSS will generate a simple descriptive cross-tabulation of the data:

Sentence * Gender Crosstabulation

Count

		Gender		Total
		Male	Female	
Sentence	Absolute or conditional discharge	13	26	39
	Fine	28	22	50
	Community rehabilitation order	10	19	29
	Community punishment order	14	9	23
	Suspended sentence	2	2	4
	Immediate custody	23	9	32
Total		90	87	177

This tells us, for instance, that there were 177 people in the sample overall, 90 of which were male. Also, 13 of the 90 male people in the sample got an absolute or conditional discharge as opposed to 26 of the 87 women in the sample. The cross-table becomes more informative with percentages included. To generate these, go back to the **Crosstabs...** dialogue and then select **Cells...** In the Crosstabs: Cell Display dialogue box, tick the Column box under Percentages:

SPSS crosstabs cell display

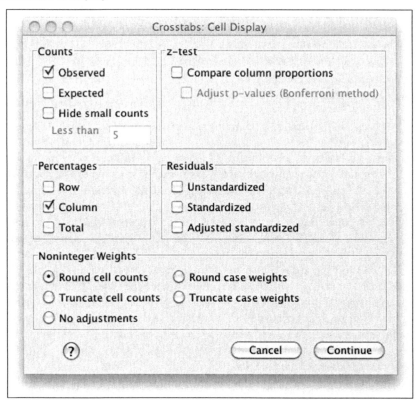

Click Continue, then OK. SPSS will then produce a cross-table with percentages:

Sentence * Gender Crosstabulation

| | | | Gender | | Total |
			Male	Female	
Sentence	Absolute/conditional discharge	Count	13	26	39
		% within Gender	14.4%	29.9%	22.0%
	Fine	Count	28	22	50
		% within Gender	31.1%	25.3%	28.2%
	Community rehabilitation order	Count	10	19	29
		% within Gender	11.1%	21.8%	16.4%
	Community punishment order	Count	14	9	23
		% within Gender	15.6%	10.3%	13.0%
	Suspended sentence	Count	2	2	4
		% within Gender	2.2%	2.3%	2.3%
	Immediate custody	Count	23	9	32
		% within Gender	25.6%	10.3%	18.1%
Total		Count	90	87	177
		% within Gender	100.0%	100.0%	100.0%

It is now much easier to see that, for instance, over twice as many female offenders got an absolute or conditional discharge than male offenders, and over twice as many male offenders received immediate custodial sentences than females.

Pearson's *r* test

Pearson's *r* test is used to examine relationships between ratio variables. This provides a measure of the correlation between variables. For instance, we might look at the relationship between poverty and convictions for property offences. We might predict that poorer individuals might be more likely to engage in acquisitive crime than richer ones and so, as poverty increases, levels of conviction for property offences would also increase. This is an example of a **positive correlation** (as one variable increases, so does the other). Alternatively, we might consider the relationship between level of education and criminal behaviour, and find that as levels of education increase, levels of criminality decrease. This is an example of a **negative correlation** (as one variable increases, the other decreases).

Pearson's *r* gives an indication of the strength and direction of the correlation. A value of $r = 1$ denotes a perfect positive correlation. As one variable increases, the other increases by the same amount and neither are related to any other variable. Similarly, a value of $r = -1$ denotes a perfect negative correlation. As one variable increases, the other decreases by the same amount and, again, neither are related to any other variable. A value of $r = 0$ denotes that there is no correlation at all between the variables and that the variation is due to other variables outside the scope of the analysis.

The different values of Pearson's *r* can be depicted by graphing the data points:

Here, $r = 1$ and there is a perfect positive correlation between variable 1 and variable 2.

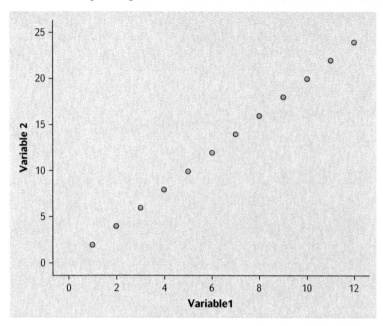

Figure 14.12 Perfect positive correlation

In this case, $r = -1$ and there is a perfect negative correlation between variable 1 and variable 2.

Perfect correlations (either positive or negative) do not generally occur in criminological studies. However, plots such as those in Figures 14.14 and 14.15 are still useful in showing whether there is *some* positive or negative correlation between a pair of variables.

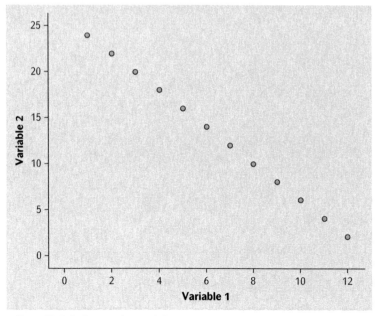

Figure 14.13 Perfect negative correlation

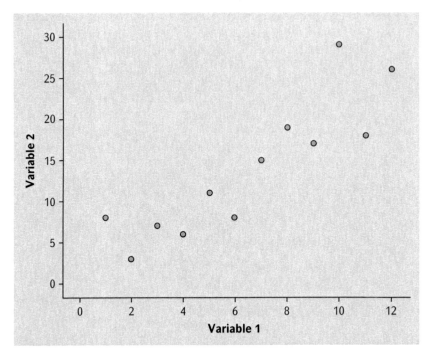

Figure 14.14 Strong positive correlation

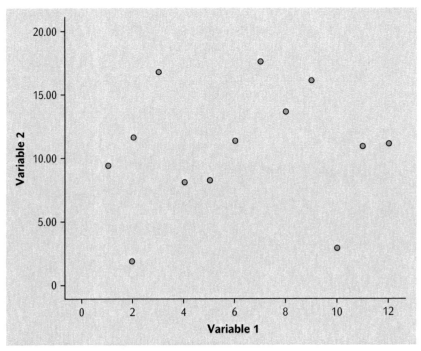

Figure 14.15 Virtually zero correlation

This plot demonstrates a strong positive relationship which is clearly evident from the points on the chart. In this instance $r = 0.884$, meaning that the variables are closely (but not perfectly) connected. There is some other extraneous variable which accounts for some differences in their relationship.

This plot shows two entirely unconnected variables. In this case $r = -0.036$: virtually zero. It can be calculated using SPSS by going to the **Analyze** menu and then selecting **Correlate** followed by **Bivariate...** which will display the Bivariate Correlations dialogue box.

SPSS bivariate correlations

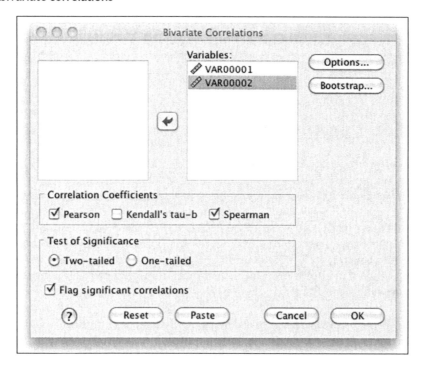

Here you can select the variables to use in the usual way, tick the 'Pearson' box and click OK.

Spearman's rho test

Spearman's rho test (which you may see written using the Greek letter ρ) is similar to Pearson's *r* in that it gives a measure of correlation between variables. The value of Spearman's rho will also vary between –1 and 1. It is used when one variable is ordinal (capable of being ordered but where the distances between categories are not equally spaced) and the other is ratio (orderable and equally spaced) or ordinal. It is also generated from the Bivariate Correlations dialogue within SPSS.

Bivariate analysis methods: a summary

This section has covered various methods of bivariate analysis which can be summarized in the following table:

		Variable 2		
		Ratio	Nominal	Ordinal
Variable 1	Ratio	Pearson's r	Cross-table	Spearman's rho (ρ)
	Nominal	Cross-table	Cross-table	Cross-table
	Ordinal	Spearman's rho (ρ)	Cross-table	Spearman's rho (ρ)

Statistical significance

We have already seen in relation to the mean that there will always be some variation between the characteristics of the population as a whole and those of the sample. The idea of the standard error in the mean gives you an indication of how confident you can be that the actual mean of the population lies within a certain range of values.

This is also true when we are looking at bivariate analysis. We need to be able to give some indication of how certain we think our findings are when examining the relationship between two variables. Therefore, we need to perform a confidence test to decide the extent to which we can be confident that there is a relationship between the two variables in question; that is, to decide whether the differences could have occurred by chance, or whether some other explanation must be required.

There are various tests which can be used to say whether or not the findings are **statistically significant**. Statistical significance is a term that is often misunderstood: it has nothing to do with 'significance' in the ordinary usage of the word. A statistically significant result is one that is unlikely to have occurred by chance, rather than one which is important.

The way in which the tests work can be depicted as shown in Figure 14.16.

Null hypothesis

The **null hypothesis** is a proposition of the default position: that the two variables are not related in the population from which the sample was selected. For instance, that there is no relationship between gender and sentencing disposal. It is typically paired with the **alternative hypothesis** which proposes that there *is* a particular relationship between the variables in the population as a whole.

Directional hypotheses

The alternative hypothesis can be **directional** or **non-directional**. A **directional hypothesis** states that not only will there be a relationship between the variables, but also states the direction of that relationship (positive or negative). For example: more aggressive three-year-old children are more likely to be convicted of violent crime in adulthood. Here, not only does

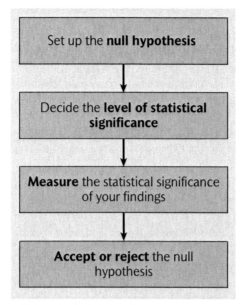

Figure 14.16 Statistical significance testing

the hypothesis state that there will be a relationship between childhood aggression and later conviction, but also that it will be a positive relationship.

A **non-directional hypothesis** also states that there will be a relationship between the variables, but does not state its direction. For example: the likelihood of conviction for violent crime will depend on levels of aggression at the age of three. In this example, the hypothesis is that conviction rates and childhood aggression are linked, but there is no mention of whether this will be positive (aggressive children are *more* likely to be convicted in adulthood) or negative (aggressive children are *less* likely to be convicted in adulthood).

Decide the level of statistical significance

The way in which statistical significance testing works assumes that the null hypothesis is true; that is, that there is no relationship between the variables in the population. So, even if the sample data lead you to conclude that there is a relationship between the variables, then, if the null hypothesis is true, then this would be a false conclusion and the apparent relationship between the variables in this particular sample occurred by chance. The level of statistical significance is a measure of the risk that you are prepared to take in concluding that there is a relationship between two variables in a population from which your sample was taken when such a relationship does not actually exist.

The level of risk usually taken in quantitative data analysis in criminology is 5%. This means that you are prepared to accept that there are five samples in 100 that might exhibit a relationship between the variables when there is no such relationship in the population. The level of statistical significance is expressed in terms of a probability value (denoted by p). The example of a 5% significance level would thus be expressed as $p < 0.05$ (that is 5/100): in other words, provided that the probability of the sample results occurring by chance is less than 0.05, it is reasonable to conclude that, if the sample infers a relationship between the variables, then there is also one in the population.

One- and two-tailed tests

You will recall that hypotheses can either be directional or non-directional. Each of these has an associated statistical model: that for a directional hypothesis is known as a **one-tailed test** and that for a non-directional hypothesis is a **two-tailed test**.

For a directional hypothesis, you are looking at only the one end (or tail—hence the name of the test) of the distribution that you have predicted in your hypothesis (either positive or negative) at the $p < 0.05$ level (Figure 14.17).

Since non-directional hypotheses could either be positive or negative, you have to consider both ends (or the two tails) of the distribution: however, to maintain the $p < 0.05$ standard, this probability has to be split across the two tails of the distribution, with 0.025 at the positive end and 0.025 at the negative end (Figure 14.18).

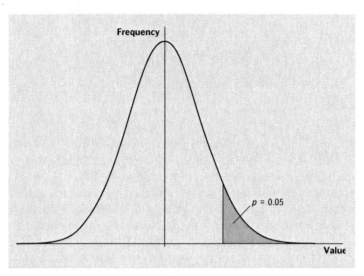

Figure 14.17 One-tailed test

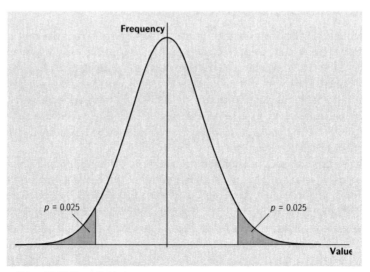

Figure 14.18 Two-tailed test

Measure the statistical significance of your findings

Measuring statistical significance of two cross-tabulated variables is usually done via a **chi-square** test (you may see this written using the algebraic form χ^2). The precise detail of how it is calculated is beyond the scope of this chapter, but in essence it compares the actual values in each cell of the cross-table with those which would be expected by chance alone. SPSS can provide a chi-square value for a cross-tabulated set of data and relate this to a *p* value.

This can be achieved by clicking the **Statistics...** button in the Crosstabs dialogue box to open the Crosstabs: Statistics box. Select Chi-square:

SPSS crosstabs—statistics

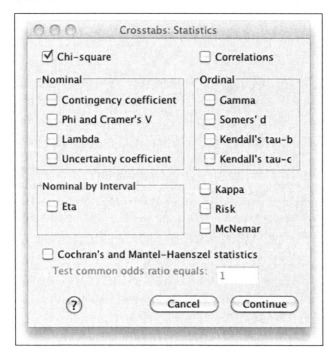

Once you have done this, click Continue, followed by OK. SPSS will then generate a table of results. Here are the results of the chi-square test for the gender and sentencing data:

Chi-Square Tests

	Value	df	Asymp. Sig. (2-sided)
Pearson Chi-Square	15.012[a]	5	.010
Likelihood Ratio	15.361	5	.009
Linear-by-Linear Association	8.381	1	.004
N of Valid Cases	177		

[a] 2 cells (16.7%) have expected count less than 5. The minimum expected count is 1.97.

You will see that the chi-square value on its own is 15.012. This means nothing, until it is related to its value of statistical significance, shown in the column headed 'Asymp. Sig.' which shows that $p = 0.010$.

Accept or reject the null hypothesis

The statistical significance $p = 0.010$ means that there is only one chance in 100 (that is a 1% chance) that the relationship in the sample appeared by chance.

We can therefore say that the results are statistically significant at the $p < 0.05$ level (which is the level of risk that we allowed ourselves to take) and that therefore the null hypothesis should be rejected in favour of the alternative hypothesis: that there *is* a relationship between gender and sentencing disposal.

Multivariate analysis

So far, this chapter has covered some of the techniques for looking at single variables (univariate analysis) and pairs of variables (bivariate analysis). In reality, the world is not such a simple place. There are a whole range of factors that can influence the behaviour of variables. Say that you were analysing factors that underpin domestic burglary. You might consider social demographic and financial position as motivating factors, but there could be a range of other variables that can explain propensity to commit the offence, such as drug use or seeking a personal thrill from the danger. So, there are complex relationships between multiple variables and their effects cannot really be interpreted in isolation: they need to be considered together.

Multivariate analysis is used for analysing complex data sets containing many independent and/or dependent variables all of which may be interrelated to varying levels. For instance, you might wish to consider the relationships between income, alcohol consumption, and convictions for domestic violence.

Various statistical techniques exist for the simultaneous measurement of multiple relationships (such as partial correlation, factor analysis, logistic regression, and logarithmic linear analysis). Multivariate analysis is therefore an umbrella term for a range of different tests and approaches, all of which are based on extensions of the univariate and bivariate techniques already covered in this chapter. The power of computer technology has allowed this branch of statistics to flourish, as calculations can be complex. Multivariate analysis theory has existed for some time, but it is only relatively recently that statistical packages like SPSS have been readily available to enable non-specialists to perform multivariate analysis.

Multivariate analysis is commonly used to determine:

- whether or not an apparent relationship between two variables is real, or whether it is produced because each of the variables in question are related to a third extraneous variable;
- whether there might be an intervening variable so that the relationship between two variables occurs as a result of that intervening variable;
- whether a third variable moderates a relationship between two variables; that is whether a relationship between two variables is true for certain values of the third variable but not the others.

A simple (and often cited) example that illustrates the interference that a third variable can introduce is the proposition that consumption of ice cream causes drowning: since it can be shown that there is a relationship between increasing ice cream sales and an increasing rate of deaths by drowning. However, ice cream sales increase in the summer (because it is warmer), and people are also more likely to go swimming in the summer (because it is warmer). The increased drowning deaths are simply caused by more swimmers, not ice cream. Assuming an equal probability that someone will drown when out swimming, it follows that increased numbers of deaths by drowning will result from having a greater population of swimmers. Of course, the probability of any single swimmer drowning is not constant. It may well depend on variables such as age, length of time swimming, depth of water, type of water, time of day, alcohol consumption, drug consumption, and temperature: and so it goes on. In other words, correlation does not imply causation—otherwise we could say that, for instance, eating prison food causes imprisonment, since most people that eat prison food are incarcerated.

Multivariate analysis is an advanced topic with which we will not engage in any further detail for the purposes of this chapter. For now, you need to know that it exists and the types of question it exists to answer. If you are required to engage in multivariate analysis as part of your course, it is very likely that you will have access to a more detailed quantitative research methods module that will consider multivariate analysis in much greater detail.

CHAPTER SUMMARY

Types of variable

- Ratio variables have equally spaced categories and can be ranked from zero
- Interval variables have no fixed zero point
- Nominal variables have no inherent value
- Ordinal variables have unequally spaced categories but can still be ranked

Univariate analysis

- The mean, median, and mode are all measures of centrality
- A normal distribution has equal mean, median, and mode and is uniformly distributed about the mean
- Positively skewed distributions have proportionately more instances of lower value; negatively skewed distributions have more higher values
- Range and standard deviation are measures of dispersion
- Roughly two-thirds of cases are found within one standard deviation of the mean; roughly 95% of cases are found within two standard deviations
- The standard error and confidence interval give a measure of the mean of a whole population based on the mean of a population sample

Bivariate analysis

- Cross-tabulation is a versatile method of analysing relationships between pairs of variables, particularly when percentages are included
- Pearson's *r* test provides a measure of the correlation between ratio variables
- Spearman's rho (ρ) test is similar to Pearson's *r*, and is used when one variable is ordinal and the other is ratio or ordinal

- The null hypothesis presumes that two variables are not related in the population from which a sample was selected
- The alternative hypothesis may be directional or non-directional
- The level of statistical significance (denoted by probability p) is a measure of the risk taken in rejecting the null hypothesis
- The chi-square (χ^2) test is a commonly-used measure of statistical significance which can, in turn, be related to a p value
- One-tailed tests are used for testing directional hypotheses and two-tailed tests for testing non-directional hypotheses

Multivariate analysis

- Multivariate analysis is a complex means of exploring the effects of third variables on the apparent relationship between two other variables

 FURTHER READING

- Dancey, C. & Reidy J. (2008) *Statistics without Maths for Psychology*. 4th Ed. Harlow: Pearson. Although this book was written with psychology students in mind, it does a good job of guiding students through the process of using statistics without mathematical formulae and offers a guide to using SPSS.

- Field, A. (2009) *Discovering Statistics Using SPSS*. 3rd Ed. London: SAGE. This book covers SPSS versions 16 and 17 and walks students through from introductory level to advanced level concepts. It is the best comprehensive guide to SPSS available.

 GLOSSARY

The **alternative hypothesis** is the proposition that two variables are related in the population from which a sample was selected.

Binary variables are nominal variables with only two possible categories. They are also known as **dichotomous variables**.

The **central limit theorem** says that the larger a number of samples, the closer the average of their means will be to the mean of the whole population.

Centrality is a term used to describe where the centre of a distribution lies.

The **chi-square (χ^2) test** is used to measure the statistical significance of two cross-tabulated variables.

A **confidence interval** represents a range of plausible values for the mean of a population based upon that of a sample.

A **cross-table** (also known as a **contingency table**) represents the variation between two variables in a tabulated grid form.

Descriptive statistics give a general indication about the characteristics of data.

A **directional hypothesis** states that there will be a relationship between variables, and also states the direction of that relationship (positive or negative).

Dispersion is a term used to describe the amount of variation from the centre of a distribution.

Interval variables have equal spacing between their categories but cannot be ranked from a zero point.

The **(arithmetic) mean** of a set of values is the total sum divided by the number of values.

The **median** of a set of values is the mid-point of the set.

The **mode** of a set of values is the most frequently occurring value.

In a **negative correlation** one variable decreases as the other increases.

Nominal variables have no inherent order and cannot be ranked. They are also known as **categorical variables**.

A **non-directional hypothesis** states that there will be a relationship between variables, but does not state its direction.

The **normal distribution** is a theoretical frequency distribution in which the mean, median, and mode are the same. It is also known as a **Gaussian curve**.

The **null hypothesis** is the default proposition that two variables are not related in the population from which a sample was selected.

One-tailed tests are statistical models used for testing a directional hypothesis.

Ordinal variables may be ranked in order, but the spacing between the categories is not equal.

Pearson's *r* is a measure of correlation between ratio variables.

In a **positive correlation** one variable increases in line with the other.

The **range** of a set of values is the difference between the maximum and minimum values measured.

Ratio variables have equal spacing between categories and can be ranked from a zero point.

A **skewed distribution** is one in which the mean, median, and mode are different.

Spearman's rho (ρ) is a measure of correlation between an ordinal variable and a ratio or ordinal variable.

The **standard deviation** measures the degree of dispersion from a mean.

The **standard error** is the standard deviation of a set of hypothetical sample means from the mean of a whole population.

Statistical significance is a measure of confidence in a result. A statistically significant result is one that is unlikely to have occurred by chance.

Two-tailed tests are statistical models used for testing a non-directional hypothesis.

15 Qualitative analysis

INTRODUCTION

The data generated by criminological research will fall into one of two categories: quantitative or qualitative. Quantitative data, discussed in chapter 14, are absolute data that are capable of being measured on a numeric scale. By contrast, qualitative data are all other data that are not capable of such precise measurement: in essence, qualitative data covers all non-numeric data such as words, images, attitudes, feelings, and reactions. There are many research methods in criminology that produce qualitative data: for example, interviews, participant observation, documentary analysis, and focus group discussion. This chapter will build on the discussions about gathering data in chapter 13 by explaining how the data that have been collected can be coded and then covers different approaches to qualitative analysis.

Since many forms of criminological study give rise to qualitative data, the ability to understand the principles relating to qualitative analysis is a key skill for criminology students. It is certainly no less important than quantitative analysis. Even if your degree programme does not require that you carry out your own qualitative analysis, it is still important that you understand the different methods of coding and analysis so that you can understand and evaluate the work of others that have used this method.

LEARNING OUTCOMES

After reading this chapter, you will be able to:

- Understand the role of qualitative analysis in criminology research

- Distinguish between qualitative and quantitative data and appreciate the different types of qualitative data that are produced from various research methods

- Recognize the key differences between thematic analysis, content analysis, grounded theory, and analytic induction as frameworks for data analysis

- Devise a coding scheme for data derived from different research methods and apply codes to texts

- Choose an appropriate method for coding your data—either manually or computer-assisted

What is meant by 'qualitative data'?

Qualitative data are extremely varied in nature and include virtually any non-numeric information. Qualitative data are commonly gathered in many research methods used in criminology. Table 15.1 will give you a reminder of the purpose of some of the research methods which were covered in chapter 13 on gathering data together with examples of the sorts of qualitative data that each might produce. A more detailed discussion of each of these methods can be found in chapter 13.

Qualitative data analysis is the means by which some form of explanation, understanding, or interpretation of the people and situations under investigation is sought from the qualitative data that have been collected. It is an interpretative exercise which attempts to give meaning to the data. In a criminological context, qualitative methods provide important insight into the social aspects of criminality and how the responses to crime operate in the social context. By contrast to quantitative analysis, small focused samples are more often needed than large samples. Qualitative research is quite exacting in nature and has suffered from problems of validity compared to quantitative research which is founded on well-established statistical tests. However, qualitative research—provided that it is done rigorously and thoughtfully—is a valid and accepted method within the social sciences.

By way of illustration, you may have interviewed a number of people to gain insight into attitudes towards domestic burglaries—perhaps a sample of reformed criminals, victims,

Table 15.1 Research methods as sources of qualitative data

Method	Purpose	Examples of qualitative data produced
Documentary analysis	Examines existing documents relevant to the topic of interest	Newspapers Magazines Books Film Websites
Questionnaires	Seeks responses to a range of questions	Closed-question answers (pre-determined) Open-question answers
Interviews	Probes the ideas of the interviewees about the topic of interest (in a one-to-one interaction)	Audio recording Video recording Transcriptions
Focus group discussion	Probes the ideas of the interviewees about the topic of interest (in a facilitated one-to-many interaction)	Audio recording Video recording Transcriptions
Participant observation	Gains an understanding of the topic of interest without actively questioning the participants	Audio recording Video recording Still photographs Transcriptions
Experiments	Depends on the nature of the particular experiment	Audio recording Video recording Transcriptions

police officers, and magistrates. A possible list of things that you might want to discern from your interview transcripts could include:

- Someone's point of view about burglary;
- Why they hold that point of view;
- How they came to that point of view;
- Their role in relation to domestic burglary;
- How they conveyed their view of their role;
- How they identify or classify themselves and others in what they say.

Unlike quantitative analysis, in which the tests and procedures are both standard and well-defined, there is less standardization of qualitative analysis methods. As such, there are various approaches that can be taken to qualitative analysis.

Before getting into any detailed discussion on these approaches, it is first necessary to look at the key qualitative analysis process that is common to all of them: **coding**.

Coding

This section will explain what is meant by coding in qualitative analysis and how it is done.

What is coding?

Coding is the process of reviewing and examining the raw qualitative data, extracting sections of text (words, phrases, sentences, or paragraphs), and assigning labels, usually referred to as codes, to parts of the text. Once fragments of data are coded, they can easily be retrieved at a later stage for further comparison and analysis, and to help you to begin identifying any patterns within the data. Coding data is a simple process that you will undoubtedly already know how to do. When you read a book or article and underline or highlight passages, or make notes in the margin, you are 'coding' it—you are labelling fragments of text with a means of consolidation and easy retrieval. That, put simply, is the basic idea of coding qualitative data.

What does this actually mean on a practical level?

Practical example: the meaning of coding

Imagine that you carried out research into the experiences of burglary victims by means of 20 semi-structured interviews.

At the end of the data gathering process, you have transcripts of these 20 interviews so, at this point in time, your data is organized on a person-by-person basis as you have generated data for each research participant. As such, you might have a series of separate documents entitled Interview 1, Interview 2, and so on.

In order to make this more useful to you, it is necessary to reorganize the data. You do this by assigning codes to parts of the transcript that enable you to spot commonalities between the experiences of the 20 participants.

The end result of this process is that you will have reorganized your data so that the parts of it that are relevant to your research are indexed not by participant but by reference to aspects of the experiences and feelings of the participants. This could give rise to a series of extracts headed 'Feelings of Anger', 'Fear of Repeat Victimization', 'Financial Consequences', and so on.

As this example demonstrates, coding enables you to sift through the mass of raw data, filter out that which has no bearing on your research, and organize that which remains into easily navigable sections based on themes that emerge from the data.

How is coding done?

There are some basic principles that should be followed to ensure that coding is effective. These are illustrated in the example that follows, concerning interviews conducted with burglary victims which assumes that you have interviewed 20 victims, that the recording of each interview has been transcribed, and that you are carrying out your coding after all of the interviews have been conducted.

Practical exercise: stages of effective coding

1. Start by reading through a few of the interview transcripts in their entirety to familiarize yourself with the data before attempting to code it. This will give you a general feel for your data.

2. Select your first transcript for coding. Allocate a number or other reference code to the transcript ('interview 1' will be fine) and ensure that the pages are numbered.

3. Read the transcript carefully and slowly, picking out words, phrases, or sentences that seem significant and assign a label to them. You can use a code for this or a straightforward explanatory word such as 'fear' or 'distress'. It might be useful to keep notes to remind yourself why you thought each theme was relevant or interesting.

4. Keep a separate list of your codes separately from the transcript and record the place where the relevant text can be found: for example, interview 1, page 1, line 14. Once you get used to your system of recording, you can abbreviate it further so that this would become 1–1–14.

5. Once you have completed your first transcript, you can apply the codes to the next transcript. Remember, though, that subsequent transcripts may reveal themes that did not emerge in previous transcripts so you will need to check back through to see if there is data relevant to these new themes.

6. When you have completed several transcripts, it would be a good idea to review your codes to make sure that they are not too wide or too narrow. For example, if you start to record all negative responses to burglary under a single theme, it is likely to be too wide to reflect the various emotions that victims will experience: after all, there are very few positive reactions to burglary! Look out for overlap between codes and consider splitting these into separate categories.

7. Remember to revisit earlier transcripts if you combine or split codes to make sure that all your data is coded in the same way.

 You will find some interview transcripts on the Online Resource Centre for you to have a go at coding. Compare your results with those provided. Remember though, that coding is impressionistic so it is entirely possible that you will have coded the data differently.

Different approaches to coding

There are three main options when it comes to the task of coding data. You could code manually by marking up paper copies of your data, you could move text about between documents on your computer, or you could use one of the pieces of specialist software that exists to facilitate data analysis.

Coding by hand

If you have a hard copy of your data, such as a printed version of an interview transcript, you could code it manually by highlighting or underlining the relevant passages of text and making a note of the relevant code in the margin. This approach is illustrated in Figure 15.1.

	Text	Code
R	You say that the insurance company was unhelpful. Why was that? What did they do that made you feel that way?	
P	Well, the problem that we had was that <u>you don't realize that a lot of things are missing until much later</u> when you look for them and can't find them. <u>You think that the insurance companies would know that and be a bit helpful. I mean, you pay them enough in premiums.</u> Anyway, I think when you first realise that you've been burgled, you look for the obvious things like the stereo and your laptop but there are other things that you don't think of. Our big thing was <u>bicycles</u>. They were in the garage right at the back – the garage is built on the side of the house and you get to it from the hallway – and we didn't think that the burglars had gone in there. I mean, the rooms they'd been in were all messed up where they'd been searching but the garage looked just as it always was. Anyway, because it was winter, we didn't have a reason to look for them and it wasn't until, I don't know, three months or so later that one of the kids wanted his bike out and we realized they was all gone. Then we got onto the insurance and they were, like, 'well why didn't you claim for them at the time?' and <u>made me feel like we were lying to get more money or something. That just adds insult to injury. Someone else stole all our stuff and we're honest and hard-working but there was this woman on the phone that was basically accusing me of insurance fraud.</u> I tell you what, though, <u>if I ever see anyone riding down the road on any of our bikes, I'll run them straight off the road,</u> I'll tell you that for nothing.	*Response to burglary* *Insurance problem* *Items stolen* *Insurance problems/anger towards insurance company* *Desire to confront/get revenge on burglar*

Figure 15.1 Coding by hand

There are a number of practical considerations to bear in mind if you are using this approach:

- Coding by hand tends to take longer than the other methods. This will be a particular problem if you make a mistake or make alterations to your themes as you may have to print the whole transcript out again and start from scratch.

- It is usual for themes to divide and amalgamate as the coding progresses, which means that the earlier transcripts need to be recoded. This can be very confusing when you are coding by hand as it results in a great deal of annotation in the margins which can be very confusing.

- If you are transcribing by hand, it is useful to convert your text into a table and add a separate blank column in which you can make a note of the code that is allocated to a particular piece of text.

- It can be difficult to find a method that makes the different themes stand out from each other as all underlining looks the same and there is only a limited number of different coloured highlighters.

In essence, coding by hand is a perfectly valid approach but it can be time-consuming and difficult to correct amendments so it is probably best used if you have a small amount of data and expect to find a limited number of themes. Having said that, some researchers find that coding the first couple of transcripts by hand helps them to really engage with the data and makes them more efficient when they then move on to one of the other methods of coding.

Coding by computer

Although specialist software exists that has been designed to facilitate the process of coding and analysing data, some researchers may feel that they do not have the time or the technical expertise to master its use (although, as you will see in the section that follows, most of the software is quite straightforward to use). An alternative approach is to make use of techniques that you can already use to help you with your data coding.

For example, you can copy sections of your transcript from the original document and paste them into a new document, creating a fresh document for each theme. This will be particularly useful if a section of text is relevant to more than one theme as it can be duplicated as many times as necessary. It will be relatively straightforward to shift text between different theme documents or to create new documents if you decide to divide a theme into two or more new themes. As with coding by hand, this method tends to be easier if your transcript is put into table form as you can then keep a column free to note where in the original transcript the text can be found. Alternatively, you could paste text into a spreadsheet.

Specialist computer software

As well as manual methods of coding and analysing qualitative data, there are also a number of different software packages that can be used to assist. There are many free examples of such software (such as Compendium, WEFT QDA, RDQA, and CAT) as well as several commercial packages (including NVivo, Atlas.ti, XSight, Hyper RESEARCH, Ethnograph, and MAXQDA). Given that there are so many different options, it is beyond the scope of this chapter to explain how these tools are used in detail. However, there are many features that these packages tend to have in common. Most of them allow you to search content, code and link textual fragments together, annotate research data, and query and report on the data: in essence, all the processes that are involved in manual coding and analysis. You must remember that such packages do not analyse—they merely sort and organize data according to the instructions of the user. The human researcher still analyses the results, but the software can assist in making the data appear clearer.

Such packages undoubtedly make the process of coding and retrieval quicker which is a great benefit, particularly if you need to analyse large sets of data. Of course, you should remember that you will need to spend time learning how to use the software and you will have to factor this into your overall research plan. Your institution may have training available in one or more of the packages, so it is worth asking in your department or in the library to see if any training is available and whether you can have access to the software. Many institutions have site licences that cover all its students, which is a great advantage, since the commercial packages can be quite expensive.

Even if you only have a relatively small amount of data, computer-assisted analysis might be useful, particularly if you think that you will be analysing a much larger data set in a future piece of research and you want to use the smaller sample as an opportunity to learn the ropes of your chosen package. That said, for smaller data sets, remember that manual coding techniques can be a more efficient use of your time.

If you have a choice of packages, you should also note that the commercial software vendors invariably offer trial versions, but remember that these are usually limited in the amount of time before the evaluation licence expires, or the number of codes that can be used or the volume of documents that can be worked on, or may have limited reporting capacity, or not have the ability to save documents, or some combination of the above! Trial versions do give you the opportunity to have a go and see if there is one that you find easier to use than others.

The basic processes of coding, analysis, and reporting are done within the software. Typically you will load up transcripts of your data and develop and assign codes on the screen as you go. The systems allow you to add, merge, and delete codes quite flexibly and to report easily across multiple transcripts. Although the software might seem daunting at first, if you remember the basic principles of qualitative analysis, you should find them quite intuitive to use. Have a look at the two screenshots which show the same extract from the transcript used as an example of hand-coding in Figure 15.1. You will see the main body of the transcript in the centre of both screens with codes assigned in a strip down the right hand side. This is a virtually identical approach to the hand-coded example shown earlier.

ATLAS.ti

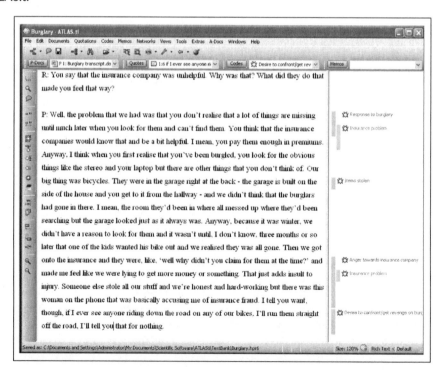

NVivo

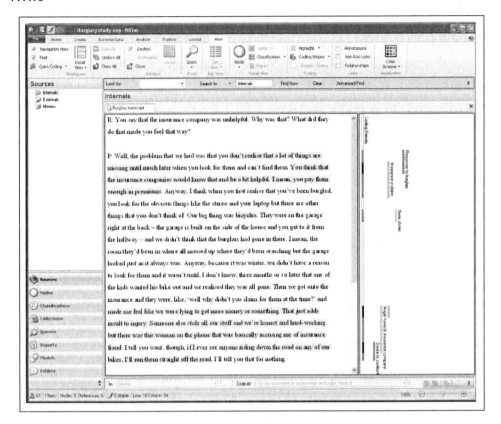

Although qualitative data analysis software can be extremely useful in many research projects, you should also bear in mind that some concerns have also been expressed about its overall usefulness. One such concern is that the data may become over fragmented and will lose context since the software makes it so easy to code and retrieve excerpts. This is particularly relevant in relation to focus group analysis where the interaction between participants may be of interest in itself (Kitzinger 1994). You should be mindful of these criticisms when coding.

Coding different types of data

In chapter 13, you will find an account of different methods that can be used in criminological research to gather data. The sections that follow explain how the data generated by each method would be coded.

Documentary research

It is tempting to think of a document as a collection of words on paper such as a Government report, but, as outlined in chapter 13, documentary research covers any printed, electronic, audio, or visual source material that was not produced for the purpose of being used in research. So, for example, the case law of the Court of Appeal and Supreme Court are documents for the purposes of criminology research but articles published about those cases are not included. In essence, documentary research focuses on primary, rather than secondary, source material.

The approach taken to coding documents will vary according to the nature of the document and the purpose of your research. If your aim was to identify policy priorities from a series of Government reports into the prison service, you could code each document in the same way that was described earlier in relation to interview transcripts. There are also examples earlier in this chapter of approaches to coding used in content analysis in relation to crime reports in newspapers, and media depictions of crime.

If you are coding audio or visual recordings without a written transcript, you must remember to make a note of the precise time at which the verbal or non-verbal content occurs in the recording.

Practical exercise: stages of effective coding

 Listen to the audio clip on the Online Resource Centre and try to code it. Once you have done this, open the transcript of the recording that you will also find and code the transcript. Compare the two to check for similarities—if your coding is thorough then your coding and the text that you have identified should be the same. Most people find that they do have differences though and that it was much easier to work from the transcript rather than the raw audio.

Questionnaires

It is usually the case that questionnaires generate quantitative data by the use of closed questions. As the use of closed questions—that is, questions to which the answers are pre-determined by the researcher—involves selecting an answer from a range of pre-determined responses selected by the researcher, the questions can be pre-coded to speed up and ease the process of analysis (since the researcher knows before any data is gathered what responses could be forthcoming). However, there is potential for questionnaires to include some open questions in which respondents are free to enter their own response. Now, this could be treated as quantitative data if you simply list the different responses and count the frequency with which they occur but it is also possible, and often preferable, to treat such data as qualitative data and group it together by theme. This is often necessary as respondents may use slightly different terminology to describe the same or similar things.

Practical exercise: coding responses to open questions

You will find a sample questionnaire on driver attitudes towards motoring offences in the Practical Exercise in chapter 13. The final question here is designed to elicit opinions about priority areas where changes are needed to improve road safety: what would your priorities be if you were Minister for Road Safety? Imagine that you received the following responses. How could you code them?

- Something needs to be done about speeding near schools and in residential areas.
- All drink drivers should be sent to prison. No exceptions.
- I think there should be better enforcement of existing laws. I am always seeing people talking on mobile phones when they are driving.
- Standards of driving seem to be poor. People develop bad habits so there should be retesting every five years.
- I would raise the legal age for driving to 21.
- Young drivers are reckless and show off a lot. You'd think that cars were toys not forms of transport.

- Selfish parking from people dropping off and picking up children at school should be policed and punished.
- Noisy car radios are very annoying. I live by some traffic lights and am disturbed all the time. Is that an offence already? It should be!
- I think that drink driving is still a massive problem.
- Uninsured drivers cause a lot of harm. There should be more checks and their cars should be impounded.
- Something needs to be done about boy racers in souped-up cars with their radios blaring, particularly late at night.
- This might be controversial but I think that disabled people who think that their blue badge means they can park wherever they like is a big issue.
- Five year bans for drink drivers. One year bans for using a phone when driving.

 You will find some suggestions on how these responses could be coded on the Online Resource Centre.

Interviews

By far the easiest approach to coding data generated by interviews is to make an audio recording of the interview and work from a typed transcript of the recording. There are plenty of illustrations on this earlier in the chapter by reference to the coding of transcripts of interviews with burglary victims.

In terms of timing, it may be that it might not be possible to start coding until all the data are collected. For example, recorded interviews may need to be sent for transcription which then arrives in a single delivery, whilst a researcher who conducts three interviews a day for two weeks will probably be too weary to think about coding until all the data are collected.

Focus groups

In some respects, the process of coding data gathered from focus group discussion is the same as that which applies to interview transcripts. The aim is to identify themes that occur across all the group discussions. However, the added interest in focus group discussion hinges on its ability to provide insight into the way that opinions are expressed, defended, and altered as a consequence of interactions within the group. This can be explored easily by using the identity of each participant as a separate code. In other words, in addition to coding the transcript in its entirety, it can also be divided so that there is a separate transcript for each participant. This will enable you to gain insight into the level of input of each participant, whether they changed their views as the discussion progressed, and, if so, what influenced this.

Participant observation

This method of data collection could generate either quantitative or qualitative data. For example, it may be the case that the observation involves the researcher sitting at fines court and recording the number of cases that result in remission of fines and the sum of money involved, thus generating quantitative data. However, if the researcher also made a note of the explanations given by the defendants for their failure to pay the fine as required and whether or not this was successful in leading to a remission of the fine, this would generate qualitative data that could be coded using the methods outlined earlier in this chapter.

On a practical note, it may not always be possible to capture the precise details of data gathered using participant observation, particular if covert methods are used, and this may impact upon whether or not data is gathered that is suitable for coding and analysis.

Experiments

It is usual for experiments to produce quantitative data that is subjected to statistical analysis. However, it is possible to conduct experiments that generate qualitative data. One example that is particularly pertinent to criminology is the trial simulation approach which exposes participants to some form of stimulus that replicates a criminal trial—this may be transcripts of testimony, video clips, or re-enactments using actors—and then requires them to discuss the issues as a group and reach a verdict in a way that simulates jury deliberations.

Practical example: trial simulations

Finch and Munro (2005) used trial simulation methods to exploring jury decision-making in rape cases involving intoxicated consent. This involved nine different trial simulations in which the nature of the intoxicant and the method by which it was ingested by the victim was varied. The transcripts of the resultant deliberations by the mock juries were coded and analysed, leading to the finding that juries seemed disposed to blame the victim rather than the defendant in all but the most blatant cases of drink-spiking as part of a deliberate plan to carry out a drug-assisted rape.

Approaches to qualitative analysis

One of the key considerations that will shape your approach to analysis of qualitative data is whether your starting point is a theory that you hope will be supported by your data or whether your aim is to start with an open mind and develop a theory as a result of the analysis of your data. So, the first key question to ask yourself is 'what comes first?'—the data or the theory?

To complicate matters further, qualitative analysis methods divide into two main types. There are those which form part of a particular theoretical position (that is, a theory of how to do analysis, not the particular theory that is part of your study). In other words, the method forms part of a prescribed framework and there is relatively limited scope for deviation from that framework—these include the two frameworks of grounded theory and analytic induction that will be considered later in this chapter. On the other hand, there are some methods that are largely separate from any theoretical framework, including thematic analysis,

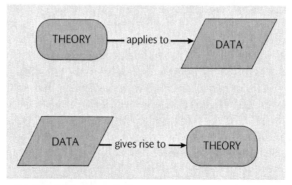

Figure 15.2 What comes first?

which will also be covered. This theoretical independence means that the method can be used much more flexibly while still retaining the ability to describe detailed and complex qualitative data.

The different characteristics of the frameworks covered in this chapter are shown in Table 15.2.

Table 15.2 Frameworks for qualitative data analysis

Framework	What comes first?	Is the method prescribed?
Thematic analysis	Data	No
Grounded theory	Data	Yes
Analytic induction	Theory	Yes

Each of these frameworks for qualitative analysis will be covered in the sections that follow.

Thematic analysis

Thematic analysis is a very commonly used method of qualitative analysis. It is a method for identifying and analysing patterns, or themes, within data. It is predominantly used when dealing with narratives that reflect the individual perspectives of the research participants. There are very few formalized techniques available for performing a thematic analysis, and much of the criminological literature that is based on thematic analysis does not contain enough methodological detail to be especially useful. Therefore, although thematic analysis is widely used, there is no consensus on how you go about doing it. As such, it does not require you to have the same level of detailed theoretical and technical knowledge required for some of the other approaches. This makes it quite appealing for many qualitative researchers.

As its name suggests, thematic analysis requires you to identify particular themes which reflect the general characteristics of the data that you are examining. This process of 'thematizing meanings' (Holloway & Todres 2003: 347) will provide you with core analytical skills that can be used in other forms of qualitative analysis. Some go so far as to claim that thematic analysis is not a specific method in its own right, but is simply a tool that can be used in other more well-defined methodological frameworks (Boyatzis 1998; Ryan and Bernard 2000).

Coding—as described earlier in the chapter—is one of the most important steps in thematic analysis. You should begin by taking a first sweep through your data to compile a long list of different codes (or labels) that you identified as you went through your data. It may be beneficial to embark on some trial coding before all the data has been collected as this will provide an opportunity to check that your method of data collection is generating the sort of data that your research requires. There is nothing worse for a researcher than realizing once all of the data has been collected that there was a question that they could have asked that would have added a further valuable dimension to their data.

It may also be the case that your data collection process is spread over a period of months. In this case, it can be useful to code the data as is it collected both to break down the task of coding and analysis into manageable chunks and to ensure that coding takes place whilst the data is fresh in your mind.

The next step in thematic analysis is to sort this list of different codes into potential themes, and to collate all the relevant coded data extracts within those themes. Themes can be defined as units derived from codes encompassing aspects of the data such as 'conversation topics, vocabulary, recurring activities, meanings, feelings, or folk sayings and proverbs' (Taylor & Bogdan 1989: 131). Themes are identified by 'bringing together components or fragments of ideas or experiences, which often are meaningless when viewed alone' (Leininger 1985: 60). This phase refocuses the analysis at a broader level.

The potential themes can then be reviewed and refined. It may be that there are not enough data to support some of the potential themes, or potential themes that seemed separate to begin with might combine into a single theme, or some broad potential themes might need to be broken down into separate themes.

Content analysis

Content analysis is a means of analysing documents and texts. Here, the term 'text' is broader than its everyday meaning. It does not just include printed words, but also audio or visual material. It is most commonly encountered in criminology in the analysis of mediated depictions of crime and policy documents.

....

Content analysis is the objective, systematic and quantitative means of making inferences from the manifest specified characteristics of communications (Berelson 1952: 18; Holsti 1969: 14).

....

You might be surprised to find the word 'quantitative' used in the description of content analysis. There are certainly some quantitative measurements that can be produced in a content analysis: this can be as simple as counting the number of times that a particular word or phrase is used. However, content analysis is also a rich source of qualitative data as it can focus on the tone or style of the text and the words used to describe and explain the subject matter of the text. It involves a search for social, cultural, and historic insights from the text itself.

For example, if you were doing a simple analysis of media reported crime, you may decide that you want to consider a few basic variables:

- Type of crime
- Gender of perpetrator
- Age of perpetrator
- Gender of victim
- Age of victim
- Harm caused
- Outcome.

This would give you some basic insight into the types of perpetrators that commit certain crimes and an elementary typology of victimization. Content analysis also involves the definition of codes which can be applied to each of the variables. These codes and their associated variables are usually defined **before** the analysis begins, in a coding scheme which could look something like Table 15.3. The researcher makes a decision about what data they are looking for in the source document and formulates codes to reflect this decision.

Table 15.3 Outline content analysis coding scheme

Variable	Code
Type of crime	1. Murder, manslaughter
	2. Non-fatal offence against the person
	3. Rape
	4. Other sexual offence
	5. Criminal damage
	6. Burglary from a dwelling
	7. Theft
	8. Motoring offence
	9. Fraud
	10. Drug-related offence
	11. Other
Gender of perpetrator	1. Male
	2. Female
	3. Not reported
Age of perpetrator	Numeric value or not reported
Gender of victim	1. Male
	2. Female
	3. Not reported
Age of victim	Numeric value or not reported
Harm caused	1. Death
	2. Physical injury
	3. Financial loss
	4. Damage to property
	5. Other
Outcome	1. Conviction and imprisonment
	2. Conviction and community penalty
	3. Conviction and suspended sentence
	4. Acquittal
	5. Non-detection
	6. Arrest
	7. Conviction and a fine
	8. Other

Practical exercise: coding content analysis

 Look at the two news reports that follow. Use the outline scheme shown in Table 15.3 to code each of them and compare your analysis with that provided on the Online Resource Centre.

Burglar used homes as toilet

December 10, 2010

A burglar who was so drunk he urinated in one house, defecated in another and then fell asleep on a dumped sofa in the street has been ordered to carry out 80 hours unpaid work.

Roman Rebosz, of Victoria Road, Wargrave, was also told he must pay compensation to the victims of his foul crimes.

The 42-year-old had initially entered a house in Westbrook Road, West Reading, on the afternoon of June 5, this year, and defecated on the sofa and carpet.

Later that night, he broke into a house in Beecham Road, West Reading, where he drank a bottle of vodka, some wine and cola and stole a phone. He had also urinated on a duvet.

Rebosz was found the following morning asleep on a dumped sofa in nearby Alma Street with the phone on him.

An earlier court hearing had been told Rebosz had little recollection of the incident but had admitted criminal damage and burglary.

Judge Bruce McIntyre was told at Reading Crown Court on Friday, November 26, Rebosz has not had a drink since June.

He said: 'I hope you have given up the drink because it seems to me that this was a very, very bad period for you.'

'You were drinking far too much and as a result committed these offences which were very unpleasant for the people whose houses you entered, for reasons only you understand.'

Judge McIntyre gave Rebosz a community order with a requirement for 80 hours unpaid work and ordered him to pay the two householders £150 each in compensation, plus £200 costs.

Three face conspiracy to murder charge
March 10, 2011

Three men have been charged with conspiracy to murder as part of an investigation into a shooting in Lower Earley last year.

Imran Khan, 33, from Wickham Road, Lower Earley, Jaspal Kajla, 35, from Hepworth Road, Coventry, and Amjed Mahmood, 30, from May Street, Coventry, appeared at East Berkshire Magistrates' Court on Saturday.

The charges relate to an incident where a taxi driver was shot three times outside his home in The Delph in Lower Earley on Monday, September 27, last year. He has since made a full physical recovery from his injuries.

The three men were remanded in custody to appear at Reading Crown Court on Monday.

A 26-year-old man and a 34-year-old man, both from Coventry, have been released on bail to return to Loddon Valley police station on April 27.

A 27-year-old man, from Coventry, has been released without charge.

A distinction can also be drawn between **manifest content** and **latent content**. Manifest content is, as its name suggests, material that is factually present in the data. All the variables in this example are types of manifest content. Latent content is content that is interpreted by the researcher—it is a more subjective and qualitative interpretation of the content. Latent content could include material such as words used to describe the victim and offender, or quotes from the victim, offender, police officer, judge, or general 'vox pop' comments from the public about crime.

The example above used a very simple coding scheme with only seven variables. In practice, the number of variables used is much greater. For example, Boots and Heide (2006) provide a detailed content analysis of 226 news reports of parricide (that is, the act of murdering one's father or mother) in the media from various countries. In total, they used 73 variables.

Finally, remember that content analysis is not solely used to interpret the written word. It can equally well be applied to other content.

Practical example: content analysis of television programmes

Monk-Turner, Martinez, Holbrook, and Harvey (2007) examined eight hours of episodes of the American documentary television series COPS that follows police officers, constables, and sheriff's deputies during patrols and other police activities. They coded the gender and race of the police officer and the perpetrator, and the type of crime committed. They demonstrated that the majority (92%) of officers portrayed were white males and most offenders (62%) were non-white males. Black men were most likely to be shown in thefts, burglaries, and drug-related crime, whereas white offenders were most likely to be shown in alcohol-related offences or as part of a domestic disturbance. The researchers argue that the media images depicted in the television programme are not in line with official crime statistics and thus reinforce stereotypes and myths surrounding the nature of crime in the United States.

Grounded theory

Grounded theory starts with the data and seeks a theory that explains them.

....

Grounded theory is an approach in which a theory is 'derived from data, systematically gathered and analysed through the research process' (Strauss & Corbin 1998: 12).

....

In essence, then, the theory is the end result of the process of data analysis: it is the discovery at the end of the exploration of the data.

Practical examples: grounded theory

Becker's (1953) research into marijuana use is an example of a grounded theory approach that pre-dates the formulation of grounded theory as a theoretical framework for qualitative research by Strauss and Corbin. Becker carried out interviews with 50 marijuana users to explore the social factors behind the use of the drug as he believed that the dominant theoretical explanation based upon inherent predisposition was *too* theoretical as it took no account of the experiences and motivations of drug users.

Plummer (2001) used grounded theory to explore the impact of homophobic bullying on the development of sexual identity in adulthood by conducting interviews that explored the uses and meaning of derogative terminology in childhood experiences.

Nee's (2003) article may help your understanding of grounded theory. She argues that research on burglary has (often unintentionally) used this approach by interviewing burglars and allowing their experiences to lead the way in formulating theories about this offence.

The basis of grounded theory as the framework within which qualitative data is analysed in criminology is the use of what Strauss and Corbin termed 'constant comparative method'. This involves an initial comparison of a small quantity of data to identify similarities and differences which then provides the inspiration for subsequent lines of enquiry and further data collection. In other words, the direction of the research is influenced by discoveries made by analysing data that has already been collected.

The key features of grounded theory, then, are that:

• the theory is developed from the data (and not the other way around); and

• data collection and analysis are done in parallel and continually cross-refer to each other.

There is some terminology that is particular to grounded theory which it will be useful to grasp before moving on.

Theoretical sampling

Unlike quantitative research and some other qualitative methods, in which the sampling strategies are decided and set before data collection is commenced, sampling in a grounded study requires you to decide what to sample next on the basis of analysis of the data collected so far. The key here is that you sample in order to test the emerging theoretical ideas, hence this method is called **theoretical sampling**.

....

Theoretical sampling is 'the process of data collection for generating theory whereby the analyst jointly collects, codes, and analyses his data and decides what data to collect next and where to find them, in order to develop his theory as it emerges'. (Glaser & Strauss 1967: 45).

....

The process of theoretical sampling can be depicted as shown in Figure 15.3.

Once the data is gathered, then it needs to be analysed. As with thematic analysis, this is started by coding and it is in this stage that you will really start to get to grips with the textual data that you have collected.

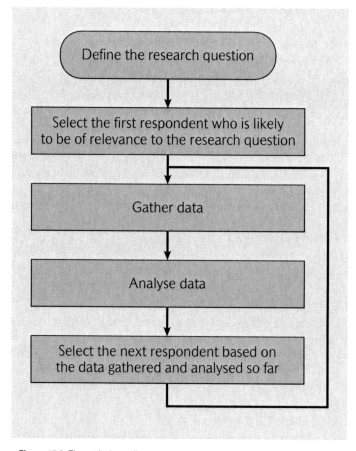

Figure 15.3 Theoretical sampling

Concepts and categories

Coding is the key to the overall development of a grounded theory. The approach taken to coding and the terminology used differs somewhat from other approaches used in qualitative research but, despite these differences, the basic idea of scrutinizing the data to identify particular ideas is the same.

In grounded theory, coding involves two distinct stages: the first generates **concepts** and the second builds on this to identify **categories** that may ultimately lead to the emergence of a hypothesis that explains the relationship between the categories. Concepts are 'the building blocks of theory' (Strauss & Corbin 1998: 101) and these are identified by an initial process of **open coding**.

....

Open coding is the process of breaking down, examining, comparing, conceptualizing, and categorizing data (Strauss & Corbin 1990: 60).

....

There are many guidelines that have been developed in relation to coding (Lofland & Lofland 1995) that might help you to identify concepts: these might be events, relationships, experiences, ideas, emotions, actions, places, or anything else distinct that you can identify in the source material. In essence, the concepts that you identify will depend on the subject matter of your research and the content of your data.

Once you have done your initial coding, you will probably find that you have a large number of concepts within which you may be able to identify groupings or patterns—these are the categories that will become the basis of your grounded theory. This is demonstrated in Table 15.4 with examples taken from interviews with burglary victims in which a single category of anger is used to cover a range of concepts including a desire to confront the burglars, disgruntlement with the police attitudes, negative feelings towards neighbours, and dissatisfaction with insurance companies.

Table 15.4 Quotes from burglary victims

Concept	Quote	Reference
Desire to confront burglars	I just want to see them face-to-face so that I can shout at them for what they've done to my home and my family.	Interview 2, page 4, lines 2–3
	I like to think that if I'd caught them in the act, I'd have laid into them and made them pay for breaking into my house.	Interview 3, page 6, line 17
	I wanted to go to court when they were sentenced so that I could confront them outside the courtroom.	Interview 5, page 2, lines 8–9
Disgruntlement with police attitudes	I waited 45 minutes at the police station only to see a civilian clerk who gave me a form and a crime reference number and told me to sort it out with my insurance company. I didn't even get to speak to a policeman.	Interview 1, page 5, lines 24–25
	The police couldn't have been less interested. They didn't even come out to my house. I thought burglary was supposed to be a criminal offence.	Interview 3, page 9, lines 2–3

This sorting of concepts into categories forms part of what Strauss and Corbin call 'axial coding' (1990: 96).

Axial coding comprises a set of procedures whereby data are put back together in new ways after open coding, by making connections between categories.

In this way, the concepts identified in open coding are compared and combined in new ways as you begin to gain a deeper understanding of the research topic. Axial coding supports the further development of a more sophisticated theoretical framework that has emerged from the raw data. The exploration of the relationship between categories should allow the advancement of hypotheses about the way in which those categories are connected.

Concepts and categories are often confused and can be best illustrated as shown in Figure 15.4.

One of the features that sets grounded theory apart from other approaches to qualitative research is its emphasis on the amalgamation of the data collection and analysis processes. In order for a theory to emerge from the data, it must be analysed as it is collected so that emerging concepts can be explored and potential research participants identified. As such, it is necessary that the data is gathered incrementally and coded as it is gathered so that these new avenues of enquiry can be identified and pursued as the data gathering process continues.

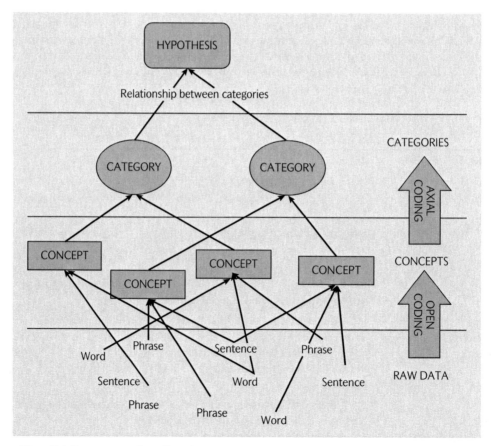

Figure 15.4 Concepts, categories, and hypotheses

Theoretical saturation

There is one fairly obvious problem with Figure 15.3: there is no point at which the sampling stops! Theoretical sampling could continue for ever, selecting respondent after respondent to see if the data gathered affected the emerging theory in any way. The way in which this is avoided is by introducing the concept of **theoretical saturation**.

As you have seen from the process of theoretical sampling, the theory that emerges from the data determines the selection of the next respondent, which refines the theory, and so on. It follows that, eventually, there will be no point in collecting further data since it will not add any further insight into the theoretical concept that has emerged.

....

Theoretical saturation is the stage in the research at which

(a) no new or relevant data emerge regarding a category;
(b) the category is well developed in terms of its properties and dimensions demonstrating variation; and
(c) the relationships between categories are well established and validated.

(Strauss & Corbin 1998: 212)

....

Therefore, the process of theoretical sampling can be better depicted as shown in Figure 15.5.

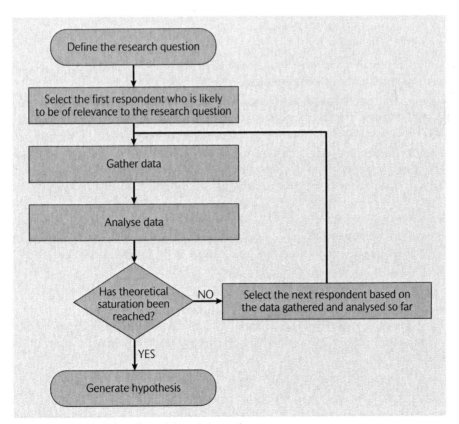

Figure 15.5 Theoretical sampling and theoretical saturation

Once the hypothesis is established, it can be tested by gathering further data (via theoretical sampling as before): if supported it becomes a substantive theory.

Analytic induction

In some respects, analytic induction is an inversion of grounded theory. As you have seen, grounded theory starts with data and seeks a theoretical explanation from them, whereas analytic induction starts with a hypothesis and seeks support for it within the data. It was first described as a method of qualitative analysis by Znaniecki (1934).

....

Analytic induction is an approach in which data are continually collected and tested against a hypothesis until no cases are found to be inconsistent. It seeks universal explanations of criminological phenomena.

....

This is a method of analysis that is scientific in style as it starts with a hypothesis and seeks to prove it by examining the data. A hypothesis is an initial theory about connections between events or explanations for particular behaviour; for example, you may start with the idea that all alcohol-related violence is committed by people who witnessed similar events in their childhood. This hypothesis is tested by the examination of individual cases and, if necessary, modified.

The basic process of analytic induction is shown in Figure 15.6.

The steps in the process are as follows:

- **Define the research question**. The process of analytic induction starts with a definition of the research question. All criminological research aims to address a particular question.

- **Examine the raw data and formulate a working hypothesis**. After coming up with the research question, the raw data can be examined in order to provide a working hypothesis that purports to answer the question.

- **Examine particular cases**. Once there is a working hypothesis, then specific cases are tested against that hypothesis one at a time. If the case confirms the hypothesis, then new cases are examined in turn. If all cases confirm the hypothesis, then it is accepted as valid and correct.

- **Refine/reformulate the hypothesis.** If, however, a 'deviant case' is found that does not confirm the hypothesis, then either the hypothesis is reformulated to include the case or redefined in order to exclude the case (so that it no longer forms part of the area in question).

As you can see, analytic induction is a very rigorous method of analysis: it refines a hypothesis on a case-by-case basis until it reaches a conclusion that is supported by data. Any case that does not fit with the hypothesis requires that the hypothesis be redefined. Moreover, in order to test the hypothesis as rigorously as possible, a sufficiently wide range of data must be collected.

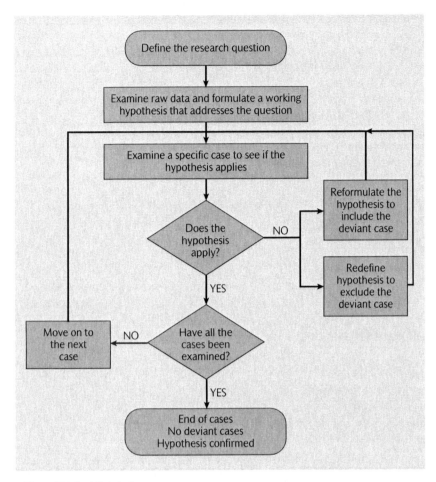

Figure 15.6 Analytic induction

Practical example: analytic induction

In his research into white collar crime, *Other People's Money*, Cressey (1953) advanced a hypothesis that embezzlement is caused by 'non-sharable financial problems'. In other words, he believed that a person will embezzle money if they are living beyond their means but feel that it would damage their reputation if others knew that they were experiencing financial difficulties. He used analytic induction to test the hypothesis by interviewing 133 prison inmates who had been convicted of embezzlement. This supported his hypothesis and allowed him to identify three conditions necessary for embezzlement to take place: opportunity to violate trust, knowledge of the workings of a specific enterprise, and the ability to rationalize the act by formulating a justification or excuse for the conduct.

There are limitations to analytic induction. Firstly, there is no means of telling how many cases must be used to test the hypothesis before it can be confirmed: there is always a possibility that an undiscovered deviant case may exist. Secondly, the use of data to test a pre-determined hypothesis could be quite limiting if cases disclose interesting points that have no bearing on the hypothesis. Certainly, analytic induction allows for the modification of the hypothesis as new data emerge but it is less able to accommodate unexpected discoveries that are worthy of investigation but which open up new lines of enquiry that do not relate to the hypothesis. Of course, such new ideas can always be followed up in a separate piece of research but this lack of flexibility is one of the reasons that many researchers prefer to use an alternative method.

Like grounded theory, analytic induction also necessitates a combination of coding and collection as it is only by examining the data that has been collected that you will be able to determine whether more cases are needed to prove the hypothesis.

CHAPTER SUMMARY

- Qualitative data are extremely varied and are gathered in many research methods used in criminology
- Most data that is analysed in criminology research are documentary and are in the form of written words, but qualitative data analysis techniques can be applied to non-written texts, such as audio or video sources
- Coding is the process of reviewing and examining raw qualitative data, extracting sections of text and assigning labels or codes to those parts of the text
- Coding can be done before, during, or after data collection depending on the analytical framework that is being used
- Coding can be done manually or with the assistance of computer software
- There are various frameworks for qualitative data analysis—some are led by data and others by theory
- Thematic analysis is a method for identifying and analysing patterns, or themes, within data and is predominantly used when dealing with individual narratives
- Thematic analysis is widely used but there is no consensus on the precise method by which it should be approached
- Content analysis is a means of analysing documents and texts, particularly mediated depictions of crime and policy documents
- Grounded theory starts with data and seeks a theory. Data collection and analysis are done in parallel and continually cross-refer to each other
- Theoretical sampling in grounded theory is the process of determining the next data sample on the basis of the analysis of the data gathered to date
- In grounded theory, data are first open coded to conceptualize and categorize, then axial coded to explore relationships between those categories. Ultimately a hypothesis may emerge that can be further tested
- Theoretical saturation is reached when the new data add nothing to existing categories or their inter-relationship with other categories
- Analytic induction is a hypothesis-led framework in which data are continually tested against a hypothesis until no cases are inconsistent. This may involve modification or reformulation of the hypothesis throughout the process

FURTHER READING

- Charmaz, K. (2006) *Constructing Grounded Theory: A Practical Guide through Qualitative Analysis*. London: SAGE Publications. This is an excellent resource for anyone planning to use a grounded theory approach to their research. It is not just an explanation of grounded theory—it is also packed with practical suggestions and worked examples that will help you to understand how to apply the theory to your own research.

- Krippendorff, K. (2004) *Content Analysis: An Introduction to Its Methodology*, 2nd Ed. London: SAGE Publications. This is a detailed exploration of content analysis. The book is divided into three parts, dealing with the history of content analysis and then moving to more practical considerations, such as the best way to design a research study based upon content analysis as well as clear guidelines on coding and analysis.

- Saldana, J. (2009) *The Coding Manual for Qualitative Researchers*. London: SAGE Publications. A comprehensive exploration of approaches to coding that covers 29 different methods of varying complexity that span the full spectrum of types of qualitative data. It is written in a really engaging manner and makes excellent use of examples.

GLOSSARY

Analytic induction is an approach in which data is continually collected and tested against a hypothesis until no cases are found to be inconsistent. It seeks universal explanations of criminological phenomena.

Axial coding comprises a set of procedures whereby data are put back together in new ways after open coding, by making connections between categories.

Content analysis is the objective, systematic, and quantitative means of making inferences from the manifest specified characteristics of communications (Berelson 1952: 18; Holsti 1969: 14).

Grounded theory is an approach in which a theory is 'derived from data, systematically gathered and analysed through the research process' (Strauss & Corbin 1998: 12).

Open coding is the process of breaking down, examining, comparing, conceptualizing, and categorizing data.

Theoretical sampling is the process of data collection for generating theory whereby the analyst jointly collects, codes, and analyses their data and decides what data to collect next and where to find them, in order to develop their theory as it emerges.

Theoretical saturation is the stage in the research at which
   (a) no new or relevant data emerge regarding a category;
   (b) the category is well developed in terms of its properties and dimensions demonstrating variation; and
   (c) the relationships between categories are well established and validated

REFERENCES

Becker, H. (1953) Becoming a marihuana user. *American Journal of Sociology*, 59(3), 235–42.

Berelson, B. (1952) *Content Analysis in Communications Research*. New York: Free Press.

Boots, D. & Heide, K. (2006) Parricides in the Media: A Content Analysis of Available Reports Across Cultures. *International Journal of Offender Therapy and Comparative Criminology*, 50, 418–445.

Boyatzis, R. (1998) *Transforming qualitative information: Thematic analysis and code development*. Thousand Oaks, CA: SAGE.

Cressey, D. (1953) *Other people's money*. Glencoe: Free Press.

Finch, E. & Munro, V. (2005) Juror stereotypes and blame attribution in rape cases involving intoxicants: the findings of a pilot study. *British Journal of Criminology*, 45(1), 25–38.

Glaser, B. & Strauss, A. (1967) *The Discovery of Grounded Theory: Strategies for Qualitative Research*. Chicago: Aldine.

Holloway, I. & Todres, L. (2003) The status of method: flexibility, consistency and coherence. *Qualitative Research*, 3(3), 345–357.

Holsti, O. (1969) *Content Analysis for the Social Sciences and Humanities*. Reading: Addison-Wesley.

Kitzinger, J. (1994) The Methodology of Focus Groups: The Importance of Interaction between Research Participants. *Sociology of Health and Illness*, 16, 103–21.

Leininger, M.M. (1985) Ethnography and ethnonursing: Models and modes of qualitative data analysis. In: M.M. Leininger (ed.) *Qualitative research methods in nursing*. Orlando, FL: Grune & Stratton.

Lofland, J. & Lofland, L. (1995) *Analysing Social Settings: A Guide to Qualitative Observation and Analysis*. 3rd Ed. Belmont: Wadsworth.

Monk-Turner, E., Martinez, H., Holbrook, J., & Harvey, N. (2007) Are reality TV crime shows continuing to perpetuate crime myths? *Internet Journal of Criminology*. [Online] Available at: http://www.internetjournalofcriminology.com/ijcprimaryresearch.html.

Nee, C. (2003) Research on Burglary at the End of the Millennium: a Grounded Approach to Understanding Crime. *Security Journal*, 16, 37–44.

Plummer, D. (2001) The quest for modern manhood: masculine stereotypes, peer culture and the social significance of homophobia. *Journal of Adolescence*, 24(1), 15–23.

Ryan, G. & Bernard, H. (2000) Data management and analysis methods. In: N.K. Denzin & Y.S. Lincoln (eds.) *Handbook of Qualitative Research*. 2nd Ed. Thousand Oaks, CA: SAGE. 769–802.

Strauss, A. (1991) *Grundlagen qualitativer Sozialforschung: Datenanalyse und Theoriebuildung in der empirischen Sozialforschung*. Munich: Verlag in Sarantankos, S. (2005) *Social Research*. 3rd Ed. Basingstoke: Palgrave Macmillan.

Strauss, A. & Corbin, J. (1998) *Basics of Qualitative Research: Techniques and Procedures for Developing Grounded Theory*. Thousand Oaks: SAGE.

Taylor, S. J. & Bogdan, R. (1984) *Introduction to qualitative research methods: The search for meanings*. New York: John Wiley & Sons.

Znaniecki, F. (1934) *The method of sociology*. New York: Farrar & Rinehart.